SECURITY MANAGER'S DESK REFERENCE

Richard S. Post, CPP
David A. Schachtsiek, CPP

Butterworths
Boston London Durban Singapore Sydney Toronto Wellington

Library of Congress Cataloging-in-Publication Data

Post, Richard S.
  Security managers desk reference.

  Includes index.
  1. Police, Private—Handbooks, manuals, etc.
2. Industry—Security measures—Handbooks, manuals,
etc. 3. Security consultants—Handbooks, manuals,
etc. I. Schachtsiek, David A. II. Title.
HV8290.P62 1986   363.2′89   85–29072
ISBN 0–409–90014–1

10 9 8 7 6 5 4 3 2 1

Butterworths
80 Montvale Avenue
Stoneham, MA 02180

Printed in the United States of America

To our wives, Penny and Sharon, for their ever-present caring and support; and to our editor and friend, Greg Franklin, for his continued help and enthusiasm.

Contents

About the Authors

Richard S. Post and David A. Schachtsiek, who have combined their talents to produce this management reference, bring to the readers a comprehensive report on up-to-date security procedures for every type of industrial and commercial operation.

Richard S. Post

Dr. Post is currently director of corporate security for the American Can Company in Greenwich, Connecticut. He has served with the United States Army Military Police Corps and was affiliated with the Central Intelligence Agency.

Post was also a police management consultant for Michigan State University, chairman of Criminal Justice Studies at the University of Wisconsin and general manager of security services for Oak Security, Inc.

He has also served as consultant for numerous state, federal and local law enforcement and security organizations and as a loss-prevention consultant to business and industry. He was a consultant to the National Advisory Committee on Criminal Justice Goals and Standards—Private Police. The Task Force Report was issued by the Department of Justice.

Post has authored numerous books and articles in the security field and conducted many studies on security, loss-prevention, crime prevention and police management.

He is a member of the American Society for Industrial Security, currently serving on its executive board. He is also a Certified Protection Professional.

David A. Schachtsiek

David Schachtsiek is presently Director of Safety and Security for a 900-bed teaching hospital in the midwest. In addition, he has spent over ten years in higher education, as both faculty member and administrator. As a teacher he has given courses and seminars on a wide variety of loss prevention and security management subjects.

Schachtsiek also has an extensive background as a management consultant, having worked with organizations in both the public and private sectors. His experience as a consultant includes projects with state government, the transportation and petroleum industries, retail stores and shopping malls, financial institutions, public housing complexes, utility companies, colleges and universities, and health care facilities.

Schachtsiek has also devoted a great deal of time to preparing policy manuals for new and reorganized security programs. He has developed and presented many training programs ranging from basic Security Officer Training to those on advanced supervisory and management topics.

He is also the author of several other articles and publications about private security, criminal justice, and crime prevention.

Schachtsiek is a member of the American Society for Industrial Security, currently serving as a chapter chairman. He also belongs to the Academy of Criminal Justice Sciences and the Academy of Security Educators and Trainers. He is a Certified Protection Professional.

Introduction

This reference book is designed specifically to assist the manager who has responsibility for providing security services. It offers information that will help both develop and manage programs that protect company assets and prevent losses that impact on the company.

In particular, the major objectives of this book are to:

1. Provide the analytical tools necessary for identifying potential or actual loss situations.
2. Provide a guide to help in critically analyzing existing security problems so that appropriate solutions can be implemented.
3. Provide forms, checklists, and guidelines useful in establishing effective security policies, procedures, and programs.

Further, this book offers to security managers those materials needed in order to:

- Evaluate existing security programs
- Determine specific security-related problems
- Identify existing or potential security resources
- Develop meaningful cost estimates and comparisons
- Organize efficient security/loss prevention and emergency/disaster plans
- Implement effective protection and prevention measures
- Administer efficient, cost-effective security programs

Each section of this book brings together a distillation of information used by successful security managers working in all areas of our profession. It is, in effect, a resource guide that can have application in virtually all organizations regardless of size or purpose.

SECTION I: MANAGEMENT CONSIDERATIONS

Although every security manager must develop a program appropriate to the unique setting in which it is to function, there is, nonetheless, certain information generic enough to give benefit to virtually everyone. There are basic principles, practices, and even problems about which security managers will inevitably have to know if they are to be effective in their jobs.

Crisis management and problem avoidance are styles of management used today by far too many in positions of authority and responsibility. Too frequently these managers operate without needed information or viable strategies. As a result, the people and programs for which they are responsible suffer. It is, therefore, the intent of this section to offer relevant material to assist in developing and maintaining both a quality security program and a professional mode of management.

SECTION II: SECURITY AUDITS AND SURVEYS

No organization can expect to remain profitable without taking precautions to reduce or prevent losses. Similarly, no security program can expect to remain efficient without taking steps to ensure that it keeps pace with the ever-changing needs of the organization in which it operates. For these reasons managers have long been conducting audits and surveys in order to identify accurately both present and future needs and the resources available to meet them.

The specific reasons for conducting audits and surveys typically vary from one situation to another. There are those that are initiated in order to uncover when and how employee thefts are occurring. Others may concentrate on identifying deficiencies in physical security systems. Still others are routinely conducted to assist management in developing new security measures needed in the organization and in evaluating those that are already in place.

Even though audits and surveys, like security programs themselves, must be designed to meet situation-specific objectives, there are nonetheless several basic *outline formats* that can be applied almost universally. Section II will present a series of these outlines as well as information on the principles of good auditing.

SECTION III: POLICIES AND PROCEDURES

Policies and procedures can be simplistically considered the tracks on which the *organizational train* runs. Without policies and procedures to give direction to an organization and its varied functions, it wanders aimlessly, having no well-defined purpose or prescribed destination.

Unfortunately however, with alarming frequency, managers forget the importance of policies and procedures and hence forget to prepare new ones or to keep existing ones current. The result of such complacency is like a *train* speeding pell-mell through the countryside in search of a catastrophe, a catastrophe that could well involve the loss of operational or administrative control, the disintegration of image and reputation, the increase of profit-reducing, unproductive time, or the damage of employees' morale and their faith in management's ability to run the organization efficiently. This brief list of consequences, however, does not include perhaps the most damaging consequence of all. In today's professional world those who ignore the very real possibility of encountering liability as a result of negligence in not adequately identifying and documenting operational parameters to govern the actions of all within the organization are naive indeed.

Therefore, to aid in developing and maintaining good policies and procedures, Section III offers a checklist identifying those typically found in progressive security programs. Additionally, this section also provides specifics on both the construction and presentation of policies and procedures applicable to security functions.

SECTION IV: BUDGETING AND FISCAL MANAGEMENT

This section discusses those budgetary and financial matters most closely related to a successful security operation. Now, perhaps more than ever before, security programs are in the position of having to get the most out of every budget dollar—cost effectiveness.

Given this very real operating constraint, security managers today must have a good working knowledge of both the budgetary process and specific fiscal issues that could impact on a security operation. Consequently, cost considerations that affect such important issues as program development, security personnel, and hardware are presented.

SECTION V: SECURITY AND THE LAW

Even though the legal issues that security managers must confront are many and varied, this section, nonetheless, offers capsulized comments on those most likely to be encountered. Basic issues concerning security's susceptibility to tort liability are discussed along with key judicial decisions that deal with criminal liability.

SECTION VI: SECURITY PERSONNEL

Almost no other single element within a security program has the potential for determining the overall quality of that program more than does the makeup of the security personnel. Therefore, Section VI presents material on a series of relevant subjects that must be considered in a comprehensive personnel management plan.

Since many more organizations are having to decide between proprietary and contractual security staffs, the operational advantages and disadvantages of both are identified in this section as well.

SECTION VII: SECURITY TECHNOLOGY

With monetary restrictions having an ever-increasing impact on both the quality and quantity of security hardware that can be purchased, systematic approaches to these purchases can make a very real difference. Although there is no easy way to offer definitive information on specifically what type or brand of hardware is best suited for an individual situation, certain guidelines for those decisions do exist and are presented in this section.

Further, the advances and improvements that the high technology industry has brought to security hardware have created, for security managers, a situation where better equipment is available. Yet, far greater care is also required in order to select that which will best meet specific protection needs. To assist security managers in successfully dealing with these advances, Section VII also provides basic technical information on alarm systems, electronic access control devices, and closed circuit television (CCTV).

Additionally, checklists to aid in selecting security hardware that is, in fact, appropriate to individual environments and circumstances are provided as well. These checklists include important questions that should be asked, and answered, prior to making final decisions on the purchase of hardware and devices that are routinely considered elements in effective security programs.

SECTION VIII: SECURITY SITUATIONS AND PROCEDURES

Even though every security program must be designed, implemented, and maintained to confront those unique and ever-changing problems that adversely affect individual organizations, there are also those that are likely to in some manner affect almost all organizations. For example, such problems as employee theft, burglary, and robbery prevention; disaster planning; and access control are basically generic in nature. Consequently, Section VIII discusses these and other issues of importance in practical terms, offering, in addition, examples of procedures that can be adapted to fit specific business settings.

REFERENCE BIBLIOGRAPHY

The importance of doing careful research into a security-related problem, its causes and solutions, cannot be overemphasized. Effective, results-minded managers, prior to deciding on solutions to their problems, first take time to review critically what others have learned about them and any solutions that may be recommended. These managers do not attempt to reinvent the wheel every time that they are confronted by a problem; they go instead to the professional literature.

For this reason, we have provided a reference bibliography. It is not intended to be an all-inclusive list of publications. Instead it will provide a very good starting point for this very crucial management task.

Finally, if material on specific subjects cannot be found by looking in the Contents, do not forget to check in the comprehensive topic index at the end of the book.

SECTION I

Management Considerations

Each security manager must develop a program appropriate to the unique setting in which he or she works. There is also basic generic information applicable to all settings. The basic practices, standards, and policy considerations are common in most organizations. The skill with which they are applied and the thoughtfulness of the manager makes the difference between a successful program and one that merely looks good.

Common management styles, which avoid solving problems or *fighting fires* rather than addressing basic issues and strategy development, are not acceptable. They are often the result of a lack of the management skills, tools, or confidence in the required abilities to make successful analysis and program change.

It is the purpose of this section to provide relevant materials to assist in the development and maintenance of professional security management and the operation of a quality security program.

1

CHAPTER 1

Philosophy for Effective Security Management

PROGRAM PHILOSOPHY

Understanding what is to be done and agreement on it by management is basic to the management of any security program. To accomplish this, a discussion with key management about what it is trying to accomplish by having a security function in the company is in order. Agreement on what you are doing and what you should be doing to protect the assets of the company is necessary for an effective program philosophy. Defining what assets the company really values will allow you to apply the resources of the company to those assets most efficiently. Program philosophy should, therefore, set the framework in which the program's efforts will be focused, responsibilities defined, and goals established.

Developing a philosophy is not just theorizing about what it would be nice to do. The value of a well-constructed and rational program philosophy will tie the security department's plans and programs in to the operating needs of the company. Without such a linkage, program value is somewhat limited. It is not enough to say that the security function is there to protect the company. The underlying assumptions about the company's desire to lower its losses, treat employees in a sensitive and ethical manner, determine which aspects of its business are most critical to success or survival, and the evaluation of risks and threats all point the way to a philosophy of protection for the company. This philosophy should also be consistent with the company's business strategy.

DEVELOPING THE PHILOSOPHY

The development of a philosophy for a program is not a theoretical undertaking. Just as in the operation of a program, you don't just let the things happen. You decide in advance what it is you are trying to accomplish, and you do it. But more importantly, the philosophy allows both the security professional and corporate management to understand precisely why programs are being organized and their relationship to overall corporate goals and strategies while focusing attention on why the program is organized in a certain manner.

It is certainly possible to analyze how time is spent on a function and to ascertain the operational philosophy for programs. Many of the evaluation methods discussed in this book assist in getting at questions of what is being done and how assets are being used rather than having forced choices in programs between prevention and enforcement or using electronics or guard personnel for specific assignments. The agreement on basic approaches to protection will allow the development of multiple programs within a philosophical approach. A company whose human resources philosophy stresses employee participation, involvement, and support for programs will likely require a security program consistent with that philosophy. Consequently, a security philosophy in such an organization will reflect management's disposition toward minimum visibility for security operations, a very visible profile for the function in the corporate structure, and a relatively weak enforcement capability. The benchmarks of an effective philosophy for program operation include (1) consistency, (2) clarity, (3) rationality, (4) logic, and (5) pragmatism. Let's apply these criteria:

1. *Consistency*. The human resources philosophy that stresses employee sensitivity, involvement, and participation must apply to security operations for it to be viewed as consistent in both overall philosophy and operation of the program. Security deals with major employee relation issues in the company. To have an open and participative system, but a highly rigid and autocratic or regimented security function, is not in keeping with the company's philosophy of employee relations. Consequently, the two approaches must be integrated.

2. *Clarity*. The philosophical approach to operating the company, management style, or corporate culture, if clearly stated, is something that all employees will understand and either accept or reject (and, therefore, leave the company.) Likewise the goals and programs of the security department, if clearly stated, will be understood and supported by management and understood by employees. A policy, for example, of prosecution in cases of employee or external theft may be based on a company's philosophy that it expects honesty from its employees in all of their dealings with the company and customers. Thus a clear understanding is developed based on what is expected and what the company's approach will be to violation of this accepted standard of behavior.

3. *Rationality*. A rational set of beliefs, which are clear, consistent, and make sense within the company's operating environment, is essential. If rules and company statements do not make sense or are out of touch with reality a gap will develop that will result in lack of effective communication, and employee disregard for work rules or security regulations.

4. *Logic*. If a philosophy is not logical, employees will disregard it. The linkage between what an employee does and the consequences must be

direct and unequivocal and seen as one step logically following the last. Just as employee grievance procedures are established, so too should the security procedures be clearly understood. Reporting of security incidents, for example, should be done in a orderly fashion based on type and seriousness of incidents.

5. *Pragmatism.* All policy and philosophy should be pragmatic. If it is not useful to the company in furthering its goals, it should not be used. A policy of complete background investigations on all employees, for example, is an expensive and unnecessary invasion of privacy unless there is a compelling reason. Background investigation for all employees in high-risk and sensitive jobs is critical and should, however, be done.

The philosophy that is developed should be pragmatic, logical and rational, and if applied consistently, all employees should have a clear understanding of why it is being done, of its value to the company, and of the consequences of not meeting the standard.

Multiple goals and programs are possible within a given philosophical approach. Regardless of the number of different programs, the entire company approach should be consistent with the company's philosophy of protection and provide an opportunity for the creative application of sound security principles and procedures.

CHAPTER 2

The Security Program

To be able to successfully develop and initiate a new security program or to evaluate and upgrade an existing one, a good practical understanding of exactly what goes into a security program is essential. For sound and intelligent decisions to be made about the existing or future state of security within any organization, those making the decisions should be informed enough about certain factors to make those decisions as worthwhile as possible. Those factors include:

- the security needs of the organization.
- the organization's potential for meeting those security needs.
- the organization's vulnerability to security problems in the future.
- those alternatives available for use by the organization in meeting its security needs.

In hopes of making these decisions easier, the following is offered as an explanation of exactly what is a security program. It will give a foundation upon which information presented later in the text can be built.

 What is a **security program**? It is a combination of systems and elements joined together to meet the specific needs of any business, industry, institution, or organization for:

- Protection
- Prevention
- Detection
- Enforcement
- Investigation
- Emergency service
- Public service

A security program is, in essence, no more than a series of operational measures enacted to protect an organization—its assets, property, employees, clients, customers, or guests. This protection, typically obtained by implementing a security program, can be adjusted to cover such diverse problems as:

- Burglary and robbery
- Theft
  External, such as shoplifting
  Internal, such as employee pilferage
- Vandalism and trespassing
- Fire and arson
- Accidents and safety hazards
- Natural disasters: flood, rain, snow, wind, hurricane, and tornado
- Losses due to mismanagement or carelessness
- Losses as a result of libelous or negligent actions

Even though a security program is primarily implemented to protect against these problems, it can more specifically be said that such a program is initiated to meet at least one of three needs that an organization might have.

1. Physical
2. Personnel
3. Information

Physical security needs are those most often considered by managers when they think of security at all. Consequently, these needs are the predominant focus of the private security industry. As the words imply, physical security deals with those measures initiated to protect an organization's facilities and their contents. It involves that part of a security program that concentrates on the protection of a company's plants, labs, stores, parking and loading areas, warehouses, and offices as well as its equipment, machines, tools, vehicles, products, and goods or materials.

Personnel security involves those measures taken to safeguard a company's employees and those coming to a place of business either for business reasons or as guests. Personnel security can further include access control systems that are designed to control access in and out of specific premises. Various identification card systems, passes, and permits used by companies also typically fall under the heading of personnel control. Probably the most recent concerns classified under personnel security are executive protection and background investigation.

Information security is that portion of a security program that is concerned with protecting an organization's communications, both verbal and written. The scope of information security is much broader than many would imagine when one considers that each of the following can easily fall under the dominion of information security:

- Research blueprints, diagrams, and plans
- Employment records
- Government or other important contracts
- Laboratory notes and formulas

- Critical correspondence
- Intraorganization memoranda
- Price lists for products
- Computer data and stored records
- Customer mailing lists
- Telephone conversations
- Interviews with media
- Private conversations during meetings

To be complete, information security must also be expanded to include protection for storage facilities—records handling, retention and destruction.

A security program can be as simple as having a single security officer in a guardhouse or as complex as establishing elaborate alarm systems that not only keep out unauthorized intruders, but also let in authorized personnel. Security programs can be designed to protect an entire facility and its perimeter or any portion thereof. Regulations and procedures can make a security program so inflexible that it cannot adapt, or so flexible that it lacks the stability necessary to make it effective. Consideration of each of these varying aspects of a security program will be dealt with separately later in the text. What follows is simply an overview that explains how they can fit together to form one integral security program.

Security programs are typically constructed of three component parts, and depending on how the program is viewed, these components can be either:

1. Physical Security		1. Security Officers
2. Personnel Security	or	2. Hardware and alarms
3. Information Security		3. Procedures and controls

Each of these components can be implemented alone as an entire program, or in conjunction with some or all of the other elements. These elements are also so diverse, in themselves, that almost any one of them can be used in a multitude of different ways. Figure 2–1 provides a schematic of the security program development process. In it, each component is shown in its relationship to all others.

SECURITY OFFICERS

A security force is probably the most visible part of almost any security program and is typically one of two basic types—*contractual* officers hired by an organization through a security service company or *proprietary* officers that are hired directly by the company for whom they will work (see Figure 2–1). Whichever type of officer is used, they are normally the link that joins the other elements together to make the program as integrated as possible. No matter what other elements are used, humans must be involved to guarantee that there is coordination and that mechanical security devices operate smoothly

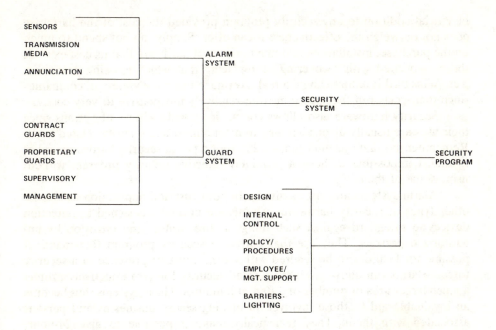

Figure 2–1 Relationship of security program development components.

and efficiently. For these reasons security personnel can be very important to almost any security program.

The other components of a security program are used primarily for protection and prevention and are not designed to eliminate a situation once it has developed. An alarm system cannot stop a burglar once he trips the alarm nor can a fire detection system extinguish a blaze. However, security officers can catch the burglar and put out the fire. Similarly, procedures and controls can be developed and initiated to see that order is maintained within an organization, but it will take the actions of security officers to see that these procedures and controls are followed and obeyed.

What is important to remember, since so much depends upon the security force, is that care should be taken to see that the officers are as up to date, professional, and efficient as are the other components of your program. Since officers are such an integral part of a security program, everything possible should be done to see that they operate at peak effectiveness. Security officers who operate effectively also can, in many instances, take up the slack of other less effective elements of a security program.

HARDWARE AND ALARMS

Security hardware includes fire doors, fences, locking devices, nonbreakable windows, and high-intensity lighting systems. This hardware can be a very beneficial addition to any security program provided the cost of the hardware does not outweigh the effectiveness it can offer. Simply, do not spend so much on the purchase, installation, and maintenance of hardware that its cost exceeds those associated with recovering or replacing that which is being protected. Yet, items of this nature can be a real advantage to a wide variety of companies since their costs run the spectrum from relatively inexpensive to very costly.

Security hardware also allows companies a wide variety of options since their uses are usually diverse enough to meet almost any security-related need. Remember too that this multitude of different types of security hardware makes it almost impossible to have a genuinely effective security program without using some of them.

Alarm systems are just as diverse in both cost and application as are the other types of security hardware. Alarms are normally designed as detection devices to safeguard against such things as fire, water, and intrusion by unauthorized persons. They are that part of a security program that makes it possible for facilities to be secured without the constant presence of a security force. Alarms can allow a relatively small security force to effectively protect a much larger area or number of different buildings. These systems thus become an invaluable aid to those involved in making secure businesses and persons associated with them. They realistically make it possible to give 24-hour, multipurpose protection to almost any type of facility with only minimum support given by a security force.

PROCEDURES AND CONTROLS

Procedures and controls seem to go hand in hand as they attempt to keep order effectively and to provide conditions where protection of persons and property is possible. Procedures establish written standards governing the behavior of employees and others on company property. They can be as simple as setting aside specific areas for smoking or as complicated as formulating actions during disasters or fires.

The principal control encountered in a security program is typically access control. Generally, a control is no more than a system implemented to regulate some type of activity. Specifically, access control deals with any system that is implemented to control entrance and exit at a company facility. An identification system, or passes and permits issued by security personnel also fall under the classification of *controls*. Other types of *controls* include fire, traffic, inventory, risk, and customer control.

DEVELOPING AND IMPLEMENTING THE PROGRAM

The following discussion on the development and implementation of security programs can be just as applicable to companies with existing programs as it can to those organizations wishing to develop totally new security programs.

Simply because a security program has been in existence for some time by no means implies that it is efficient and cost effective, or that it meets the changing needs of the organization. For that reason alone, these programs, also, should be considered for a *redevelopment process*. This type of redevelopment would center on the addition of more elements to the security program, making changes within the existing program, or deleting nonessential elements.

When discussing the formation of a new security and safety program the predominant concern should be that the program fit easily and comfortably into the mold formed by the needs of the organization. This new program should be an integral part of the entire makeup of the organization. Whatever the specific needs of the organization might be, its security and safety program should be able to easily and effectively cope with them. The whole purpose of having a protection program is to lessen the burden on the organization whose *primary* concern should be on the industrial or commercial endeavor in which it is engaged, and not on the protection of its property, employees, and customers.

The function of security is to protect life and property and to prevent their loss. Therefore, it is extremely important to emphasize at this early point that security is not meant to be punitive in its nature. What it is supposed to do is to keep secure all interests of an organization. To successfully meet this a security and safety department must have interdepartmental jurisdiction and cooperation. A failing of security is neither more or less than an insufficiency on the part of the total operation. Even though protective services is the primary consideration of only one department of an organization, its success or failure will most definitely affect the whole. For that reason, if for no other, total commitment from every level of management and staff is mandatory.

As mentioned before, a security program is the combination of interacting components, all of which are required for successful operations. It can be noted in Figure 2–2 that the basic security program components, with employee support added, form the four sides of a protective block. Consequently, an absence of, or weakness in, any of these components can seriously hamper the effectiveness of any or all of the other parts. If, for example, a company uses only security personnel and hardware to protect itself, it does not have a genuine program because it has not used all required protective components to form a truly effective protective block around itself. It is highly likely that in such a situation, even though no losses might have occurred as yet, a significant risk does nonetheless exist. A simple test for establishing the risk level for an existing program is located in Section II. Remember, too, the higher the risk level, the more desirable the development of effective controls, policies, and procedures.

The process of developing and building an effective security program is not unlike any other program-building process undertaken by management. It must be a painstaking process carried out with meticulous care. As is the case in other program development processes, a hastily-done job is quite often more costly than no program at all. So, too, is the case of security and safety.

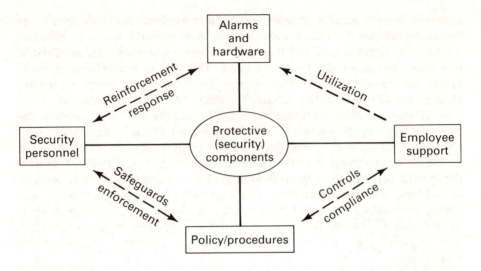

Figure 2–2   Interaction of security components.

The program must be developed with enough patience to ensure that, when finally initiated, it has all the components necessary to satisfy all the safety and security needs of an entire organization. It is important to remember that a protective services program should not be developed solely to satisfy the demands of the security department but rather to serve every segment of the organization. A security program must become an integral part of both the operations and management systems of an organization.

Unlike most other components of an organization, a security department directly affects every other component and thus must be extraordinarily concerned with the comprehensive quality of the programs it offers. A security program must have been developed well enough so that it can efficiently cope with its two primary concerns:

1. A security program must be able to meet the expectations of management in terms of services rendered and the cost effectiveness of those services.
2. It must also be able to meet the expectations of the operational and functional entities within the organization regarding the quality and quantity of services given to each.

In essence, private security is in the unenviable position of having to answer to two masters. On one hand, management is scrutinizing security to ensure that the quality of service is comparable to the money spent to obtain it. Unfortunately, in all too many instances management looks at its security program in the same way as it would any other business-oriented function. If the process or function does not show favorable results, it is looked upon as an economic burden. In this business philosophy lies part of a security program's problem.

If a program is totally effective in achieving its goals of preventing loss and protecting assets, it often appears that there is no further need for the program. *The better the job done by a security program, the harder it often becomes to explain the need for its existence.* Therefore, it is important that management be made to fully understand that security must be an ongoing process and that a temporary success in the battle does not mean a war won. Effective security, truly successful security, means a total commitment to protection and prevention tasks undertaken by a comprehensive security program.

There must be close interaction and cooperation between security management and the organization's administrator if they are to remain equally informed about the desires, needs, and expectations of each other. It requires a willingness on the part of both groups before any program can be expected to function at its peak level of efficiency.

On the other side of the coin, the operational and functional elements of an organization look upon security programs in terms of their ability and potential to fulfill the more immediate needs that they might have. Employees who work in these areas of an organization often are not concerned with the long-term objectives and effects of a security program, or with its cost effectiveness. These individuals are more interested in the protective services afforded them at present, and they are far more concerned about the protection given their cars in the parking lot or their possessions in the locker room.

They probably do not see a security program as the means to affecting an end as higher management might, but rather as simply an extension of management's control over them. This seemingly prevalent attitude has created problems for the security program that is implemented. Even though there is some truth in this attitude, it need not be totally detrimental to security. A security program should be in a perfect position to act as a catalyst to bring about favorable interaction between management and employees. A good, efficient, employee-oriented security program can go a long way toward showing management's sincere interest in those who make the organization work smoothly day after day.

Employees can easily be the biggest supporters of a security program or the biggest hindrance. The only factor that will ultimately determine which attitude they take is the quality of the protective services offered. It then becomes the responsibility of management to see that a security program is developed that coincides with the needs of the organization and its employees. Secondly, it is the responsibility of the security department to implement the program in such a fashion that it meets the expectations of both management and employees.

Not only is it important to see that the security program fits in as an integral part of the framework of the entire organization, but also that its own components fit together so that each element complements the others.

The main objective of a security program should be to produce an integrated program that deals with problems as a unified whole rather than to attempt to fragment the various elements of the program and treat them separately. A well-integrated, properly organized program will be infinitely more effective and efficient, both in terms of performance and budget (cost effectiveness), than one that is not. It is impractical to attempt to deal with fire and safety, theft and criminal activity, access control, emergency planning, and security administration one at a time, under different supervisory areas or departments, or with completely segregated programs.

IN BRIEF

1. A security program provides the procedures and means for accomplishing desired security objectives. It is a combination of elements—audit, evaluation, recommendations, implementations, training, and hardware.
2. A security program is action resulting from a planned approach to loss prevention.
3. A security program is designed for specific protection purposes with definite objectives and time limitations that are clearly communicated to all interested parties. It also provides a controlled method of implementing security systems, devices, and controls.
4. A security program is a system of logical procedures to utilize safeguards against all identified risks.
5. A security program is a controlled method of protection.
6. A security program is a series of specific components designed with specific objectives in mind to protect the assets, personnel, and information of the organization with feedback to indicate degree of success.
7. Assisting in providing an environment conducive to furthering the objectives and/or goals of an organization, a security system is the basis for control within that organization.
8. A security program is a combination of personnel and hardware balanced to provide protection for assets and lives.

CHAPTER 3

Program Planning

Planning is without a doubt the most effective way of achieving long-term success with a security program or of correcting programs that are unsophisticated, unproductive, or unorganized. The planning function is essential to both the development and implementation of protection programs, and should, therefore, be the center of any good security management operation.

The allocation of important, but limited, resources for effective organizational operations makes planning even more important for the continued success or existence of those operations. Despite the fact that an organization's protection operation affects all its levels and activities, only minimal consideration is typically given to planning for such operations. Even though organizations are willing to expend large sums on planning for product output, expansion of facilities, employee changes, or program development, planning for safety and security seems to be largely ignored. As a result of the prevalence of this type of situation, private protective services are falling short in their attempts to meet the needs of client organizations or parent companies.

Since security and safety are viewed principally as secondary considerations to an organization, proper solutions to present and future problems often go unresolved. Available expenditures for planning efforts are logically used primarily to improve the marketability of products or to enhance the conditions of the total organization, leaving protective services to fend for themselves. Consequently, the rest of the organization advances on a reasonably well-defined course while safety and security are left trailing behind in a forest of uncertainty, not knowing which route they are expected to follow.

To show the relevance of, and need for, planning in the operation of a security and safety program, it is important that management realize exactly what the planning process is and what it can accomplish for an organization. Planning is actually a process that, when done correctly, will show where an organization is, where it should or wants to go, and what alternatives can be used to get from here to there. It is a continuing process which examines the conditions of an organization and its functions in hope of developing realistic objectives, alternative means of attacking problems, and those conditions or operations that are best suited or most adaptable for present and future needs.

For planning to be effective, there are five basic principles that must be adhered to:

1. Planning must be *continuous*
2. Planning must be *comprehensive*
3. Planning must be *participatory*
4. Planning must be *integrated*
5. Planning must be *experimental*

1. *Continuous.* By its nature planning is a future-oriented process. Therefore, management must remember that planning must take on a dynamic quality. It must be an ongoing process.

While the results of planning can limit an organization's activity by maximizing efforts toward a particular goal, it should never be assumed that an organization has reached an ideal level of performance. Management should be willing nonetheless to strive toward the ideal by using effective ongoing planning.

2. *Comprehensive.* Planning must be inclusive. Planning must be done for the benefit of the entire organization and not simply for its subdivisions. Fragmenting the organization for the purpose of planning makes it very easy for certain segments of the organization to outdistance others. The result of this can be that the smooth functioning of the organization is put off course.

3. *Participatory.* To achieve the maximum benefits from planning, all concerned parties must be represented and those representatives allowed to participate. Simply put, who better knows the way the organization works than those who make it work?

Since planning must also be comprehensive, it is important that management be willing to accept knowledgeable input from all levels and subdivisions of the organization. The responsibility of management, then, is to see that the information offered through this participation is as useful as possible. This can best be done by seeing that it is offered in a professional fashion.

Further, this *participatory planning* will go a long way toward ensuring that programs or systems implemented as a result of these planning efforts will be well received. Those who participate in designing new programs—or who have representation in such designs—are a great deal more likely to give much-needed support and cooperation.

4. *Integrated.* For all practical purposes, the integration of the planning process is simply the expansion of the comprehensive quality of planning. Not only is it important that planning consider all elements of the organization, it is also essential that these elements be coordinated so that the progress moves at compatible speeds. When some operations outdistance others, problems result. Marketing should not outdistance production just as production should not outdistance sales. In another sense, the expansion and growth of the organization should be planned so that it is coordinated with the capabilities of the Security Department.

5. *Experimental.* Planning is experimental for the simple reason that it has got to analyze conditions and then offer alternatives to be tested meticulously and objectively.

In particular, the security planning process seeks to identify those conditions during a security risk survey—a security audit. It then offers alternatives to help eliminate or reduce the security hazards identified. As shown in Figure 3–1, planning is cyclical in that data collected through security audits becomes input for developing alternatives for eliminating problems or hazards. Audits are again used to evaluate the success or failure of the approaches that have been implemented. This evaluation should contain a redefinition of the organization's goals that will start the entire cycle moving again.

Although these five planning *principles* have relevance to all such efforts, when one specifically undertakes planning for security or loss control efforts, the following basic *assumptions* must also be considered. These, if adhered to, will considerably increase the likelihood of achieving long-term successes.

1. *There is no one single cause of losses.* Losses can be the result of many different things including carelessness, negligence, inadequate employee supervision, lax access control provision, unenforced security procedures, or intentional criminal activity. When considering the totality of losses suffered

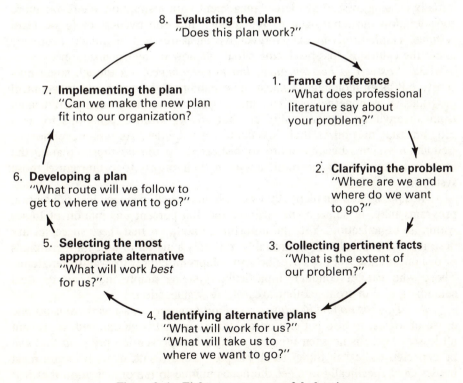

Figure 3–1 Eight steps to successful planning.

by an organization, it is, therefore, inappropriate to arbitrarily assume that any one condition is responsible for all losses. Invariably several factors impacting together on a situation create the loss. For example, inadequate supervision may have given a potentially dishonest employee the opportunity to leave his or her work area and go alone to the tool storage room. Once in the storage room, poor record-keeping practices allow the employee to remove an expensive electric drill without having to sign for it. Finally, ineffective access control procedures enable the employee to leave the plant with the drill, undetected. Even though the end result is the loss of the drill, the contributing causes of that loss are numerous. So it is with almost all losses encountered.

2.   *Loss causation is a complex issue.*   The multiplicity of causes that affect losses within an organization creates for management a complex situation where *hatchet* attacks on loss-related problems rarely bring acceptable results. Consequently, if this complexity is not realized, the effects of corrective efforts can often produce *overkill,* decreased productivity or problem displacement, rather than long-term prevention, reduction or control.

The complex nature of loss causation is further typified by the multitude of preventive and corrective measures that have been used over many decades in attempts to curtail losses suffered by those in both the public and private sectors. The sophisticated techniques used by those committing crimes or initially causing losses have left management with a situation where far more consideration must be given to the quality and effectiveness of loss-control systems. Haphazardly-invoked preventive measures will no longer positively affect the calibre of loss-producing situations now facing organizations.

3.   *Losses can be controlled, but not eliminated.*   Although some may construe it as an indictment against the capabilities of security and loss-control programs, it is nonetheless a fact that losses can never be totally eradicated from an environment. In reality all that an organization can hope for is a program that maximizes their loss-control capabilities. As loss-prevention or -reduction systems become more sophisticated, so too do those creating the losses readjust to become more adept in their efforts to compromise those systems.

It is possible, even likely, that well-planned, well-managed loss-prevention programs may, at some point, achieve the 100 percent elimination of losses within an organization. Yet, the unfortunate reality is that these successes are destined to be short lived. Regrettably, it is only a matter of time until criminals or dishonest employees discover how to compromise most loss-control systems. Those who cannot conquer a particular system, simply move on to steal something else or from another area of the organization.

4.   *There is no one best loss-prevention program.*   Just as there is no one cause of losses, so also is there no one program that is guaranteed to prevent all losses. There is no such thing as a single loss-prevention program that can be expected to be "all things to all people." As a result, every program must be designed specifically to meet the needs unique to the organization that it is to serve.

Even the most successful loss prevention program cannot be uprooted and transplanted elsewhere and expected to flourish as well as it did in its original setting. Similarly, it cannot be arbitrarily assumed that programs effective in controlling a certain type of loss will work as well in combatting others. As losses suffered by retail stores because of lax employee procedural controls are not assumed to be identical to those experienced by other retailers, so the programs needed to curb those losses should not be expected to be the very same either. Losses *are* unique to the environment of which they are a part and the loss control programs employed to curtail them should be similarly unique.

5. *Sound program planning and evaluation will make the difference.* As mentioned earlier in this section, crisis management and reactionary decision making no longer have a place in quality, efficient management systems. On the other hand, sound planning and objective program evaluation can greatly enhance the overall effectiveness of a loss control program and its management.

The sporadic and temporary successes characteristic of poor management practices need not be the only ones experienced. A carefully thought out plan for the control program can bring consistent and long-term successes in the fight against security-related losses. The comprehensive evaluation of a loss-control program can then aid management in maintaining an environment conducive to continued, effective loss-control efforts as well.

No organization is expected to be able to totally predetermine all of its protection needs for the future when it is developing its protection program, yet every reasonable effort should be made to see that the program is as applicable to its needs as possible. Simply, it becomes a basic matter of cost effectiveness—you only get what you pay for.

If only a minimum and haphazard attempt is made at developing a security and safety program, the results will almost certainly fall short of adequately meeting all of the needs for which it was, at least in theory, designed. To avoid this type of dilemma, a well-thought out plan of attack should be decided upon well in advance of any action toward program implementation. Therefore, developing a protection program must be a meticulous undertaking, done thoughtfully and carefully, so that every contingency is allowed for. It is much easier to plan for some eventuality before it takes place than to be forced to eliminate it after it has occurred.

The main purpose of a protection program is to offer the best possible service and protection to its parent organization. But, should less than a wholehearted effort be shown by the organization during the planning process, it is more than likely that the protection given will be less than adequate.

Only those organizations that have a genuine desire to have a successful and efficient program should undertake the exhaustive task of developing one. Although the cost of a safety and security program is an important factor, it varies considerably with demands for efficiency placed on the program and the number of components in the program. What should be examined is the time and patience required to develop a good program and then the ease with which it can be put into operation. Most organizations have funds that can be allocated for security services, but what they often unintentionally fail to allocate is the time and effort to see that the funds are spent wisely in the development and implementation of such a program. In many respects a bad security program is worse than none at all. Bad security programs make it terribly easy for organizations to be lulled into a false sense of security. They allow management to think that safety and security actions are successfully meeting all the organization's needs when in reality they are not.

DEVELOPING THE PLAN*

The eight steps discussed below (see also Figure 3–1) provide an orderly means for the development of plans, be they large or small, long-range or short-range. These provide a framework for the consideration of all aspects of planning.

1. *"Frame of reference."* This is based on a careful review of the literature relating to the situation for which plans are being developed, and opinions or ideas of persons who may speak with authority on the subject of concern. Definitive views of the security director, officers, and other organizational officials are important. In effect, data gathered provide an outline of the best available information on the situation.

2. *Clarifying the problem.* This requires identifying the problem, and understanding both its record and its possible solution. A situation must exist for which something must and can be done. For example, a plant is victimized by a series of burglaries. There is need for reaching the preliminary decision that burglaries may be reduced at the plant and that the security department can reduce them.

3. *Collecting all pertinent facts.* No attempt should be made to develop a plan until all facts relating to it have been gathered. In the series of burglaries, all information should be carefully reviewed to determine *modus operandi,* suspects, and such other information as the public police will provide. Facts relating to such matters as availability, deployment, and use of present personnel should be gathered, as well as such other data as may be needed— a review of general and special orders, and pertinent literature on burglary coverage. After all data has been gathered, a careful analysis and evaluation must be made. This provides a basis from which a plan or plans are evolved. Only such facts as may have relevance should be considered.

4. *Identifying alternative plans.* In the initial phases of plans development, several alternative measures will appear to be logically comparable to the needs of a situation. Persons responsible for plans development may overlook or fail to consider important factors. As the alternative solutions are evaluated, one of the proposed plans will usually prove more logical than the

---

* Adapted from "Mechanics of Planning," U.S. Dept. of Justice Planning Project #122, 1967.

others. For example, one plan may call for the use of off-duty patrolmen for "stake-outs" in the burglary case, and other plans for use of increased site-hardening and electronic protection with better communication to response force personnel.

5. *Selecting the most appropriate alternative.* A careful consideration of all facts usually leads to the selection of a "best" alternative proposal. In the burglary case, the "best" plan may call for use of hardware with maximum use of police for "stake-outs." Sometimes a synthesis or a compromise between plans may provide a solution.

6. *Developing a plan.* A plan, to be effectively carried out, must be accepted by all personnel concerned. This requires involving all persons concerned at the appropriate level of the plan's development. For example, in the burglary case, the security director may be preparing the plan. At the outset, the police department is concerned and should be consulted. As the planning develops, there may be need to involve the patrol personnel, and communication units, as well as company officials. Lastly, all personnel to be involved in the "stake-out" should be thoroughly briefed and involved, as necessary, in the making of minor (and, in some instances, major) changes in the plan. In other words, all involved personnel should be "sold" on the merits of the plan before its implementation in order to reduce possible chances of failure or disruption.

7. *Implementing a plan.* The execution of a plan requires the issuance of orders and directives to involved units and personnel, the establishment of a schedule, and the provision of manpower and equipment for carrying out the plan. Briefings must be held and assurance must be received that all involved personnel understand when, how, and what is to be done.

8. *Evaluating the effectiveness of the plan.* The results of plans should be determined. This is necessary in order to know whether a correct alternative was chosen, whether the plan was correct, which phase (if any) was poorly implemented, and whether additional planning may be necessary. Also, the effects of the executed plan on other operations and on total departmental operations must be determined. Follow-up is the control factor essential for effective departmental management.

IN BRIEF

The following format can be used for all Security Plan Development activities.

To:

From:

Subject:

1. *Problem.* A concise statement of the problem written in the form of goals or objectives to be met.

2. *Assumptions.* Any assumptions necessary for a logical discussion of

the problem must be identified and explained. (If there are no assumptions, this paragraph may be omitted.)

3. *Facts bearing on the problem.* A logical presentation of all essential facts about the problem must be shared with all those participating in the development activity. (If there are no facts, omit this paragraph and renumber subsequent paragraphs accordingly.)

4. *Discussion.* A concise and logical analysis of the essential facts and assumptions must be undertaken in order to arrive at sound recommendations and conclusions.

5. *Conclusions.* A presentation of the results derived from the judgements reached during the discussion is provided in an objective manner. Various alternatives considered in the discussion are eliminated in this section and a reasoned judgement presented. (This paragraph may be omitted in brief studies. If so, renumber the paragraphs accordingly.)

6. *Action recommended.* Recommendations should be completed and concise statements of any actions suggested or recommended presented in a form that only requires approval or disapproval.

CHAPTER 4

Management Techniques

This section provides a variety of proven management techniques for analyzing conditions, problems, and incidents affecting the security of an organization. These techniques provide the means for developing solutions to problems as well as assistance in the reorganization of existing security programs.

The following techniques will provide management in any organization with a series of procedures that can be useful in the planning, implementation, administration, and evaluation of protection programs. The management techniques that will be discussed below are universally applicable to virtually any size or type of program. Further, with minor adjustments, they all should be considered evolutionary in nature and suitable to continuous changes as new methods are developed and evaluated as satisfactory for implementation.

This text will, in the following pages, present various perspectives on organizational management systems that will hopefully provide a basis for comparative analysis and also allow for utilizing selectively the information presented in formulating individual programs and systems. Enormous technological changes have taken place in the industrial and commercial sectors of the economy, particularly in terms of the principles by which operations can be technically managed and organized. These changes have also been far more drastic and obvious than those occurring in the protective services field, which have been, at best, discreet. Yet, there is considerable evidence that indicates that this situation is rapidly changing.

In any event, these changes have, nonetheless, greatly affected the management of general operations in such diverse areas as organizational planning, control budgeting, and staffing. For this reason, if for no other, private protection must make every effort to keep pace with the environment in which it must function. To more readily achieve an acceptable level of professional service, each protection program should consider organizing its operation around an individualized management system that will effectively minimize errors while still keeping the security and safety functions advancing at an acceptable pace so that needs for service are met. The following systems are offered only as examples since each organization is, in fact, unique unto itself in its conditions and needs.

RISK MANAGEMENT

In the total environment of protective services, one of the most used methods for recognizing, appraising, and anticipating critical loss is the technique known as *risk analysis* or *risk management.* Although this management system was originally developed primarily as a tool for complex aerospace programs, the logic and principles of risk management have many applications in other areas, including safety and security. Risk management requires the identification, tabulation, evaluation, and solution of all conceivable hazards. **Hazards** can be defined as any conditions that have potential for causing losses, and, further, they are concerned with the followup activities that are designed specifically to guarantee that all remedial measures implemented will either control or eliminate those hazards that have infiltrated an organization's operation.

The initial step to take in initiating any risk management program is to conduct some kind of analysis or audit designed to determine the total potential for hazards or losses occurring within the organization. Such an audit should contain, but not be limited to, the collection of security and safety data including material on accident and incident analysis; existing specifications on protection programs, operations, and personnel checklists used during the period of analysis; and plans, concepts, and proposed operating systems for present and future. As the audit continues, it should also serve as a descriptive catalogue of all existing and potential hazards.

Identifying these hazards primarily involves making determinations about what will happen, good or bad, in any given situation within the confines of your organization. According to the Public Security Center, a division of the International Association of Chiefs of Police, there are five different types of risks with which organizations consistently have to deal:

1. *Dynamic risks* fluctuate under certain conditions such as weather or location.
2. *Static risks* remain constant, without regard to other factors, such as regulations, laws, or standards.
3. *Inherent risks* are unavoidable and are associated with a certain product, industry/business, or procedure.
4. *Speculative risks* are those which an organization subjects itself to when it initiates any new program, procedure, or operation, and also, when it enters into any activity which might subject it to any other risk.
5. *Pure risks* are those risks to a system—such as natural disasters or criminal acts—that do not fall into any of the above categories.

The same document goes on to say that these risks can be more systematically identified if the sources of the risks are known. Normally, these basic sources can be placed into one of the following categories:

1. *Human factors,* probably the greatest single source of risk, including both human error and failure.

2. *Mechanical factors* are sources of risk resulting from any reliance on some type of machinery or equipment.
3. *Environmental factors* include both physical environment—weather and climate—and social environment—crime rates and civil disorders.
4. *Procedural factors* are those sources of risks caused by the use of certain procedures, routines, or operations.

Once hazards are identified and catalogued, the next step in a risk management program is to determine the probability or likelihood that any of the hazards might occur. In this type of system two kinds of determinations can be made:

1. Factual determinations
2. Relativistic determinations

Factual determinations of probability are made by measuring the actual occurrences of a particular hazard over a significant period of time to make the sample reliable. This sample may be taken either from within the organization or, if necessary, from a whole of which the organization is but a part. Should conditions dictate, a sample may be taken from a similar organization, although this should be considered the least acceptable method of data collection.

Examples

If data on an organization's crime status indicates that one of every 20 employees is caught stealing company property, the corresponding probability is 1/20.

If government statistics show that every day one of every eight employees will take off ill, the probability of the occurrence will be 1/8.

Relativistic determinations of probability are actually made from a rating scale that uses predetermined numerical values assigned to various probabilities:

*   The event will *certainly* occur   — 4/5
*   The event will *most likely* occur   — 3/4
*   The event is *moderately probable*   — 2/3
*   The event is *not likely* to occur   — 1/2

To add even more credibility to these relativistic determinations, it is most beneficial to have those that identify the hazard make value judgments about which of the five categories is most applicable.

No matter which of the two systems is used to determine probability, both require that fractional figures be converted to percentage figures. Once percentage figures are given and a tabulated list is made, ranking the hazards from high to low, the list will then readily show the comparative severity of each, making decision making easier.

What should be noted here is that both of these probability systems, even though valuable evaluation tools, are limited in their uses. Factual determinations are best suited for those situations where the hazard can be analyzed through some type of reliable statistical or mathematical data that applies directly to the hazard. Those hazards that occur with enough frequency to make it possible for statistics to be gathered and then analyzed are best examined with factual determinations.

On the other hand, relativistic determinations are best used to appraise hazards occurring with less frequency. Normally, hazards appraised using this type of determination are those that, without regard to consequence or loss, cannot have their future occurrences predicted.

William T. Fine's article in *Lifeline* Magazine, added another dimension to risk management with the explanation of his *Risk Score Formula*. This formula allows for the existence of economic risks in hazards, and he, in turn, injects into the system the consequences of a possible loss or accident due to such a hazard. **Consequence,** as part of the Risk Score Formula, is defined as the most probable result of a hazard.

According to Fine's Risk Score Formula, once a consequence is determined, it is categorized and then given numerical ratings as follows:

Severity of Consequence	Rating
Catastrophe	100
Extensive damage-loss over $1,000,000	
Several fatalities	50
Loss/damage $500,000 to $1,000,000	
Fatality	25
Loss/damage of $100,000 to $500,000	
Extremely serious injury	15
Amputation, permanent disability	
Loss/damage of $1,000 to $100,000	
Disabling injury	5
Loss/damage up to $1,000	
Minor injury	1
Cuts, bruises, minor damage	

In connection with the consequence ratings add the following probability ratings:

Hazard will most likely occur	10
50/50 chance that the hazard will occur	6
Would be unusual if the hazard occurred	3
Hazard's occurrence is only remotely possible	1
Extremely remote that a hazard will occur but possible	.5

Even though Fine has a third scale for his formula, it is complicated and adds little more to the credibility of the formula than the two already given.

Once a hazard has been identified, determine which of the five categories on both scales that it falls into, and then multiply the consequence rating by the probability rating to obtain a risk score. *What must be remembered, though, is that there is no particular significance to any risk score unless other scores for hazards are computed using the same criteria for making decisions and judgments.* When there are a series of risk scores to deal with, comparative analysis is possible just as in the case of relativistic and factual determinations of probability.

When final mathematical calculations are made on determined hazards of an organization, it then becomes the responsibility of management to make a decision as to the status of each hazard. Under most circumstances there are five general options open to management as they anticipate dealing with individual hazards.

1. *Accept the risk.*   For whatever the reason, there are certain risks that cannot be avoided or eliminated. There are those that are simply too expensive to act against and those that are unavoidable just because they are inherent in a particular industry.
2. *Avoid the risk.*   Avoiding a risk can be accomplished in either of two ways:
    A.   eliminate the hazard or
    B.   eliminate the activity that contains or causes the hazard.
3. *Reduce the risk.*   A risk can be reduced by either lessening the probability of its occurrence or by lessening the severity of the hazard.
4. *Redistribute the risk.*   A risk can be redistributed by changing operations, procedures, or activities so that the hazard is spread throughout the system. By doing so, the impact of a hazard on any one part of the system can be appreciably lessened.
5. *Transfer the risk.*   The difference between risk redistribution and risk transference is that the latter uses the assumption that the risk or hazard is transferred to some outside source. Transferring a risk is ordinarily done by obtaining appropriate insurance, thereby putting the burden of the risk on the insurance company.

Even though these five alternatives for coping with security and safety hazards were mentioned as part of an explanation of risk management, they are universally applicable no matter what type of management technique is used. *The only consideration that must be allowed for is that the severity of some hazards tends automatically to make some of the five options unacceptable or less acceptable.*

Even after management decision-making techniques are implemented within an organization, security managers and management planners often still find it difficult to isolate those factors that cause the day-to-day problems that their organizations are faced with. Nonetheless, their responsibilities for the safety and protection of their organizations make it necessary that they be knowledgeable about the many hazardous situations, problems, crimes, and loss conditions that they might encounter. Unfortunately, most managers have limited amounts of time to do needed planning and analysis and an even more restricted amount of financial assistance specifically allocated for isolating these problem situations to analyze them or to implement solutions for them.

By definition, analysis is a process of breaking up, dividing, or separating a condition, process, or activity into component parts. The analysis and data collection process normally includes the gathering of information such as data or documents relative to the problem under consideration, the classifying and subdividing of the information into appropriate groupings, and the summarization and tabulation of data within these groups. Finally, it is the formulation of conclusions and possible interpretations of the evaluation results in order to show the effectiveness, desirability or usefulness of a program's improvement or modification.

Requirements for effective analysis should also include:

1. A realization that there is a need for some type of analysis or evaluation to take place
2. Adequate facilities, funds, equipment, personnel, and time for gathering necessary data and conducting the analysis
3. A competent knowledge of the techniques for data collection that will be employed
4. A true desire on the part of both staff and management to see that the analysis/evaluation is done well
5. An agreed upon commitment to seeing that situations deserving change, brought to light by the analysis, are readily and properly acted upon

---

IN BRIEF

One of the most critical problems affecting the success of risk management efforts is ensuring the proper detection of risks. Frequently, managers make decisions on risk conditions too quickly or move from analysis and evaluation to resolution without giving adequate attention to all of the factors that created the risk. Unfortunately, lack of due care and caution can have near catastrophic consequences for the manager in a hurry. Not only can important hazards be overlooked, but emphasis can also be inappropriately placed on the wrong types of risk conditions. Because one is concentrating on the consequences of risk conditions rather than on the risk and its causation, adequate attention may never be given to the most important element in the process—the accurate identification of risks.

Time is invariably our greatest ally when we strive for accurate risk detection and subsequently successful risk management.

PARTICIPATORY MANAGEMENT

Participation is one of the most misunderstood ideas that has emerged from the field of human relations. Therefore, dealing with what participatory management is *not,* is the first essential step toward understanding what it is.

First, participation need *not* cover every phase of management. Some areas are suited to group decision making while others are best left to management discretion alone. Common sense, invariably, will be the best guide in deciding which method to use and when to use it.

Second, every member of the group is *not* equal. While this method encourages input from the total staff and strives for consensus, this does not mean equal influence is exerted by everyone, nor do decisions necessarily have to reflect the point of view of the least competent members.

Finally, the use of participatory management does *not* mean that there is no place in an organization for individual leadership. There is still much room for evaluation and decision making on the part of management. Management is still likely to be held fully accountable and responsible for the quality of all decisions, their implementation, and the results they yield. An increase in *group power* is not necessarily obtained at the expense of management's ability to exert control. Participatory management should be seen as a welcome sharing of responsibility and work load rather than as a usurping of power or a weakening of authority.

Participatory management is a state of mind, an attitude that is shared by managers and subordinates alike. Rensis Likert's System 4, Douglas McGregor's Theory Y and Joseph Scanlon's Scanlon Plan are all attempts to combine the same basic elements to achieve organizational harmony. All these men, through their theories, have recognized the most necessary and fundamental force in the human organization as people. We all have both social and individual needs that, if met, allow us to experience greater job satisfaction and increased productivity at work and lead toward greater personal happiness and achievement.

The key is simple. Employees have feelings that are as important as, if not more important than, economic factors. Consequently, a management that correctly identifies and fulfills these needs is the one that most often reaches desired organizational goals and objectives. Conversely, systems that ignore employee satisfaction very likely will not have an operationally successful staff no matter how good the salaries. Participatory management, therefore, sees employees as more than mere production statistics or workhorses. They are, in fact, considered the most vital resources in the organization.

Any work climate, to be genuinely successful, must meet a wide range of these personal needs. Effective participation offers an opportunity for each member of an organization to contribute his or her brains and ingenuity, along with his or her physical effort, both to meet these needs and to improve organizational effectiveness.

Gone is the old theory that if people would only do more of what they are supposed to do, then productivity would be increased. Management must now take into account the valuable contribution that can be made by workers who can draw from their own creativity, unique work and life experiences, and common sense judgments. At the same time it should also recognize the employees' needs, and even their right to have reasonable control over decisions that directly affect them in the workplace.

Allowing the individuals active and responsible participation in decisions that affect their careers or job situations can, first of all, be easily defended as the right thing to do. Every other aspect of our life, especially in the United States, is based upon the principle of personal participation. Our national and local governments, most social organizations, and church groups are all run through some form of either direct or indirect representation by the people involved. Then, should such a large part of an individual's life, his job, be the only area excluded?

Further, the practical fact is that management systems using group decision making and supervision are more productive and successful in achieving desired goals and objectives. The body of professional management literature supporting this fact is convincing and increasing rapidly. Summarily, it concludes that the most efficient and productive management systems are also the ones most satisfying to employees. This is not to say that there won't be disagreements. These differences, however, will be out in the open and settled by group discussion.

Group decision making is not only an advantage to management by increasing worker interest and efficiency, but it is also a good problem-solving tool. A group of employees with varied educational levels, backgrounds, and interests but with the same practical job experience, can sometimes do a better job of identifying problems and their solutions than can a manager with only one point of view and who may also be removed from the actual work environment. Additionally, people like to be consulted about, and participate in, actions that will personally affect them. In short, employees want to be treated as belonging to, and being an integral part of, some group.

Through participatory management these needs are met and in turn employees fulfill management's major need—a successful, cooperative, and productive organization.

All of this may sound like an unattainable management never-never land. But it is being done and not only in large factories. It is more often found in public service organizations with higher staff-education levels than exist in large business.

Yet, with the push for security professionalism raising the educational levels within individual departments, participatory management is just the method to meet the demands of a more informed and progressive staff.

Not only employees but managers as well are calling for the security department to become both a more open and a more participative organization. Participatory management is indeed an effort to engender professional pride, improve labor-management relations, and elevate departmental performance. Consultation with union committees on such issues as uniform changes, officers' safety, loss control, and job enrichment appears to have provided stimulation and challenge for security officers working with top management.

Participatory management can work, even in a quasimilitary, crises-oriented structure like the modern security department. It takes a skillful manager, an administrational will to at least give him or her the benefit of the doubt and a medium-size flexible work group willing to work cooperatively to reach agreed-upon goals.

Undercover investigations, stake-outs, surveillance, or even routine investigations require security personnel to be in and out of the office and not always under close supervision or in touch with coworkers. Group management would provide their link to the unit's affairs while giving them personal motivation to put forth their best efforts in achieving the unit's goals, making close supervision unnecessary.

The most important decision facing the head of a security department who wishes to institute this system is how much supervision to use and when to use it. Security work often requires action without much discussion. As a result, participation must be both feasible and realistic in terms of what needs to be accomplished. The degree of its use, therefore, will depend on a variety of factors.

Probably the most basic variable is size. A department with 25 officers is going to have a different amount and style of participation than one with only 5. A larger department should be divided along division, bureau, section, or shift lines into participation groups of no more than 10 and no less than 5. This allows a workable size but a variety of viewpoints. The larger the unit the less direct the participation, often making some form of indirect employee representation necessary.

Another factor is how immediate is the need for a decision. A manager can ill afford to spend a half hour talking over which officers to assign to a major on-the-job accident when employees on the scene are calling for assistance as soon as possible. Here the rule of thumb must be that problems that require quick decisions or ones where time is a factor, such as assignments while in the field or emergencies, are to be made by the superior alone. Later, perhaps the group can be given a chance to discuss how the decision was made and voice complaints or suggestions for the future. Most of the staff will be able to recognize these instances with no question. However, a written policy, drawn up with representative members of the unit having a chance for input, should spell out as definitely as possible specific situations where group participation is forbidden.

Another consideration is the staff itself. What are their levels of *experience*? What are their individual *backgrounds*? How much *education* have they had? How *independent* are they? It is foolhardy to take 10 people unaccustomed to working in a group setting or to making major decisions and suddenly dump a large batch of problems into their laps for solutions. The result might well be poor decisions, bad feelings, and chaos.

Success depends upon the manager's ability to gauge subordinates' capabilities. If they are not experienced enough, it is wise to start small and pick things directly related and important to everyone. Then, as they learn through experience, let them branch out into other areas. It will take time to evolve a group able to create solutions easily and efficiently, but it will be well worth the effort.

The mechanics of operating a security department using participatory management is not as complicated as one might expect. Since the nature of participatory management leaves a lot of the specifics open and flexible, different departments will be able to implement what works best for them.

Yet, there are two forms of participation that should be developed and used equally. They are group and individual participation.

The cornerstone of the group method is the regular weekly meeting of the entire security staff. All members from every shift, whether on duty or not, should be required to attend these sessions. Also, they should be scheduled for the same day and time each week so there is no confusion. If at all possible, a private room away from the noise and constant interruption of the office should be used. If there is no civilian to take care of the office during this period, it may be necessary to rotate officers for this purpose. A written record of the meeting should be kept. This assures that there will be no misunderstanding as to what was discussed and what was decided. These minutes should be typed up by the unit secretary with a copy for the supervisor and a copy to be put where everyone has access to it.

The department manager is the one who will be instrumental in the success or failure of these group sessions. He must realize that genuine group participation is not merely his listening to the investigators' ideas. He must be willing to responsibly consider and use them if at all possible. It is also necessary for him to allow the staff complete control over some decisions. Most importantly, he must make clear the distinction between "we'd like your opinion" and "the final decision is up to you."

Don't ask the staff to decide on anything unless the decision is really up to them. Going back on promises and misrepresenting the issues is the surest way to lose the trust and confidence that is critical to group decision making.

Managers' principle function at these meetings is not that of leader. They should keep a low profile. If there is a subject they wish to discuss they should introduce it and then allow the others to take over. Remember that managers who dominate the staff and manipulate the conversation are not practicing participatory management. They are practicing puppeteering.

However, there is a need for some control. All groups, especially at first, have a tendency to wander from their purpose. There should be a chairperson whose job it will be to keep the discussion on a constructive track with a minimum of idle talk, one who should make sure everything is clear and understood and that everyone has a chance to speak. Responsible decisions can be made only if there is widespread participation. A few vocal members should not be allowed to take over. Therefore, the chairperson should make it a point to solicit opinions from those members who do not volunteer.

The supervisor is not the best choice for this position. Often, there will be an officer in the unit who will have the skills and personality for this job. Here is a good opportunity to uncover and build leadership potential in members of the unit. A chairperson should be chosen by election at the first meeting. Periodic reelection thereafter insures everyone who wishes a chance for the position, prevents one person from obtaining too much power, and gives the manager an opportunity to evaluate the leadership capabilities of a number of his staff.

The actual procedure for these meetings is the group's responsibility. However, the manager must have already decided his personal goals and objectives for these staff sessions. This is at least a mental, if not a written, plan to be developed and used much like any other management system. It must designate what areas the group will cover and how participation is appropriate and feasible.

Individual participation promotes employee satisfaction. It stimulates job growth. The staff will actually seek to extend their responsibilities and workload, rather than shirking extra duty. Allowing individuals the right to have a hand in shaping their own job future will give them the incentive to put forth their best effort in achieving the goals they and their supervisor have set together.

Participatory management can also involve individual participation. An officer should be able to discuss with his immediate manager, and in some cases cooperatively make decisions on, areas that affect his day-to-day work atmosphere and his future job status. This element of participatory management is fostered by an open-door policy by the manager. Employees must be able to walk in and discuss any aspect of their job with the supervisor and not feel they are wasting their breath. Yearly job evaluations are not enough. Often, officers see these simply as gripe sessions with the manager listing all of their deficiencies. More frequent meetings, where job satisfaction, career opportunities, or training can be discussed should be scheduled. A busy department head may find it difficult to fit everyone in, but the rewards will be worth it!

No management system can be all things to all people, and this system may not be for every department. There are disadvantages to participatory management. Decisions take longer, responsibility is more scattered, and there is less central control. These faults, however, can be handled and far outweighed by its advantages.

The security manager who effectively uses group methods of decision making, group supervision, and individual participation will find his organization will display greater group loyalty, higher performance goals, greater cooperation, more assistance to peers, fewer feelings of unreasonable pressure, more favorable attitudes toward the supervisor, and higher job motivation.

IN BRIEF

To be effective in using participatory management, you must recognize and accept the fact that employees cannot always participate in decision making. Consequently, it is very important to carefully decide when and to what extent it is appropriate for them to be involved.

At one extreme, managers can exercise virtually autonomous control over the decision-making process, while at the other extreme, they use almost none. In between there are infinite degrees of compromise. The amount of authority invoked by management or the freedom given to employees, therefore, should be determined by critical evaluation of the situation's sensitivity, the employees' objectivity and ability, and finally, management's willingness to implement change based on the recommendations of the group.

MANAGEMENT BY OBJECTIVES

Although Management by Objectives (MBO) has been used in business for a number of years, its use in the private security field has not been that prevalent. While the implementation of MBO might be more difficult in larger security departments, its principles are nonetheless adaptable to all.

Like the other management techniques that have been offered, MBO does not represent a solution to all management problems. It is suggested as only one additional management technique that has proved workable in the past.

The essence of MBO can be summarized and expressed using five key phrases:

1. System
2. Common goals
3. Results
4. Identification
5. Appraisal

1. *System.*   MBO, to be successful, requires that the following determinations be made:
    A. What is the organization doing to achieve its objectives?
    B. What steps are required to accomplish its objectives?
    C. How much will it cost to meet those objectives?
    D. What constitutes a level of satisfactory performance by the organization?
    E. How much progress is being achieved towards reaching objectives?
    F. What is being done to keep the organization's operation *on track* toward its objectives?

    Thus, MBO can really be classified as a planning process, by virtue of steps A and B, and a controlling function as shown in the remaining four steps.

2. *Common goals.*   This term relates to the definition given to the primary function(s) of the organization. This function (or these functions) should then give direction to the goals and objectives that the organization sets for itself.

    In addition, each subdivision within the organization will have its own goals and objectives that must be in line with both the functions and goals of the organization.

3. *Results.*   According to MBO, each goal should be translated into a series of objectives. These objectives then become the measurable targets to be achieved by the specific areas of operation. Consequently, various results can be compared with the previously determined objectives so that the need for modification or redirection can be seen more easily.

4. *Identification.*   When MBO is not used, goals and objectives are often identified by only individual managers or by only one level of management. As a result, the goals and objectives that have been decided upon often filter down through the system in the form of mandates that then meet with resistance from lower-level management and the general employee population.

    MBO, by contrast, gives the responsibility for developing and implementing goals and objectives to those in management who also have the responsibility for seeing that they are achieved. Each manager and his subordinates jointly identify the basic functions they are to perform and the specific results that they plan to achieve. By working in this manner, it becomes much easier for subordinates to perceive their places within the total management picture. Similarly, the coordination between superior and subordinate is greatly enhanced, and the distinction between the two groups is appreciably lessened.

5. *Appraisal.*   This part of the MBO process constitutes the management function of controlling the organization's direction. Since the objectives in MBO can be used as standards against which progress can be judged, it is easy for management to make its determinations on the course the organization should take to achieve goals.

This controlling function can be better accomplished if superiors and subordinates agree to meet regularly to mutually determine levels of progress in the various subdivisions of the organization. During these meetings potential and actual problems should be identified and then corrective action decided. If necessary, top-level management may have to develop an appropriate schedule for these meetings.

Although MBO has been characterized as a technique promoting a democratic form of management with little management-level control, this is not the intent or purpose of the system. It is rather a system that aids management in identifying its goals and objectives so that the responsibilities for achieving those goals and objectives can be designated more efficiently and effectively. These goals and objectives need not be equivalent but they *must* be compatible. The best way of achieving harmony throughout the organization is to make certain that each managerial and operational level adequately contributes to the objectives of the next higher level of the organization.

In applying the MBO technique, it is imperative that well-ordered steps be followed. The original step in MBO is that of *planning*. Meticulous care should be taken during this phase, since it is here that management must determine:

1. Why the organization exists?
2. What should it be accomplishing?
3. What should it accomplish in the future?

While these questions appear initially to be fairly simple, the answers require considerable thought about the role security is to play now and in the future. They require taking a close look at the more traditional role of security as compared to the evolving, more innovative requirements being placed on security by business and industry. The answers to the questions may show that methods, programs and procedures previously accepted, and therefore unchanged, are now completely outdated and unworkable.

The result of such discussions and planning should be a revised set of appropriate and applicable goals and objectives. As these goals and objectives determine the long-range directions for the entire organization, it becomes obvious that management's authority has not been undermined. They have, instead, enhanced management's position as it now takes on the additional role of coordinator of the efforts undertaken to reach these new levels of activity and accomplishment.

Once the goals and objectives have been formulated, the next step is to *communicate* them downward through the organization. It is recognized that businesses or departments vary in organizational structure, and for this reason the roles of management and its subunits will be simplified for use in this MBO description. In most organizations, top-level management would confer with division heads and explain and clarify the new goals. Each division head would then meet with his immediate subordinates to determine the functions his unit must perform in order to achieve the revised goals. Divisional objectives would then be formulated to support the organizational (or departmental) goals. The division heads would then convey their newly formulated objectives back to top-level management and an in-depth exploratory conference would follow. During this conference, the proposed objectives would be discussed. Many proposals would be rejected until the divisional objectives were *mutually* agreed on by both top management and divisional administrators.

The divisional administrator would then confer with his immediate subordinates to discuss the new objectives. Each progressive sublevel of the organization's management system should then see that the objectives were transmitted downward throughout the entire organization.

As these new objectives filtered down, it would be vitally important that the supervisors at each sublevel explain, in detail, the effects of the changes on the employees and, in turn, their responsibilities in meeting the new objectives. The result would be that each employee of the organization would know his relationship to the new goals and objectives.

With MBO, progress is primarily determined by the degree of success or achievement realized as a result of implementing new objectives. Therefore, at regular intervals, progress within an organization or its subunits must be examined and measured regularly by management. This process should really be one of review and should involve a detailed look at the progress made during the preceding period toward receiving stated objectives. Basically, management must examine the objectives and what effort has been expended to reach them.

As MBO progresses, emphasis can then be directed where it is needed, new priorities initiated, and even better, more up-to-date objectives can evolve. Objectives must not remain static but must, out of necessity, change if progress is to continue. Objectives must be continually evaluated and revised, and then the entire operational procedure of the organization must be adapted. This process will not necessarily result in an abrupt change in the direction of the organization, but it may very well make a present direction easier to follow.

IN BRIEF

Advantages of MBO

- MBO forces management to look at the future—to do long-range planning.
- MBO forces management to set priorities.
- Intraorganization cooperation and coordination is stimulated.
- MBO is easy to understand and easy to implement.

Disadvantages of MBO

- Goals and objectives can become ambiguous as they filter down through the organization.

Similarly, it is very difficult to obtain up-to-date, reliable, and accurate basic data about hazardous conditions that exist within an organization making it difficult for quality decision making to take place. Thus, if the collection and analysis phases of a problem-solving cycle are to be made more effective, the task of identifying problems and developing solutions should be to make the difficult and tedious process easier. The following proven techniques are offered as guides to compiling your own system for problem identification and problem reduction:

- Brainstorming
- Nominal group process
- Fault tree analysis

BRAINSTORMING

Creative techniques that can be used for problem solving are lagging behind the more quantitative techniques like cost effectiveness. But it is these more creative techniques that are needed to solve the more difficult and complex problems that all too frequently face the security manager. Even though the quantitative techniques give the manager a certain level of security because of their simplicity, they can often lead to ineffective or misleading conclusions.

Managers often look upon quantitative techniques as foolproof methods of problem solving and/or decision making simply because they are based on the firm foundation of mathematics, statistics, and logic. What they fail to realize is that errors often occur, not in the methodology itself, but rather in the calculations and computations within the operation. Consequently, managers who have been complacently going about problem solving in this fashion, find that this ease of operation does not always bring about the success that they expected to achieve.

Brainstorming was originally developed in the early 1950s to help develop creative new ideas in the field of commercial advertising. The purpose of the process is just as the term implies—to use the human brain to *storm* a problem. This storming approach is, accordingly, supposed to manifest itself in an intrepidly bold attack made against actual or potential problems.

Even though brainstorming is a relatively new technique for discovering and solving problems, it is by no means a unique concept. Many Roman and Greek philosophers and academicians used a comparable concept by having their students meet in small, intimate groups so that a more open and uninhibited learning process could take place. Those early teachers theorized that the interaction between students could also enhance their education and make the whole learning process a more unique and worthwhile experience. They felt that each could learn valuable things from the others in the group.

The philosophy behind brainstorming is much the same. Brainstorming is based on the assumption that the interaction between those involved in a management session can breed more and better alternatives to existing problems as well as bringing to light the potential for other problems or hazards.

Brainstorming is essentially no more than a meeting of a group of managers and employees who have an appropriate awareness of safety and security as well as the need for its effective operation and who are in a position that allows them to offer intelligent input regarding an organization's protective services program. It is of little value to offer suggestions as to who should be invited to participate in brainstorming sessions since every organization has its own management procedures that it has to consider. Yet, it is important to mention that often those who work closest to a problem area are more apt to recognize hazards and then propose worthwhile alternative solutions. What can also be done, if circumstances warrant, is to have certain midlevel management personnel brought into these sessions on a rotating basis or, better still, whenever the areas being considered relate directly to their work or to an area in which they have expertise.

Still, what is more important than *who* participates is *what* takes place during each session so that the most worthwhile information possible is obtained. It must be made clear to everyone participating that these brainstorming sessions are to be, above all else, open and creative. One man's silly conception of a problem may lead another to realize a true hazard that may have otherwise gone completely unnoticed.

To ensure that the most benefit possible is achieved from brainstorming sessions, Dr. Fred Luthans of the University of Nebraska detailed in his text, *Organizational Behavior,* the following basic rules for conducting these sessions:

1. Invite inventive and creative thinking.
2. The more ideas the better—promote quantity.
3. Encourage interactions among participants.
4. Withhold criticisms of ideas and suggestions.

If you expect to gain the full benefit of brainstorming, everyone participating must be encouraged to get involved. Make it clear that all ideas are welcome no matter how extravagant they might seem at first. Rarely are great ideas conceived so perfectly that they do not need at least some minor revisions. Success is much more likely to be achieved if everyone works together constructively.

Encourage staff and management to openly discuss problems and possible solutions. Many, many crisis situations have been avoided when a simple, but previously overlooked problem, was brought to light and then solved through intelligent discussion and interaction. Actually, the whole premise behind the verbal interaction that is sought in brainstorming is put best in the well-used cliche that "two heads are better than one."

One man's thought process is often limited by a number of different variables, making his opinions more subjective than others. Unknown biases and prejudices affect one's thinking as well as other mind-narrowing attitudes that can often inadvertently creep into a person's subconscious. For this reason, it is often much better to have the objective views of others, not so involved with the actual problem, to act as a counterbalance to any subjectivity.

Creative thinking is also something that must be cultivated to make brainstorming effective. Every person involved in the sessions must be treated as a knowledgeable professional who is *expected* to have quality ideas on problem areas and the possible solutions for them as well. Let all those participating know that free wheeling thinking is welcome and that they should feel free to make all of their ideas known. What must be remembered, though, is that by nature people often hesitate to voice their opinions for fear that they might be subjected to criticism as a result. Consequently, it is important to limit criticism and instead promote suggestions. Explain how the good ideas of others can be made better, and how several mediocre ideas can be combined into an outstanding one if everyone *works together* without allowing animosity, dislike, or retaliation to creep into the process through inappropriate criticism.

In addition to the guidelines for brainstorming already mentioned, we suggest considering the following:

- Sessions should last only 60–90 minutes.
- Problems should be clearly stated and should be concise enough that the discussions can *key* on the problems.
- General problem areas to be discussed should be revealed in advance of the meeting.
- The group should be small enough to promote good interaction among participants.

Sessions lasting less than 60 minutes are too short and often keep participants from voicing their ideas or opinions because they do not want to be the one stringing out the meeting. An hour normally allows everyone ample opportunity to speak their minds without being stigmatized. If a good session is underway and good quality ideas are being brought to light, a meeting should be allowed to continue. Similarly, a sluggish, nonproductive session should be halted as it is time wasting. The thing to remember is that once the momentum slows down and things begin to stagnate, it is best to end the meeting.

Even though the time limitations are arbitrary, they seem fairly well suited for most circumstances. Yet, like so many other techniques, conditions within your own organization will have to dictate which one you finally decide to work with.

Remember also, that if problem areas to be discussed are too broad, participants can spend an entire session simply picking away at small pieces of a larger whole. They can find themselves immersed in a seemingly endless discussion on the complexities of a problem rather than on the problem itself. Here too, it is often beneficial to let participants know in advance what topic is to be considered in a forthcoming brainstorming session so that they can give some thought to what their individual plans of attack will be. An hour before a particular session begins seems to be a reasonably sufficient amount of time to identify and explain what problem is to be discussed. The participants come prepared to tackle a specific problem area without having to spend valuable time in the session psyching themselves up for what is to come. On the other hand, an hour is not so long that it allows for overzealous time to research and prepare a canned speech on a problem. To fully meet the requirements within a brainstorming session, a large degree of spontaneity is needed.

To help ensure this spontaneous atmosphere, it is important that the number of participants be kept at a level where vocal exchanges of ideas will flow freely. Too many participants make it easy for arguments to start or for confusion to overtake the discussion. Conversely, allowing too few to participate makes it possible for the discussion to become very limited in scope and depth.

The type of, or severity of, the problem to be discussed should always be taken into account when deciding on the size of a particular session. The problem itself should also dictate who should participate and how long a session should last. If an extraordinarily critical problem must be confronted, it is quite possible that you might elect to allocate more than one session to the problem, or have various different administrators or experts invited to participate, thereby allowing more than six, eight, or ten opinions to affect the final decision. Still, limit attendance at individual sessions to small numbers but, on a rotating basis, have several sessions where everyone can have at least one opportunity to interact with everyone else. However, if this is done, make sure that the same moderator from management can be involved in all sessions so that the entire process can be effectively coordinated.

This way, brainstorming encourages participation by those who are directly concerned with a system and its operations. Those who have valuable insights into its problems because of their intimate familiarity with equipment, activities, procedures, or operations provide an outstanding resource to draw from during analysis. This is particularly significant since faults, errors, hazards, and malfunctions are best isolated by those who operate within a system, and who often experience the problem on a recurring basis.

IN BRIEF

Advantages of Brainstorming

- Those who know the most about problems or hazards are allowed to correct them
- Simplicity of operation
- Can be used to identify problems and to determine alternate solutions

- Interaction during brainstorming creates cooperation among management
- Low cost—no expense other than time

Disadvantages of Brainstorming

- Technique is only applicable to problem areas where decisions do not have highly technical considerations
- Time consuming

NOMINAL GROUP PROCESS

A rather sophisticated offshoot of both the brainstorming management technique and participatory management is a small group activity known as Nominal Group Process (NGP). NGP was developed by two academics—Andrew H. van de Ven and Andre Delbecq—both from the University of Wisconsin. It was originally conceived with the objective of maximizing the benefits and minimizing the problems associated with various kinds of problem-oriented, small group interaction.

The process involves the implementation of six steps implemented in the following structured sequence:

1. A *silent* generation of ideas in writing.
2. A roundtable listing of those ideas on a flip chart.
3. A serial discussion of those ideas.
4. A preliminary vote listing the priorities or ranking of the ideas *(done in silence)*.
5. A discussion of the vote.
6. A final, *silent* vote including a re-ranking of the priorities.

This structured process is based on social psychological research which indicates that this type of procedure is clearly superior to more conventional discussion groups in terms of generating higher quality, quantity, and distribution of useful information.

NGP is designed to attack a single issue or problem by affording an opportunity for interaction among Experts, where the final outcome is the most equitable solution as determined by the consensus vote of the group. It should be explained that here we define **experts** as those who have an appropriate level of knowledge to enable them to offer viable alternative solutions to the problem.

In one respect, NGP is really no more than a controlled brainstorming session. The direction of this small-group process is achieved through the use of a moderator whose only role is to maintain the structure of the process. Since he does not take an active part in any of the discussions or voting, the moderator need not be an expert in the subject area being discussed. Even though this is the case, it may be advisable to choose a moderator who has an administrative position at least comparable to those on the panel. This makes it easier for him to maintain the maximum control that is necessary for success in NGP.

The moderator's primary function is to walk the experts on the panel through the six steps of the process, so that they can devote all of their energies to the problem without having to be concerned with the rules of NGP. An explanation of each of the steps will better show the structure of NGP and the role the moderator plays in it.

Once the problem has been identified and clarified by the moderator:

Step 1: This 15 minute period is to be used for silent group activity. During this time, panel members will be asked to make a written list of items (solutions) that they feel are appropriate to the problem. It is important to ask participants to work singly and silently and to compose their lists in key words or phrases—not sentences or paragraphs.

Step 2: This step consists of a roundrobin recording of all items on the participants' lists. All items are to be recorded on a flip chart or chalk board, with each participant offering one item from his list in the roundrobin fashion. The moderator should list the items on the flip chart. Thirty minutes is allotted for this phase of NGP.

Step 3: The next step of the process is a 15 minute discussion period. The objective of this phase is the clarification of the items that have previously been listed. In this phase it is important to keep in mind the time constraints—the moderator must insist that participants be brief and concise, not only in clarifying their items when asked to do so, but also in asking for clarification from others. Also, do not collapse or condense items, simply add them on as new items.

Step 4: This step of the exercise consists of a preliminary vote on the importance of the items listed. During this 10 minute period, panel members will be asked to choose, in their opinion, the five most important items. The normal procedure for this voting process is to have each participant list one item on each of the 3 × 5 file cards supplied to them. Tabulate votes on new pages of the flip chart or a different section of the chalk board, so that panel members now realize that they are to give consideration only to those items receiving votes.

Step 5: Following the preliminary vote, there should be a second discussion period lasting 10 minutes. The purpose of this discussion period is the same as the first, and consequently the same cautions given with the first also apply here. The objective here is only to seek clarification of those items shown on the second list.

Step 6: This last step of the process is a 10 minute period given to a final voting procedure. Here again, panel members are supposed to vote on the five items they feel are most important. The difference between this vote and the preliminary vote is that the participants are to rank order their choices with this final vote.

As you can see from the description, every minute of the hour and a half NGP is accounted for. As a result, management receives maximum productivity with a minimum of effort. The structure of the process, kept intact by the time constraints and the moderator's instructions, guarantee that the value of such a management-level gathering is not lost through superficial discussions, conversations, or petty bickering.

Like other group processes, NGP can be adapted to meet the needs of the user. Although panel members should never be less than four, it can go as high as thirty or forty as long as no more than six or seven participants are put at one table and all tables are adequately separated so as not to interfere with each other. Similarly, vote items need not be limited to five. If more specificity is required, two or three items may be requested on either or both votes. As long as the steps are followed, even the time parameters can be slightly expanded to fit a larger panel.

To ease preparation for an NGP session, the following supplies will be needed:

- 36 × 48 lined flip chart or *ample* chalk board space
- easel
- masking tape (to tape completed sheets to wall)
- red marker (for second, tabulated list)
- black marker (for original list)
- pencils (two per person)
- 3 × 5 file cards (five per person)
- 8 ½ × 11 paper, blank except for the issue/question printed across the top
- 8 ½ × 11 paper, blank (used for final vote)

IN BRIEF

Advantages of Nominal Group Process

- Structured and easy to operate
- Minimum expense of time
- Even larger groups can be adapted to NGP
- All participants have "an equal vote"

Disadvantages of Nominal Group Process

- No way to control the actual responses of participants
- Participants must be willing if NGP is to work

FAULT TREE ANALYSIS

Since the collection and analysis of information is often the most time-consuming and expensive part of a problem-solving process, Fault Tree Analysis (FTA) is useful in providing accurate and complete data about problem conditions/hazards fairly efficiently.

Like risk management, FTA is also the result of aerospace technology. It was originally developed and used by NASA for analyzing of risks (hazards) in operating systems and for developing safety programs for those systems. The basic concept of FTA is to provide an ordered way of thinking about a system, process, or action. This makes it particularly significant to protective services programs since they, too, are operating systems that have operations difficulties that can be isolated for analysis.

The outstanding value of the FTA technique is that it allows the managers to concentrate on a specific problem area or hazard without interference from conditions or situations unrelated to the particular event or activity under analysis. It is based on the premise that an undesired event or condition within an operating system can be identified and isolated. Then all of the major factors contributing to the problem or hazard are arrayed in such a manner that all are graphically represented, and all components contributing to the problem are shown. This graphic representation of relationships is most beneficial since the logic of the relationships are then easily visible. The symbols used to represent this logic in the system's operation are, in effect, a shorthand representation of the way in which the system operates in reality. These symbols are identified for you in Figure 4–1.

To better explain the benefit of using FTA, it might well be appropriate to cite the old cliche that "one picture is worth a thousand words." This is essentially what FTA does—it offers a visual picture of a system's problem with only a minimum number of words.

As can be seen in Figure 4–2, FTA provides a very graphic representation of the conditions leading up to an undesired event. It can be noted that crime is an undesirable event caused by a combination of a perpetrator, a victim, and a loss. Notice in Figure 4–3 on *Employee Theft* that the FTA diagram presents a more detailed presentation of all possible problems that could occur either at the first, second, or subsequent levels of a system, subsystem, or component operation. Basically, FTA very clearly details the system relationships between components of a process, event, or activity.

Conducting Fault Tree Analysis

Step 1. The selection of the problem to be analyzed is undoubtedly the most critical aspect of FTA or any other analytical technique for that matter. Assuming that the correct problem or hazard is identified, it should be considered the undesired event—the *crime* in our example.

Step 2: This step involves the array of *all* major elements which contribute

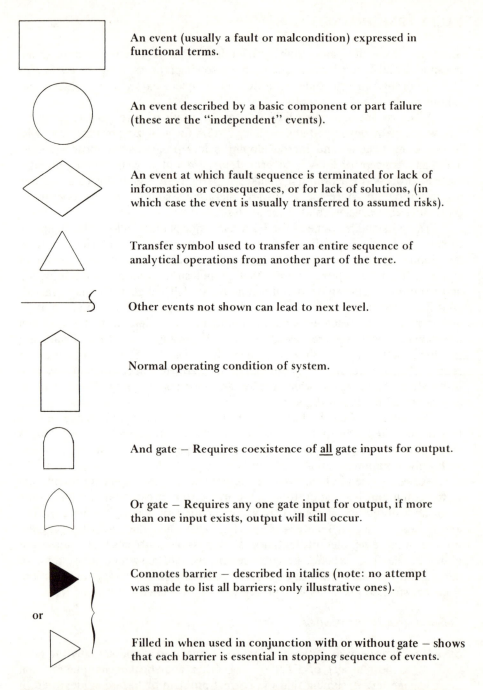

An event (usually a fault or malcondition) expressed in functional terms.

An event described by a basic component or part failure (these are the "independent" events).

An event at which fault sequence is terminated for lack of information or consequences, or for lack of solutions, (in which case the event is usually transferred to assumed risks).

Transfer symbol used to transfer an entire sequence of analytical operations from another part of the tree.

Other events not shown can lead to next level.

Normal operating condition of system.

And gate — Requires coexistence of <u>all</u> gate inputs for output.

Or gate — Requires any one gate input for output, if more than one input exists, output will still occur.

Connotes barrier — described in italics (note: no attempt was made to list all barriers; only illustrative ones).

or

Filled in when used in conjunction with or without gate — shows that each barrier is essential in stopping sequence of events.

Figure 4–1   Fault tree analysis symbols. This partial listing of fault tree analysis symbols is to be used when conducting an analysis using FTA, in order to give additional clarity to the process.

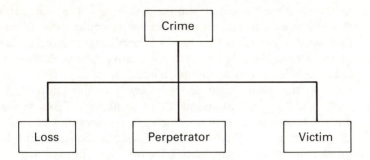

Figure 4–2 Fault tree analysis.

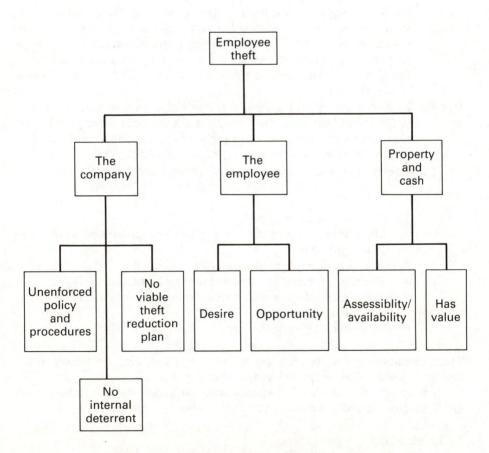

Figure 4–3 Fault tree analysis of employee theft.

to the undesired event. By looking at Figure 4–3, you can observe that the analyst has identified three major contributing factors to the undesired crime. This first level of specifications indicates those primary or most directly observable causative factors that contribute in some *significant* way to the undesirable event.

At this point, each of these *primary* contributing factors can, and should, be considered as a tree of its own. From this level on, each subsequent level of specification will array all of those factors that contribute to this first level of specifications. Figure 4–3 gives an example of how contributing factors to the primary factors should be listed. Figure 4–4[c] shows how all subsequent levels of factors should be listed.

Step 3: The fault tree can continue to additional levels, depending upon the type of problem to be examined. Under most circumstances three levels of specification are considered sufficient but, should a specific problem require additional levels, these can be easily added. The transfer symbol (see Figure 4–4[c]) is used to continue portions of a fault tree that are more detailed and might detract from the basic system presentation. However, when a transfer symbol is used, a second fault tree should be started completely separate of the first. In Figure 4–4[d] the collusion should be the undesired event that begins the second fault tree.

Step 4: FTA can also prove useful in the selection of alternatives once a problem has been identified. It allows management to graphically see the options open to them in eliminating a particular problem. Selecting alternatives at any level, however, is difficult but if the following factors are considered, the process can be made somewhat less involved.

1. The severity of the problem
2. The economic costs of each alternative as compared to the cost of the problem
3. The ease of implementation of each alternative
4. The time involved in implementing each alternative
5. The effects of each alternative on the system and on the organizational operation
6. Estimates of success for easy alternatives

These conditioning factors must be considered in the selection of any alternatives, whether FTA is applied and used or not.

When selecting the level of specification for various factors to be placed in a fault tree, follow the guide given in the following outline:

1st Level: Major categories/types
   Few alternatives: possible effect more difficult to assess
   (depending on problem)

2nd Level: Contributing factors (primary)
    More alternatives: effects can be assessed
    (usually)
3rd Level: Basic units/factors (unusually)
    Most alternative: effects directly assessed without significant difficulty

    Array all alternatives for each factor at the appropriate level.

Level 1:
    General Problem Statements
    Relationships of causal factors less clear
    Postbenefit not always observed
    Little logic available
Level 2:
    Major contributing factors
    Relationships/logic clearer
    Cost/benefit observable
Level 3:
    All relevant factors present
    Relationships/logic most clear
    Tradeoffs made with full knowledge

To bring this technique into clearer focus, Figure 4–4 is an example of how our FTA works with a specific security-related problem—employee theft.
    The fault tree analytical technique can be easily adapted for use by any or all of the following groups.

1. Administrators and managers
2. Planners
3. Analysts
4. Field personnel
5. Supervisors
6. Employees

    FTA can be used by administrators and managers to isolate problems and to identify alternative solutions for each. For the planner it can facilitate the development and monitoring of operational plans and procedures. The analyst can develop a basic understanding of relationships within operating systems. Field personnel and supervisors can analyze problems and conduct field problem solving using FTA. Using FTA they can all further develop an awareness of problems or potential problems, and actual or contemplated plans to eliminate them.
    Employees can learn system operations and its problems in a very graphic fashion using FTA. It is also particularly useful for demonstrating why problems occur as well as providing an opportunity for direct employee input into protective services program development or improvement.

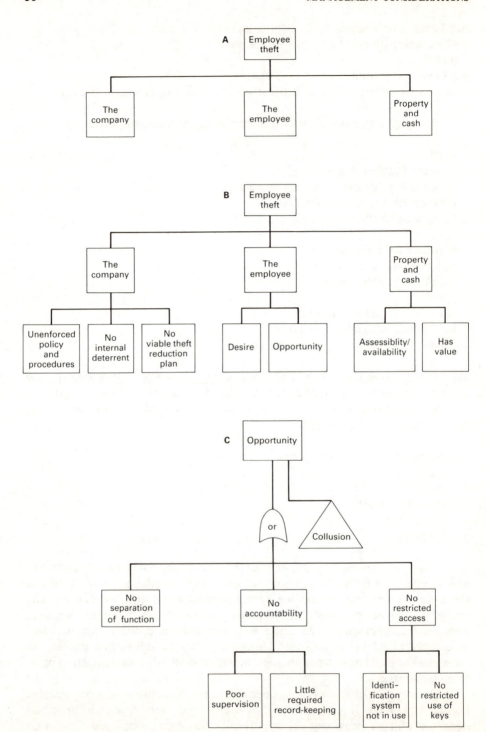

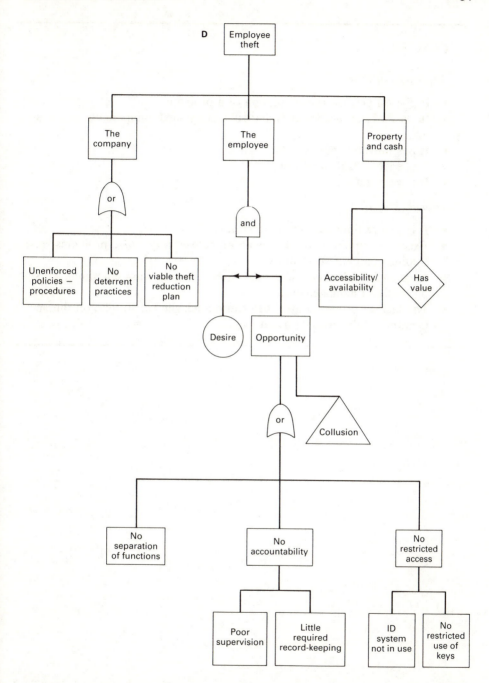

Figure 4–4   Progression of a fault tree analysis. (A) The first level. (B) Expansion with more detail. (C) Detail of a single element. (D) The complete fault tree analysis of employee theft.

IN BRIEF

Advantages of FTA

- It gives a graphic representation of a problem.
- It shows relationships between subsystems and components of a system.
- It has universal application.
- It is easy to learn and use.
- It is very detailed.

Disadvantages of FTA

- It is a very time-consuming operation.
- Excessive emphasis on achieving objectives may cause problems, including competitive hostility.
- Excessive emphasis on achieving objectives may cause emotional stress on midlevel management.
- The lack of proper control can cause management to take on the appearance of dictatorial slave drivers.

CHAPTER 5

Security Management Problems

Many current protection programs are beset by fundamental and inherent weaknesses that have hindered their progress for years. Still, many of these weaknesses can be countered by an effective program of safety and security that is developed after a well-planned, indepth audit and careful planning for implementation.

Problems such as the following are indicative of those affecting the entire industry. Yet, if proper management techniques are applied, even these can be dealt with efficiently. Three specific problem areas seem typically to directly affect security program development or improvement.

- Narrow view of security and protective services
- Universal cures
- Inadequate training

NARROW VIEW OF SECURITY AND PROTECTIVE SERVICES

For years considerable progress in the private security industry has been impeded by a prevalent preoccupation with safety, and in particular with the prevention of personal injury. Management has long felt that the losses incurred through injuries to employees, in terms of down time, and to visitors or customers, in terms of losses through civil litigation, made safety and accident prevention a factor to be dealt with resolutely. Even though most of these programs include measures for fire and disaster protection, in-plant and on-the-job safety, industrial sanitation, and, more recently, environmental safety, they have overlooked such considerations as access control, product and facility security, criminal activities, and industry-related investigations.

This type of channel vision has blinded management to the realization that more is involved in making an effective protection program than simply accident prevention. In terms of dollars lost, theft, fire, and accidents, respectively, rank one, two, and three. Yet, simply because the three elements are aligned as they are does not mean that every organization will confront them in similar order. Management must realize that peripheral vision is required so that they can see the entire picture surrounding their organization and thus make more accurate determinations about their specific safety and security needs. No longer can management simply form a protection program around accident or injury prevention and expect to meet all of the needs of the organization.

This singular preoccupation with accident prevention has also caused management to give less thought to the premise that organizations have individual and varied needs. Granted, the accident prevention element of any protection program is important and certainly must not be played down or overlooked, but these other needs must also be taken into account. Each organization must independently and intelligently appraise its needs, and then plan and develop its program accordingly.

No longer is it appropriate for every organization to systematically implement programs that are no more than mirror images of those others have. A security program must be unique to the organization that it is to serve. A mercantile establishment is likely to be more concerned with theft than is an industrial firm engaged in the manufacture of tractor parts. Although they both must be concerned with the same elements of a protection/security program, they must still make them conform realistically to their individual needs.

During this type of scrutiny, a security audit can be of immense value. When it becomes necessary to evaluate an existing program or to implement a new one, a well-executed audit can offer a considerable amount of information about conditions, problems, strengths, weaknesses, and needs of an organization and its security operation.

Management should also remember, when undertaking the development or remodeling of a protection operation, that no longer can security and safety functions be arbitrarily separated. It is impractical to think that the program can be implemented to do either one without the other and be effective. Security and safety must form a single, integral program.

UNIVERSAL CURES

These universal cures seem to take on two forms, both of which waste time and effort by offering solutions that often have no appreciable positive impact on the environment in which they are used or by requiring that more effort be put into a situation than is really necessary. The shotgun approach is used to blast away at problem situations hoping for random hits, rather than systematically keying on specific components of the problems and then gradually working toward successful results.

It is far more effective to pinpoint problem areas and then seek professional assistance with the expertise to offer equitable solutions that are realistic for both the organization and the situation. Implementing various protection operations, and randomly hoping for success is a very poor approach to achieving a good safety and security program. True success is attained through careful planning and is not by accident.

Arbitrarily installing an alarm system or retaining a guard service is far less likely to solve an organization's loss problem effectively than taking the time to survey the entire operation properly and then take appropriate action. Programs must fit the organization not only in its ability to meet its needs, but also for a cost that it can afford. *Planning* is the key to making it all happen. "It worked for the other guy" is a philosophy that has led many an organization down the path to even more problems and expense. This approach is based on the assumption that a solution that remedies one organization's protection dilemma can, in turn, solve similar problems for others.

An organization has to allow for many different variables when it is preparing to implement a security program all of which are unique to that organization. There are geographic, climatic, physical, personnel, and legal differences that make each organization's position distinctive to it alone. Although any security component is apt to cope very effectively with an organization's protection problem, it still has to be remembered that the solution was undoubtedly designed specifically to meet the need of that particular organization.

Simply because the installation of outside security-type lighting appreciably lessened vandalism and theft from one company's dockyard does not mean similar satisfaction will be obtained by implementing the same type of program elsewhere. A new, well-travelled highway passing nearby may realistically have done as much to eliminate the problem as did the lighting system. Also, a similarly constructed, priced, and implemented system used to cover a yard in a desolate, unpopulated area is, logically, less likely to achieve success unless complementary security components are initiated in conjunction with the lighting.

Commercial advertisements dealing with various security devices also contribute to this problem by allowing the reader of the ad to get the mistaken impression that the product is a cureall for their security problems. This does not imply that the industry lacks an abundance of top-quality equipment. The point being made here is that it is important that management be able to understand their security needs and then be able to seek intelligently the best alternative to solve them. Consequently, the best possible solution for overcoming a security problem is to appraise, slowly and meticulously, current situations, develop realistic objectives, and then implement a program capable of meeting both current and future needs.

INADEQUATE TRAINING

One of the biggest obstacles preventing the true professionalization in the private security industry is the lack of adequate training for its personnel. The private sector has long had an infamous reputation for using retired men on social security and pensions or younger, unskilled persons who work for lower wages. This has, in turn, led most law enforcement agencies to have little confidence in the job that security and safety personnel can do. Consequently, the cooperation and assistance that they offer to private security officers is, unfortunately, often minimal.

Similarly, the general public also holds little respect for private security personnel. Even while crime is increasing and the need for additional protection is more apparent, many people seem hesitant to think that the private sector can offer an acceptable level of service to counter the rising crime rate. Again, this attitude is probably due, in large part, to the quality of the individuals working in the private security field in nonmanagerial capacities.

More importantly, what do client companies and parent organizations think of their own security and safety operations? Do they realize that improvements must come first from within? Do they understand that each organization must first make a wholehearted effort to upgrade its own program before the industry can ever be looked upon with real acceptance?

Standards can, and should, be implemented and enforced to guarantee that more top-quality people are employed and that wages are improved to get a better caliber of personnel. Further, it takes a sincere desire by organizations and their managers to bring real quality to private protective services. Times change and, accordingly, needs change. Thus, it is up to management, through the use of proper administrative practices and techniques, to see that their part of the private sector keeps pace with change. This bit of realism is as applicable to management as a whole as it is to security and safety administrators.

The private security industry has been challenged to provide more effective service at a time when the growing desire for public safety is surpassed only by the increase in the cost of providing that service. These costs are reflected in the growing nationwide expenditures spent on protective services. In response to this mounting fear of personal harm, loss of property, and public disorder, costs for providing these protective services have increased appreciably in the last few years. Unfortunately, though, a great many organizations still do not have unlimited funds to give to their security efforts.

These fiscal facts of life have forced many an organization to recognize that the demand for more and better service cannot be met simply by expanding the size of their operation. Rather, management must learn to use more effectively what resources they do have. They must be able to formulate appropriate management systems that make effective fiscal and operational management possible.

Fortunately, the last few years have indeed brought about considerable improvement in the quality of security personnel and the work they do. In 1984, almost $300 billion was spent on activities directly related to security and loss prevention in the United States alone. Additionally, professional standards now exist to both identify and certify those in the security industry who are well-prepared to confront effectively security-related problems.

SECTION II

Security Audits and Surveys

No organization can expect to remain profitable without taking precautions to reduce or prevent losses. Similarly, no security program can expect to remain efficient without taking steps to ensure that it keeps pace with the ever-changing needs of the organization that it serves. For these reasons managers have long been conducting audits and surveys in order to identify accurately both present and future needs and the resources available to meet them.

The specific reasons for conducting audits and surveys vary. Some are initiated in order to uncover when and how employee thefts are occurring while others may concentrate on identifying deficiencies in physical security systems. Still others are routinely conducted to assist management in developing new security measures needed in the organization and in evaluating those already being used.

Even though audits and surveys, like security programs, must be designed to meet situation-specific objectives, there are several basic *outline formats* that can be universally applied. This section provides a series of these outlines as well as information on the principles of using them effectively.

CHAPTER 6

The Security Audit Process

Briefly, an audit is used to identify and highlight deficiencies in the operation of the organization that adversely affect the quality of security protection.

Under most circumstances, the audit should be separated into three separate phases:

1. An assessment of current loss-control measures, if any
2. An assessment of vulnerabilities to loss and/or theft
3. Recommendations that are appropriate for implementation to curb losses attributed to dishonest employees

Assessing existing loss and/or theft prevention efforts, when done carefully, should provide even more valuable information both on the effectiveness of existing loss reduction activities and on the extent and severity of any theft problem affecting the organization. After completing the first phase of the actual audit, you should be able to make decisions on the continued usefulness of those loss-control measures already in use. In many cases, management will discover that a number of the activities or methods that they have depended upon to curtail losses and theft were partly or totally ineffective and certainly not worth continuing. This particular portion of the audit can also help identify people or resources that have not previously been part of the theft prevention program but possibly ought to be.

The second phase of the audit should concentrate on identifying those areas of the security system that are particularly vulnerable to either loss or theft. Here, it is also important to analyze why current theft-control measures are failing. This analysis should look not only at the failure of procedures and techniques, but also at whether there are some less obvious reasons that ordinarily-good controls did not bring anticipated success. For example, the best system of cash transfer will not be successful if the business office employees consistently fail to lock the safe once the money has been placed inside.

One might also have to evaluate the amount of training given to employees as part of theft-reduction efforts. Even the best loss-control program, improperly implemented by untrained employees, is likely to experience only mediocre success in this instance. Simply remember, when auditing, that it is very crucial to evaluate component parts of a program with meticulous care. You most certainly have to look beyond the obvious. The following checklist should help in this endeavor.

The last phase of the audit process is to develop recommendations for change or modification. Keep in mind two things when making recommendations:

1. Recommendations should be realistic in terms of cost, time, environment (situation), and outcome.
2. Recommendations should be consistent with the needs, culture, and style of the overall organization.

The audits, surveys and check-lists found in this chapter are to be used for conducting a full-scale audit of a company to determine its security problems. Each question that applies to the facility should be answered and the data recorded.

SELF-ASSESSMENT

Although professional assistance will be needed, in most cases, in order to accurately identify the specific security needs of an organization, self-assessments can also prove beneficial. Self-assessments, like the example that follows, can provide management with a preliminary view of just how inclusive or responsive its security efforts are.

These self-assessments typically use the format of a questionnaire and ask for responses that can then help evaluate objectively the status of a security operation. Yet, a great deal of depth and detail is not always found in them.

First, self-assessments are intended only to generate thought—or perhaps, more appropriately, concern—on the part of management. Thereafter, critical decisions should be made concerning what amount of additional, indepth auditing is needed to learn more about specific problem areas.

Secondly, these self-assessments can be easily done internally by managers within the organization. However, even though objectivity can usually be assured by carefully selecting those who will be doing the self-assessment, they are not likely to have the expertise to do much more than collect general information and basic facts needed to answer the questions that are asked. As a result, the subsequent appraisals of individual security defects and deficiencies should be left to security professionals who can also propose appropriate solutions or improvements.

Finally, the actual use of this type of self-assessment, for all of its potential value, is still only intended to offer a starting point. Concerted effort by a group of carefully-selected and concerned managers can do a lot to appreciably improve the overall quality of almost any security operation. However, indepth auditing, done cautiously and thoroughly by security professionals, will invariably tell the final tale.

SELF-ASSESSMENT CHECKLIST

A. Does your company have a formalized, operational security program?
  1. Is security for your company provided by a proprietary staff?
      a. Are candidates for security positions carefully screened prior to hiring in order to confirm:
         1) Previous work experience?
         2) Educational background, both academic and professional?
         3) Lack of criminal convictions?
         4) Mental stability and emotional maturity?
      b. Do you offer your security personnel an *initial* orientation program and thereafter *regular* job-related inservice training?
      c. Is there a prescribed plan, with appropriate policies and procedures, that govern:
         1) The supervision of security personnel?
         2) The scheduling and assignment of security personnel?
         3) The evaluation, promotion, and disciplining of security personnel?
      d. Does your security program include actual procedures for, or activities that concentrate on:
         1) Physical security?
         2) Fire safety and prevention?
         3) Fire suppression?
         4) Emergency and disaster planning?
         5) Accident and loss prevention?
         6) Secured parking areas for specific groups such as employees? visitors?
         7) Restricted access to critical areas?
      e. Is your security program *regularly* audited or evaluated in order to determine efficiency? cost-effectiveness?
         1) Are these audits or evaluations conducted by those inside of the company? outside of the company?
         2) Does your company's top management mandate the careful review of recommendations and, subsequently, the appropriate implementation of recommended improvements?
  2. Is your company's protection provided by a contractual guard service?
      a. Does your company require that the contractual service maintain a specified level of liability insurance?
      b. Does your company require that contractual security personnel have a predetermined amount of professional training

prior to their working on company property? What about regular, inservice training thereafter?

    c. Does your company reserve the right to:
- 1) supervise contractual personnel?
- 2) schedule contractual personnel?
- 3) evaluate the performance of individual contractual guards?

    d. Does your company critically review the performance of the contractual security service on a *regular* basis (as least annually)?

B. Do security personnel provide protection for your company utilizing patrol activities?
1. Are these patrols varied by both time of day and routes taken?
2. Are punch-key (Detex) clocks used during security patrols?
    a. Are these *clock patrols* done only to accommodate insurance requirements?
    b. Are the location of keys regularly evaluated, and is placement changed if needed?
3. Does your company use motor vehicles for patrol activities?
    a. Are there specific criteria used to determine which security personnel will be assigned to motorized patrol?
- 1) Driving record?
- 2) Rank or classification?
- 3) Past performance?

    b. Does your company place operational restrictions on the use of security patrol vehicles?
    c. Is there a formal process for security personnel to use to report promptly safety and security hazards discovered while on patrol?

C. Does your company employ physical security measures in order to safeguard your assets and employees?
1. Does your company utilize *high-security* grade hardware (locks, doors, fences, and so forth) to protect your property's perimeter?
2. Is your property, including parking lots and other critical areas, properly illuminated using systems specifically designed to offer protective lighting?
    a. Are all exits properly lit?
    b. Is there adequate emergency lighting for both inside and outside areas?
3. Are critical and vulnerable areas of your company under constant surveillance utilizing closed circuit television (CCTV)?
4. Are intrusion alarms used to protect your company's perimeter and other sensitive or restricted areas?
5. Are your company's assets protected by a fire alarm system? Smoke detectors?

D. Does your company have a system to manage the distribution and duplication of company keys?
   1. Does this system include:
      a. A formalized, up-to-date record-keeping system that properly documents key distribution, exchanges, and so forth?
      b. Specific controls on the duplication keys?
      c. Well-defined accountability measures for keys that are issued?
E. Has your company identified critical or sensitive areas that need special attention?
   1. Does security make an extra effort to patrol those areas?
   2. Are security devices used to provide *extra* protection or access control for these areas?
F. Does your company have a system to control access and to properly identify both employees and nonemployees that come onto the property?
   1. Are employees and nonemployees required to display company identification badges while on the premises?
   2. Do employee identification badges/cards contain a current photograph?
   3. Are security personnel given the responsibility for verifying identification badges and passes?
   4. Are employees and nonemployees required to enter and exit through specified doors?
   5. Are nonemployees required to sign a register each time they enter or leave?
   6. Are entrances and exits manned by security personnel?
   7. Is there an after-hours policy that controls access to company property during nonworking hours?
G. Are security personnel authorized to make unannounced inspections of personal property brought onto or taken from company property?
   1. Does the company have a policy that details this inspection process?
   2. Is this process properly publicized so that employees and nonemployees alike are adequately acquainted with its provisions?
      a. Are visitors informed through appropriately-placed signage?
      b. Are employees made aware of the inspections during employee orientations and inservices? via employee/company publications?
H. Does your company have a plan for dealing with disasters, fire, or other emergencies?
   1. Does your plan include:
      a. Emergency notification lists?
      b. Emergency operating procedures?

       c.   Coordinated arrangements with police, fire, and other public service or emergency agencies?

   2.   Do security personnel have specific duties and obligations in the event of an emergency or disaster?

   3.   Are all company employees instructed about their specific roles during and after emergencies and disasters?

I.   Does your company have prescribed policies for handling incidents of theft?

   1.   Are security personnel specifically designated to investigate all cases of theft?

   2.   Does your company prosecute nonemployees caught stealing? employees?

SECURITY PROGRAM GOALS DEVELOPMENT CHECKLIST

The Security Program Goals Development Checklist is designed to assist in the identification of security problems associated with the attainment of goals and objectives. It is divided into two parts:

1. Program goals
2. Program activities

The two questions in part one and the three questions in part two must be completed in detail. This data can then be used for determining the degree of compatibility between the desired objectives and existing problems. The Self-Assessment Guide that follows the checklist provides a format for making this comparison.

Part One: Program Goals

A.   List the major goals of the security functions in the organization.

   1.   Example

       a.   Staff

          1)   coordinate protection for V.I.P.'s.

          2)   recommend procedures to improve security weaknesses.

       b.   Operational

          1)   patrol the facility to reduce criminal opportunity.

          2)   report defective locking devices.

          3)   inspect fire extinguishers regularly.

B.   List your corporate philosophy of security. (If area is not developed for the organization, it is essential that an attempt be made to describe clearly what is expected from such a program.)

    1. Examples:
       a. To provide a safe and risk free environment for conducting business.
       b. Protect employees, customers, and the corporation against criminal damage or loss.
       c. Guard against losses and accidents.

Part Two: Program Activities

A. Describe the major protective functions currently performed by security personnel.
    1. Enforcement of security regulations
    2. Protection of assets and personnel
B. List the three "top priority" security problems in your corporation.
    1. Examples:
       a. Reducing losses due to pilferage in the warehouses.
       b. Eliminating unauthorized personnel from entry into work areas.
       c. Reducing theft losses in employee parking area.
C. List supplementary protective or security functions performed in the organization. (Identify as many as possible.)
    1. Examples:
       a. Receptionist performs access control.
       b. Maintenance personnel inspect locking devices and replace defective equipment.
       c. Foremen provide emergency first aid.
    2. Prevention of losses or crime
    3. Investigation of losses or breaches in security
    4. Inspection of equipment, measures, and controls
    5. Handling emergency situations
    6. Reporting violations, hazards, malfunctions, and related incidents

GOALS DEVELOPMENT SELF-ASSESSMENT GUIDE

Problems	Goals
List problems from 2— PROGRAM ACTIVITIES	List objectives from 1— SPECIFIC PROGRAM GOALS

Variances in compatibility between security objectives and priority problems indicate a less than effective use of protective resources. To evaluate where program emphasis should be placed, list the *Program Activity* function in its appropriate problem or objective category.

Problems		Goals	
Example		Example	
Enforcement	1	Enforcement	5
Investigation	2	Investigation	4
Inspection	1	Inspection	5
Emergency	4	Emergency	2
Reporting	3	Reporting	3
Protection	2	Protection	4
Preventing	1	Preventing	5

PRELIMINARY DATA-COLLECTION WORKSHEETS

The Preliminary Data-Collection Worksheets can be used in two major ways:

1. to collect data prior to initiating a full-scale security audit
2. to assist an external consultant in order to:
   A. Reduce data collection time for the consultant
   B. Reduce consulting costs

Specifically, there are four major areas in which data must be collected for the development of a preliminary view of an organization's state of security. These areas are:

1. *General information.* A great deal of general information about the physical plant, neighborhood, key control, ID system, and so forth are required. This list is designed to obtain all relevant data about the general condition of the organization.
2. *Alarm and monitoring equipment inventory.* The collection of information relative to existing alarms and equipment monitoring devices to determine the need for additional or supplementary equipment.
3. *Crime incidence inventory.* This provides for the collection of information from the security office, personnel, and police agencies relative to various categories of criminal activity, unauthorized building entries, and equipment or material losses.
4. *The attitude survey.* This information, obtained by questionnaire, determines the general attitudes of employees toward the company security program.

If an independent security survey is to be conducted prior to the arrival of a consultant, the preliminary data collection should be completed. It can reduce costs and the amount of time required for data collection. If consultants are to be utilized, notification should also be sent to all employees to inform them of their presence in the company, and to ask them to extend help and cooperation to those doing the audit.

General Information

Security Office
1. Number of security officers
2. A detailed list of duties performed by each security officer on each duty shift (prepared under the supervision of the Director of Security).
3. An inventory of security equipment including radios, weapons, and vehicles
4. A list (including location) of any Detex and time clock stations or routes
5. A detailed list by type and location of all fire fighting equipment
6. A complete description of identification card programs
7. A list of all the parking regulations
8. A detailed description of the lock and key system
9. A copy of the emergency operating plan

Physical Plant/Maintenance Department
1. Blueprints, maps, and line drawings
   A. Overall map showing property lines
   B. All major highways and access roads leading to and from property
   C. Blueprints showing all electrical routing, underground and overhead wiring, master control panels, telephone systems, and location of the source of electrical power supply for all facilities
   D. Obtain maps or blueprints showing all sanitary and storm sewer systems.
      1. Show all underground tunnels, manholes, and controlling tunnels.
   E. Obtain maps showing steam, water, and gas systems.
      1. Indicate all master cutoffs, meters, underground tunnels showing access points, above ground systems, monitoring systems, and sources of power.
   F. Obtain information on how, who, and when each of the above systems are monitored.
   G. Obtain floor plans of each building.
      1. Plot location of each of the following:
         a. Doors—general condition
            1) Indicate fire doors.
            2) Indicate exit doors.

      3) Indicate if locked.

      4) Indicate if monitored.

b. Windows

      1) Indicate if locked.

      2) Indicate if monitored—general condition.

      3) Indicate if basement and first floor windows are screened.

c. Fire Alarms

      1) Indicate type.

      2) Indicate condition.

      3) Indicate location.

d. Lights (exit)

      1) Indicate type.

      2) Indicate condition.

      3) Indicate location.

e. Lights (security)

      1) Indicate type.

      2) Indicate condition.

      3) Indicate location.

f. Fire fighting equipment

      1) Check tags for inspection validation initials of fire inspector.

      2) Note if equipment is operative.

g. Hazards

      1) List on separate paper all buildings' hazards.

      2) Indicate if hazards are for security, fire, or safety.

h. Time clock stations

      1) Indicate the use of time clock stations by security personnel.

i. Secured areas within each building

      1) Administrative offices

      2) Equipment storage areas

      3) Boiler rooms

      4) Laboratories

      5) Vaults and safes

      6) Production areas

      7) Master cutoff switches

         a) Electric

         b) Fire Alarms

         c) Gas

         d) Water

         e) Heat or Steam

            (1) Indicate if these systems are monitored.

      8) Computer or EDP center

      9) Research and development areas

    10) Classified records

H. Make provisions to have copies made of blueprints, maps, and line drawings from:
   1. Administrative offices
      a. It may be necessary to have line drawings made for floor plans.
   2. Security offices
2. Physical building inspections will be necessary in order to plot:
   A. Fire alarms
   B. Exit lights
   C. Security lights
   D. Doors (locked)
   E. Windows (locked)
   F. Window screens
   G. Fire fighting equipment
   H. Time clock stations
   I. Security areas (within each building)
   J. Hazards (very important)
   K. Master control panels or access to such areas
   L. Cut off switches for:
      1. Gas
      2. Water
      3. Fire alarms
      4. Heat
      5. Electricity
      6. Telephones
      7. Steam
      8. Sewerage

Alarm and Monitoring Equipment Inventory

The purpose of the Alarm and Monitoring Equipment Inventory is to accurately determine technical data relating to the presence of various types of alarm and equipment monitoring devices. This inventory should be completed under the direction of the building or maintenance superintendent. To aid in this effort, the chart in Figure 6–1 includes the majority of equipment monitoring devices commonly used in physical plant maintenance.

All categories of equipment should be checked as either not present or specific detail data given if a particular item of monitoring equipment is present.

One inventory sheet should be used for each building (or area). Use any coding designated by the company in addition to building names. This will also aid in converting the data into computer format.

If additional monitoring equipment is present that is not included on the inventory list, insure that this information is also provided by attaching supplementary sheets to the inventory.

Building by Name _____

Building by Number _____

CODE:

RR - Rate of Rise	A - Audio Identification
SD - Smoke Detectors	BP - Bypass Switch
RC - Remote Control	VP - Variable Parameters
I - Interior Devices	SC - Supervisory Circuit
	(failure of circuit line)

CATEGORIES	SENSORS			TRANSMISSION		ANNUNCIATORS			DATE OF INST.
	No.	Type	Brand	Wire	Other	No.	Type	Brand	
1) Fire Safety									
2) Exhaust Ventilators									
3) Gas Meter On - Off									
4) Exit Doors									
5) Transformer Hi-Temp Alarm									
6) Power Dist. Air Flow									
7) Exhaust Fans Air Flow									
8) Compressed Air Low Alarm									
9) Steam Main Pressure Drop Low Side									
10) Air Supply On - Off Control									
11) Area Temp.									

CATEGORIES	SENSORS	TRANSMISSION	ANNUNCIATORS	DATE OF INST.
12) Water Pumps				
13) Environment Chambers Temp.				
14) Environment Chambers Humidity				
15) Storage Vault Vent Fans Air Flow				
16) Water Distillers (Low Level)				
17) Intercomm. Stations Mech. Equip. "to Where"				
18) Sump Pumps Hi - Level				
19) Elevators Alarm (Where Sound?)				
20) Environment Chambers Personal Alarms				
21) Emergency Lighting				
22) Emergency Generators				
23) Air Conditioners				
24) Intrusion Devices				

Figure 6–1   Alarm equipment inventory chart.

Crime Incidence Inventory

In gathering crime information, it is necessary to contact the Director of Security and the Chief of Police of local jurisdictions.

The purpose of contacting these people is to gather all of the pertinent information relating to the services performed by the security officers as well as the frequency, location, and types of incidents occurring on company property. The need for all pertinent data relating to the security function is to determine what are the best hours for shifts, how many men are needed for each shift and where trouble areas are located.

The data to be collected should be categorized as follows:

1. Incident, such as theft, vandalism, accident, call for service, employee incident
2. Location of incident
3. Hour of day
4. Day of week
5. Vandalism and theft amount

Data for one calendar year should be gathered so as to show a complete view of security problems. Once the data has been collected, it should be presented in chart form. This chart would consist of 9 spaces on the vertical axis and 27 on the horizontal axis. The vertical axis is for the days of the week, total for that day and percentage of total for each day of all incidents for the year. The horizontal axis contains the 24 hours of the day, the total for each hour and the percentage per hour of the number of incidents for the year.

To find the percentage for each day of the year and each hour of the day, each column is added separately to find the total for each day and each hour. This total is then divided by the total number of incidents for the year. The percentage found is then placed in its proper column for each day and each hour of the day. Once these percentages are found, the two percentage columns should add up to 100 percent. Once this chart is completed, it will present which are the most active days of the week and which are the most active hours per day. With this information, the Security Department can prepare a realistic manpower distribution chart as shown in Figure 6–2.

Proportionate need is used to determine the shift hours and the number of men per shift. The chart previously referred to is used to determine proportionate need. In determining proportionate need, the researcher should try a variety of possible shift arrangements, i.e., 8 to 4, 4 to 12, and 12 to 8; or 7 to 3, 3 to 11, and 11 to 7; or any other combination as long as there are always eight continuous hours to a shift. For each combination, the percentage of the total for each hour of the eight-hour shift should be added. The shift to be utilized is the one with the smallest deviation between the three shifts, i.e,

8 to 4 – 32% of total	7 to 3 – 20% of total
4 to 12 – 33% of total	3 to 11 – 30% of total
12 to 8 – 36% of total	11 to 7 – 50% of total

Time	Sunday	Monday	Tuesday	Wednesday	Thursday	Friday	Saturday	Total	% of total
12 am to 1 pm	TCM	V	M		IC	TA		9	5.77
1-12	C	V		C		M		3	1.92
2-3									
3-4	MC								
4-5									
ETC.									
Total	12							156	
% of Total	7.69							100%	

KEY: C-Crimes; M-Maintenance; V-Vandalism; T-Thefts; I-Student Incidents; H-Accidents.

Figure 6–2 Example of a total incident chart.

The deviation per shift is found by subtracting the percentage of the total from 33.33, which is the average percentage of need for each shift. These three figures are then added together. Once this is accomplished, the shift with the smallest percentage of deviation is selected as the desirable shift.

If the problem should arise that two or more shift possibilities are close together in their percentage of total deviation, the highest percentage of total from one of the shift possibilities should be chosen and subtract each of the other shifts in that shift possibly from it. Once these two figures are found, they must be added to find a total. This is to be done for all the shift possibilities.

Once the shift hours have been determined, the number of men that will be needed for each shift should be determined. This is accomplished by finding the total number of men on the force and subtracting from this figure the number of men used for auxiliary purposes, i.e., radio dispatch, and so forth. This figure is the total men assignable to security activities. Next, this figure is multiplied by seven, which represents a complete week. The product, called *man-day-per-week,* is found and put into a percentage basis. Then the percentage of need per day, which must be carried out only to the tenths place, is multiplied by the man-day-per-week. This product is the total men for a shift. Finally, the total men figure is divided by 1.5 to find the number of men available for duty that day, and this is a relief factor. A relief factor is the number of men on vacation, sick leave, off duty, and so forth. This process must be repeated for each day of the week.

To determine how many men are needed for each shift, first multiply the number of men available for that day by three, which represents the number of shifts per day. This will find the man hours per day and place this product into a percentage. Then multiply the percentage of need per shift by the man hours per day. This will find the total manpower per shift. Then divide the manpower per shift by three to find how many men are needed for a shift. This must be repeated for each shift of the day.

Attitude Survey

A Company Security Study Committee is currently working to improve the protection of both employees and company assets. It now seeks your assistance in learning about employee attitudes about security and protection. All responses are strictly confidential; no names are to be placed on the form.

The Committee is working with management in an attempt to evaluate opinions and suggestions about the quality of the security program. Therefore, any problems, concerns, or information you wish to provide will greatly assist in insuring a safe and secure work environment.

The Committee wishes to thank you for your cooperation in completing this opinion questionnaire. Your immediate response is required to enable us to complete our data collection by _____ , 19____.

1. Have you ever been the victim of a crime while at work? Yes ____ No ____
   If yes, please describe (date, type of crime).
2. Have you ever known of any thefts from the company? Yes ____ No ____
   If yes, please indicate type and other relevant particulars.
3. Are all of the crimes committed against the company known and reported to management? Yes ____ No ____
   If no, indicate which ones have not been reported.
4. Are you aware of the functions of the Company security department? Yes ____ No ____
   If yes, what in your opinion does security do?
5. Do you feel it is necessary to maintain a company security department? Yes ____ No ____
   Comments:
6. Have you ever had any dealings with the Security Department? Yes ____ No ____
   Areas of Satisfaction.
   Areas of Dissatisfaction.
7. Please list the major ways in which you feel security of the company could be improved. (List as many as you wish.)
8. Do you feel that the company should prosecute employees caught stealing from the company? Yes ____ No ____
   Comments.

9. Do you feel that security adequately protects the company, and all of its assets and employees? Yes ____ No ____
   If no, please explain.
10. In your current job in the company, is there anything that you can do to improve your personal protection from crimes?
11. In your present job in the company, do you know of ways to prevent thefts from the company? Yes ____ No ____
    If yes, please indicate how.

LOSS HAZARD IDENTIFICATION GUIDE

The following list presents the major categories of events, conditions, and activities that can cause loss or considerably raise the probabilities of risk to an organization.

Natural
Cold
Darkness
Earthquakes
Explosions
Fire
Floods
Heat
Wind
Hurricanes
Tornadoes

Human
Absenteeism
Accidents
Carelessness
Collusion
Disloyalty
Dissatisfaction
Espionage
Pilferage
Sabotage
Theft
Vandalism

Organizational
High vulnerability
High value products/materials
Inadequate management
Inadequate internal controls
Inadequate lighting
Inadequate barrier systems
Inadequate access control
Inadequate protective policy
Poor employee communications
Poor employee relations
Poor housekeeping
Poor organization for security/loss prevention
Ineffective management
Uninterested management

SECURITY AUDIT CHECKLIST

The following checklist is a guide to security auditing and surveying. Since each audit should be a unique process fitted to suit a specific situation, this outline is written in general, easily adaptable terms. Each organization can then carefully adapt the outline so that it conforms to its specific needs.

Section I: Preliminary Data

A. Is the request for the audit appropriate? Is the audit necessary?
    1. Is there sufficient time allocated to do a worthwhile audit?
    2. Is there adequate money available for the audit?
B. What is the reason for conducting an audit?
    1. Are there specific problems that prompted the audit?
C. What kind of final report is the audit expected to produce?
    1. Is the report to be limited in its scope and/or its recommendations?
    2. Are specific areas or conditions to receive special consideration?
    3. What is to be the format for the presentation of the final report?
        a. Written
            1) Narrative form
            2) Outline form
        b. Oral presentation

      c. Combination written and oral
    4. Are there monetary restraints on either the report or the recommendations?
D. Have there been other audits or surveys done?
    1. Who did them and when were they done?
    2. Why were they done?
    3. What recommendations were made? And were they adhered to?
    4. Are written reports of former audits available for study?
E. Determine what will be necessary, in terms of material and equipment, to undertake the audit.
    1. Maps, blueprints, floor plans, and so forth
    2. Necessary passes, identification badges to guarantee access to areas, and free mobility within the facility
    3. Photographic and reproduction or copy equipment
    4. Vehicles
F. Are interviews of personnel necessary for the success of the audit?
    1. Who *can* be interviewed and when?
    2. Who *should* be interviewed? Are these people available for interviews?

Section II: The Installation

A. Research the facts of the installation's past.
    1. When was it built?
    2. Expansions?
    3. Examine physical characteristics such as sewers, canals, caves, tunnels, and so forth.
    4. Did the installation have a use or serve a function other than its current one?
B. Why was the installation opened in its present location?
    1. What product is made or what service is rendered?
    2. Does the purpose of the facility's existence contribute to its safety and security problems?
C. Does the location of the facility make it vulnerable to safety and security problems?
D. How important is the property (material, products, and information) stored in the facility?
    1. Does any of the property stored in the facility present a security or safety problem?
    2. What would it cost to replace the property stored inside the facility? (Can it be replaced?)
E. What is the importance of the facility?
    1. Can it be replaced and at what cost?
    2. How important is the installation to the total operation of the organization/corporation?

F. What are the topographic features in and around the installation?
   1. Are natural conditions a help or a hinderance to safety and security operations?
G. What are the critical areas in and around the installation?
   1. Motor pools, airport/heliport, communications equipment, fuel storage facilities, and so forth.
   2. Hospital, police, ambulance, fire dept., and so forth. (How accessible are these?)
   3. Are critical areas within the installation properly safeguarded?

Section III: Physical Security

A. Are perimeter barriers used around the facility?
   1. Are the perimeters of the entire installation well defined by barriers?
   2. Are signs posted in appropriate locations to identify company property?
B. Do buildings or other permanent structures make up any of the perimeter barriers?
   1. Do all or any of these structures belong to the company?
   2. Do any of these structures present a security problem?
C. Is the installation operated under an open, closed, controlled, or semi-controlled system for access control?
D. Are fences used as perimeter barriers?
   1. Are the fences used simply to identify perimeter boundaries or for security purposes?
   2. What kind of fences are used and where are they located? (Describe fences in detail.)
      a. Type of fence
      b. Height of fence
      c. Type, angle, and width of overhang
      d. Number of wires and distance between them
      e. Distance between bottom of fence and ground
      f. Is fence alarmed?
   3. Describe the type of terrain that surrounds all the fences that are used.
      a. Hills, mountains, ditches, and so forth
      b. Tunnels, culverts, above-ground sewage or drainage pipes, and so forth
      c. Rivers, streams, canals or other waterways that run next to or through perimeter
      d. Railroad tracks and/or public or private roadways passing next to or through the perimeter barriers
   4. What is the general condition of the perimeter fences?
      a. When were they installed?

        b. How often are they inspected and repaired?

        c. Is there a road that allows easy access to the entire perimeter fence area?

    5. Are specific clear/restricted zones marked off and identified on both sides of all perimeter fences?

        a. How are the clear/restricted zones marked and identified?

        b. How wide are the zones?

        c. Are the zones free of all obstructions?

        d. What are the topographic characteristics of the zones?

        e. Are there permanent structures that eliminate or shorten the width of any zone areas?

    6. Are guard towers or control posts used in conjunction with the perimeter fence?

        a. How many and what type of posts or towers are in use?

        b. Where are they located and what are their specific functions?

        c. Are any precautions taken to give protection to security personnel in outlying towers or posts?

        d. Do all towers have an acceptable field of view, without blind spots?

        e. Are searchlights mounted in towers or posts for use at night? (Describe capabilities of the lights.)

        f. Are all towers and posts connected to each other and to security headquarters through a communications system? (Explain system in detail.)

E. Is perimeter lighting used for security and protection?

    1. When were the lights installed and where are they located?

    2. What kind of lighting system(s) is (are) used? (Direct, indirect, glare projection)

    3. What kind of lamps are used as a part of the system? (Mercury vapor, quartz, bulbs, sealed beams, and so forth)

    4. What is the wattage and/or candlepower of each lamp and what is the foot-candle power that they project to given areas such as gates, entrances, storage areas, and so forth?

    5. How are perimeter lights controlled and what is the primary power source?

    6. Where are power lines supplying the perimeter lighting and communication system located? (Overhead, underground)

    7. What is the overall condition of the perimeter lighting system and how effective is it at performing the function for which it was designed?

Section IV: Personnel Security

A. Identify all top-level administrators by name, title, and address. It may also be advantageous to identify those in midlevel management who hold positions that are vital for the smooth operation of the organization or facility.

B. Identify the Security Department, using the names and titles of all of its managers and supervisors.

C. If appropriate, identify and list those with top security clearances and those who are authorized to review, give, or revoke security clearances.

D. How many individuals are employed by, or assigned to, the facility?
    1. Give an analysis of personnel distributions and assignments.
    2. Show the organization of the facility.

E. Have there been any political, racial, religious, or labor problems that have affected the safety or security of the facility?
    1. What types of problems were they and what were the causes?
    2. What steps averted or stopped those past problems?

F. Based on data gathered or company-supplied information, is there any indication of employee problems within the facility that could create a security problem?

G. Does the facility have a set of emergency procedures that provide for action in the event of fire, natural disaster, civil disturbances, evacuations, and so forth? (Obtain copies.)

H. Describe in detail the process for granting a "security clearance" for access to sensitive company materials.
    1. Employment pre-screening—(obtain copies)
    2. Background investigations (who does them, type)
    3. Polygraph or psychological stress evaluation (PSE) examination
    4. Use of patent or secrecy agreements (obtain copies and review)

Section V: Personnel Control and Identification

A. Is there any facility-wide identification system for personnel?
    1. If no identification system is in use, are guards expected to identify personnel on sight?
        a. Are guards expected to identify personnel by name?
        b. What procedures are used for visitors, customers, and so forth?
    2. Are security personnel notified when individuals are no longer to be allowed access to the facility?

B. If an artificial or mechanical identification system is used, describe the system used. (Badge, card, pass, and so forth)
    1. What type of identification document is in use?
        a. Size and shape
        b. Color or coding scheme
        c. What is the instrument made from?
    2. Does the document have any or all of the following?
        a. Name, weight, height, and color of hair and eyes of the bearer

      b. A legible fingerprint of the bearer

      c. His signature

      d. A photograph of the bearer in color or black/white

3. Is the identification document (card or badge) issued for a specific time period or an indefinite length?

      a. Explain any time parameters that are used in connection with the system.

      b. Explain circumstances for renewal, recovery, and so forth.

4. Are there set procedures to follow when identification cards are lost or stolen?

      a. Are employees acquainted with these procedures?

      b. Is there any type of instructions printed on the card or badge to explain the procedure for returning lost cards/badges should they be found?

5. Is there an accurate record kept of who has been issued an identification card or badge?

      a. How many has each person been issued and when?

      b. Are individuals required to sign for an identification card or badge when it is issued?

      c. Who is responsible for the issuance of identification cards or badges?

      d. Who collects identification documents upon employee termination?

6. Is there any type of coding system used in connection with the identification cards or badges?

      a. Color, shape, size, and so forth

      b. Explain the system in detail.

7. Are identification cards or badges used for any other purpose?

8. Are there any security safeguards built into the identification that can deter unauthorized reproduction or alteration? Explain those safeguards that are used.

9. Do security personnel visually or electronically examine all company identification credentials as personnel enter the facility or any of its restricted areas?

C. Does the facility employ any type of structured customer or visitor control?

  1. How are customers/visitors identified as they enter the facility?

  2. Is access to the facility by customers/visitors limited to certain entrances and/or certain periods of time? Who enforces this procedure?

  3. Is a register of customers/visitors kept?

      a. What information is required of those who sign the register?

      b. Who is in charge of the register and how many are kept simultaneously?

  4. Are signs posted in appropriate locations throughout the facility

that inform customers/visitors about where they can and cannot go or what they can and cannot do?

D. Is there a set of procedures in use governing the escorting of visitors or customers, messengers, truck drivers, and so forth?
1. Who is escorted and under what circumstances are they escorted?
2. Who is assigned to escort duty? (Are specific security personnel or company employees given escort tasks, or do those to be visited have the responsibility to escort?)
3. Explain the escort system, in detail.

E. Are visitors or customers, messengers, truck drivers, and so forth issued special passes or identification credentials when they enter the facility?
1. Who issues these passes?
2. Describe the type of pass system in use.
3. Are these persons spot checked while inside the facility?
4. Are any actions taken against unauthorized persons found on the premises?
5. Are permanent records kept on who passes are issued to, when, and why they are issued?

Section VI: Work Area Security

A. How are buildings, structures, and other designated areas safeguarded?
1. Describe each building, structure, or area that is to be audited.
    a. Kind of building or area. What is it used for?
    b. How is the building or area laid out? (It may be beneficial to include a map or blueprint.)
    c. What are the physical characteristics of the building, structure, or area? Entrances, windows, gates and their dimensions, location, and purpose.
2. Which of these inner buildings, areas, or structures are enclosed by a clear/restricted zone? (Refer to Section III, 5 for information on clear/restricted zones.)

B. Are there any restricted buildings, structures, or areas inside the perimeter area that contain secret or highly sensitive material?
1. Explain the significance of each restricted or sensitive building, structure, or area. Closely examine each.
2. Explain the extent to which each of these is safeguarded. Examine the safeguards.
    a. Are they protected by security fences or alarms? Examine and explain.
    b. Are they under the protective responsibility of guards? Do

they patrol or maintain stationary security posts at these locations? Examine and explain.
c. Is there any special system of access control for these locations? Examine the system and explain it in detail.

Section VII: Information Security

A. What type of classified proprietary material is stored in the facility?
   1. Is a system for identifying the security classification of written
      material used? Examine the system and explain it in detail.
   2. How much of each classification is kept in the facility?
B. How are these classified proprietory materials stored?
   1. Is there a difference in the security of storage given material de-
      pending on the security classification of the material? Examine
      the storage facilities and explain.
   2. Are floor safes or vaults used to store classified material?
      a. Where are they located?
      b. Are these safes and vaults secured with combination locks?
         Who has the combinations and when or how often are they
         changed? Examine and explain in detail the entire process.
C. Are accurate and up-to-date records kept on:
   1. What classified material enters and leaves the facility? How and
      why it enters or leaves?
   2. Where classified material is kept?
   3. Who has access to and/or obtains classified material?
D. Are registers kept complete, with all required information included?
   1. Are separate security registers kept at each location where sen-
      sitive material is kept, and/or are individual registers kept for each
      different class of security material? Examine and explain them in
      detail.
   2. Who maintains security registers?
E. Is there a set of definite procedures for receiving and disseminating
   security material? Examine and explain them in detail.
   1. Who receives and disseminates the material?
   2. Is it necessary to sign for material upon receipt of it?
   3. How is security material transferred within the installation?
   4. How is it stored when not in use?
F. Is there a security procedure in force for the security of document
   reproduction and to prevent unauthorized reproduction or copying?
   Examine the procedure and explain it in detail.
G. Are all security materials properly destroyed or disposed of to safeguard against unauthorized control of them? Examine the procedure
   and explain it.

1. Are classified materials:
   a. Burnt in an incinerator?
   b. Shredded in a machine?
   c. Both?
   d. Other?
2. Who is responsible for destroying or disposing of the security material?
3. Are there authorized witnesses to the destruction?

H. Are security couriers used to transport classified material outside of the facility?
   1. Who are the couriers and do they have a security clearance commensurate with the material that they carry?
   2. How is the classified material secured in transit?
   3. Is the public mail ever used to send classified material?

I. Electronic data transmission
   1. Encryption or encoding used?
   2. Facsimile, Telex, word processing, and EDP system communication protection?

J. Is there any central location that is always used for the distribution of classified proprietary material both inside and outside of the facility?
   1. How many are assigned to this center and what department are they assigned from?
   2. Do those handling classified material in this center have appropriate security clearances?

K. Are all personnel employed within the installation notified of the proper security procedures currently in use regarding the handling of classified material? Examine the procedure for informing employees and explain it in detail.

L. Secrecy/noncompetition agreements in effect?

M. Release of sensitive, proprietary, classified information to governmental agencies, clients, or other companies?

Section VIII: Vehicle Identification and Control

A. Are all vehicles owned by the company and/or driven onto company property by employees required to be registered?
   1. Who are vehicles registered with and who is responsible for maintaining these registration records?
   2. Is there a specific set of procedures that govern the registration process?
      a. Are registration stickers issued to vehicles?
      b. Are they issued for a specific period of time?

B.   Are employees requested or assigned to use specific entrances/gates when entering the installation? Examine and explain the procedure.
C.   Are parking areas and/or parking spaces assigned to employees? Where are these areas located? Do they present a security problem?
D.   Are controls exercised over the vehicles driven onto company property by nonemployees such as:
    a.   Visitors, guests, or customers
    b.   Delivery vehicles and commercial trucks
  1.   Are these vehicles required to be registered as they enter the facility?
    a.   Who are they registered with?
    b.   Are permanent records kept of those who enter and why?
    c.   What information is entered on the register(s)?
  2.   Are these vehicles required to enter through specifically designated entrances/gates?
  3.   Are these vehicles, their drivers, and other occupants required to carry special passes when they enter the facility? Examine and explain the procedures.
E.   Are vehicles inspected by security personnel as they enter and leave the facility?
  1.   What vehicles are inspected?
  2.   How often are they inspected?
  3.   What is involved in the inspection?
  4.   Are signs posted at all entrances and gates to explain that all vehicles are subject to inspection?
    a.   What do the signs say and where are they posted?

Section IX: Security Personnel

A.   What kind of security officers are used in this installation?
    a.   Proprietary
    b.   Contract
    c.   Both
  1.   Examine and explain the security operation currently in use.
    a.   How many are on the security force?
    b.   From what source are security officers selected?
    c.   What is the distribution and assignments of security personnel?
  2.   What is the preemployment process that guard or security applicants must submit to? Examine the process.
  3.   Do officers and other security personnel possess security clearances?
    a.   What types of clearances are given to security personnel?

       b.   Who has security clearances and for what reasons?

       c.   Who makes the decision about which guards or security personnel get security clearances?

B.   What is the general condition of the security department and its security officers?

   1.   What is the level of morale?

   2.   What is the general appearance of the security personnel?

       a.   Well-groomed?

       b.   Physically fit?

       c.   Median age?

       d.   Neat in appearance?

   3.   Are there labor, disciplinary, or wage disputes or problems going on between either contract or proprietary security personnel and the organization that could create a breach of security?

C.   Are security personnel required to attend any type of organized/training program on security services *before* they start active duty? Examine and explain the program that is used.

   1.   How many subjects are taught? What subjects are taught? Who teaches the course?

   2.   Is there a required number of hours of training that must be successfully completed?

   3.   Are security personnel disciplined or discharged if they fail to complete their training successfully?

   4.   Are regular and/or continuing courses on important phases of protective services offered throughout the year?

D.   What kind of training is provided to security personnel *after* officers are hired?

   1.   What is the content of the training? How many hours?

   2.   Are there advanced courses offered periodically?

   3.   Who provides the training?

   4.   Is it certificated?

E.   What type of supervision is given to security officers and other security personnel?

   1.   Explain the chain of command. Include an organizational chart.

   2.   Are supervisors members of the security department or the organization's management or are they hired on a contract basis?

   3.   How do supervisors insure an effective operation?

F.   Is there a published policy and procedures manual used to govern the activities of the security department and its personnel?

   1.   Who formulated and wrote the manual?

   2.   How often is it audited and updated?

   3.   What procedure is used to update, add to, or make changes in the manual?

G.   What is the function of the security department and its security officers?

1. Are they assigned to fixed posts for access control, and so forth?
2. Are they assigned to vehicle and foot patrols?
3. Are they given special duties—escort duties, fire protection, and so forth?
4. Who assigns security personnel?
   a. Is any specific criteria used in assigning guard personnel? Examine and explain.
   b. Are security personnel assigned 24 hours a day and 7 days a week?
5. What is the duration of a security officer's tour of duty?

H. Are roving vehicle and foot patrols used? Examine and explain the patrol process and its function.
   1. Are regular or random patrol routes used? Examine and explain the patrol processes.
   2. How many men are assigned to the patrol operation?
   3. Who reviews patrol plans and evaluates their effectiveness?

I. Are security officers equipped with radio communications equipment so that they can converse with each other and with their headquarters? Examine and explain the system now in use.
   1. Is the communications frequency used by the security department on a FCC private channel?
   2. Does the radio communications equipment available permit security personnel to communicate with public police and/or fire departments? Examine and explain the system.

J. Are vehicles used by and/or specifically assigned to the security department?
   1. How many vehicles are in use by the guard force? How many vehicles are authorized for use?
   2. What kind of vehicles are used?
      a. Cars?
      b. Trucks?
      c. Motorcycles?
   3. Where are they stored and who is responsible for the upkeep and maintenance of the vehicles?
      a. Is a regular maintenance plan used?
      b. Are vehicle expenses on security vehicles part of the security department's budget?

K. Are dogs used? If so, how many?
   1. Are they contracted for or do they belong to the Security Department of the organization?
   2. Who is responsible for handling the guard dogs?
      a. Are the dog handlers trained specifically with the dogs they use?
      b. Are the dogs always used with a handler, or are they allowed to run loose?

3. Where are the dogs kept when not in use?
4. Is the area posted to indicate that dogs are used?

L. Are security personnel issued weapons to carry while they are on duty? Examine the system and explain the procedure that governs the use of weapons.
1. Are they equipped with:
    a. Hand-guns? (real or dummies)
    b. Rifles and/or shotguns?
    c. Nightsticks, billy clubs, blackjacks, and so forth?
    d. Nonlethal chemical devices such as mace or tear gas?
2. Who is allowed to carry a weapon?
3. Who determines which security officers do or do not use weapons?
4. Are all officers who are issued weapons first given training with those weapons?
    a. What type of training is offered? Examine and explain the program.
    b. Who are the instructors for the weapons training?
    c. How much training are officers *required* to have *before* they are issued a weapon?
5. Are officers given, or required to take, any type of physical training in self-defense tactics? Examine and explain the program.

M. Are security personnel required to participate in any type of physical fitness program? Examine and explain the program.
1. Are security personnel expected to be able to meet certain physical standards? Is any disciplinary action taken if they do not do so?
2. Are personnel working in, or assigned to, the Security Department required to submit to regular medical examinations?
    a. How often are personnel required to take a physical?
    b. Who is the physician that administers these examinations?
    c. Is any action taken if security personnel fail to pass their physical examinations?

N. Are officers required to take a civil service style test before they are eligible for rank advancement? Examine and explain the testing system.
1. Is there a specific set of procedures that governs advancement through the various ranks of the security organization? Examine and explain the procedure.
2. Who makes the decision about the advancement of an officer?

Section X: Alarm and Detection Systems

A. Are intrusion detection alarms used in the installation? Examine and give an overview of the system.

    1. On what buildings, structures, or outside areas are alarms used? Examine and explain.
    2. Are the perimeter barriers protected with intrusion alarms? Examine and explain.
B. What kind of alarm system(s) is used? Examine and explain in detail.
    1. Local alarm systems?
    2. Central Station Alarm Network?
    3. Proprietary? Obtain specifications.
    4. Contractual? Review contract.
    5. What type of power source is used to operate the system? Are emergency power sources instantly available? Examine and explain.
    6. Who is responsible for the repair and maintenance of the detection systems?
C. Are there set procedures or systems that govern who responds to an alarm call?
    1. Are permanent records of each alarm response and the outcome of the alarm call kept?
    2. What is the percent of false alarms as compared to the total alarms signaled?
    3. What is the average response time of security personnel to alarms? Of police to alarms?
D. If a central station is used, who mans the monitor? If a central station is not used, where do the alarm signals ring?
    1. Where is the central station located?
E. What is the total cost of the alarm system?
    1. Initial installation cost
    2. Cost of the equipment
    3. Contract maintenance cost
F. Does the system meet, or qualify for, *Factory Mutual* type rating and/ or insurance discounts?

Section XI: Fire Protection

A. Is there a fire protection/prevention program within the installation? Examine and describe.
    1. Is the fire protection function a part of the Security Department?
    2. How many individuals are assigned to fire protection/prevention?
    3. Are security personnel expected to participate in fire protection or are individuals specifically assigned or hired for the job?
    4. Is there a volunteer fire brigade? Describe.
B. Are individuals hired especially as firemen and fire fighters or does the organization recruit from within the organization?
    1. What criteria are used for the selection of potential firemen?

      a. Age?

      b. Previous training or experience?

      c. Education?

  2. Are fire fighters given any special training in fire protection/prevention prior to their beginning work?

      a. How long is the training period and what are the subjects taught?

      b. Who teaches the program?

      c. Is any disciplinary action taken if personnel do not pass the course?

  3. Is any regular, followup inservice training given to firemen or to those assigned to fire protection/prevention?

  4. Do fire fighters receive special security clearances?

C. What type of fire fighting vehicles are available within the installation?

  1. Are fire trucks used within the installation?

      a. How many and what kind of fire trucks are in use?

      b. Who mans the fire trucks?

      c. Where are fire trucks kept?

      d. What type of equipment is placed on each vehicle?

  2. How often is equipment inspected and tested to guarantee that it is in proper working order?

D. Are arrangements made with local fire departments to offer emergency service should it become necessary? Examine and explain the procedure for notifying the fire department.

E. Are fire alarms incorporated into the fire protection system?

  1. What type of fire alarms are used?

      a. Are local alarms used?

      b. Are central station alarms used?

      c. Are automatic sprinkler alarm systems used?

      d. Where are specific systems used?

  2. Who monitors fire alarms?

  3. Are fire alarm systems obtained on a contract agreement or have they been purchased?

      a. What type of maintenance agreement is used?

      b. Are regular checks made to inspect the proper workability of alarms?

F. What steps are taken to provide an ample amount of water for fire protection?

  1. Where does the water come from?

  2. Is the water system for fire protection separate from the installation's principal water system?

      a. What is the water pressure on the system? (Pressure must be checked at several locations.)

      b. Where are hydrants, sprinklers, and control valves located on the system?

3. Is there an emergency water supply or storage reservoir available?
   a. How much water is available for use?
   b. How is water transported and/or sent away from the storage facility?
4. Is there a regular inspection program that examines the condition and workability of the water system(s) used in fire protection and control?
   a. How often are the inspections made?
   b. Who makes these inspections?
   c. Are permanent records kept of these inspections?

G. What other types of fire fighting equipment is readily available within the installation?
   1. Are fire extinguishers available for use?
      a. What types and classes of fire extinguishers are available? How many?
      b. Where are the fire extinguishers located?
      c. Are employees shown the proper procedures for using fire extinguishers? Are operating instructions placed with each extinguisher?
   2. Are hoses, ladders, axes, buckets, and so forth, strategically placed throughout the installation that are specifically designated as fire fighting equipment?
      a. Where is this equipment located?
      b. Are security personnel and employees taught the proper procedures for using this equipment?
   3. Is all of the fire fighting equipment within the facility regularly inspected?
      a. How often are these inspections made?
      b. Who makes these inspections?
      c. Are permanent written records kept of these inspections?

H. Does the installation have an emergency fire/disaster plan? Examine and explain the plan.
   1. Who is responsible for the development of this plan?
   2. Are there emergency fire plans for each building, structure, and area within the installation? Examine each plan and explain in detail.
   3. Are certain employees assigned specific tasks during fire or disaster evacuations?
   4. Are all employees instructed in, and familiar with, the emergency plan?
   5. Are written copies of the emergency fire/disaster plan posted in appropriate locations throughout the installation? How many are posted and where?
   6. Are evacuation routes and emergency escapes clearly marked and free of obstructions?

      a. Do all fire exits open outward?

      b. Do all fire exits have easily visible and operable fire lights over them?

      c. Do all exits meet state and local fire codes?

I. Are fire sprinkler systems incorporated into the installation's fire protection system?

    1. What type of system is used?

    2. How is water for the system supplied?

      a. What is the water pressure within the system?

      b. Where are the sprinkler heads and control valves located?

    3. How is the sprinkler system activated?

    4. What buildings or structures are equipped with sprinkler systems? How extensive is the system in each?

J. Is there a *regular* training program on fire prevention offered to all employees?

    1. Who supervises this training program?

    2. How often are sessions held?

    3. Are fire drills held regularly as part of the training program?

      a. Who participates in, and supervises, the fire drills?

      b. Does the local fire department and/or the company fire protection squad respond during fire drills?

    4. What subject materials are presented at training sessions?

K. Are regular fire safety inspections conducted in connection with the training program?

    1. Who conducts these inspections? How often are they conducted?

    2. Are employees notified by inspectors about safety hazards that are discovered?

      a. Are employees expected to correct safety deficiencies?

      b. Who supervises followup actions?

L. Are fire safety regulations posted in appropriate locations throughout the installation?

Section XII: Public Utilities

A. What is the source of electrical power furnished to the installation?

    1. Is power purchased from a public utility company?

      a. What type of transmission lines are used to bring the electricity onto the installation?

        1) Overhead wires?

        2) Underground cable?

      b. What is the peak load request for electricity?

    2. What type of electrical facilities are maintained inside the installation?

    3. Is any power generated at the installation?

    4. Who is responsible for the maintenance of electrical equipment on the installation?

    5. What kind of security precautions are in use to protect electrical equipment?

    6. Is there any provision made to provide emergency electrical power to the facility?

       a. Is an emergency generating station located inside the installation?

       b. What are its capabilities in terms of performance and duration of effective use?

       c. Where is the emergency power supply located and how is it secured?

B. What is the source of the installation's water supply?

    1. What is the demand for water within the installation? (Are there any special processes that require special water supplies?)

    2. How is water brought onto the facility for use?

       a. Is the supply adequate to demand?

       b. Is there any storage facility inside the installation?

       c. Are there any pumping equipment or control valves inside the installation?

    3. Who is responsible for the maintenance of water pipes, storage facilities, pumps, and so forth?

    4. What kind of program is used to safeguard the supply of water and its quality? Examine and explain the program.

C. What is the principal system of communications within the installation? Examine and explain.

    1. Are any supplemental communication systems in use? Examine and explain.

    2. Who owns, controls and maintains each of the communication systems?

    3. Does the installation have any type of operator/switchboard system?

    4. Is there any *major* communications equipment inside the installation?

    5. How is the communications equipment and telephone system safeguarded?

RECOMMENDATIONS

No audit has any lasting value to the organization if the security and safety deficiencies that are discovered are not eliminated. To aid in this effort, meaningful recommendations must be developed. These recommendations should afford management the opportunity to consider feasible, realistic alternative solutions to problems.

IN BRIEF
Alarms and Perimeter Security Devices:
Audit Requirements

There are numerous devices available that can provide alarm protection and physical barriers to delay or detect unauthorized entry. A number of them have been found effective for use in protecting employees and assets while others have been found to be ineffective or excessively costly. To be assured that employees are provided with secure working environments and assets are protected, minimum requirements for alarms, fences and gates, security lighting, and closed circuit television (CCTV) have been developed for use in various types of facilities.

Alarm Standards

A. *General offices* requiring them should be equipped with access control systems. These systems should include card readers with program capability to record entry during normally closed periods and intrusion detection systems for critical or sensitive areas. The Security Department should conduct appropriate surveys and assure that adequate systems are designed.

B. *Manufacturing plants* are to be equipped with monitored alarm devices on doors designated as exit doors. Other perimeter pedestrian doors that are used for ventilation should be equipped with Security Department approved ventilation enclosures.

Sensitive manufacturing areas, laboratories, data processing, and office areas are to be equipped with monitored Security Department approved alarm devices. The Security Department will conduct surveys and develop specific recommendations for the areas covered.

C. *Warehouses and sales offices.* Those warehouses normally used to stock merchandise susceptible to theft, or hazardous in nature, are to be equipped with Security Department approved intrusion detection systems. Alarm coverage may be extended beyond the building walls to detect attacks upon merchandise and conveyance equipment or exterior storage areas. General standards for these systems are:

   1. All intrusion detection devices used are to be U/L listed but the system itself need not be U/L certified.
   2. Alarm signals are to terminate in a central station whenever possible.
   3. Systems are to be leased or purchased from suppliers.
   4. Areas of coverage are to be zoned to enable shutoff in specified areas while leaving the other areas active. This will allow normal activities to occur in one area while providing protection to areas of the facility that are not occupied.

5. Monitoring will be conducted in such a manner that the facility manager is provided with regular reports of opening, closing, and other entries into the facility. The reports shall be provided for periods not exceeding one calendar month.

6. Overhead bay doors need not be equipped with electromagnetic contacts, but they must be backed up with an interior space protection device. This device can be sound activated, ultrasonic, passive infrared, or photoelectric beam, depending on existing environmental conditions.

7. Exterior pedestrian doors must be equipped with electromagnetic contacts. Interior pedestrian doors may also be equipped with electromagnetic contacts should this be desirable in the particular location.

8. Company employees must have the capability of knowing the system is armed at close of business.

9. As a minimum, the alarm supplier must provide next-business-day service when alarm malfunctions occur.

10. All false alarms shall be investigated to ascertain their cause. The investigation shall be conducted by the supplier and a facility representative. The Security Department is to be advised if the cause cannot be determined or if the rate of false alarms exceeds one per 30-day period.

11. Visible or audible local alarm devices are desirable and should be used when possible.

12. Intrusion systems shall be walk-tested once per quarter by facility and supplier representatives.

13. Alarm suppliers shall prepare proposals that conform to the standards set forth.

D. *Retail Locations and Warehouses.* Intrusion detection devices shall be acquired for those retail locations and warehouses that have a history of burglary attacks that reasonably could be eliminated or losses minimized by the acquisition and use of such systems. The Security Department and the business sector will identify the location requiring such systems. The following standards shall be forwarded to potential alarm suppliers by the Purchasing Division:

1. All equipment must be U/L listed but the intrusion system itself need not be U/L certified.

2. Exterior pedestrian doors must be equipped with electromagnetic contacts. Interior pedestrian doors may also be equipped with electromagnetic contacts should this be desirable in the particular location.

3. Overhead bay doors need not be equipped with electromagnetic contacts, but they must be backed up with an interior space protection device. This device can be sound activated, ultrasonic, passive infrared, or photoelectric beam.

4. Interior space protection devices must be included for sales

room, office, and warehouse areas. Should more than one location be protected or should the location be of such a size that zoning is required, this provision should also be included.

5. Signals should terminate in a U/L certified central station or with a direct police connection.

6. Company employees must have the capability of knowing the system is armed at close of business.

7. Service on the system to correct malfunctions shall be provided by the suppliers the next business day.

8. All false alarms shall be investigated to ascertain cause. The investigation shall be conducted by the supplier and a facility representative. The corporate Security Department should be advised if the cause cannot be determined. The Security Department is to be advised if false alarms occur at a rate greater than one per 30-day period.

9. Optional Features
   a. Opening and closing records
   b. Local annunciators, either visible or audible

10. Fire detection devices shall be utilized where economically justified. Suppliers will describe in detail the code of standard used.

11. Intrusion systems shall be walk-tested once every 60 days by facility employees coordinating efforts with the supplier.

Alarm suppliers will furnish the following information in addition to that called for above:

1. Cost of either lease or purchase, or both, of the system proposed.

2. A blueprint or scale drawing will be provided the company to assure uniform scale is used by all suppliers. The blueprint or scale drawing of the facility shall be marked to indicate the location of all devices with area of coverage included.

3. A narrative description of system functions, including opening and closing procedures.

4. Lead time for installation.

5. Information about the supplier's business as requested by the Purchasing Division.

E. *Other facilities.* Installation of alarms for other facilities shall be determined by a security survey and vulnerability assessment done by the Security Department.

Closed Circuit Television

Use of closed circuit television (CCTV) is a method of achieving visual monitoring areas both inside and outside facilities. The equipment can reduce personnel expense while maintaining or increasing monitoring for security purposes.

The equipment available is constantly improving. Usable viewing can be accomplished under very low light levels. Video tape recorders, with or without time date generators, can be used and the cameras can be equipped to pan, tilt, or zoom automatically or on command.

Security Lighting

Security lighting can be an effective deterrent to criminal attack. Both interior and exterior lighting must be considered when using light as a portion of the security plan.

A. *Interior*. Many facilities have large ground-floor windows making viewing into office areas possible during closed periods. Night lighting should be on a circuit that cannot be shut off when the facility is closed. These lights should be near an interior wall causing the light to project forward toward the exterior walls and windows. This arrangement will highlight an intruder by causing a large shadow, thus making the intruder's presence easily visible to an observer. By maintaining this type of arrangement, the number of lights and total wattage used can be minimized while maintaining lighting effectiveness for security purposes. Additional lighting to illuminate sensitive areas such as safes, sensitive record storage, and sensitive equipment should be added.

B. Exterior

    1. *Parking and storage areas*. Parking lots that are used during hours of darkness and exterior storage areas should be equipped with pole-mounted lighting of sufficient wattage to project a minimum of two foot candle surface illumination in the darkest area. These poles should be of sufficient height and arrangement to allow visibility between parked vehicles. Pole spacing should be arranged so that burn out of a light source will not reduce illumination below one foot candle surface.

        Parking areas that are not normally used during hours of darkness can be illuminated at approximately one half the foot candles required for those used during hours of darkness.

    2. *Building illumination*. Floodlighting of building vertical surfaces and creating an illuminated clear zone around the perimeter will provide proper building illumination. The floodlights are to be ground mounted and should be placed a minimum of 30 feet from the building. This arrangement will highlight the presence of an intruder well before reaching the building.

        Exit doors are to be equipped with overhead lighting positioned to illuminate both the doorway and the areas immediately adjacent to the door. This will assist in observing activity near exit doors and help employees and others approaching or exiting the building.

3. *Perimeter lighting.* Roadways and approaches to facilities are to be illuminated using overhead pole-mounted lighting. The illumination on roadways should be a minimum of one foot candle; walkways, a minimum of two foot candles.

Perimeter lighting should illuminate the area from the roadway to the building. Care should be taken to remove or trim shrubs and trees to eliminate shadowed areas that offer concealment to intruders.

Outside storage tanks containing flammable or hazardous chemicals and electrical substations should be illuminated in a manner similar to that used for buildings.

Security Fencing and Gates

Security fencing shall be nine-gauge wire mesh. The openings shall not exceed two inches. The wire mesh shall be at least 8 feet high. The posts shall be set in concrete. Post spacing is not to exceed 10 feet. The fabric shall be securely anchored to posts and lower wire to prevent raising. The fencing shall be topped with a minimum of three strands of barbed wire facing *outward* on a 45 degree angle. On those areas of security fencing around finished product storage that has high theft susceptibility, a second interior fence should be provided. This interior fence is to be at least 10 feet high, constructed equivalent to the fence described above with a three strand outrigger facing *inward* at a 45 degree angle.

Security gates can be electrically operated, manually operated, and swing type or slide action. These gates shall be constructed of suitable material having the same degree of deterrence as the fence in which they are located. Security gates, when closed, shall be secured with suitable locking devices and security anchors that render the gate strength equivalent to that of the fence line in which they are located.

When buildings are used as a portion of the perimeter, the buildings shall be of masonry construction without windows or doors on the perimeter. If windows or doors are present, they shall be barred or suitably protected to enhance their deterrence to attack equal to that of the surrounding masonry surface. The walls should extend a minimum of 20 feet in height. If the walls are less than 20 feet, the roof should be equipped with suitable security devices to prohibit penetration by ladders or climbing.

If local ordinances prohibit the use of required security fencing, the perimeter fence line deterrence factor can be enhanced by utilization of outdoor intrusion alarm systems or secondary fence lines, thereby creating a more effective deterrent to criminal attack.

CHAPTER 7

Physical Security

Physical security systems should be designed and implemented for the sole purpose of denying access to a facility for any unauthorized purpose.

- Burglary
- Theft
- Vandalism
- Sabotage

- Arson
- Robbery
- To do physical harm to anyone

Physical security is based on the simple principle of self-protection.

The following checklist is offered as a basic guide to help determine what physical security needs your organization might have.

PHYSICAL SECURITY CHECKLIST

A. Physical security barriers are intended to delay an intruder's entry time or to prevent it altogether. Their purpose is also to ensure that access to restricted or sensitive areas within the facility cannot be made easily. Does your organization use any of the following types of barriers in its protection program?
1. Natural (topographic) barriers such as rivers, cliffs, canyons, or other kinds of terrain that are difficult to traverse.
2. Structural barriers that are permanent or semipermanent structures used to create a physical or psychological deterrent. These barriers fall into four general categories:
   a. Perimeter barriers such as chain-link fences
   b. The outer walls of buildings
   c. The inner walls of buildings
   d. Security containers such as safes or vaults
3. Energy barriers that fall into three primary categories:
   a. Protective lighting
   b. Protective alarms
   c. Audio and/or visual surveillance equipment (CCTV, for example)

B. Physical security should be applied in three specific overlapping areas at three different levels. Does your protection program include components from each of the following?

   1. *Deterrent protection.* These systems are designed to create a mental deterrent effect on the minds of potential intruders. This effect can be generated using three methods:

      a. *Visual deterrents.* Walls or fences, protective lighting or alarms, CCTV, security personnel—any security deterrent that can be seen.

      b. *Audible deterrents.* Alarm annunciators such as horns, bells, or sirens—any sound that has a deterrent effect.

      c. *Publicized deterrents.* Signs, posters, decals, articles in company publications—anything that, when read, will serve to discourage people.

   2. *Interior protection.* These measures are designed and implemented in order to provide for the safety and security of an organization's assets. Examples include intrusion or fire alarms, CCTV, locking devices, or fire suppression systems.

   3. *Internal security.* These concentrate on eliminating or at least curtailing the incidence of employee dishonesty. The use of security containers, access control systems, and individual door alarms would be applicable here.

C. The effectiveness of structural security barriers are determined by:

   1. Their architectural design. Are those used by your organization constructed in such a manner as to adequately protect and/or deter?

   2. Their locking devices. Are the locks used by your organization of such a quality or construction that they can be classified as *security grade?* Do they actually produce an *acceptable* entry time delay?

   3. Their back-up systems. Are *intrusion alarms* used to detect attempts to compromise your structural security barriers? Do *security personnel* regularly inspect the integrity of structural security barriers? Are the areas where structural security barriers are used properly lighted?

D. Security fences, to be effective deterrents, must be properly constructed?

   1. Are your chain-link fences constructed using 11-gauge wire with openings no larger than two inches?

   2. Are fences at least seven feet tall with an appropriately constructed top guard set on top? (Top guards, at a minimum, should contain three strands of barbed wire set on arms that are angled at 45° *away* from the property being protected.)

   3. Are all fence posts sunk in concrete? Is the fence itself sunk in a trench at least four inches deep so that the bottom cannot be pried up?

4. Are there clear zones, free of all obstructions, at least ten feet wide located on both sides of the fence so that no one or nothing can be hidden there?

E. To be totally effective, all openings in structural barriers must be properly secured.

1. Are all doors, windows, and other openings with a diameter larger than 18 inches on the first two floors of all buildings properly secured and/or alarmed?

2. Are the rooftops of buildings properly protected and secured?

3. Are all openings in perimeter fences, including culverts, drainage ditches, and pipes with diameters larger than 18 inches, properly secured?

F. Almost all sensitive or restricted outside areas require some type of security lighting to ensure adequate levels of protection at night. Does your organization utilize security lighting to protect:

1. Parking lots?

2. Perimeter fences?

3. Exterior doors?

4. Sensitive/restricted areas such as:
   a. Fuel storage facilities?
   b. Equipment parts or supply storage areas?
   c. The outside of buildings?
   d. Other sensitive or restricted areas?

1. Which types of security lighting systems does your organization use?

   a. *Incandescent* (the common light bulb). These lights provide instant illumination and have a lamp-life of approximately 2,000 hours.

   b. *Gaseous discharge* (two types).

      1) Mercury vapor lamps put off a strong bluish light. Although they do not provide instant illumination like incandescent bulbs do, they are, nonetheless, brighter. Their lamp-life is also longer than incandescent bulbs—an average of 15,000 to 20,000 hours.

      2) Sodium vapor lamps put off a soft yellow-orange light and are considered by most to be more efficient than mercury vapor lamps. Sodium vapor lamps are also four times brighter than are quartz lamps. They have a lamp-life that averages 10,000–15,000 hours. (Since these lamps, with their yellow-orange light, penetrate fog, they work very well for lighting parking lots.)

      3) *Quartz* (Halogen). These lamps have a very high wattage rating and put off a bright, white light that is comparable in intensity to mercury vapor. Their illumination is virtually instaneous when turned on. However, their relatively short

lamp-life (2,000–4,000 hours) makes their use somewhat expensive. (Quartz lamps do provide good lighting for perimeter protection.)

2. Do your security lighting systems meet the following standards to ensure ongoing quality and effectiveness?
   a. Are they free from glare? Do lights provide a clear, undistorted view?
   b. Are lights and fixtures easy to maintain? Can maintenance workers get to fixtures easily to replace burnt-out bulbs or to repair defective equipment?
   c. Are lights and fixtures secure from compromise or attack? Are lights placed on the ground where they are readily accessible or on light poles or the roofs of buildings?
   d. Do the lights provide overlapping illumination?
   e. How are your security lights turned on and off?
      1) Manual on/off switches? (Not effective because they must depend upon the human element)
      2) Photo-electric cells or electric eyes? (Not effective because rapid light changes from lightening, automobiles, and so forth can drastically affect their effectiveness.)
      3) Timers or time clocks? (Effective because they are automatic and can be adjusted to compensate for natural changes in the hours of light and dark.)
   f. Is the intensity and dispersion of illumination adequate enough to provide a satisfactory level of security lighting? (A minimum of 2.0 foot-candles of light is needed to readily identify people, and at least 1.0 foot candle of light is needed where vehicular identification is important.)
   g. Are your security lighting systems equipped with backup power supplies that will function in the event of a power interruption? What power source is utilized? Batteries? Emergency generators? How long will the backup power supply keep security lighting systems operational?

G. General considerations
   1. Are exterior doors kept to an absolute minimum? Are exterior doors opened only during those hours when it is absolutely necessary?
   2. Is public access controlled? Are walkways, streets, and driveways properly secured so that access control can be effective?
   3. Is exterior landscaping designed to complement physical security systems? Is it kept such in a condition that it does not afford hiding places?
   4. Are employee parking lots situated at least fifty feet away from the entrances/exits that employees use? (To reduce the possibility

of pilferage, employees should not be given convenient access to their personal vehicles during working hours.)

5. Are the foyers of your buildings open to permit maximum observation, pedestrian control, and traffic flow?

6. Are intrusion alarms used to protect important, valuable, or sensitive assets within your organization? Have you taken necessary precautions to ensure that there are prompt and *guaranteed responses* to intrusion alarms that are activated?

CHAPTER 8

Perimeter Security

The Physical Security Perimeter Checklist provides a convenient means for analyzing weaknesses in the perimeter barriers of the facility. The forms should be completed at the time of the inspection. The actual inspection should be made by walking around the entire perimeter and inspecting it.

The data from the inspection should then be used to determine the requirements for improvements in the physical plant, repairs, modification, and maintenance.

PHYSICAL SECURITY PERIMETER CHECKLIST

Facility:

Location:

Agency or department conducting survey:

Individual(s) conducting survey and title:

Date of survey:

Date of any previous survey: (Obtain and review reports)

Purpose of survey (State reasons for survey):

1. Is the perimeter of the facility or location secured by a fence or other physical barrier?
   Yes _____   No _____   n/a _____
   If no, explain why there is none:
2. If a fence is utilized as a perimeter barrier, does it meet the minimum specifications for security fencing?
   Yes _____   No _____   n/a _____
   If no, explain:
3. Is fence of chain link variety?
   Yes _____   No _____   n/a _____
   If no, explain:
4. What gauge wire is used? (Should be 11 gauge or heavier)

5. What is opening of mesh? (Should be no larger than two inches)
6. Is top of fence strung with barbed wire and angled out at a 45° angle?
    Yes _____   No _____   n/a _____
    If no, explain what is current condition:
7. Is bottom of fence within two inches of the ground in all locations?
    Yes _____   No _____   n/a _____
    If no, give condition and location:
8. Is fence free of damage or deterioration that would make it ineffective as a security barrier?
    Yes _____   No _____   n/a _____
    If no, give condition and location:
9. If masonry wall is used, does it meet minimum specifications for security fencing? (At least 7 feet high with barbed wire rolled or strung at a 45° angle outward on top)
    Yes _____   No _____   n/a _____
    If no, give present condition:
10. If a building forms a part of the perimeter barrier, does it present a hazard by allowing illegal or unauthorized entry?
    Yes _____   No _____   n/a _____
    If yes, explain circumstances:
11. If a river, lake, or other body of water forms any part of the perimeter barrier, are additional security measures provided?
    Yes _____   No _____   n/a _____
    If yes, explain measures used:
12. Are openings such as culverts, tunnels, man-holes, and so forth, which permit access to a facility, properly secured?
    Yes _____   No _____   n/a _____
    If yes, how secured:
    If no, give condition and location:
13. Are there sufficient entrances through the perimeter barriers?
    Yes _____   No _____
    If yes, how many and of what type:
14. Do gates and/or other entrances in the perimeter system exceed the number required for safe and efficient operation?
    Yes _____   No _____
    If yes, explain circumstances:
15. Are all perimeter entrances equipped with secure locking devices?
    Yes _____   No _____
    If yes, explain locking systems in use:
    If no, explain deficiencies and location(s):
16. Are all entrances always locked/secured when not in use?
    Yes _____   No _____
    If no, explain and give location(s):
17. Are all perimeter gates of such material and installation as to provide

protection equivalent to the perimeter barriers of which they are a part?

Yes _____   No _____

If no, explain deficiencies and location(s):

18. Are all gates and/or other entrances that are not in active use frequently inspected by security personnel? (Inspected a minimum of once every eight hours)

Yes _____   No _____

If no, explain:

19. Who is responsible for key control of locks on perimeter entrances?

20. Explain key control system in detail:

21. Who has keys issued to them allowing them authorized entrance to facilities inside the perimeter barrier?

22. Are any other measures of perimeter access control used?

Yes _____   No _____

If yes, explain:

23. Have any perimeter gates or entrances been permanently (or temporarily) established since the last survey? Have any been permanently closed? Permanently opened?

Yes _____   No _____

If yes, explain and give location(s):

24. Are all normally used pedestrian and vehicle gates or other perimeter entrances effectively and adequately lighted to assure that:

    A. Proper identification of individuals and their credentials can be checked:

    Yes _____   No _____

    B. Vehicles and their interiors are clearly lighted:

    Yes _____   No _____

    If no in A or B, explain:

25. Are any gates and/or entrances manned by security guards?

Yes _____   No _____

If yes, explain and give hours and location(s):

26. Are there any perimeter access gates or entrances open and not manned by security personnel?

Yes _____   No _____

If yes, explain and give location(s):

27. Is closed circuit television or any other type of electronic system used for monitoring and/or surveillance of vulnerable perimeter areas, gates, or entrances?

Yes _____   No _____   n/a _____

If yes, explain and give location(s):

If CCTV is used, who monitors the equipment?

Is the system strictly visual or does it have audio capabilities?

    Visual only _____   Audio/visual _____

Explain system:

Do cameras have fixed field of view or can their angle of sight be remotely controlled?

    Fixed _____   Remote control _____

Explain:

28. Are <u>all</u> perimeter barriers well lighted during hours of darkness?

    Yes _____   No _____

If no, explain:

29. Is the perimeter regularly patrolled by security personnel?

    Yes _____   No _____   n/a _____

If no, explain:

If yes, are rounds recorded using checkin key stations, key clocks, or some other type of similar device?

    Yes _____   No _____   n/a _____

If no, explain what system is used:

30. How often is the perimeter area of this location/facility required to be checked, examined, and/or patrolled by security personnel?

31. Is there a system in force for governing which entrances or gates are opened during which hours and/or days?

    Yes _____   No _____   n/a _____

If yes, explain system/procedure:

32. Are all outside entrances and perimeter barriers, where public access is readily possible, under constant surveillance?

    Yes _____   No _____   n/a _____

If yes, explain procedure:

If no, explain deficiencies and give location(s):

33. Are outside perimeter, emergency exists in operable conditions?

    Yes _____   No _____   n/a _____

If no, explain and give location(s):

    A. Are they constructed in such a fashion as to prevent opening from the outside?

        Yes _____   No _____

        If no, explain and give location(s):

    B. Are emergency exit doors wired with an alarm to indicate their being opened?

        Yes _____   No _____

34. Are all perimeter entrances, gates, doors, and windows equipped with proper intrusion detection alarms?

    Yes _____   No _____

If yes, explain system:

If no, explain and give location(s):

35. Are there adequate and appropriate signs posted to indicate restricted areas around, on, or inside the perimeter?

    Yes _____   No _____

If yes, explain system:

If no, explain and give location(s):

36. Are these restricted areas and their entrances monitored continuously either visually or electronically?

   Yes _____   No _____

   If yes, explain monitoring system:

   If no, explain deficiencies and give location(s):

37. Is there any parking allowed near any of the perimeters?

   Yes _____   No _____

   If yes, where is parking allowed?

   A. Is this parking supervised by security personnel?

      Yes _____   No _____

   B. Is parking in these areas restricted?

      Yes _____   No _____

      If yes, explain:

CHAPTER 9

Access Control

The Access Control Checklist provides a method for collecting information necessary for developing or improving an access control system. All questions should be answered that apply to the facility and the data recorded on the form. This information can then be used to develop appropriate policy statements and procedural guidelines. It can also form the basis for any equipment modifications or purchases that might be indicated to meet company access control objectives.

ACCESS CONTROL CHECKLIST

Facility:

Location:

Agency or department conducting survey:

Individual(s) conducting survey and title:

Date of survey:

Purpose of survey:

1. Are in/out logs or registers maintained at <u>all</u> entrances used by visitors, customers, and/or employees?
   Yes _____   No _____   n/a _____
   If yes, explain procedure:
   If no, explain and give location(s):
2. Are separate logs maintained for employees and nonemployees?
   Yes _____   No _____   n/a _____
3. Who is responsible for maintaining these logs?
4. Does nonemployee register show <u>all</u> deliveries and/or pickups made at the facility?
   Yes _____   No _____   n/a _____
5. Is there a badge or identification card system used in this facility that requires the card/badge to be worn in plain sight at all times?
   Yes _____   No _____   n/a _____

6. Are identification cards/badges issued to each employee at the beginning of his employment or as they start each day's work and then collected at the end of the work period?
    a. Issued at employment? _____
    b. Given out at start of work? _____
7. Who issues identification cards/badges?
8. Are records kept of identification cards/badges that have been issued?
    Yes _____   No _____
    If yes, who maintains these records?
9. Are employee badges or identification badges coded, either by color or design, to indicate access privileges and/or limitations?
    Yes _____   No _____   n/a _____
    If yes, explain coding system:
10. Do employee badges or identification cards:
    a. Include the signature of the employee?
        Yes _____   No _____
    b. A photograph of the employee?
        Yes _____   No _____
    c. The date of issue (and expiration)?
        Yes _____   No _____
    d. Are cards laminated or constructed in such a fashion as to prevent alteration or tampering?
        Yes _____   No _____
11. Are security officers constantly posted at gates and entrances where persons or vehicles pass in or out?
    Yes _____   No _____   n/a _____
    If no, explain and give location(s):
12. Are all visitors, including delivery persons, escorted to and from their destination by employee or security personnel?
    Yes _____   No _____   n/a _____
    If no, explain:
13. Are packages, briefcases, lunch boxes, tool kits, and other similar articles inspected upon entering or before leaving the facility?
    Yes _____   No _____
14. Is there any standard procedure for inspecting persons entering and leaving the facility that is actively enforced?
    Yes _____   No _____
    If yes, explain procedure:
15. Is there any standardized procedure actively enforced for inspecting vehicles entering and leaving the facility?
    Yes _____   No _____   n/a _____
16. Are there adequate and appropriate signs posted to indicate restricted areas at or near all entrances to these areas?
    Yes _____   No _____   n/a _____

17. Is there restricted access to restrooms, tool rooms, labs, and so forth, which may otherwise cause a breach of security?

Yes _____   No _____   n/a _____

If yes, explain procedure and identify restricted location(s):

If no, explain and give location(s):

a. Are <u>all</u> restricted areas properly identified and adequately posted?

Yes _____   No _____

If no, explain deficiency and give location(s):

b. Are accesses to buildings, perimeter barriers, or other facilities immediately adjacent to sensitive or restricted areas controlled or monitored?

Yes _____   No _____   n/a _____

If yes, explain system/procedures:

If no, explain and give location(s):

18. Are keys to access entrances and gates given out according to a specific security procedure?

Yes _____   No _____   n/a _____

If yes, explain procedure:

19. Is a keyholder list maintained for all keys to access or restricted areas so that keys can be recovered should the need arise?

Yes _____   No _____   n/a _____

If yes, who maintains this list?

How often is the list verified and updated?

When was the last time that it was verified and updated?

20. Are all outside entrances and gates provided with specially designed security locking systems?

Yes _____   No _____

If no, explain deficiency and give location(s):

21. Are all outside entrances and gates covered with adequate overhead security lighting to allow easy identification of individuals and vehicles that pass through them?

Yes _____   No _____   n/a _____

If no, explain deficiency and give location(s):

22. Are terminated employees required to return identification cards, badges, keys, and keycards?

Yes _____   No _____

If no, explain deficiency:

CHAPTER 10

Information Security

Even though the protection of proprietary information is a very important security responsibility, it is also a much-neglected one. In order to determine how well any particular organization is dealing with information security, the following checklist is offered.

The purpose of the checklist is to help identify specific areas that need to have the safeguards of applicable policies and procedures in force to protect proprietary data.

INFORMATION SECURITY CHECKLIST

A. Does the organization have policies and procedures on information security that deal with the following:
    1. Research and development data
        a. Blueprints and design drawings?
        b. Product formulae?
        c. Project data?
        d. Schedules for future research and development projects?
        e. Negative information
            1) Projects that did not work?
            2) Projects that are too costly?
    2. Projection and manufacturing data
        a. Technical data?
        b. Information on operational problems?
        c. Data on hardware and equipment in use?
        d. Production timetables?
        e. Information on expansion programs?
        f. Data concerning cost-benefit analyses?
    3. Marketing and distribution information
        a. Information on advertising plans?
        b. Information on product promotion campaigns?
        c. Data from test-market surveys?
        d. Sales records?

       e. Mailing lists
          1) Catalogue customers?
          2) Priority clients?
          3) Customers to be billed?
   4. Bookkeeping records
       a. Data on accounts payable?
       b. Data on accounts receivable?
       c. Payroll data?
   5. Computer records and software?

B. Additionally, companies should also have appropriate policies and procedures that place security safeguards on the following:
   1. The use of company telephones
   2. Contacts with vendors and sales representatives
   3. On-the-job conversations, meetings, and conferences
   4. Materials given out and conversations held during sales meetings or trade shows
   5. Information given out through press releases or during press conferences (media encounters)
   6. The disposal of trash
   7. Information exchanges during:
       a. Joint ventures with other companies
       b. Proposed merger discussions
       c. Plans for buy-outs or acquisitions
   8. Pertinent information given out during job interviews
   9. Plant tours
  10. The use of consultants
  11. Inhouse newsletters and publications
  12. The use of copying machines
  13. The implementation of a *clear desk* policy
  14. Speeches given in public by company employees and managers
  15. The use of security classification codes for documents containing sensitive information

---

The policy and procedures that follow offer guidelines for providing information to the news media about incidents that occur on company property. It will also serve as an example for other policies that may need to be prepared on information security.

PUBLIC RELATIONS

A. *Purpose.* The purpose of this general order is to set forth guidelines for the release of information to the news media. Such disclosures may be on individual violators of the law, incidents and happenings, or a combination of both, that either occur on company property or involve the company and its personnel.

B. *Policies.*
1. The company shall cooperate with representatives of the news media. However information disclosed shall be limited to that allowed by this general order and by the law as it pertains to the rights of those persons charged with violations of the law.
2. The company shall release information only during the times that it is open. At all other times, designated personnel shall release previously approved information to any inquiring news media representatives only after they have properly identified themselves.
3. Any exceptions to paragraph 2 above will be made by the Director of Security or his designate.

C. *Designated personnel.*
1. The following listed personnel are authorized to release information to the news media:
   a. Director of Security
   b. Company Public Relations Director
2. In cases of questionable deaths, all news inquiries will be referred to the coroner.
3. Other situations may require the Director of Security or his designate to issue a statement for release to the news media.

D. *Guidelines.* The following guidelines shall apply to what information will be released to the news media:
1. Criminal cases
   a. The following shall apply from the time a person is arrested and charged with an offense until proceedings are terminated. Designated departmental personnel may disclose the following:
      1) The defendant's name, age, residence, employment, marital status, and similar background information
      2) The substance or text of the charge, such as: the complaint, incident, or law violated
      3) The circumstances involving a criminal incident, such as: burglary, theft, armed robbery, hit and run, and so forth
      4) The identity of the arresting and/or investigative agency
      5) The status of the case, such as: still under investigation, has been investigated, police (agency) are continuing to look for the suspect, or investigation has been completed
      6) The circumstances immediately surrounding an arrest including the time and place of arrest, resistance, pursuit, and possession and/or use of weapons
   b. Disclosures should include only factual matters

    c. In cases where disclosures of any of the above information may hamper the apprehension of a violator, such information will not be released

    d. Any information that would be prejudicial and that does not serve a law enforcement function, will not be released. Designated personnel will refrain from making available the following:

        1) Observations about a defendant's character, physical appearance, or dress

        2) Statements, admissions, confessions, or alibis made by the defendant

        3) Prior criminal records of arrested persons

        4) Defendant's association with, or membership in, any radical, militant, subversive, or criminal organization

        5) Opinion and/or subjective observations about the defendant

        6) Statements concerning evidence or arguments in the case whether or not it is anticipated that such arguments or evidence will be used at a trial

        7) Statements about investigative techniques, processes, or procedures

    e. Department personnel will take no action to encourage or assist news media in photographing or televising a defendant or accused person held or transported in departmental custody.

2. *Unnatural deaths.* When an unnatural death occurs (such as homicide, suicide, or accident) the following action will be taken:

    a. Refer all initial inquiries to the coroner

    b. The Public Relations Officer, or his designate, will prepare a written statement for release to the news media about the facts and circumstances surrounding the death

    c. Supervisors will be briefed as to what information can be released to the news media

    d. Field personnel will refer all news inquiries to the shift supervisors

3. *Juvenile cases.* All information pertaining to arrested juveniles may be released as in other cases except:

    a. Identification of child's name, parent or guardian name, and place of residence

    b. Confidential information exchanged between officers, school officials, welfare agencies, juvenile authorities, and other law enforcement agencies

4. *Other information.* The following steps will be taken when inquiries are made on subjects not covered herein. Such inquiries may be about an accident, rumor, bomb threat, fire, and so forth.

a. Inquiries will be referred to the company when it is open
b. All information on subjects listed above will be transmitted to appropriate company officials when the facility is open
c. When the company is closed, inquiries may be answered by department-designated personnel following the appropriate guidelines.

CHAPTER 11

Security Investigations

The purpose of this summary is to set forth some general guidelines on how to handle an investigation when an employer suspects that one of his employees is misusing or concealing drugs or intoxicants or has misappropriated company property.

What can you legally do when you suspect that an employee is concealing on his or her person or effects (i.e., lunchbox, handbag, briefcase, locker) stolen company property, intoxicants, or drugs?

Basically, the law is clear that all employers have a legitimate right to protect their property from damage, theft, or misappropriation by another, as well as to establish reasonable safety regulations and employee sobriety and mental stability standards. Therefore, to protect company property from theft and to insure that employees are not using intoxicants or drugs on company property, *based upon a reasonable suspicion,* you may require your employees to submit to an interview and search. Yet, suspicion must be reasonable and *not* merely conjecture. In other words, you cannot conduct a wholesale *shake down* of all employees just to see what might turn up. Therefore, before subjecting any employee to a search and interview there must be some independent information—perhaps from other employees or supervisors—that the suspected employee is concealing drugs or intoxicants on company property. (However, *wholesale shake downs* on premises should not be confused with the normal inspections that take place during normal entry and/or exit from company facilities. These inspections are intended to serve as a deterrent. A frequent question that arises is, "How should you approach the employee that is suspected of concealing prohibited items?" As was previously stated, all employers—and their security personnel—have the right to require their employees to submit to *reasonable* searches and interviews to substantiate their innocence. If it is suspected that an employee is concealing prohibited items on his or her person or in something that the employee is carrying (e.g., lunchbox), it is most appropriate to first confront the employee privately and ask permission to search the employee, and whatever he is carrying. Care should be taken *not to accuse* a suspected employee of any wrongdoing during the investigation. If an employee is prematurely or wrongfully accused of a wrongdoing, the company may become vulnerable to a libel or slander suit for damages. Therefore, be careful in how you phrase your need to search the employee or the employee's possessions! It is also advisable to have one other security staff person or the employee's supervisor present during the conversation. Fortunately, in most cases an employee will consent to be searched in any case.

If an employee does not give consent, what can be done? First, you should *not* force a search of the employee's person or personal effects because an involuntary, forced search of the employee may result in a civil suit against both you and the company alleging *technical battery,* assault, or invasion of privacy. However, you may inform the employee that failure to cooperate may result in serious disciplinary action. Numerous arbitration decisions recognize that an employer may discipline or discharge, depending on the facts, an employee who fails to cooperate in an investigation. In addition, if you suspect that the employee is about to leave the facility with stolen company property, you should inform the employee that if he or she refuses to consent to your search, you may have no other recourse than to call the police. Additionally, remember that an employee may be detained for a reasonable length of time, pending the arrival of police.

Another situation may arise when you suspect that an employee has contraband or stolen items in his or her locker or automobile. Again, first try to obtain the employee's consent for the search. This solves many problems. If you have a *reasonable suspicion* that the employee has intoxicants, drugs, or stolen property in the locker, you may open the locker without the employee's permission and examine its contents to find stolen property, intoxicants, or drugs. This search does not violate the employee's rights because you have a right to protect your property; and, because the constitutional safeguards against unreasonable searches and seizures do *not* apply to searches between private individuals (i.e., nonpolice personnel). If the suspected goods are in the employee's car and the employee will not consent to allow you to search it, you should not force a search. However, again, you should inform the employee that the employee's failure to cooperate may result in serious disciplinary action and possible involvement of the police. Remember, too, that an employee may be detained for a reasonable length of time, pending the arrival of police.

If your investigation necessitates an interrogation of the suspected employee, three considerations must be kept in mind. First, you should move the employee to an isolated area away from other employees before you begin questioning the employee. It may be well, however, to have a second security person or company supervisor as a witness to the questioning. Second, although you may detain and interview the suspected employee for the purpose of conducting an investigation, you should do so only for a reasonable time. Detaining an employee—even one suspected of a serious crime such as theft—for a long time or restraining the employee, such as by questioning the employee in a locked room, may subject the employer and you to a damage suit for false imprisonment. Typically, the courts have ruled that *reasonable time* falls in the vicinity of one hour. Third, certain other considerations must be taken into account if a union represents the suspected employee. A U.S. Supreme Court case stated that, when an employer conducts an investigatory interview with an employee, the employee may request and must be granted the right to union representation during the interview. However, the union representative may not interfere with your investigation. Again, it may be well to have a second security person or company supervisor participate in such a meeting.

All employees should understand that, from a management standpoint, you are concerned about the problems of theft of company property and the illegal use and possession of drugs or intoxicants by employees. Therefore, *all* officers, in enforcing company rules, should be conducting inspections of employee lockers, packages, handbags, briefcases, lunchboxes, and so forth. This procedure will insure employee safety while at work as well as protecting company property. Such employees (both hourly and salary) are expected to cooperate and to obey all plant rules. Refusal to cooperate would be sufficient grounds for disciplinary action.

In addition to investigations of a criminal nature routinely conducted by security personnel, the following should also be included in the list of investigations performed:

1. *Preemployment investigations* conducted in order to better ensure that those that are hired by an organization have all of the personal characteristics and professional traits that the organization desires in its employees.
2. *Postemployment investigations* initiated to ensure that employees already in the employ of an organization continue to conduct themselves appropriately, both personally and professionally. These investigations are also conducted in order to determine that those about to be promoted have all of the traits required to perform the duties associated with the new position capably.
3. *Claims investigations.* There are typically two types of claims investigations, those conducted in order to verify facts concerning:
    a. Claims against the company for reimbursement or compensation (Worker's compensation claims or civil suits, for example)
    b. Claims of loss, by the company, against others
4. *Employee misconduct investigations.* These investigations are concerned with allegations of such procedural violations as:
    a. Gambling on the job
    b. Drinking or using drugs on the job
    c. Falsifying time sheets or other company records
5. *Malfeasance investigations* conducted in order to determine whether or not managers are abusing their positions. Such investigations may include concerns about:
    a. Kickbacks from vendors
    b. Sexual harassment

     c. Selling company secrets
     d. Abusing management perks
     e. Conflicts of interest

6. *Disaster investigations.* These are typically concerned with reconstructing the facts associated with disasters. For example:
     a. Fires
     b. Natural disasters
     c. Bombings, sabotage

CHAPTER 12

Security Consultants

There are three lists in this section. They include:

1. What can a security consultant do for a client?
2. How do security consultants work with clients?
3. Guidelines for obtaining a quality consulting assignment.

WHAT CAN A SECURITY CONSULTANT DO *FOR A CLIENT?*

1. Identify problems
2. Clarify problems
3. Simplify problems
4. Planning guidance in solving problems
5. Eliminate problems
6. Suggest alternative solutions to problems
7. Offer professional specialized resources
8. Offer a medium for exchange of experiences
9. Offer a medium for exchange of techniques
10. Offer a medium for exchange of information
11. Training programs for guards
12. Assist in safety, fire, and other related jobs
13. Help with group programs or decisions
14. Provide security managers on time-sharing basis
15. Provide a security check-up audit
16. Provide reference material
17. Provide educational seminars
18. Solve problems
19. Train clients in management of risk or loss
20. Design systems or programs
21. Reports—objective results of unbiased surveys and audits
22. Develop programs that reduce risks or loss
23. Develop programs that promote awareness or accountability
24. Provide problem-solving services for the clients

25. Provide services that increase the company's ability to survive within its environment, whether it be social, economic, or political
26. Provide service that should increase the economic stability of the company
27. Provide service that will give a company a deeper, better understanding of the program it has
28. Advance their theories
29. Provide educational programs
30. Audit existing programs or systems
31. Conduct evaluations or investigations
32. Analyze situations
33. Prepare operational manuals
34. Prepare management manuals
35. Develop applicable policy and procedures
36. Implement programs or systems

HOW DO CONSULTANTS WORK *WITH* CLIENTS?

1.   Help find the most economical solution to problem(s)
2.   Define and/or point out other problems they are not currently aware of
3.   Provide supportive services or provide direction in administrative and operational areas of their company
4.   Suggest possible services offered by supplier firms
5.   Determine training needs and satisfy those needs
6.   Gather the necessary data from the client and other sources to try to solve problem(s) or give them viable alternatives to the solution of their problem(s).
7.   Act as advisors for their problems or programs
8.   Keep in contact to insure that the solutions presented are working and for possible followup services.
9.   Provide the expert advice that the client is unable to obtain from within the organization.
10. Develop programs or systems that are based on objective thinking and knowledge

GUIDELINES FOR OBTAINING A QUALITY CONSULTING ASSIGNMENT

Proposals

1.   The proposal and its review is the most important phase of obtaining a quality assignment. It should be specific and realistic as to what will and will not be accomplished during the project.
2.   When possible, management should participate in drafting the proposal.

3. The proposal should allow for developing a work plan and provide sufficient time for preparing and presenting a quality report.

Work Plan

4. The plan should be developed by management and the consultant.
5. The work plan should be designed for the client's needs. It should be expandable and not too structured or elaborate for the situation.
6. The work plan should include the work to be done by the clients as well as that by consulting personnel.
7. The plan should be reviewed with management and they should also be provided with a copy.

Work Performance

8. Effective staff orientation and training are essential to assure a high level of work performance.
9. The consultant must assume responsibility for his or her activities and his or her own development as a professional, but should expect company management to contribute.
10. Personal conduct must reflect high standards and be compatible with assignment rules and customs.
11. The quality standards for a project should be explicitly defined by the management and consultant managers.
12. Complacency or a desire to *do-it-myself* are a real threat to quality performance.
13. Continuing communications are necessary to coordinate the efforts of both management and the consulting personnel working on an engagement.
14. The client should be involved in the project during the study phase to develop his rapport with consultant personnel.
15. Client participation in a project should be planned and scheduled. Client involvement should be used to prepare people for implementation and maintenance.
16. Progress should be reported to the client regularly on both formal and informal bases.

Organized Recommendations

17. The consultant must judge the degree of quality that is necessary in each client situation.
18. A number of alternates should be analyzed before fixing on the optimum alternative.

19. There is a need for considerable judgment in checking or testing possible solutions with the client.
20. On group assignments there is a need to check to be sure that all persons involved are aware of all recommendations being made to avoid overlap, redundancy, and conflict.
21. Both management and the consultant should be alert to the possibility of a loss of objectivity during a long association on a project.

Reporting

22. All project activities should be documented. The minimum requirement would be a (file) memorandum stating what was done.
23. Working papers should be purged and put in good order and indexed, if necessary, when the report is completed.
24. The report should be outlined early in the study phase. It should be based on the work plan and constructed to satisfy the objectives in the proposal.
25. The contents of the report should be accumulated and the outline expanded, when necessary, as the study progresses.
26. On a group engagement, report writing assignments should be made very early in the work performance.
27. The writing of the report should begin during the performance of the work.
28. A standard report format should be followed in report writing. It should, however, be tailored to fit the specific situation.
29. All reports should strive to be clear, concise, and brief.
30. The report should describe *how* the proposed changes can be accomplished as well as the time required for implementation.

Planned Implementation

31. Implementation should begin during the study phase.
32. Followup visits by consultants should concentrate on auditing the status and progress of the project.
33. A regular audit or evaluation process should be built into any program that is implemented.

SECTION III

Policies and Procedures

Policies and procedures are often considered the *tracks* on which the *organization train* runs. Without them to give direction to an organization and its varied functions, it wanders aimlessly, having no well-defined purpose or prescribed destination.

Unfortunately, however, with alarming frequency managers forget the importance of policies and procedures and do not prepare new ones or keep existing ones current. The result of such complacency is a *train* speeding through the countryside in search of a catastrophe, a catastrophe that could well involve the loss of operational or administrative control, the disintegration of image or reputation, an increase of profit-reducing, unproductive time, or damage to employee morale and their faith in management's ability to effectively run the organization. This brief list does not, however, list the most damaging catastrophe of all—liability. Today's profession must clearly document programs, policies, and actions taken.

Section 3 provides checklists to aid in developing and maintaining effective policies and procedures including sample formats that can be modified for any organization.

CHAPTER 13

Developing the Policies and Procedures

In order to fully appreciate the purpose of policies and procedures within an organization, one must also understand the purpose of goals and objectives. To develop and implement policies and procedures without taking into account the goals and objectives of the organization is most inappropriate. They are, indeed, intended to be interrelated.

In practical terms, policies and procedures direct the activities of an organization toward the successful attainment of goals and objectives. Consequently, having a basic knowledge of these terms—and how they are to be applied—is essential.

GOALS AND OBJECTIVES

Technically, a **goal** is the *end result* toward which action is directed. An **objective** is a *specific* target toward which efforts are directed. A goal is the final destination to be reached, while objectives are intermediate stops en route.

To transform these definitions into a simple example consider a trip beginning in Boston and ending in Los Angeles. Travelling the entire 3,000-mile distance between the two cities becomes the goal for those undertaking the cross country trek. Reaching Cleveland within eight hours or driving the 1,000 miles between Denver and Los Angeles in twenty hours become the specific targets—the objectives—to be reached along the way (see Figure 13–1.).

POLICIES AND PROCEDURES

Similar to goals and objectives, **policies** are *general* statements and **procedures,** *specific* statements. Policies and procedures translate an organization's philosophy into action and guide it toward achieving the goals and objectives it has set for itself.

As goals and objectives explain *what* is to be accomplished, policies and

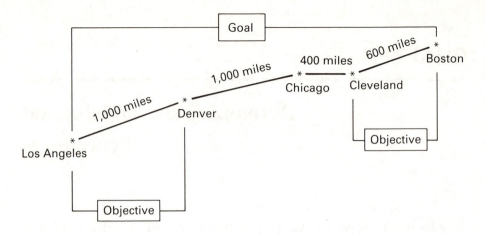

Figure 13–1   Goals and objectives.

procedures explain *how* it will be accomplished. Again, referring to our hypothetical trip, as the goals and objectives identify the results strived for—travelling the 3,000 miles from Boston to Los Angeles with intermediate targets en route—then policies and procedures will spell out such things as mode of travel, specific routes to be used, behavior while travelling, and driving time. For example:

Policy (General):
- The trip from Boston to Los Angeles will be made using an automobile.

Procedures (Specific):
- No one will drive the car in excess of 55 mph.
- No one will drive more than two hours without taking at least a 30-minute break.
- No one will drive more than 8 hours in any 24-hour period.

In order to better clarify how goals and objectives and policies and procedures relate to the security function, the following scenario is offered:

A retail store is concerned about its losses from theft and wants very much for its security staff to operate more efficiently. As a result, the store's security manager was asked to develop a specific plan that would curtail losses due to theft.

In part, the security manager's plan suggested the following:

Goal: Reduce the incidence of theft that occurs at the expensive department store.

Objective: Within months, increase the number of shoplifting apprehensions by one-third.

Objective: Within one year increase the number of successful prosecutions by 50 percent.

Objective: By the end of the fiscal year, reduce by 25 percent the dollars lost through shoplifting.

Policy: All those who shoplift from the expensive department store will be prosecuted.

Procedure: Security personnel are to promptly notify city police whenever a shoplifter is detained. Upon their arrival, the city police are to make the actual arrest of the subject.

Procedure: Security personnel are to totally and accurately complete copies of both the expensive department store's *Security Incident Report* and the *Apprehension and Detention Report* for each shoplifter apprehended. These reports are to be completed *prior to* the end of the work day on which the incident occurred.

Policies and procedures, as important as they are, can lose a good deal of their value if they are not properly written and presented. Further, care must also be taken to ensure that policies and procedures are implemented to deal adequately with all situations that security personnel are likely to encounter.

The checklist that follows will help in that task. It is to be used to determine if your organization has up-to-date policies and procedures that relate to specific security-related matters or functions. It is *not* intended to be used merely to identify functions that are now a part of your security operation/ program.

POLICIES AND PROCEDURES CHECKLIST

Code:
1 = *Yes* there is a policy/procedure and the effective date of it
    is _____
2 = *No* there is not a policy/procedure because it is not applicable to our situation
3 = *No* there is not a policy/procedure. However, there should be one.

Check the appropriate column. If your response is YES, *provide effective date(s) on applicable policy/procedures.*

Topic	1	2	3
Department:			
Functional responsibilities			
Principles and philosophy			
Operational objectives			
Operational/administrative accountability			

Topic	1	2	3

Personnel and staffing:

Organization structure
Job classifications
Position descriptions
Scheduling, preparation of
Scheduling, changes in
Overtime, use of and compensation for
Time off, requests for
Recruitment and selection of security staff, format
Recruitment and selection of security staff, criteria
Payroll/salary scales
Performance evaluation, format
Performance evaluation, criteria
Disciplinary action
Absenteeism and tardiness
Professional conduct, standards for
Training, inservice
Training, requirements for job retention
Training, seminars and workshops

Uniforms and equipment:

Dress code
Uniform badges
Security master keys
Firearms, possession and use of
Nonlethal weapons, possession and use of
Night sticks/riot batons, possession and use of
Handcuffs, possession and use of
Patrol vehicles, assignment of
Patrol vehicles, care and use of
Telephones, use of
Telephones, answering
Supplies, requests for
Supplies, purchase of

Duty assignments:

Assigned duties, by shift
Assigned duties, by unit
Public service responsibilities
Security for vehicles and parking areas
Priorities for security services
Punch-clock (DETEX) patrols
Strikes and labor disputes, security responsibilities
    during
Intrusion alarms, response to

Topic	1	2	3
Securing buildings or property, perimeter control/security			
Interior patrols of buildings			
Key control			
Access control, employees			
Access control, nonemployees			
Access control, vehicles			
Access control, passes and permits			
Guard post functions, by assignment or location			
Patrol functions, on foot			
Patrol functions, by vehicle			
Security reporting, of incidents			
Security reporting, of investigations			
Logs and records, visitors			
Logs and records, after-hours			
Logs and records, communications			
Logs and records, daily/shift			
Investigations (criminal), performance of			
Investigations (internal), requests for			
Investigations (internal), performance of			
Interviews, employee			
Interviews, nonemployee			
Outside agencies (police, fire, and so forth), assisting			
Confidentiality standards			
Courtroom conduct			
Company regulations, enforcing			

Safety:

Unsafe conditions and practices			
Accident prevention			
Safety responsibilities, OSHA			
Accident, injury, or death cases, involvement with			
Accident investigations, pedestrian			
Accident investigations, vehicular			
Accident investigations, employee/nonemployee			

Fire safety:

Fire extinguishers, inspection of			
Fire extinguishers, service and maintenance of			
Fire suppression equipment, care and use of			
Fire drills, participation in/responsibility for			
Fire alarms, response to			
Reporting a fire			
Fire codes, compliance with			
No smoking regulations			
Fire department response, security's role in			

Topic	1	2	3

Support services:

Services to disabled vehicles
Valuables, receipt and protection of
Lost and found articles
Deliveries, receipt for and distribution of
Deliveries, off property
Executive protection
Maintenance and janitors, assistance to
Escort services
Inservice training, nonsecurity employees

Emergencies and disasters:

Internal disasters, power/utility interruptions
Internal disasters, weather-related
Internal disasters, bomb threats/sabotage
Internal emergencies, labor disputes, strikes
External disasters/emergencies
Reporting disasters or emergencies

Compliance statement:

IN BRIEF

Guidelines for the Development of a Corporate Security Policy

1. Essentials of security policy formation:
   a. Definite, positive, and clear
   b. Translatable into practice
   c. Flexible, yet highly permanent
   d. Covers all foreseeable situations
   e. Founded on facts and sound judgment
   f. Conforms to laws and organizational interests
   g. General statements rather than detailed procedures.
2. Policies should be reduced to writing:
   a. Lessens misinterpretations and error
   b. Provides a checklist
   c. Constitutes useful instructional device
   d. Failure to write is admission of weakness

3. Responsibility for formulating policy:
   a. Control must lie at top management level
   b. Policy-maker seeks staff aid and guidance
   c. Security is not only a concern of the security officer
4. Steps in the development of security policies:
   a. Determine objectives
   b. Outline problems
   c. Consider practical aspects
   d. Test and analyze
5. Prescribing procedures and rules:
   a. Consider objectives, problems, and policies
   b. Make it a job analysis
   c. Make it extensive enough to maintain uniformity
   d. Be as brief as possible with clarity
   e. Follow standard pattern
6. Examples of operational areas needing policy formulation:
   a. Access control
   b. Use of company vehicles/equipment
   c. Document control
   d. Political activities
   e. Disbursement of funds
   f. Check cashing

CHAPTER 14

Format and Presentation

It would be unrealistic to propose that all security organizations adopt identical formats for the presentation of their policies and procedures. Of primary importance is the prudent construction, proper organization, and prompt dissemination of the policies and procedures. *How* they appear during the delivery or dissemination process is only of secondary importance.

Since no two security programs are arbitrarily expected to be alike, the policy and procedures manuals that provide operational parameters for them are also given the same latitude to be individualized. In fact, they are expected to be individualized—to fit the environment that they are to control.

For this reason, no single format for their construction is offered. Rather, a number of different examples are presented. Only the specific needs of individual security programs will ultimately determine which format is most appropriate.

Even the simplest of policy statements, with accompanying procedures, can serve to explain to employees security-related restrictions on their on-the-job behavior. The following is an example.

EXAMPLE 1: COMPANY RULES AND POLICIES

XYZ Industries tries to operate with a minimum of rules and regulations, and attempts to create as pleasant a working environment as possible for all its people. History has shown XYZ employees have a high sense of responsibility and understanding for each other's rights.

However, when a group as large as ours must be in close contact every working day, we must have certain rules to be sure our employees are protected from occasional trouble-makers. (Infractions of these rules may bring disciplinary action up to and including discharge.)

1. Reporting for or working while under influence of alcohol or drugs, or possession of any alcoholic beverage or narcotics on company property
2. Theft of company or personal property
3. Gambling or playing games of chance on company premises

4. Destroying company property deliberately
5. Fighting, horseplay, and disorderly or immoral conduct
6. Providing false or misleading information intentionally to obtain employment, or the making of false, vicious, or malicious statements concerning any employee, the company or its products
7. Being late or absent from work without notifying your supervisor or the Personnel Department, continued tardiness or absenteeism
8. Loafing on the job or idling in washrooms or other areas during working hours
9. Stopping work before quitting time, inefficient or unsatisfactory performance of duties
10. Punching a fellow employee's time card, or permitting another to punch your card
11. Submitting false time records or work tickets
12. Entering unauthorized areas or walking in plant without proper authorization
13. Smoking in unauthorized areas or otherwise violating fire regulations
14. Violating safety or health regulations
15. Failing to carry out instructions of your supervisor
16. Collecting money for gifts, flowers, parties, memorials, or selling of merchandise or tickets without written approval of the Personnel Department
17. Unauthorized carrying or possession of firearms on company property
18. Bringing cameras on company property without the approval of the Personnel Department
19. Playing radios or TV except as approved by the Personnel Department
20. Oral solicitation or distributing literature on company premises by nonemployees
21. Oral solicitation by employees during working time
22. Distributing literature by employees during working time
23. Distributing literature by employees in working areas at all times, posting or the removal of notices, signs or writing in any form on bulletin boards or company property without specific company approval
24. Receipt by the company of three or more wage assignments or deductions in a twelve-month period
25. Using company telephones for personal calls without proper authorization

---

As requirements for protection increase, so too do the policies and procedures that govern those efforts. Therefore, the examples of policy statements—and accompanying procedures—that follow are a bit more sophisticated.

EXAMPLE 2: POLICY AND PROCEDURES MANUAL

Date:
To:
From:
Re:

Arrest: Policy and Procedures

To arrest is to deprive a person of his liberty or freedom of movement, i.e., his freedom of choice to come or go. It may be effected by taking, seizing, or detaining a person. An arrest can also be accomplished by an act indicating an intention to arrest or conveying the impression to an individual through word or act that he is under restraint. It is not necessary to touch the person unless it is required to control him and then no more force than is necessary may be used. It is necessary that the person arrested realize that he is being placed under arrest by another person who is authorized to arrest. This knowledge may be imparted to the person being arrested by the following means: (1) Telling him he is under arrest and why, and (2) Depriving him of his freedom to leave—taking him into custody.

EXAMPLE 3: GUARD OPERATIONS: POLICY AND PROCEDURES

A. *Policy Statements.* The duties of a security officer are many and diverse. Some are dictated by directive, some by custom, and others by courtesy and the exercise of reason and good judgment. Whatever the causes for the existence of these duties, the security officer must always remember that he is an employee of _____and, thus, a representative of both this company and the client company (agency).
    1. A security officer must perform his or her duties in keeping with the objectives for providing protection, outlined in this manual. An officer's conduct, bearing, personal appearance, and associations with the public must be such that he is recognized as a responsible employee of _____who can capably carry out the assignments of his office or station.
    2. In addition to a security officer's responsibility to protect the client company's property, he must, also, be prepared to protect the wellbeing of employees and visitors to the facilities of the client company (agency) and to assist them in every fashion appropriate to the extent that such assistance may be accomplished without detriment to the discharge of an officer's official responsibilities.
    3. While on duty every security officer is charged with the responsibility of preventing unauthorized entry into the client company's

premises; preventing any malicious acts; and safeguarding all other buildings, employees, and visitors through the enforcement of the client company's regulations and those of _____ .

4. Should the needs of the client company dictate, security officers should conduct appropriate patrol activities either on foot or by motor vehicle. In all instances, plans for patrol activities must be originally approved by the Director of Security before they are initiated.

5. Plant and building protection includes the physical measures for the prevention of theft and damage to grounds, buildings, and equipment by fire, water, or natural disasters; malicious or thoughtless acts of individuals; trespass by unauthorized persons; and compromise of client company property and that of _____ to the extent entrusted or charged to the care of security officers or _____ .

6. Although the basic duties of a security officer vary with assignment, his basic responsibilities are the same:
   a. Assistance
   b. Deterrence
   c. Prevention
   d. Protection
   e. Safety

B. *Procedures.* The following general instructions are applicable to all guard stations and must be adhered to at all times.

1. All personnel must be identified by a badge or pass before being permitted entry into company facilities. Identification badges issued to company employees will be recognized as interchangeable throughout all company locations. In connection with the enforcement of these instructions the security guard will:
   a. Prohibit unauthorized persons from gaining access to company premises and property.
   b. Detect and detain individuals who have gained unauthorized entry. (In this event, report the facts to the Security Control Center and request instructions regarding release or disposition of the individual being detained.)
   c. Prevent unauthorized removal of company owned or controlled property.
   d. Challenge the presence and prevent the entry of individuals who do not display their identification badges properly. (Challenge such individuals saying "Excuse me, may I see your badge.")
   e. Spot check persons wearing area specified identification badges to assure that they are in their assigned work area as noted on the badge.
   f. Challenge persons wearing a special identification badge (issued to commercial vehicle drivers and their helpers) if their

presence is detected inside a company building. These persons are normally restricted to the vicinity of loading or unloading areas and are not authorized access to, or permitted entry inside, company buildings except to use rest room facilities. (In the event that any of these persons are found inside a company building, their presence will be questioned and a report (report no.) prepared on the incident.)

g.   Permit company officers and division heads access to all areas without restriction. Instructions issued by these officials will be complied with immediately. After complying with the instructions, the guard will prepare a report (report no.) quoting the instructions issued and action taken.

2. *Visitor escort.*

a.   When the visitors do not voluntarily surrender their badges, the guard will question them, or their escort, as they exit each building to determine if their visit is being terminated. If the answer is yes, the visitor will be asked to surrender his badge.

b.   Whenever an outgoing visitor arrives at a guard station without an escort, when one is required, the guard will ask the visitor to surrender his badge and determine the specific reason that he was allowed to move about the building unescorted.

EXAMPLE 4: POLICY AND PROCEDURES MANUAL

Civil Disturbances Directed Against Company Facilities: Policy and Procedures

During a situation brought about by civil disturbances, demonstrations, or strikes that may interfere with normal operations, it is necessary to provide a continuity of protective plans and operations for employees and property of the facility.

All planning will be directed toward keeping the plant and offices open for business as usual, to afford physical protection measures against damage to the facility, and to protect the rights and property of the company and all employees by peaceful and lawful means.

Three situations requiring protective measures are covered in this plan. These are defined as follows:

A.   *Civil Disturbances.* Unlawful activities perpetrated by unruly mobs or hit and run groups with the intent of damaging or destroying the facility or any part thereof.

B.   *Demonstrations.* Picketing and disruptive activities by outside dissident groups whose protests are bent on obstructing the flow of employees and vehicles through the gates. Attempts may also be made to breach security barriers with the further intent of disrupting operation.

C. *Strikes.* Labor/management disputes involving picketing activity and attempts to prevent access of employees and vehicles through the gates.

Emergency operations will be conducted within normal management channels. Specific functions that are contrary to normal operations and responsibilities are set forth in this plan.

A. Planning
   1. Establish and maintain call lists of key management officials, security personnel, and the guard force.
   2. Develop plans for expansion of plant protection activities with additional post assignments, special duties, and other related emergency functions.
   3. Maintain close relationships with local, county, state, and federal law enforcement agencies for intelligence purposes and assistance.
   4. Conduct special training programs for plant protection and auxiliary personnel.
   5. Conduct physical security inspections of the facility to assure maximum capabilities of fencing, lighting, and other protection equipment.
B. Execution
   1. Notify the designated key management officials on the Emergency Call List.
   2. Establish and maintain liaison, as directed, with
      a. Local police
      b. Contract guard service (where utilized).
   3. Maintain a written log and submit periodic reports of developments to the plant manager.
   4. Establish special prescribed procedures for control of entry of personnel and vehicles.
   5. Alert or call in staff personnel as needed for supporting services.
   6. Maintain communications with key management officials.
   7. Provide material assistance as required.

EXAMPLE 5: POLICY AND PROCEDURES MANUAL

Security of Vehicles and Parking Areas: Policy and Procedures

Regular, yet random, patrols should be made through all facility parking areas, both on foot and by vehicle, in order to ensure proper protection of persons in those areas as well as vehicles parked in them.

1. Regular and random patrol rounds are to be made routinely through all parking areas in order to provide maximum protection for both people and vehicles. All such patrol rounds are to be properly reported to the Desk Officer and then properly documented on the *Security Shift Log.*

2. If anything or anyone suspicious or out of the ordinary is discovered while on such patrol rounds, reasonable investigative efforts should ensue and proper documentation on the *comments* section of the *Security Shift Log* should be made by the Desk Officer. If appropriate, a *Security Incident Report* should also be completed. Such decisions should be at the discretion of the Charge Officer on duty.

3. When vehicles are involved, when possible, reasonable efforts should also be made to contact the owner(s) of any vehicle(s) involved.

4. Under no circumstances will any vehicle be forcibly entered without the owner's permission.

IN BRIEF

The following questions are to be asked when policy or procedures are to be developed regarding protective services.

Program objectives:
1. What objective is this program designed to attain?
2. Is this objective sound and desirable?
3. If the program is successful, will it attain the objective?
4. Is the program feasible?
   a. Is it reasonable to expect success?
   b. Can it be done with existing personnel?
   c. Does it involve cooperation of outside personnel/agencies?
5. Can the success of the program be determined? If so, how?
6. Are there supplementary advantages?

Program problems:
1. In what ways can the program fail? What are the foreseeable difficulties?
2. What are the penalties for failure?
   a. Will it embarrass the corporation if it fails?
   b. Will it embarrass the security department if it fails?
3. Are there disadvantages to the program?
   a. Is it contrary to sound security policy?
   b. Is it contrary to corporate policy?
   c. Is the expense too high in relation to the possible gain?
   d. Can it embarrass top management? Sales? Production? Research? Public relations?

Program rationale:
1. Why do it at all?
2. Is it worth attempting?
3. Why do it now?
4. Is there any reason for moving rapidly?
5. Why do it this way?
6. Are there other methods of approach that are more promising?
7. How much will it cost? Is it cost effective?
8. Where will funding be obtained?
9. Is this the best way that the amount of money involved could be utilized to promote security of the corporation?

Program approvals:
1. Who, if anybody, outside the Security Department must approve the project?
2. Who, if anybody, outside the Security Department must be informed?

CHAPTER 15

Content of Security Manuals

Policies and procedures, by nature, are generally intended to be as unique as the organization whose operations they are designed to control. Just as security programs must be unique to the environment in which they function, so too must its policies and procedures.

Consequently, no attempt will be made to dictate the contents of a specific policies or procedures manual. Rather, tables of contents from various policy manuals are offered.

These Tables of Contents represent a cross section of manuals used in a variety of different settings. They should, therefore, provide ample support on which to build new manuals or to revise existing ones.

BASIC SECURITY POLICY MANUAL

   I Command structure
  II Regulations
 III Personal conduct
IIIa Personal appearance
  IV Operations
   V Training
  VI Guard patrol
 VII Emergency procedures
VIII Report writing procedures
  IX First aid and safety
   X Authority and jurisdiction
  XI City fire/police departments and security force relationship

---

INDUSTRIAL SECURITY MANUAL

Policy	Procedure No.	Title
I	–	No standard
II	I	Access control procedures
	II	Master keyed lock and key stystem
	III	Photo ID card/badge program
	IV	Security guards
	V	Alarms and perimeter security devices
	VI	Storage cabinets, safes, and vaults
	VII	Holdup and burglary protection
	VIII	Property controls
	IX	Cargo security
III	I	Proprietary and sensitive information
	II	Release of privileged information to government agencies
IV	I	Emergency operations, formats, and principles
	1.1.1	Emergency operations organization (sample)
	1.2	Emergency security plan
	1.3	Emergency evacuation plan
	1.4	Fire, explosion, and escaping gas warning procedure
	1.5	Employee emergency procedures
	1.6	Emergency call lists
	1.7	Job descriptions (sample)
	1.8	Test/training
	1.8.1	Fire training
	II	Procedures
	2.1	Bomb threats
	2.2	Chemical spills
	2.3	Civil defense plan
	2.4	Civil disturbances directed against company facilities
	2.5	Closed plant operations
	2.5.1	Plant shutdown procedures
	2.6	Fire, explosion, and escaping gas plan
	2.7	Severe weather and flood emergency plan
	2.7.1	Severe weather and flood emergency operations center
	2.8	Medical emergencies
	2.9	Natural disasters
	2.9.1	Natural disaster plan
	2.10	Industrial accidents
	III	Protection of resources
	3.1	Maps and diagrams

Policy	Procedure No.	Title
	3.2	Dangerous material storage
	3.3	High risk area list
	3.4	Fire fighting equipment
	3.5	Products
	3.6	Proprietary documents
	3.7	Capital equipment
	3.8	Office equipment
	IV	Emergency evacuation
V	I	Self-inspection checklist

GENERAL OFFICE BUILDING COMPLEX SECURITY MANUAL

Foreword
Introduction
Part I: *General office complex: Its buildings, its people*
Organization chart: General office complex
Organization chart: Security department
Map of building locations
Part II: *Organization of security services*
Responsibilities of Director of Security, Security Sergeant, Security Officer
Part III: *General duties of the security force*
General outline of duties of members of security force
Part IV: *Authority as a special deputy*
Right to arrest
Right to detain and question
Part V: *Deportment and general appearance*
Code of ethics
Deportment
Personal appearance
Part VI: *Special police equipment*
Use of baton, handcuffs, chemical mace, walkie-talkies
Part VII: *Preventive patrolling*
Preventive patrol, building patrol
Aggressive patrol
Part VIII: *The things security officers must keep in mind*
Increasing your powers of observation
Part IX: *General orders for security officers*
General orders: How they are given and how they are to be carried out
Part X: *Investigation reports*

Daily security report
Who, what, when, where, how
Index to sample reports
Sample reports
Part XI: *Special emergencies*
Fires
Disasters, internal and external
Bomb threats

Summary

AIRPORT SECURITY POLICY MANUAL

Armed guard instruction
Uniform guard instruction
General security information
Regulations
Training
Report writing
Firearms
Records of firearms
Preboarding screening and training
Security inspectors instruction
Regulations
Time cards
Training
Personnel selection and assignment
Responsibilities and duties of security inspectors
Baggage search procedure
Predeparture screening
Classified document and handicapped persons screening procedures
Weapons detector
Micro dose X-ray inspection regulation
Training X-ray equipment
Relief periods
Work practices
Uniform and personal appearance
Nonunion, Nonmanagement employee benefits

HOSPITAL SECURITY DEPARTMENT POLICIES AND PROCEDURES MANUAL

1. Foreword
2. History of the hospital
3. Description and mission of the hospital

    a.   Department

    b.   Company

4.   Code of ethics

5.   Emergency notification system

6.   Security 10 codes

7.   Radio procedures

8.   Security organization chart

    a.   Graphic

    b.   Descriptive

9.   Department description of responsibilities and duties

    a.   Day shift

    b.   Evening shift

    c.   Night shift

10.   Job descriptions (all job classes)

11.   Policy on press releases

12.   Public and community relations policy

13.   Security department relationship to other departments and employees

14.   Appearance, regulations, and conduct

15.   Smoking regulations

16.   Identification badge requirement

17.   Hiring agreement

18.   Firearms waiver

19.   Weapon safety

20.   Arrest, search, and seizure

21.   Securing of evidence

22.   Notification of emergency services

23.   Civil disturbance plan

24.   Offense reports and forms completion

25.   Reporting of major incidents

26.   Fire department notification procedure

27.   Fire plan and duties

28.   Fire drills and reporting

29.   Accidents

30.   Altercations

31.   Visitor passes

32.   Guidelines for after hours visiting

33.   Policy in event of possible gas leaks

34.   Public utility shutoff locations

35.   Care of patient valuables

36.   Lost and found policy

37.   Parking regulations

38.   Towing of vehicles

39.   Tornado policy—Storm procedures

40.   Policy for civil defense

41.   Disaster plan

42. Bomb threat plan
43. Infection control policy
44. Secondary employment policy
45. Information on firearms and uniforms
46. Security of the hospital pharmacy
47. Legal information
48. Patient and visitor rights
49. Policies on the release of medical information
50. Housekeeping responsibilities
51. Office and department supplies
52. Key control policy
53. Emergency key use
54. Package inspections
55. Employee attendance records
56. Conclusion

**UNIVERSITY DEPARTMENT OF PUBLIC SAFETY
ORGANIZATION AND OPERATIONS MANUAL**

Foreword
Code of ethics
Title I: Orientation
Chapter I: Introduction to the Department of Public Safety
Chapter II: Defining terms
Chapter III: Origin of authority
                3.1.   Department jurisdiction
Chapter IV: Organization
                4.1.   Organizational chart
                4.2.   Delineation of authority
                4.3.   General duties and responsibility by order of rank
Chapter V: Personnel
                5.1.   Qualifications and prerequisites for employment
                5.2.   Recruiting
                5.3.   Occupation contracts
Chapter VI: Department rules and regulations
                6.1.   General orders
                6.2.   Special orders
                6.3.   Uniforms and equipment
                6.4.   Department vehicle operation
                6.5.   Discipline
Title II: Operating procedure
Chapter VII: Reports and report forms
                7.1.   Report writing

CONTRACTUAL GUARD SERVICE MANUAL OF POLICY AND PROCEDURES

3-3   Emergency procedures
      (a) Fire
      (b) Natural disasters
      (c) Bomb and explosions
      (d) Building evacuations
3-4   Reporting procedures
3-5   Safety and first aid
3-6   Special duties for clients

SAMPLE POLICY MANUAL

To provide a general conceptual idea of what information a policy manual might contain, the following is offered. It represents those policies and procedures that might be in place to support the security operation in a fictitious corporation.

Alpha Corporation: Employee Security-Safety Handbook

Letter from the President
Introduction
Security
        Security areas
        Need to know
        Information classification
        Alpha facilities
        Reporting incidents
        Identification cards
        Protective Services Director
        Departmental responsibility
        Supervisor's responsibilities
        Employee responsibilities
        General regulations
        Personnel in restricted, limited, and controlled areas
        Motor vehicles
                Safety regulations

Introduction

Every employer has a moral responsibility to his employees to remove as much of the temptation to steal as is humanly possible. Likewise, every employee has the same moral responsibility toward his fellow employees.
        Mr. S. J. Curtis, a professional security expert, feels that: "In many

instances—perhaps the majority—the individual would not have turned dishonest had reasonable, precautionary methods been exercised. To take steps that will successfully prevent this dishonesty is to save many lives from ruin."

The Alpha Corporation, recognizing that its employees are its greatest asset, has developed the Employee Security-Safety Handbook. This handbook is designed to acquaint you with our security practices.

Many of the losses suffered by both the employees and the company are caused by the uninformed or neglectful employees.

Careful inspection and constant supervision are necessary on the part of supervisors and foremen; continuous observance of security practices is required of each employee to reduce the temptations that contribute to the losses of employee property and the ruination of lives.

Study and know your Security-Safety Handbook and remember that everyone is subject to temptation and that it is the responsibility of each one of us to help each other by observing security-safety regulations.

Report all unsafe and insecure conditions and security violations to your Supervisor; report all losses at once.

Security and Safety suggestions are welcome, in fact, requested. If you know how to improve the security system for yourself and others, inform your supervisor. It will *pay you* to do so! Additional security policies will be issued from time to time by the Protective Services Department or by your department.

Violation of any security regulation may subject you to disciplinary action.

Security. Security provides those means that serve to protect and preserve our environment. It allows for the conduct of our activities without disruption.

Security Areas. The security system of the Alpha Corporation has designated certain areas that only authorized personnel are permitted to enter. The areas are classified according to their criticality and vulnerability to the Alpha Corporation.

The three classifications are:

Restricted. This is a tightly controlled area where only selected personnel are allowed. An example would be the Research and Development area.

Limited. This is an area of sensitive nature. Employees other than authorized personnel may walk past but may not enter. An example of this would be a records area.

Controlled. This is an area where all employees are permitted. It may be defined as the widest possible area with least risk of damage or loss of knowledge. Only authorized personnel are allowed.

The restricted areas are conspicuously marked with signs designating their classification.

Need-to-know. A determination made by the possessor of classified information that a prospective recipient, in the interest of state defense, has a requirement for access to, knowledge of, or possession of the classified information in order to perform tasks or services essential to the fulfillment of a classified contract or program approved by a specified agency within the Alpha Corporation.

Information Classification. Certain documents and information, pertaining to the company are to be considered *company confidential.* They are for the use of only authorized persons.

All classified documents are clearly marked on their cover sheet with the notation *company confidential.* They are not to be shown to persons without a need for the information.

Alpha Facilities. Facilities of Alpha Corporation are defined as: Something that is built, constructed, installed, or established to perform some particular function or to serve or facilitate some particular end. Every employee works at one or more facilities. Drawing from the above definition, a facility includes the buildings, parking lots, and the ground around the buildings. Facility security begins when an employee enters the facility and ends when he leaves. Employees should only enter and leave by prescribed exits.

Upon entry into a work area, employees should first take a minute to see that it is as it was left the night before. If things are not in their proper order, call the Security Department and wait for their arrival. Do not touch anything or try to straighten things up.

Reporting Incidents

1. All thefts, attempted bribes, kickbacks, vandalism, mislaid property, and other security regulation violations, no matter how small, shall be reported directly to the department supervisor.
2. The supervisor will contact the Protective Services Department and complete the official form and route as directed on the form. If the supervisor is unavailable, the employee shall contact the Protective Services Department immediately and the supervisor as soon as possible.

Identification Cards. All Alpha employees must have an Alpha identification card issued under the direction of the Protective Services Department. These cards are to be used only for employment identification. When an employee transfers to a new department he may be issued a new identification card. When an individual's employment ceases, he must surrender his identification card.

Security Coordinator.   The Director of Protective Services of the Alpha Corporation has the overall responsibility for formulating, directing, and coordinating security-safety activities throughout the company. This is done through liaison with all department heads, personnel officers, and all management and through the initiation of an ongoing security awareness program.

Departmental Responsibility.   Each department must assume responsibility for an effective employee security program that shall include the following:

a. leadership and direction,
b. periodic inspections,
c. insure that all security violations are investigated,
d. post and enforce security regulations,
e. review and sign reports of security violations and performance,
f. initiate and evaluate departmental security programs and regulations that include the checking in and out of all equipment and classified documents,
g. cooperate with the Director of Protective Services on all programs,
h. plan and make known emergency exit routes,
i. organize a departmental security committee, and
j. compile an accurate account of all equipment within the department.

Supervisor's Responsibilities

a. Train all employees in security regulations within their departments and point out security hazards.
b. Make sure that the necessary security equipment and protective devices for the department are provided in proper working condition, and are used.
c. Take prompt corrective action whenever insecure conditions and actions are observed.
d. Investigate and report all violations of security regulations.
e. Conduct frequent, unannounced security inspections of all work areas and operations within the department.

Employee Responsibilities

a. Report any security violation to your supervisor.
b. Report any missing money, equipment, documents, or personal belongings to your supervisor.

c. Use all security equipment for your job without fail.
d. Follow all security regulations.
e. Report any vandalism to company or employee property.
f. Lock your vehicle in the prescribed parking lot.
g. Take your purse or belongings with you whenever you leave your work area.
h. Report anyone who is unauthorized to be in your work area.
i. Do not give any information to *anyone* who does not have a need to know.
j. Lock your desk and file cabinets when you leave your work area.
k. Report any bribe attempts even if the persons offering state they were not serious.

General Regulations

1.01 You are required to be familiar with, and to observe, all security-safety regulations. Violation of any security-safety regulation may be cause for disciplinary action.
1.02 Drinking of alcoholic beverages during working hours is prohibited. Any employee reporting for work while under the influence of alcohol shall be subject to disciplinary action.
1.03 Use of illicit drugs is strictly prohibited. Any employee who is convicted of a drug offense shall be subject to disciplinary action.
1.04 Any employee who is convicted of a serious misdemeanor or felony is subject to disciplinary action.
1.05 Any employee who is charged with a serious misdemeanor, other than traffic, or a felony must report this to his supervisor. Failure to do so within seven days counting the day of arrest will subject the employee to disciplinary action.
1.06 Employees are required to park motor vehicles in assigned places or lots. Continued failure may result in disciplinary action and most assuredly involve a parking ticket.
1.07 Employees are permitted to enter and leave their places of employment at assigned exits.
1.08 Employees must produce their identification cards upon request by a security officer and wear *badges* while in the facility. Failure to do so may lead to disciplinary action.
1.09 Packages brought into and leaving buildings are subject to inspection. Passes are required to remove anything from the facility.
1.10 Entry into classified areas without proper authorization is prohibited.
1.11 All supplies must be requisitioned by supervisors.
1.12 All supply rooms must be kept locked.
1.13 Employees must report all incidents, all security violations, and all hazardous actions by other employees in order to make all employees safe.

1.14 All Alpha equipment that may be lent out to employees must be checked out and back in.

Personnel in Restricted, Limited, and Controlled Areas

2.01 Transmission of information to people who do not have a need to know is prohibited.

2.02 All documents must be signed in and out.

2.03 Documents, when not in use, must be returned to their proper file.

2.04 All files must be locked when not in use.

2.05 All desks must be locked whenever you leave your work area.

2.06 Documents may not be removed from the building unless proper approval is given by the head of the department and documents are transported with care.

2.07 All Research and Development and sensitive material workers must use the paper shredder for destruction of notes.

2.08 Destruction of all *company confidential* documents is to be supervised by a supervisor and two witnesses.

2.09 All dials to safes or vaults must be spun three times around when the safes are locked.

2.10 All secretaries must use the paper shredder for destruction of typewriter ribbons, scrap paper, and old mail envelopes.

2.11 Communication of *company confidential* information by telephone is prohibited.

Motor Vehicles

3.01 Unauthorized use of company vehicles is prohibited.

3.02 Employees who have vehicles assigned to them should inspect them for operating condition. No one should operate a defective vehicle.

3.03 Vehicles must be checked in and out properly.

COMPLIANCE STATEMENTS

In order to better document the fact that subordinate security managers (or security personnel) understand the specific provisions of a policy manual *and* appreciate the need for adherence to those provisions, a *Compliance Statement* should be developed and used. Such written statements provide basic expectations for those who are responsible for enforcing the policies and procedures contained in the manual. Further, they provide evidence, through the appropriate signatures, that each manager understands and accepts that responsibility.

An example of one type of *Compliance Statement* is offered for your review.

COMPLIANCE STATEMENT

I have read, completely, this *Policy Manual for Safety and Security,* and I do fully understand the specific procedures and special instructions contained in each policy.

Further, I am also cognizant of the fact that it is my responsibility, as a manager, to ensure, to the best of my ability, that there is proper and consistent compliance with each of these policies and the specific procedures, and special instructions contained in them.

_____   _____
Signature: *Signature:*
Security Manager   *Security Director*

_____   _____
Date   *Date*

SECTION IV

Budgeting and Fiscal Management

Managers responsible for the execution of a company's security program are invariably also responsible for its budget. Consequently, it is imperative that they possess a strong working knowledge of budgeting and the management of funds allocated to make purchases, pay wages, and, ultimately, deliver services.

Cost considerations that affect important issues such as program development, security personnel, and technology use are presented in this section. These factors have the greatest continuing cost impact on budgets and program effectiveness. How well programs are planned, used, and paid for, will often make the difference between those that are cost effective and those that are a waste of money.

Yet, without regard specifically to how a budget is prepared, the bottom line in management is virtually always *cost effectiveness*. Managers are expected to spend wisely—get the most possible for the dollar.

One of the most perplexing problems for the security practitioner is the evaluation of what he or she does. There are few generally accepted standards for evaluation of security programs or specific security activities. Many authors indicate that lower losses, reduction of criminal attack, increased recoveries of stolen property, and number of apprehensions and successful prosecutions are measures of effectiveness of security programs. The quantification of various activities performed by the security function is quite another matter. It is difficult at best to determine, for example, the indirect monetary loss to a company associated with a theft or a burglary. It is likewise difficult to assess the value of implementing an effective access control program. How do you, for example, show the relationship between an ID card or an access control system and a directly proveable benefit to the organization? In attempting to justify budgetary increases, how does a security department show value to the organization for funds provided to it during the past fiscal period? Budget development and presentation thus become critical to Security Department effectiveness and success. The material in this section will assist in accomplishing this very important task.

CHAPTER 16

Budget Considerations

COST AND BID SPECIFICATIONS

The development of bid and cost specifications for contract security services must involve the participation of senior executives of the organization. On the surface, contracting for a service such as security might well be considered for action only by the Security Director. Guards protect property and enforce company rules and regulations and, in some cases, are present to insure compliance with various Federal regulations concerning operations of a particular type of facility. Why, then, does this relatively mundane management function require executive attention and involvement?

The Security Director has often been given complete responsibility for the development of bid specifications and contract terms to best serve the interests of the corporation. If this has been sufficient in the past, why does it now require more than his attention?

A number of very real problems exist in the development of contract terms that can affect not only the type and quality of security service, but also impact on the entire corporate structure and its ability to carry out its primary activity. Each security guard contract that is developed within an organization has inherent within it implications for the personnel function, insurance, EEO compliance, legal, purchasing, and labor union considerations that transcend the operating responsibilities of the Security Department. It is, therefore, critical that senior management develop a policy for the development of security contractual terms and the actual contracting for security services that reflects a well considered, cost-effective approach to security contracting.

It should be noted that many of the original reasons for the growth of the contract security field are still operative. Basically, contract services provide the number and type of security officers required to perform specified services at an agreed upon fee. For this contractor's fee, the contracting organization receives a specified number of security officers to perform certain tasks without any additional cost, nor the administrative, legal, insurance, and labor relations problems associated with the operation of that contract function. In general, contract security services are less expensive and to a large degree more cost effective than proprietary security operations.

The competitiveness of the contract security field has led to the philosophy on the part of purchasers of contract services that they play one company against another to receive the most favorable and least expensive terms during the bidding process for a particular contract. The process of selecting the lowest bidder on particular jobs, while a proper management decision, in many regards has expanded to include not only the desire to obtain the most favorable cost terms, but to place management restrictions and contractual relationships that go beyond the contractor-client relationship.

A relatively recent development in contract security services is the development of bid specifications that require the security company to provide X number of security officers for a given fee to be administered and supervised by the client/Security Director and his or her staff. All directions and orders being provided by the client Security Department with the contract agency providing trained, uniformed personnel to work specified hours. From the point of view of the Security Director and client, this is a significant attempt to have the best of both proprietary and contractual security personnel—in effect, getting the best of contract services by not having the administrative problems of recruitment, training, selection, uniforming, replacement, and the associated labor relations problems while on the other hand having total administrative and supervisory control over the use, placement, termination, and assignment of these personnel, as would be the case with a proprietary officer.

The situation that arises in this type of contract is that of the establishment of a coemployer relationship between the security company and the client. The implications of such a situation are potentially detrimental to both the client and the contract agency.

There have been numerous situations in the U.S. in which a contract company has made an attempt to comply with an extremely demanding guard contractual relationship and has agreed to provide personnel in such a situation only to find that neither the best interests of the client nor of the firm have been served. The development of this type of contract, in effect, places the contract agency in the role of a labor broker.

The desirability of having a Security Director and facility management control the security staff is understandable. The movement toward the structuring of bid specifications and the extremely tight and rigid set of controls of security personnel by facilities is, to a large degree, a reaction against historically poor quality of personnel and low service capabilities of security service agencies. The assumption is that the guard company cannot give good service, and the only way to assure good service is to tightly control each aspect of the operation by facility management. This is, unfortunately, a somewhat justifiable reaction to many low-quality services offered in the security industry. It similarly reflects the type of service that can be obtained in virtually every market area of the United States. Conversely, quality security services have always existed. There are literally thousands of facilities around the United States using quality contract services.

The primary question that must be faced by the potential purchaser of contract security services is that of the risk involved with purchasing security services based on the primary consideration of cost. This type of *cost* purchase has greatly increased the probabilities that a security administrator will seek highly restrictive and structured bid specifications that reduce greatly the freedom of the contract agency to conduct and control the management of the security force. The likelihood of a coemployer relationship arising in such a situation is very high.

The major questions that must be answered by the purchaser of the service are:

1. What is the probability of a coemployer relationship developing?
2. What is the risk associated with a coemployment contract?, and,
3. What will the consequences of the establishment of a coemployer situation be to the overall operation of the facility?

In essence, in the cost-risk relationship of a coemployer situation there are three outcomes.

1. Industrial relations and labor problems are almost inevitable.
2. Work stoppages and strikes could occur, initiated by the Security Department and spreading to other unions operating within the facility.
3. A loss of or suspension of operating licenses could occur through a breakdown in the security operations required under licensing agreements.

Any one of these three conditions is a justification for involving top management in its resolutions. Their involvement in the development of bid specifications is, therefore, desirable to reduce possible occurrence of these conditions.

The development of a captive unit (coemployee) by tight control of the security forces, in the contract terms, is a less than desirable condition both from a security standpoint and for overall facility management. In striving to insure that the guidelines for purchase of services are complied with, the specifications for security services have been rigorously developed. They are, on one hand, essential; conversely, the impact of such control for the overall operations of the facility have been either minimized or not considered during the development of the bid specifications and contract terms. Cost at the expense of significant loss exposure is at best a false economy.

EVALUATORS

Numerous facilities have attempted to deal with the problem of insuring quality services at a fair and cost-effective price. Various approaches have been tried, 1) in the development of performance standards and 2) with contractual terms to effect the desired protective goals of the facility.

These methods have included:

A. Specification of:
    1. Personnel physical standards
    2. Psychological standards
    3. Criminal history standards
    4. Educational standards, and so forth
B. Guard service, administration criteria. These criteria have included:
    1. Coordination of the guard force
    2. Site supervisory and management personnel
    3. Requiring the contract agency to provide all training demanded by the site
    4. Provision of all equipment specified by the site
    5. Writing a number of personnel considerations such as:
        a. The right to reject all employees before assignment to the position with a provision that all employees selected for work on the site must be interviewed and approved by the facility prior to hiring.

It is essential that specific operational, personal, and administration objections be the frame of reference for contractual terms. Security considerations, in the context of *worst case* situations, tend to be overly restrictive for both the supplier and the user. Quality services can be obtained when contract terms spell out clearly what performance is expected. The methods and techniques that the contractor utilizes to attain client protective goals must be the responsibility of the agency. Creativity in solving the client problem is the reflection of a competitive marketplace when goals and objectives are given without rigid controls being imposed.

The development of the contract is a critical aspect of obtaining the required type and level of security. The terms must be evaluated and understood by corporate management.

The view of the security force, affecting only one portion of facility operations, is restrictive and can lead to potentially damaging consequences. The corporate strategy for protection should therefore be based on marketplace competition and the contractor's creative response to client security needs.

CHAPTER 17

Program Costs

The worksheet in Figure 17–1 is provided as a guide to management so that a security program can be looked at in terms of its effects on the company's fiscal plan. Obviously no security program is cost free; like every other development program in commerce and industry, there are expenses involved in both developing and implementing an effective security program. The word "effective" is stressed because if something less than an effective program is initiated, your time, effort, *and* money are being wasted.

To insure that the final cost estimate for security protection is reflective of the actual cost, the worksheet in Figure 17–1 has been prepared as a do-it-yourself budget proposal—the only thing that is missing is your cost for each item. However, to make that determination easier, we have also included a general list of possible sources where you might find information on costs and prices.

In addition, remember that it is virtually impossible to make a security program 100 percent operational overnight. It must be a meticulous, carefully-prepared undertaking. It is probably safe to say that once you take your initial step in the implementation of an effective security program—the hiring of a Security Director who can devote all of his or her time and energy to the program—it will be at least 90 days before the program is operating at 100 percent. Therefore, every cost or expense prior to that time is a *preparatory expenditure*—an initial expense.

The Security Director who makes $3,000 per month and works the 90-day period to get the program working at a maximum level has placed his $9,000 salary ($3,000 × 3 = $9,000) under the general heading of *preparatory expenditures*. Since regular security personnel will probably not be employed until after the first 30 days have passed, only two months of their salaries will fall into the preparatory classification. *Preparatory expenditures* will be calculated in the second section of the worksheet. For now select only those expenditures required to begin operations and calculate initial expenditures.

Example

Director of Security $ _____ mo. × 3 = _____
Director of Security $ _____ mo. × 2 = _____

EXPENSE WORKSHEET
FOR
SECURITY PROGRAMS

PROPOSED ITEM	POTENTIAL SOURCE OF INFORMATION	ESTIMATED COST
Security Hardware	Supplier, Dealer	
Fixtures & Equipment	Manufacturer	
Intrusion Alarms		$_____
Detection Alarms		$_____
Fire		$_____
Smoke		$_____
CCTV System/Video-Tape, etc.		$_____
Central Station Monitors		$_____
Security Lighting Fixtures		$_____
Keys, Locks, etc.		$_____
Other Misc. Items such as:		
Equipment Maintenance Contracts		$_____
_____		$_____
Installation of Hardware,	Supplier or	
Fixtures & Equipment	Contractor	
Alarms		$_____
Electrical systems		$_____
Keys, Locks, etc.		$_____
Others		$_____
Insurance Changes *	Insurance Agent	$_____
(for personnel, vehicles, etc.)		
Changes, Adaptations	Contractor	
or remodeling of Facilities	(Landlord)	$_____
Changes in Public	Utility Company	$_____
Utilities		
Electric		$_____
Telephone		$_____
_____		$_____
Legal, Professional		
and Consulting Fees		
Appropriate licenses	Attorney or	
and/or Permits	Government Offices	$_____
Operating and	Accounting Department	
contingency funds		$_____
Equipment		
Weapons, Flashlights,	Police Supply Co.	
cuffs, etc.		$_____
Communications	Manufacturer	$_____
	Sub-Total	$_____

Figure 17–1   Expense worksheet for security programs.

ON-GOING EXPENSES	MONTHLY COST		FORMULA	
Salaries:				
Director of Security	$_____		× 12 =	$_____
Security Officer (Number _____)	$_____	× N	× 12 =	$_____
Clerical Staff (N)	$_____		× 12 =	$_____
Support Staff	$_____		× 12 =	$_____
Equipment				
Vehicles (Number _____)	$_____	× N		
Uniforms (N)	$_____		× 12 =	$_____
_____	$_____		× 12 =	$_____
_____	$_____		× 12 =	$_____
Telephone				$_____
Utilities				$_____
Supplies				
Office	$_____		× 12 =	$_____
_____	$_____		× 12 =	$_____
_____	$_____		× 12 =	$_____
Maintenance				
Gas/Oil/Service (@ .20 per car per mile/@ .12 per unit per mile for other				
Vehicles)	$_____		× 12 =	$_____
Security Hardware				$_____
Office Equipment	$_____		× 12 =	$_____
Communications Equipment				$_____
_____				$_____
_____				$_____
On-Going Legal and Security				
Consulting Fees	$_____		× 12 =	$_____
Miscellaneous Expenditures * *				
_____				$_____
_____				$_____
_____				$_____
_____				$_____
			Sub-Total	$_____
	Hardware			$_____
	On-Going		&	$_____
			Grand Total	$_____

Start up cost can be computed by extracting 25% of the yearly on-going cost. If Hardware is being employed, the entire cost must be prorated for the start-up period also.

Start-up Cost
25% Personnel Cost _____ ÷ 25% $_____
% per month total hardware _____ × 3 $_____
Total $_____

*While consulting your insurance agent it may be worthwhile to find out if the addition of a security program will decrease your rates for other coverage, i.e. fire, liability, theft.
* *Expenses such as tax, social security, pension, etc.

CHAPTER 18

Personnel Costs

A cost analysis worksheet can provide a means for analyzing the costs associated with contractual security services and inhouse protection. In most cases the cost of contractual security services is less than providing the same amount of protection on an inhouse basis. However, the difference in cost might be substantial or slight depending upon the rate of pay for inhouse officers and the prevailing rates charged by contract agencies in your particular area.

For purposes of example only, the worksheet in Figure 18–1 will provide specific cost differences. Decisions can then be made about the relative value of other factors such as control and supervision, responsiveness, quality of personnel and related administrative and operational consideration. Remember, cost is only one factor in making a decision between contract and inhouse security officers. It is, however, an important one.

SALARIES FOR PRIVATE SECURITY AND
PUBLIC POLICE PERSONNEL

One of the most acute problems in the private security industry today is the lack of good salaries that could attract quality people. Most organizations will, in order to attract high quality personnel, offer salaries that are competitive enough to attract individuals with the education, experience, and maturity to perform well. Such is not the case with private security personnel. Certainly any manager would agree that occupational problems, such as low salaries, can adversely affect employee-management relations, attrition rates, morale, and the quality of services rendered. To counter this situation the National Advisory Commission's Private Security Task Force recommends:

> In an effort to reduce the attrition rate of the industry, salaries for private security personnel should be commensurate with experience, training and/or education, job responsibilities, and other criteria related to the job performed.

In addition, many security administrators feel that the salaries paid security officers should, in fact, be commensurate with those paid to public law enforcement personnel. Were that to be the case, statistics from the U.S.

IN-HOUSE GUARD SERVICE

Direct labor costs

Rate per hour $ _____ × total

hours per week = $ _____

Overtime rate $ _____ × total

hours per week = $ _____

Total direct pay per week = $ _____ × 52 weeks = $ _____

Additional labor costs

Supervision and administration – $ _____ per

week × 52 = $ _____

Vacation pay – $ _____ per man × number of

weeks = $ _____

Paid holidays _____ × rate per man × number

of men = $ _____

Sick leave, jury duty – est. number of days × rate = $ _____

Shift differential (weekends and nights) – cost per

week × 52 = $ _____

Training and retraining per man = $ _____

Total additional labor costs per year = $ _____

Total Labor Cost Per Year.. $ _____

Figure 18–1 Security officer protection cost analysis worksheet

Insurance, taxes and operational expenses

Uniforms and equipment – (est. $350 per man × number of officers = $ _____

Liability and property damage insurance (est. 1 percent of total labor cost per year) = $ _____

Life insurance, union costs, hospitalization, pensions – (est. 13 percent of total labor cost per year) = $ _____

Workman's compensation insurance (est. $3.00 per $100 of payroll) = $ _____

Payroll taxes, FICA, state and federal unemployment (est. 9 percent × total labor cost) $ _____

Cost of recruiting replacement personnel (est. number of new employees × average cost to hire) = $ _____

Total operational expenses.. $ _____

GUARD SERVICE YEARLY TOTAL COST................................... $ _____

Figure 18–1 (continued)

Bureau of Labor indicate that security officers should be paid between $17,120 and $23,100 (see also Table 18–1).

Yet, as the *Private Security Task Force Report* indicates, attempting to identify any recommended national minimum salary would be questionable at best. Salaries in any given area are affected by any or all of the following factors mentioned by the Task Force:

1. General economic aspects of the locale
2. Availability of labor
3. Competitive aspects of private security

All of these must be considered before deciding upon a specific salary to offer present or potential employees.

    1. *General economic aspects of the locale.* Naturally, the economic condition of the area is going to bear heavily on the amount of salary offered. Common sense will probably indicate that an area with high unemployment and low annual salaries should not require an organization to offer the wages that an organization would have to if the situation were reversed.

Prices of commodities, rates of inflation, and the community's standard of living affect the salaries that must be paid if an organization is to get and keep employees as well. As always, management will, from time to time, have

Table 18–1

	Average Annual Salaries for Public Police	
	Minimum	*Maximum*
1971	$ 8,874	$10,576
1974	10,540	13,080
1981	15,159	19,066
1984	19,406	23,109

	Average Annual Salaries for Private Security	
	Minimum	*Maximum*
1971	$ 4,160	$ 6,900
1974	7,426	8,421
1981	11,006	12,754
1984	12,515	14,623

Public police salaries from the International City Mgt. Assoc. and the U.S. Dept. of Labor. Private security salaries from the U.S. Dept. of Labor.

to reevaluate the economic condition of the area and adjust its salary scale if appropriate.

2. *Availability of labor.* In a similar vein, the number of available quality applicants and employees will also affect the amount of salaries that an organization must offer. If the local labor market is saturated with adequately educated, able-bodied employees, an organization may not have to pay higher or more exorbitant salaries to get the calibre of security officer it desires. Theoretically, an organization need only offer a salary that guarantees it an ample number of satisfactory employees, but, realistically, it is also important that management consider the levels of morale, efficiency, effectiveness, and productivity of those employees. Even though there is no single formula for helping management determine how much salary is enough, cost-benefit should always be an important consideration.

3. *Competitive aspects of private security.* No matter what the economic or employment conditions of the locale are, if there are other organizations or security companies competing for available personnel, management must be willing to offer salaries that are competitive. Again, though, it will probably become a question of cost-benefit when management approaches its decision:

1. Is it necessary that your salaries be competitive with others?
2. Is it necessary that your services be competitive with others?

CONTRACTUAL VERSUS PROPRIETARY PERSONNEL: COST CONSIDERATIONS

In order to accurately appraise the actual cost of using a proprietary security force, all of the following criteria must be considered. Further, costs associated with each individual criterion must be calculated.

1. Costs associated with recruiting security staff
2. Screening, testing, and hiring
3. Preservice (orientation) and inservice training expenses
4. Salaries, including overtime
5. FICA contributions
6. Worker's compensation claims and payments
7. Unemployment insurance contributions
8. Contributions to retirement and pension programs
9. Contributions to medical, dental, and life insurance programs
10. Profit-sharing contributions
11. Payments for sick leave
12. Seniority pay
13. Vacation, holiday, and personal time pay
14. Pay for shift differentials or special duty

15. Costs connected with scheduling responsibilities and manpower distribution
16. Costs associated with the purchase of uniforms, equipment, weapons, and so forth
17. Capital purchases such as vehicles and radio equipment
18. Repair and maintenance costs
19. Costs associated with administrative and supervisory duties
20. Costs associated with liability claims and insurance

For the sake of comparison, contractual guard agencies charge an average of $10.00 to $15.00 per hour for protection provided by their personnel.

CHAPTER 19

Hardware Costs

On pages 176–179 there is a listing of various types of security hardware equipment arranged generically rather than by brand name. Included are the major methods of activating the device, the use and coverage, and the average installed cost of the equipment. All prices listed are approximate for good quality equipment. They represent average prices for the generic equipment indicated (1985 cost).

A schematic indicating the costs of alarm components is presented in Figure 19–1 so that expenses associated with the development of an individualized system can be determined as well. Section VII provides additional information on security technology that will be helpful in determining hardware costs.

LEASING SECURITY HARDWARE

The leasing of security equipment has many desirable features. A major virtue is that it frees the company's working capital. Leasing also creates an additional source of credit and offers tax benefits since lease payments are normally fully deductible as business expenses where security equipment is concerned. Tax savings may return more than half the expenditure.

The relative cost of equipment is in favor of leasing. If a manufacturer takes $100,000 out of his liquid working capital and uses it to acquire new equipment, he is obviously paying something for the use of that money. Since every dollar of liquid working capital has earning power, the investment of $100,000 in new equipment must return to the company at least the same profit that the company can earn with this $100,000 in other ways.

Every company has at least one simple choice in regard to new security equipment: to buy using their own working capital as funds or to lease. When using their own funds to buy, they obviously decrease liquid working capital. For example, if a company's working capital earns 40 percent profit before taxes, they are paying 40 percent for the use of money invested in the equipment. Security equipment can almost always be acquired at a lower cost through leasing than the manufacturer's use of his own working capital or of borrowed capital.

174

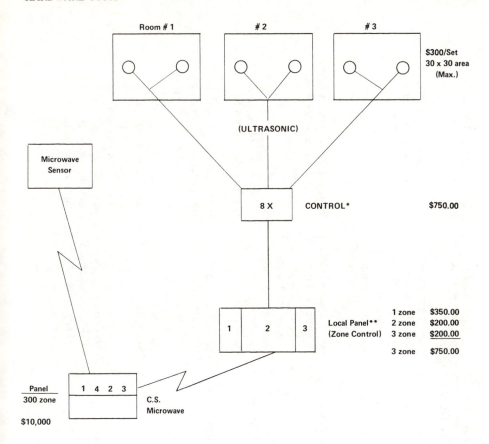

Figure 19–1   Alarm system schematic/costing.

Equipment installed is leased at a price that amortizes the cost of the equipment over the period covered by the contract. Thus, when the contract is completed (3 or 5 years), new and more efficient equipment may be available and can be readily installed in the facility.

Types of Systems to be Leased

A basic list of those systems that may be considered for leasing is:

1. COST FACTORS FOR INTRUSION DETECTION DEVICES:

Type Alarm	Method of Activation	Cost Installed	Coverage of Utilization
Magnetic contacts	Breaking of an electric circuit	Simple contacts $35–50; high security approx. $75–100 per opening add 50 percent for second window. Add 50 percent for tape/foil	Used on doors, windows, or any other opening of 96 sq. in. or greater
Current carrying strips of metallic foil	Breaking of an electric circuit	Average size window is approx. $70 per opening. Larger multipane windows are more expensive	Tape is laced around window in patterns to offer max. protection
Photo electric	Interruption of a light beam	$300–500 indoor $600–1,800 outdoor	Indoor max. 500 ft. across Outdoor max. 1,000 ft. across
Minisentry Ultrasonic	Interruption of a light beam Motion detection	$120–200 per pair $500–1,000 (Basic equipment) Extra transceivers $50–80 per set	Indoor max. 75 ft. across Basic equipment covers an area approx. 4,000 sq. ft.
Microwave	Motion detection	$500–1,000	Max. coverage 100' × 80' will penetrate thin doors, walls, and so forth
Sensitive microphone	Vibration detection	$400–500 for an area of 400 sq. ft. additional microphones $25–50 each	Microphones should be located approx. every 20 ft. around the building

Capacitance alarm	Interruption of an electromagnetic field	$350 connected to existing system, up to $800 for complete UL approved local system	Used for point protection safe; safe; vaults; containers; openings
Passive infrared (PIR)	Responds to body heat	$80–150 per detection unit	Used where contents of the protected area may absorb either ultrasonic or microwave energy
Audio detector	Sound detection	Basic equipment $700–2,000 sq. ft. may be connected to existing PA system. Additional microphones $100 each	Average microphone pickup is 2,000 sq. ft.
Heat detector	Detects fire and heat	$50 each	Can be connected to another control unit in protection zone
Holdup devices	Footrail or pushbutton	$200 each; $95 each additional unit	Covers a single cage
Console monitors	Single zone 2–10 zones 10–20 zones 20–50 zones	$500 $2,000 $3,500 $8,000	Alarms should be zoned to allow exact pinpointing of location. Fences up longer than 300' per zone
Wire	One pair per zone	$2.00 per foot	In conduit buried

Item	Wiring Installation
2. *TRANSMISSION MEDIA*	
Telephone lines (leased)	$1.25/1/10 mile/month—plus $100 installation charge
Direct bury of cable (4-strand CS grade)	.75/ft.
Pull through conduit	$4.00/ft.
Coaxial cable (CCTV/Audio)	$3.50/ft. plus installation
Ten pair CS grade wire	.85/ft. plus installation
Rigid conduit	$4.50/per foot (can vary by size)
EMT	$2.50 per foot
Single open run plain wire	.50/ft.
(Wire requests/cost must be considered on one pair basis per instrument between zone and panel)	

Item	Cost
3. *ANNUNCIATION*	
Console monitor	
Single zone	$600.000
2–10 zone	$2,400.00
10–20 zone	$5,000.00
20–50 zone	$10,000–15,000
Panels	
Per zone (included labor and handwork hookup)	
Class A	$900.00
Class B	$425.00
Class C	$300.00
Emergency power indicator (per zone)	$275.00

Event recorder
  50 zone $7,000.00
  100 zone $8,500.00
  200 zone $12,000.00
Telephone system
  Basic unit–10 zone $2,000.00
  10–50 zone $5,200.00
Basic equipment
  Building unit control $1,000.00
  Base console (10 door capacity) $850.00*
  Circuit board module (one/door) $325.00**
  Hardware for door (one/door) $250.00
  Telephones (door/base) $250.00

4. *CCTV*

Monitor $200.00–500.00
Video tape recorder $750.00–1,200.00
CCTV cameras:
  B/w camera $400.00–900.00
  B/w high resolution camera $900.00–1,600.00
  B/w low-light camera $6,000.00–6,500.00
  Color camera $900.00–1,200.00
  Low-light CCTV lens (motorized zoom) $3,000.00–5,000.00
  Wide-angle or telephoto lens $500.00–600.00
  Pan and tilt unit
    Interior $200.00–400.00
    Exterior $800.00–1,200.00
  Exterior, environmental housing $250.00–400.00

*300 Position panel approximately $10,000.00
**Module cost the same and needed for annunciation of any device.

1. Anti-intrusion electronic protective systems
2. Supervised guard tour systems
3. Electronic process surveillance systems
4. One-way and two-way communication systems
5. Closed-circuit television systems
6. Equipment used in connection with identification and control
7. Access control systems
8. Fire supervision and protective systems

Obtaining Estimates

The estimate provided should always be broken down into equipment costs and installation costs and should always include the cost of a separate maintenance contract. The installation cost would be paid in full by the client. The equipment cost would be broken down into equal monthly payments. The maintenance contract would be a separate arrangement between the client and the dealer.

SECTION V

Security and the Law

Even though the legal issues that security managers must confront are many and varied, this section offers basic information on those most likely to be encountered. Issues concerning tort liability are discussed along with key court decisions involving both criminal and civil liability.

Security and the Law

CHAPTER 20

Law and Liability

It is now a well-accepted fact that civil cases against security organizations—alleging negligence and liability—are steadily increasing. Likewise, the amounts of settlements and judgments in such cases are rising just as dramatically. Therefore, it is more important than ever that security managers have a sound understanding of those legal unpleasantnesses that can so easily befall their operations at virtually any time.

A. Liability and the damages that result are categorized based upon the type of act committed.
   1. *Negligent liability*. Liability that results when personnel act with an "absence of due care and caution"—when they fail to act as "reasonable and prudent" people. Negligent acts committed by security officers typically center around:
      a. The inappropriate or illegal use of a weapon
      b. The inappropriate or illegal use of a motor vehicle
      c. The excessive use of force
      On the other hand, security managers typically fall victim to negligent liability as a result of:
      a. Inadequate or inappropriate supervision of subordinate personnel
      b. Inadequate or inappropriate training of personnel
      c. Inappropriate management decision making
   2. *Intentional liability*. Liability that results when security personnel act in a manner *designed* to bring about an intended result that turns out to be illegal, inappropriate, or excessive. For example, a security officer who purposely harasses or invades the privacy of other employees would be likely to subject himself to intentional liability if those employees were to bring suit against him. Aggravated battery, false arrest, or unlawful detention would be additional examples of intentional liability in civil court.
   3. *Strict liability*. Liability associated with acts or activities that by their very nature are hazardous, dangerous, or harmful.
      a. High-speed vehicular pursuits
      b. Firing warning shots
      c. Firing at a suspect in a motor vehicle or in a crowd of people

      d.   Using vicious guard dogs

      e.   Electrifying a perimeter fence

    4. *Vicarious liability*. Under the legal principle of *respondeat superior* ultimate liability for an employee's actions is determined. An employer is normally considered to be vicariously liable if the employee, while "within the scope of his employment," performs liabilous acts on behalf of the employer or authorized by the employer.

B. Once an employee or the employer is found to be liable, a judgment against them will be rendered by the court. Those judgments are discussed in terms of damages.

    1. *General or compensatory damages*. As the name implies, these damages are intended to provide direct compensation for injuries, damage, or harm sustained as a result of liabilous conduct. Compensatory damages are awarded by the court on the basis of "enlightened conscience" with the intent of facilitating financial reimbursement equal to the loss or injury suffered.

    2. *Punitive damages*. Punitive damages are awarded in order to deter the guilty party from committing future liabilous acts of a similar nature. Punitive damages are *not* usually awarded in cases involving mere negligence unless the court views the conduct as "gross negligence." Gross negligence implies that the negligent act was performed in total disregard of safety considerations.

CHAPTER 21

Case Law Considerations

No one denies that both case law and statute law are important in placing legal parameters on security-related activities. However, they are unique unto themselves both conceptually and practically. Whereas statute law originates with some legislative body at some level of government, case law comes to us from the courts.

Case law is, in fact, **judicial interpretation**—rulings from the courts that define or redefine legal issues. These rulings can pertain to issues that originate in any type of law:

- Criminal Law
- Civil (Tort) Law
- Constitutional Law
- Contract Law
- Regulatory Law

Unlike statute law, case law is also considered to be current in time since pertinent judicial decisions are rendered almost continuously, thus generating near-constant refinements on legal issues. Statute law, on the other hand, once on the books, may remain so, unchanged for decades.

Consequently, most view case law as the more beneficial of the two to security managers who must develop and implement policies and procedures to control their personnel and operations, while simultaneously reducing the risk of liability. To assist in identifying specific case law issues that are likely to impact on an organization's security program, the following case interpretations and citations are offered.

Issue	Case	See Also
Security officers acting as private persons have power to arrest without warrant for felony	U.S. v. Coplon 185 F. 2d 629, 634 (2d Cir. 1950)	U.S. v. Gomez 614 F. 2d 643 (9th Cir. 1982)
Security personnel are considered to be private citizens for purposes of search and seizure done on behalf of employer	State v. Coburn 539 P. 2d 442 (Montana 1974)	

Issue	Case	See Also
Conduct of ordinary security officer is equated with that of private citizen, and this is unaffected by exclusionary rule	People v. Hormon 22 N.Y. 2d 378 (1968)	U.S. v. Francoeur 547 F. 2d 891 (5th Cir. 1971) People v. Johnson 101 Misc. 2d 833, 422 N.Y.S. 2d 980
Security officers acting on behalf of police are bound by same legal restrictions as police	U.S. v. Davis 482 F. 2d 893 (9th Cir. 1973)	
Companies are not immune from liability resulting from false arrests made by security staff	Dillard Dept. Stores v. Stukey 511 S.W. 2d 154 (Ark 1944)	
Retail merchants or their agents (i.e., security) have lawful right to search suspected shoplifters for stolen merchandise	Jackson v. State 657 P. 2d 405 (Alaska App. 1983)	Sutherland v. Kroger Co. 144 W. Va. 673, 110 S.E. 2d 716 (1959)
Search of a visitor's personal property by security must be voluntary and not coerced	People v. Matera 45 Misc. 2d 864, 258 N.Y.S. 2d 2 (1965)	
Temporary detentions, for a reasonable time, conducted in a reasonable manner, permitted to investigate suspected criminal activity on company property	Martinez v. Goodyear Tire and Rubber Co. 65 S.W. 2d 18 (Texas App. 1983)	State v. Abislaim 437 So. 2d 181 (Florida 1984)
Temporary detentions can be initiated, with cause, for a reasonable period of time	Delp v. Zapp's Drug and Variety Stores 238 Oreg. 538, 395 P. 2d 137 (1964)	Landsburgh's Inc. v. Ruffin 372 A. 2d 561 (D.C. Ct. App. 1977)
Temporary detentions, with cause, permissible off company property as well as on	Bomkowski v. Arlan's Dept. Store 12 Mich. App. 88, 162 N.W. 2d 347 (1968)	
Companies have right to evict those on their property who "act out" or behave in a manner inconsistent with purpose of business	Ramirez v. Chavez 71 Ariz. 143, 309 P. 2d 776 (1957)	

Issue	Case	See Also
Reasonable force may be used to remove *unwanted visitors* from company property	Shranek v. Walker 152 S.C. 88, 149 S.E. 331 (1929)	
Security personnel have right to use reasonable force to protect/defend themselves and others	State v. Cook 78 S.C. 253, 59 S.E. 862 (1907)	
Company can retain security, to use reasonable force, to protect private property	Simpson v. State 59 Ala. 31 Am. Rep. 1 (1877)	State v. Clay 51 W. Va. 547 41 S.E. 204 (1902)
Security personnel can be held criminally liable for ignoring their prescribed duties when injury or loss could result	Perrine v. Pacific Gas and Electric Company 186 Cal. App. 2d 442 (1978)	Powell v. U.S. 2 F. 2d 47 (Ca 4, 1924)
Companies suffer liability for damages resulting from their negligence in not providing adequate security	Estate of Ransdell v. Budget Inn et al. (Ky., 1982)	Kenney v. Southeastern Pa. Transit Authority 581 F. 2d 351 (1971)
Efforts to provide adequate security can prevent or reduce liability	Phillips v. Equitable Life Assurance Co. 413 So. 2d 696 (La. App. 1982)	Courtney v. Remler 566 F. Supp. 1225
History of criminal activity has impact on how much security is needed to be *adequate*	Klein v. 1500 Mass. Ave. Apt. Corp. 439 F. 2d 477 (1970)	Holley v. Mt. Zion Terrace Apts., Inc. 382 So. 2d 98 (Fl. App. 1980)
Employer is liable if security personnel's wrongful conduct occurred while acting within the scope of employment	Peak v. W.T. Grant Co. 386 S.W. 2d 685 (Mo. App. 1964)	Brown v. Great Atlantic and Pacific Tea Co. 89 N.Y. Supp. 2d 244 (App. Div. 1949)
Use of trained dogs to detect drugs in personal belongings does not constitute invasion of privacy	U.S. v. Place 33 Cr. L. 3186 51 LW 4844 462 US 696 (1983)	State v. Snitkin 681 P. 2d 980 (Hawaii 1984)
Employer subject to liability for negligence in hiring, training security personnel	Gonzales v. Southwest Security and Protection 665 P. 2d 810 (N.M. App. 1983)	Welsh Manufacturing Div. of Textron v. Pinkerton's 474 A. 2d 436 (R.I. 1984)

Issue	Case	See Also
Company is liable for negligent actions of their employees	McGinnis v. Chicago R.I. and P.R. Co. 200 Mo. 347, 98 S.W. 590 (1906)	Columbia Plaza Corp. v. Security Nat'l Bank U.S. App. C. 78–1496 and 78–1606 (1983)
Independent contractor lessens liability for agent's tortious acts (respondeat superior)	Globe Indemnity v. Victill Corp. 208 Md. 573, 119 A. 2d 423 (1926)	
Security may search employees' personal property if done in a reasonable manner	Commonwealth v. Leone 435 N.E. 2d 1036 (Mass. 1982)	
When employer keeps master key to lockers, and employees know it, lockers can be entered by employer at will	State v. Robinson 86 N.J. Super. 308, 206 A. 2d 779 (1965)	U.S. v. Speights 557 F. 2d 596 (1977) U.S. v. Bunkers 521 F. 2d 1217 (9th Cir. 1975)
Degree of privacy accorded to desks depends upon "exclusive use and control"	U.S. v. Blok 188 F. 2d 1019 (P.C. Cir. 1959)	
Security officers justified in retaking company property being illegally taken off the premises	Kroger Grocery v. Waller 208 Ark. 1063, 189 S.W. 2d 361 (1945)	Prieto v. May Dept. Stores 216 A. 2d 577 (D.C. Ct. App. 1966)
Company can be held vicariously liable for criminal acts of employees	Commonwealth v. Koczwara 397 Pa. 575, 155 A. 2d 825 (1950)	People v. Canadian Fur Trappers Corp. 248 N.Y. 157, 161 N.E. 455 (1928) Ex Parte Marley 175 P. 2d 832 (Calif. 1946)
Tortious liability for actions of *armed* security personnel	Horn v. IBI Security Services 317 So. 2d 444 (Florida 1975)	Lopez v. Wm. J. Burns Det. Agency 368 N.Y.S. 2d 221, 48 A.D. 2d 645 (1975)
Detention of employees for investigative purposes must be done in a reasonable manner to avoid liability	Moffatt v. Buffums' Inc. 69 P. 2d 424 (Calif. 1937)	Parrott v. Bank of America Nat'l Trust & Savings Association 217 P. 2d 89 (Calif. 1950)

Issue	Case	See Also
Private security personnel are not required to give *Miranda* warning prior to questioning	State v. Lombardo 104 Ariz. 598, 457 P. 2d 275 (1969)	People v. Deborah C. (a minor) 635 P. 2d 446 (1981) People v. Raitano 401 N.E. 2d 209 (Tenn. 1981)
Employee has right to union representative's presence during investigatory interview when such representation is requested	NLRB v. Weingarten 420 U.S. 251, 95 S. Ct. 959 (1975)	Internat'l Ladies Garment Workers' Union v. Quality Manufacturing 420 U.S. 276, 95 S.Ct. 972 (1975)
Discharged employees entitled to view reports of investigation that caused termination	Zampatori v. UPS 463 N.Y.S. 2d 977 (App. 1983)	
Employee can be terminated for refusing to cooperate in Polygraph testing	Ising v. Barnes Hospital 674 S.W. 2d 623 (Mo. App. 1984)	Everett Lumber Co. v. Industrial Commission 565 P. 2d 967 (Colo. App. 1977)
Results of a Polygraph exam is admissable in court if both parties agree	Commonwealth v. DiLego 439 N.E. 2d 807 (1983)	
Interrogation of employee by supervisor about involvement in theft does not constitute coercive action	NLRB v. St. Vincent's Hospital 729 F. 2d 730 (11 Cir. 1984)	
Employees have an obligation to employer to assist police with investigation involving the company	U.S. v. Dockery 736 F. 2d 1232 (8th Cir. 1984)	
Private employer of off-duty police officer, not the municipality, is liable for actions even when the officer is in police uniform*	Kasarda v. Tomasch 530 F. Supp. 1346 (N.D. Ohio 1982)	
Police officer, working off-duty as security guard, still considered a police officer*	State v. Feldstein 654 P. 2d 63 (Ariz. App. 1982)	Duncan v. State of Ga. 294 S.E. 365 (Ga. App. 1982)

Issue	Case	See Also
Employer can keep former employee from being hired by competitor if employee retains knowledge of *trade secrets*	Bell Telephone Laboratories v. General Instrument Corp. U.S. Dist. Ct. W. Pa., No. 83–0016 (1983)	

Note: Since the use of off-duty police officers continues to be a controversial issue, as these cases indicate, companies should evaluate their own exposure to litigation and liability.

SECTION VI

Security Personnel

The development of an effective security program depends on well-qualified personnel to operate it. The recruitment and selection of qualified officers is thus of the highest priority. Thereafter, these officers must be properly trained and scheduled so that the program continues to meet its prescribed goals and objectives efficiently. Further, to ensure that officers remain both productive and professional, they must be regularly and critically evaluated.

Are proprietary security personnel better—more effective—than their contractual counterparts? Obviously, responses to that question vary. What does not seem to vary, however, is the fact that many security managers are now being asked to decide between inhouse and contractual personnel. In the 1980s, concerns over cost containment make decisions on the type of security personnel to use virtually as critical as any other operational matter.

No other single element within a security program has the potential for determining the overall quality of that program as the personnel who staff it. This section presents materials on a series of relevant subjects that must be considered in a comprehensive personnel management plan. The major considerations between proprietary and contract security personnel are presented along with relevant checklists.

CHAPTER 22

Recruitment and Selection

The National Advisory Commission on Criminal Justice Standards and Goals recommends that every security agency should have a formal process for the selection of qualified applicants and that this selection process should include the following:

1. The primary emphasis in the screening process should be to select qualified personnel who will perform efficiently and make a career in private security.
2. In order to determine whether prospective personnel are trustworthy and capable, a preemployment screening should be initiated. Preemployment screenings should include:
   a. Screening Interview
   b. Honesty tests/integrity profiles and/or Polygraph examinations
   c. Background investigation, and other job related tests as appropriate
3. An employment application should be used to provide a basis for the screening process, and should include the following:
   a. Full Name
   b. Aliases
   c. Current Residence
   d. Prior residences
   e. Educational background
   f. Current employment
   g. Previous employment
   h. Military service
   i. Criminal/traffic convictions

Since professionalism in private protective services is also an important factor to be considered when processing candidates for security positions, the entire selections system should be geared accordingly. To guarantee the presence of a sincere sense of professionalism and dedication on the part of the applicant, those items listed above must be set up to afford the agency the best opportunity possible to observe those characteristics desired and at the same time allow the applicant the best possible opportunity to show the department that he or she does, in fact, possess the characteristics required for a professional security officer.

Today, professionalism in private security work is primarily centered around desires to improve the academic education and the specialized training of the security officer or, in this case, the potential security officer. This is, to a large extent, a legitimate approach, but authorities in the field of security administration contend that professionalism can be much better achieved if the total character and the background of the applicant is considered. With this in mind, the following guidelines are offered for use when considering potential applicants for security positions:

Residency. Since professionalism is the goal to be strived for, it seems logical to allow the concept of "lateral entry" within private security departments or agencies, especially since it is a well-practiced procedure among other professions. Therefore, it seems foolish to disqualify a security officer, already trained and qualified, from employment with a specific security agency solely because he does not live in a particular state or city. On the other hand, it seems only fair to give a security officer more credit than an individual who is from the community and who is familiar with the problems, needs, and wants of the community and its businesses. It is hard to determine which of these two factors is the more important, so in this particular case compromise will have to be the solution—allow other factors about each of those candidates that fall into these categories to make the determination as to which may be the better.

Work experience. Working daily in the outside world can have a very sobering effect on even the most idealistic of individuals. So it seems reasonable to give *fair* consideration to the work background and experience of an applicant. Along the same line, some types of work are of more value to a security department than others so it also seems reasonable that prior security work, work in other areas of law enforcement, or work in a relevant supervisory capacity should have great importance. Since professionalism is the focal point of this selection process, the more qualified that person is to do a particular job, the more foundation there will be upon which to build toward this very important professional goal.

Military service. Serving in the armed forces can furnish an individual with many of the same things that work experience can, and not the least of these is additional education and specialized training. The military is also notorious in its quest for regimentation, obedience to orders, and dedication to the service; and since private security departments have often been characterized as quasimilitary organizations, it is not totally illogical to desire applicants with prior military experience.

Education. Probably the most important single factor affecting the professionalization of any occupation is the extent of the education of the members. This being true, security agencies are striving to employ the most educated personnel possible. Proper education and training can do a great deal to advance the skill of an organization but they cannot be considered as the automatic solution to whatever problems security agencies have experienced in years gone by. Nor is education the sole criterion for success in the private security field—the persons who work within this field must temper education with experience and practical training. Thus, the education of an applicant will be given sufficiently important notice but not so much as to overshadow other important criteria.

Allowing for the fact that not all recruitment may be done in areas close to your community and for the possibility of lateral entry into your department, certain steps must be taken to allow individuals in these categories to apply for employment and yet keep any complications to a minimum. There should be no reason to limit the initial number of potential applicants, but neither should the administrators of the Security Department be overburdened with less than top-notch applicants.

To accomplish both of these goals an *Initial Evaluation Form* and a *Request for Formal Application* will be given, either in person or by mail to any individual showing an interest in applying for employment with this agency. These forms will be evaluated by the Director of Security. Then those meeting the necessary qualifications will be mailed a formal application form and a specific time and date to report, in person, for an interview with the Director of Security. By using this type of system, every possible person wanting to apply will be able to do so. Yet there will be enough limitations placed on employment to narrow the field.

CHAPTER 23

Desired Traits and Characteristics

The unique nature of security work makes it essential that those factors that identify a person with good potential for long term job stability and good performance be available. The checklists that follow provide a listing of those factors that have been identified as being associated with successful, productive security personnel. There are two checklists presented:

1. Security officer applicants
2. Desirable worker traits for security officers

DESIRABLE TRAITS FOR SECURITY OFFICER
APPLICANTS CHECKLIST
Factor 1

A. *Previous job reliability/stability.* Those whose work history indicates that they have:
   1. Stayed on previous jobs for reasonable lengths of time
   2. Avoided absenteeism and tardiness
   3. Had acceptable reasons for leaving previous positions
   4. Called in when they were going to be absent
   5. Had justifiable reasons for being absent or tardy
   6. Had never been discharged from a job
   7. Had no history of being disciplined on the job
   8. Had no record of theft or other illegal or unapproved activity on the job.

Factor II

B. *Oral communications.* Those who can communicate orally in such a way that:
   1. Others can clearly understand what is meant
   2. Facial expression, mannerisms, attitude, body language, and so forth are appropriate to the situation

3. They can clearly communicate to others instructions on how to perform a task

Factor III

C. *Employee attitudes.* Those who consider each person an individual, who respect each person's right to basic human treatment, and who would be able to deal impartially with everyone with whom they have contact.

Factor IV

D. *Desire to be a security officer.* Those who have:
1. Given serious consideration to becoming a security officer
2. Felt a definite feeling that they would receive some personal satisfaction from being a competent officer
3. A definite desire to be a security officer

Factor V

E. *Poise/self-confidence (normal circumstances).* Those who have achieved a reasonable degree of self-confidence and who are neither overconfident (arrogant) nor underconfident (meek or submissive).

Factor VI

F. *Reading ability.* Those whose reading ability is satisfactory and who would experience little or no difficulty with the aspect of security work that involves reading.

Factor VII

G. *Written communications.*
1. Those who are able to write reports in such a way that the reader can clearly understand what has been written.
2. Those who are able to write reports that include all of the necessary, relevant facts of the incident being reported.
3. Those who report only what actually took place, only on who was actually involved; i.e., any references to who, what, when, where, and how that are truthful and factual.

Factor VIII

H.   *Reactions to hostility/stress.* Those who react appropriately to hostility or stress, who take necessary, spontaneous action without overreacting, and who can keep their "cool" in hostile or stressful situations. Those who can successfully think on their feet.

Factor IX

I.   *Alertness.* Those who are fully aware of what is going on around them and who quickly identify situations or events that need attention and then react appropriately.

Factor X

J.   *Perceptions of what makes a competent security officer.*
   1.   Those whose perceptions of a competent security officer are similar to the perceptions of expert assessors.
   2.   Those who perceive a competent security officer as being honest, fair-minded, cool-headed in emergencies, and alert.
   3.   Those who perceive security officer competence as including the ability to communicate well and show empathy, reasonable self-confidence, and professional objectivity.

DESIRABLE WORKER TRAITS FOR SECURITY OFFICERS CHECKLIST

A.   Responsibility, honesty, and conscientiousness
   1.   Being morally, legally, and mentally accountable
   2.   Being fair, objective, and straightforward.
   3.   Being scrupulous and professional in the performance of his or her job.
   4.   Having teamwork consciousness—i.e., wanting to adequately fulfill one's own responsibilities in such a way that it contributes to the overall effectiveness of the entire staff, concern for the success of other programs in the organization, being in sympathy with these programs
   5.   Willingness to report on time, concern for reporting on time
   6.   Being of such moral character as to avoid involvement in theft, graft, bribery, or other dishonest activities
   7.   Having high regard for policies and procedures and rules and regulations of the organization

8. Concern for protecting confidential information
9. Personal concern about avoiding excessive absenteeism
10. Concern for doing a quality, thorough job on routine duties
11. Concern for reporting whole truth, and only the truth, about any incident involving employees
12. Concern for the safety of visitors and employees (i.e., assuring that equipment is in safe working order, seeing that employees follow work safety principles)
13. Respect for the employee's right to basic human treatment, including those guaranteed by law
14. Concern for personal hygiene and grooming as well as general appearance and demeanor

B. Reading and writing communicative skills
1. Ability to write a clear and concise report about employee actions or about an incident
2. Ability to communicate orally in a clear and concise manner
3. Reading ability at a 12th grade level

C. Leadership skills: exercising responsible authority over people and property
1. Ability and willingness to discharge duties without getting too close to employees; i.e., without getting emotionally or personally involved to the point of becoming ineffective
2. Ability to take spontaneous, appropriate action when necessary—i.e., not afraid of becoming involved when necessary, acting decisively in emergencies, and making correct decisions; the ability and willingness to defend oneself and others against physical assault.
3. Ability to recognize the development of a potentially dangerous or emergent situation; the possession of a superior state of mental alertness.
4. Ability to recognize when you are possibly being set-up for a bribe or other involvement with an element of graft or dishonesty
5. Ability to deal fairly and impartially with all employees' concerns
6. Ability and willingness to take orders from superiors without question or complaint
7. Being firm but fair
8. Ability to tell an employee to do something without making him hostile or angry
9. Ability to admonish with minimum hostility
10. Ability to withstand verbal abuse, and when such surfaces, to react in an appropriate manner
11. Ability to recognize when admonishment is necessary; willingness to admonish when necessary
12. Ability to deal with abnormal situations in an appropriate and professional fashion

      13. Ability to offer informal guidance to employees relative to their adjustment to work on security rules

      14. Forceful but not overbearing or timid.

      15. Self-confidence to a reasonable degree (neither underconfident nor overconfident)

      16. Ability to discern between minor and major problems or conditions, and then to react to either in the appropriate fashion

      17. Recognizing individual differences of employees

      18. Ability to promote socially and organizationally acceptable conduct in employees

D. Ability to make critical and acute observations

      1. Quick to be aware of changes in behavior in an employee and to wonder why the change has occurred

      2. Ability to make notes of observations

      3. Ability to relate factors in situations. (e.g., relate one individual's change in behavior to another individual's change in behavior, and so forth—i.e., ability to put two and two together)

E. Satisfactory health

      1. Having no history of mental illness that could cast doubt on the quality of performance on the job or on potential court testimony

      2. Adequate health (includes hearing and vision)

      3. Adequate physical condition

      4. Being scared when it is normal to be scared

F. Satisfactory background (i.e., having nothing in background that would interfere with effectiveness as a security officer)

      1. Having no background that could render the officer ineffective when pressured by employees or visitors

      2. History of stable employment (job hoppers not desired)

      3. Drivers' license (for some assignments)

G. Miscellaneous

      1. Willingness to be subject to 24 hour call, willingness to work nights, weekends, and/or holidays; willingness to change personal schedule if necessary

      2. Willingness to use firearms, if necessary; potential to be trained in proper use of firearms

CHAPTER 24

Duties and Functions

This section provides a checklist of generic functions performed by security officers. It is designed to permit the development of post instructions, job descriptions or to decide what is to be done by the security force. Specific tasks to be performed can be checked off for all officers or specific post assignments. Each officer then knows exactly what he is responsible for doing in general and for his specific assignment.

To use the checklist, review all tasks and check off all those that are necessary for your company or location. Next assign checks to appropriate locations (posts) e.g., 1, 2, 3, 4, or 5.

Example	*All*	*1*	*2*	*3*	*4*	*5*	
Patrol streets		√					
Inspect parking lots				√	√		
Prevent unauthorized entry	√						
Require all employees to show badges			√				

Specific tasks required at each location can then be consolidated onto a single instruction sheet. The result of these efforts will be the development of complete duty assignments throughout the company or location. Audits, inspection, and training can then be accomplished against specific assignments.

In addition, a *Security Patrol Outline* is provided in order to help determine specifically what information officers ought to know so that they can effectively handle this important function so frequently assigned to them.

GUARD FUNCTION CHECKLIST

1. Prevention

All Officers	Posts				
	1	2	3	4	5

1.1

Locking/inspecting locks

1. Secure the building by locking all exterior doors.

2. Lock the truck gate at prescribed times.

3. Close all windows in areas that are unoccupied.

4. Secure doors to unoccupied areas and turn off all lights.

5. While on patrol, check for and note all open doors.

6. Insure that fire doors are closed after areas are closed.

7. Unlock and open gates at specified times.

8. Perform routine checks on building and office.

9. Check all inside doors, tunnels, and basements.

10. Insure that all assigned areas are properly secured.

11. Unlock doors and turn off burglar alarm.

12. Obtain keys required for operations and retain.

1.2

Checking condition of doors/windows/locks/areas

1. Check parked cars for proper stickers/unlocked doors.

2. While making each patrol round, check all floors.

3. Inspect all parking lots periodically.

4. Check designated gates to keep them unlocked.

5. Patrol area to prevent unauthorized entry/vandalism.

6. Check and lock lab/work areas.

1.3

Patrolling/all types/modes/methods/except clock tours

1. Inspect the general office.

2. Patrol street outside building.

3. Patrol assigned areas on foot.

4. Make rounds in squad car and check for locked doors.

5. Patrol using a three-wheeled motorcycle.

	Posts				
All Officers	*1*	*2*	*3*	*4*	*5*

1.4					

Preventing law violations/theft

1. Prevent unauthorized activities from occurring.

2. Prevent fires, theft, and trespassing on the property.

3. Maintain close watch on known or suspected shoplifters.

4. Prevent cars from blocking emergency entrance(s).

5. Call police/building engineer if vandalism is found.

1.5					

Clock tours

1. Make clock tours as assigned.

2. Pull fire and watch box at scheduled times.

3. Perform guard duties when other guards request relief.

2. Protection

2.1					

Access control

1. Insure that all personnel show their ID cards.

2. Prevent unauthorized entry to building.

3. Insure that all employees check in and out.

4. Allow cleaning personnel to leave the building.

5. Prevent removal of property from building.

6. Require that supervisor sign for employees without IDs.

7. Require all after hours employees to show ID cards.

8. Insure that all visitors to building have passes.

9. Inspect all employees to insure that badges are displayed.

10. Insure that employees working late remain in assigned areas.

11. Insure that only Research and Development personnel enter the Research and Development area.

Posts

All Officers | 1 2 3 4 5

2.2

2.3

2.4

2.5

12. Insure that visitors to computer room are escorted by employees.

13. Identify all persons in high risk areas.

Protecting life and property

1. Protect life and property.

2. Maintain order.

3. Assist doctors and nurses in handling unruly patients.

4. Contact assistance by pulling box in emergency or fire.

5. Insure that hallway traffic moves smoothly.

6. Maintain a tornado watch when so directed.

7. Protect employees from their own actions or the actions of others.

8. Insure that unnecessary lights are turned off.

9. Stop fights using your own judgment in order to prevent injury.

Searching

1. Check all cars and trucks for entry passes.

2. Operate main gate.

3. Record passes and items in register.

4. Access control by turning off alarm during entry.

5. Process all mail received at the building as directed.

Escort/money transfers

1. Escort money transfers from parking lot to main building.

2. Transfer receipts to bank each day.

3. Guard money for special events as required by client.

Observing conditions/events

1. Check restaurant to remove boisterous patrons.

2. Observe construction workers to prevent theft.

3. Enforcement

3.1 Traffic/parking

1. Enforce parking regulations.

2. Insure that emergency entrances are kept clear.

3. Check all vehicles for proper parking stickers.

3.2 Arrest/police cooperation

1. Inform police of unusual occurrences beyond officer needs.

2. Cooperate with all law enforcement agencies.

3. Make arrests as required.

4. Detain prowlers and other individuals found on grounds.

5. Conduct search of persons when it is warranted.

6. Handle evidence and stolen property according to set rules.

7. Be familiar with state, federal, county, and city ordinances.

8. Contact supervisor/police when weapons or explosives are found.

9. Assist in serving legal processes.

3.3 Employee rules/policy

1. Enforce no smoking regulations and report violations.

2. Insure that each person punches time clock only once.

3. Insure that there is compliance with established rules and regulations.

4. Check for alcoholic beverages and drugs.

5. Issue parking tickets to lot violators.

6. Remove drunks from the emergency room.

3.4 Customer/visitor/client rules

1. Enforce *no barefeet allowed* policy.

2. Enforce tape color-code system for merchandise control.

3. Maintain and enforce control system at door-merchandise.

4. Detection

	4.1	

Equipment use/alarms

1. Set up alarm system in building at prescribed time.

2. Use magnatometer and hand metal detector.

3. Reset annunciator on fire alarm on appropriate instruction.

	4.2	

Responding to alarms

1. Check exterior of building when responding to burglar alarm.

2. Assist police in search of building interior after burglar alarm has sounded.

3. Respond to fire/burglar alarms when requested.

4. Contact subscribers if alarm call is deemed valid.

5. Perform watch tours to all designated areas on schedule.

	4.3	

Watch tours

1. Perform DETEX clock tours as required.

2. Perform watch tours according to established schedules.

5. Investigation

	5.1	

1. Protect and preserve evidence at scene of crime.

2. Investigate all assigned matters.

3. Investigate all offenses or violations of policy.

4. Conduct special investigations assigned by security director.

5. While performing supervisory duty, apply state statutes.

6. Emergency Services

6.1

First aid

1. Perform minor first-aid procedure on slight injuries.

2. Transport sick passengers to medical assistance.

3. Be familiar with medical emergency procedures.

6.2

Fire

1. Notify fire department in case of fire.

2. Recognize fire type and select proper equipment to fight fire.

3. Put out small fires.

4. Warn or rescue persons endangered by fire.

5. Return equipment to truck after fire.

6. Operate all fire fighting equipment as required.

7. Respond to all fire alarms.

6.3

Panic alarms/alarms

1. Make key calls.

2. Respond to key calls as required.

6.4

Emergencies

1. Respond to fire and emergency alarms when they are sounded.

2. Provide assistance in emergency situations.

6.5

Disturbances

1. Respond to physical disturbances.

6.6

Calls for service

1. Use two-way radio to report control center.

2. Respond to calls for service.

6.7

Bomb threats

1. Call police if bomb threat is received.

2. Instruct people where to go in case of bomb scare.

3. Pull fire alarm in case of bomb scare to evacuate building.

7. Reporting

7.1

Incidents

1. Record all unusual occurrences in log.

2. Report all vaults found open to HQ by phone.

3. Record all unnecessary open doors and burning lights.

4. Prepare written reports on unusual incidents and give to superior.

5. Prepare written reports on weapons found in screening.

6. Notify supervisor when problems are encountered.

7. Prepare written reports on all violations and incidents.

8. Prepare list of all persons in building after hours.

9. Record license number of private vehicles in lot.

7.2

Accidents/fires

1. Report evidence and take action against all fires.

2. Prepare written report on accidents and action taken.

7.3

Daily reports/activity reports

1. Prepare lost and found report.

2. Maintain log of radio calls and incidents.

7.4

Arrests

1. Prepare offense report after making arrest.

7.5

Safety/equipment conditions/alarm calls

1. Prepare written reports on unusual happenings and conditions.

2. Make report after responding to alarm.

3. Contact client if alarm is valid.

7.6

Special reports/HQ calls/contacts

1. Call HQ every half hour.

2. Contact HQ at beginning and end of shift.

3. Contact HQ if guard can't handle situation.

4. Maintain radio contact with all guards.

8. Inspections

8.1

Fire

1. Inspect fire extinguishers monthly.

2. Check for fires, smoke, or smoking in unauthorized areas.

3. Place and replace fire extinguishers and emergency equipment.

4. Inspect fire fighting equipment.

5. Discover and correct prefire conditions.

6. Insure that fire doors are not obstructed.

7. Check for fires and notify fire department if unable to stop.

8.2

Equipment

1. Insure that proper temperature exists in labs/work areas.

2. Call designated person before turning off equipment.

8.3

Safety/security

1. Insure that all entrances are unobstructed.

2. Keep all aisles clear.

3. Perform inspections for violations of policy.

4. Inspect all equipment used by shift guard.

5. Inspect vehicles for proper operating conditions.

6. Report defective locks or keys.

9. General Services

9.1

Escorting/transporting

1. Arrange for transportation of sick and injured employees.

2. Escort all employees to and from parking areas.

3. Provide escort on cash pickups from registers.

4. Escort buses and groups on the grounds.

All Officers	Posts				
	1	2	3	4	5

5. Pick up mail, supplies, and so forth as requested.

6. Keep guards supplied with necessary equipment.

Counting/catching animals

1. Count all persons in office areas after normal hours.

2. Count number of persons entering the building.

3. Trap stray animals in the building and on the grounds.

Preventing

1. Prevent the taking of photographs.

2. Insure that elevator safety conditions are observed.

3. Call cleaning service to insure properly cleaned areas.

4. Check grounds to prevent brush fires.

5. Be familiar with transporting procedures.

Assisting

1. Provide assistance when needed or called for.

2. Handle all tasks assigned.

3. Reset all electrical equipment after power failures.

ID services

1. Take and process ID cards using photo ID systems.

2. Conduct employee screening.

3. Take and process employee fingerprints.

Communications/receiving

1. Answer all telephone calls and forward to requested personnel.

2. Insure cooperative working relations with other firms.

3. Greet all persons leaving the store.

Information/direction

1. Refrain from giving specified information to visitors.

2. Help those who ask for assistance or information.

All Officers	Posts				
	1	2	3	4	5

3. Respond to employee complaints regarding security procedures.

4. When requested, explain purpose of program.

Traffic direction/control

9.8

1. Control parking lot.

2. Insure that signs are erected as required.

3. Control vehicle and pedestrian traffic at front gate.

4. Operate remote control traffic light.

5. Erect barricades for traffic control.

6. Direct traffic on the grounds.

Instruction/education/ceremonies

9.9

1. Perform flag ceremonies.

2. Instruct fire safety classes.

3. Plan and hold fire drills.

10. Administration

10.1

Actions toward the public

1. Treat all persons firmly but with courtesy.

2. Be suspicious of everyone and everything.

3. Use plant equipment with courtesy and consideration.

4. Maintain an atmosphere of safety and comfort.

10.2

Post assignments

1. Remain at designated post until properly relieved.

2. Move around without establishing a pattern.

3. Inform relief guards or required followup actions.

4. Relieve desk, main gate, and squad cars as required.

10.3

Vehicle maintenance

1. Perform maintenance on all assigned vehicles.

All Officers	Posts				
	1	2	3	4	5

10.4

Knowledge of policy/procedure/locations

1. Wear a firearm at all times while on duty.

2. Be alert at all times.

3. Remember people.

4. Know the physical facilities and equipment in building.

5. Be familiar with all emergency procedures.

6. Know the janitorial and custodial staff of the facility.

7. Qualify with assigned firearm each month.

10.5

Operate radio equipment

1. Set up radio and insure its proper operation.

2. Operate all radio equipment.

3. Drive and operate a radio-equipped squad car.

10.6

Use of judgment

1. Exercise judgment and discretion in performing tasks.

10.7

Maintaining of records/logs

1. Insure that all property is recorded.

2. Maintain a recorded traffic violation ledger.

3. Keep records of all incidents and investigations.

11. Supervision

11.1

Operations/field supervision

1. Take action on direction from supervisor.

2. Assign employees to posts.

3. Insure employees are present for work on time.

4. Supervise inspector activities.

5. Insure that correct number of employees are present.

6. Observe security problems and coordinate security resources.

All Officers	Posts				
	1	2	3	4	5

7. Make decisions regarding operational problems.

8. Enter assignments on work rosters.

9. Coordinate activities of security force in emergency situations.

10. Answer calls and assign officers to answer complaints.

11. Evaluate work performance and attendance records.

12. Insure efficient operation and performance of guards.

13. Make recommendations to prevent fires.

Training

1. Train employees to recognize weapons.

2. Conduct employee grievance meetings.

3. Conduct training programs for new employees.

4. Assist in administering and establishing fire prevention programs.

5. Instruct guards in investigative techniques.

6. Assist men in handling new or unfamiliar situations.

Inspecting/informing

1. Insure proper dress and conduct of employees.

2. Inform employees on new policies and procedures.

3. Evaluate employee performance for promotional purposes.

Dispatching

1. Dispatch guards on all calls for service.

Payroll/scheduling/issuing equipment

1. Call in additional personnel as they are needed.

2. Prepare daily assignment sheets for shifts.

3. Handle personnel and payroll problems.

4. Conduct employment interviews.

5. Supervise proper maintenance of vehicles by security guards.

The left margin grid contains the labels: 11.2, 11.3, 11.4, 11.5

All Officers	*Posts*				
	1	*2*	*3*	*4*	*5*
11.6					
11.7					

6. Record statistics on department activities.

7. Conduct roll call.

Report review/file maintenance

1. Inspect reports to insure they are properly completed.

Performing security functions

1. Relieve shift supervisor when it is required.

2. Perform all duties of security officer when the department is shorthanded.

3. Respond to, and handle, personally serious incidents.

SECURITY PATROL OUTLINE

Many facilities provide two-way radio communications for security personnel while they are on patrol. The proper use of this equipment and its coordination with patrol procedures insures that the officer's time is properly used. This policy statement should be modified to fit the specific requirements of the facility. The procedures outlined here are equally applicable either to on-foot or vehicular patrols.

A. The security patrol is for the purpose of:
1. Insuring that the company is properly safeguarded. The patrol guard will process any security violation in accordance with the operational policy.
2. The prevention, detection, and reporting of fires and safety hazards; being alert for sparks, smoke fumes and/or other indications of a hazard.
3. Protecting property. Checking doors of all areas and perimeter doors to insure they are securely locked or attended by authorized personnel.
4. Preventing vandalism and malicious mischief. Physically checking all emergency exits and perimeter doors to insure they are locked. Noting condition of locks and emergency alarms and reporting defects such as broken or cracked glass, run-down alarms, corroded batteries, and so forth.
5. Reporting suspicious actions of any person or persons and ap-

prehending intruders. Verifying that all persons are properly identified. No person is to enter the area without proper credentials and the guard will challenge the presence of unauthorized personnel attempting illegal entry into work areas or buildings.

6. Preventing any person from committing or attempting to commit a theft. Be alert for employees tampering with office equipment, machinery, reproduction machines, or any other items they are not authorized to use.

7. Reporting without delay unusual conditions such as maintenance personnel loafing in cafeterias, evidence of gambling, drinking, or large congregations of employees.

B. The *first* round is *most important* and may well be the difference between safety and disaster. The patrol guard will exercise the utmost vigilance on his or her first round. He or she must insure that the intrusion systems of unattended closed areas are operational and that controls are on the night setting.

C. The security radio patrol will be performed as indicated on the special folder for each particular building. Any deviation in this schedule must be directed or approved by an officer of the shift concerned. The *Security Operations Outline* will contain the required data.

D. Some common security violations the patrol guard must be alert to detect are:

1. Client areas not locked.
2. Lights or electrical equipment not turned off.
3. Presence of smoke or unusual odors.
5. Failure to make a complete security radio patrol will be immediately reported to the Security Supervisor and followed up with a complete written report by the reporting guard.
6. Upon completion of the final patrol the third shift guard will notify the monitor that the radio is ready to be returned to Guard Headquarters.

CHAPTER 25

Training Programs

This chapter provides both a policy statement on the need for adequate training for security personnel as well as recommended formats for providing it. As in many other chapters of this sourcebook, the recommendations of the Private Security Task Force have been followed. There are four training outlines presented:

EXAMPLE 1.	BASIC SECURITY OFFICER TRAINING	40 Hours
EXAMPLE 2.	BASIC SECURITY OFFICER TRAINING	72 Hours
EXAMPLE 3.	BASIC SECURITY OFFICER TRAINING	80 Hours
EXAMPLE 4.	BASIC SECURITY MANAGEMENT CURRICULUM	80 Hours

The training of security officers is probably one of the most deficient areas in private security. Training, as a necessary part of security operations, has suffered largely because management often feels that available monies can better be spent elsewhere in the organization. Management, by virtue of its responsibilities, is very conscientious about the money it spends. Out of necessity they look at all expenditures in terms of cost-benefit. Consequently, the security function within an organization is often pushed down the list of priorities, and the training of security officers is usually eliminated from any priority consideration.

Even so the National Advisory Commission's Task Force Report on Private Security indicated that 76 percent of the American Society of Industrial Security members they sampled felt that the training of security officers was *very important*. The report continued by saying that, until certain standards are developed and then strictly adhered to, private security training is not likely to (significantly) improve.

One suggested Task Force standard explains that: "The responsibilities assumed by private security personnel in the protection of persons and property require training in private security."

The assumption made by the Task Force is that this training will upgrade the quality of service offered by security personnel. Their assumption takes on added credibility when you also consider that, without adequate training, the potential for error by the security officer is greatly increased.

216

With this standard as a basic foundation, the Task Force also proposed more concise standards.

All security personnel, inlcuding those presently employed full-time and part-time, should:

1. Complete a minimum of eight hours formal preassignment training.
2. Complete a basic training course of a minimum of 32 hours within 3 months of assignment.

All armed security personnel, including present and part-time, should:

1. Be required to successfully complete a 24-hour firearms course that must include legal and policy restraints or submit evidence of competence and proficiency.
2. Be required to qualify at least once every 12 months with firearms they carry while performing private security duties.

Examples 1, 2, and 3 are given as three possible ways of formulating curricula for private security personnel that meet the requirements outlined in the Task Force report. These examples all include material determined to be essential for quality, effective security officer training. The fourth example is a possible curriculum for an 80-hour management program.

Even though the Task Force does not specifically recommend management training, it is nonetheless a very essential part of any successful security operation. It is of little value to have well-trained officers well-equipped, if management does not know how to properly organize and use them. The management program outlined in example 4 helps educate the administrator so that he or she efficiently manages the resources available.

EXAMPLE 1: BASIC 40-HOUR SECURITY OFFICER TRAINING PROGRAM

A. *Prevention and Protection*

1. Security organization: An introduction	2 hours
2. Security operations: An introduction	5 hours
3. OSHA and safety responsibilities	2 hours
4. Physical security	2 hours
5. Patrol procedures	3 hours
6. Fire prevention	2 hours
7. Alarms	1 hour
8. Locks and keys	1 hour
	18 hours

B. *Enforcement*

    1. Report writing   3 hours
    2. Investigations   3 hours
    3. Arrest, search, and seizure   2 hours
    4. Courtroom procedures   1 hour
    5. Civil disturbances   1 hour
                                                 10 hours

C. *Emergency services*

    1. Fire control   2 hours
    2. Disaster control   2 hours
    3. Introduction to first aid   1 hour
    4. Use of force   1 hour
                                                   6 hours

D. *Special problems*

    1. Public relations   1 hour
    2. Labor relations   1 hour
    3. Narcotics and drugs   2 hours
    4. Security vulnerabilities   1 hour
    5. Bomb threats   1 hour
                                                   6 hours

EXAMPLE 2: 72-HOUR SECURITY OFFICER TRAINING PROGRAM

40 Hours of Instruction
    Plus
<u>32</u> Hours for Weapons/Defense Tactics
72 Hours, total

Basic Security Officer Training Curriculum

A. Orientation (preassignment): 8 hours
    1. What is security?
    2. What are the duties of the security officer?
    3. Public relations
    4. Deportment and appearance
    5. Care and use of uniforms and equipment
    6. Reporting and note taking

B. Legal powers and limitations: 4 hours
    1. Introduction to the criminal code
    2. Use of force

    3. Search and seizure
    4. Arrest powers of the security officer

C. Handling emergency situations: 4 hours
    1. Procedures during floods, fires, riots, and explosions
    2. Bombings and bomb threats
    3. Ground control
    4. Automobile accident investigations
    5. Responding to alarms

D. General security duties: 4 hours
    1. Patrol
    2. Inspection
    3. Fire prevention and control
    4. Accident prevention and control
    5. Enforcement
    6. Investigations

E. Prevention/protection: 4 hours
    1. Patrolling techniques
    2. Inspections and audits
    3. Personnel control and ID systems
    4. Access control
    5. Alarm systems
    6. Police-security cooperation

F. Enforcement/investigations: 4 hours
    1. Interview techniques
    2. Crime of scene investigations
    3. Collection and preservation of evidence
    4. Enforcing company rules and regulations
    5. Enforcing parking and traffic regulations

G. First aid: 8 hours
    1. Orientation to first aid
    2. First aid training

H. Special problems: 4 hours
    1. Escort duties
    2. Vandalism
    3. Arson
    4. Burglary-theft-robbery
    5. Drugs-alcohol
    6. Handling mentally disturbed persons
    7. Handling juveniles

8. Shoplifting
9. Sabotage-espionage
10. Terrorism-bombings
11. Kidnapping-extortion

Weapons Training and Defense Tactics

A. Weapons orientation (classroom): 2 hours
1. Types of Weapons: Lethal and nonlethal
2. How do they work?
3. Care and maintenance of weapons

B. Legal constraints on the security officer carrying firearms: 2 hours

C. Proper use of weapons: 4 hours
1. Procedures governing the use of weapons
   a. Night stick
   b. Chemical mace or tear gas
   c. Shotgun
   d. Service revolver
2. Instructions for onrange, handgun training
3. Firearms safety

D. Onrange weapons training: 16 hours

E. Physical training in defense tactics: 8 hours

EXAMPLE 3: 80-HOUR BASIC SECURITY OFFICER TRAINING CURRICULUM

A. Prevention: 4 hours
1. Patrol procedures
2. Basic principles of patrol

B. Protection: 4 hours
1. Personnel control and identification systems
2. Access control
3. Vehicle monitoring
4. Physical security systems and procedures
5. Information security systems and procedures

C. Enforcement: 4 hours
1. Basic principles in criminal law
2. The collection and preservation of physical evidence: An introduction

  3. Arrest procedures
  4. Crimes and offenses

D. Detection: 4 hours
  1. Introduction to alarms
  2. Types of and uses for alarms
   a. Intrusion alarms
   b. Robbery alarms
   c. Fire alarms
   d. Assistance alarms
  3. Responding to alarms
  4. CCTV and surveillance cameras detection devices

E. Investigation: 4 hours
  1. Interviewing techniques
  2. Crime scene procedures
   a. Crime scene sketching
   b. Crime photography
   c. Crime scene searching
  3. Procedures for the collection, preservation, and examination of physical evidence

F. Emergency services: 4 hours
  1. First aid orientation
  2. First aid procedures
  3. Procedures during fires, explosions, floods, and riots
  4. Bombs and bomb threats
  5. Automobile accident investigation

G. Reporting: 4 hours
  1. Reporting forms for security
  2. Techniques of report writing

H. Inspections and audits: 4 hours
  1. Introduction to security audits and inspections
  2. Fire prevention inspections
  3. Accident prevention inspections
  4. How to conduct security inspections/audits

I. Weapons and Self-Defense: 32 hours
  1. Weapons orientation
  2. Legal policy and constraints
  3. Proper use of firearms
  4. Proper use of nonlethal weapons
  5. Personal defense tactics and training (8 hours)
  6. Onrange weapons training (16 hours)

J. General duties (orientation, preservice): 8 hours
1. What is a security officer?
2. What is expected of a security officer?
3. What is the organization of the security department?
4. Public relations
5. Cooperation with police agencies
6. Appearance and deportment
7. Maintenance, care, and use of equipment and uniforms
8. Security communication systems
9. Guard supervision

K. Special problem areas: 8 hours
Vandalism
Arson
Burglary-theft
Drugs-alcohol
Dealing with the mentally disturbed person
Rules of conduct for employees
Dealing with juveniles

EXAMPLE 4: 80-HOUR BASIC SECURITY MANAGEMENT CURRICULUM

A. An introduction to security management: 8 hours
1. Management definitions of security and protection
2. Fundamental management considerations in security
3. The problems of loss prevention
4. The systems approach to security management
5. Management's use of security inspections

B. Security weaknesses: 8 hours
1. The loss factor
2. Security hazards
3. Loss prevention inspections
4. Security hazard inspections
5. Cost-benefit analysis for security management
6. Cost effectiveness in security management
7. Management approaches to problem solving
   a. Evaluation techniques
   b. Selecting among alternative solutions
   c. Participatory management
   d. Fault free analysis
   e. Risk management

C. Defensive barriers—What kind to use: 4 hours
   1. Natural barriers
   2. Structural barriers
   3. Energy barriers
   4. Human and animal barriers

D. Locking systems: 4 hours
   1. Types of locks
      a. Warded
      b. Lever
      c. Pin tumbler
      d. Wafer tumbler
   2. Electromechanical locks
   3. Security vulnerabilities of each type
   4. Where should locks be used?

E. Alarm systems (sensors): 12 hours
   1. General introduction: 10 alarms
      a. Glossary of common terms
      b. Security applications for alarms
      c. Federal and UL specifications for alarms
   2. Categories of alarms (sensors)
      a. Electromechanical systems
      b. Soundwave and microwave systems
      c. Vibration systems
      d. Capacitance systems
      e. Audio systems
      f. Light systems (sensors)
      g. Combination systems
   3. Other applications for alarms (sensors)
      a. Fire detection
      b. Smoke detection
      c. Heat detection
      d. Water/air pressure
   4. Termination of alarms
      a. Local
      b. Central station
      c. Direct to police/fire
      d. Tie-ins (telephone)
      e. Proprietary
   5. Alarm design
   6. Factors to be considered in selecting alarm systems
      a. Engineering design
      b. Systems adaptability
      c. Cost-benefit

F. Communication systems for security: 4 hours
 1. Radio and microwave systems
 2. Intercom and telephone systems
 3. Protecting the integrity of the system
     a. Scramblers
     b. Coding systems
     c. Frequency divisions
 4. Factors to be considered in selecting communication systems

G. Access Control and identification systems: 4 hours
 1. Security applications for identification systems
 2. Criteria for effective identification
 3. Criteria for effective access control
 4. Types of identification systems
     a. Manual systems
     b. Mechanical and electromechanical systems
     c. Fully automated systems

H. Security officers and guards: 8 hours
 1. Basic functions of the security officer
 2. How many security officers do you need?
 3. Recruitment and selection of security officers
 4. Inhouse v. contract guards
 5. The training and education of guards
 6. Organization of guard forces
 7. Management's responsibilities
     a. Wages and salaries
     b. Uniforms and equipment
     c. Weapons and sidearms
 8. Legal responsibilities

I.   Traffic control and parking: 4 hours
 1. Access control for vehicles
 2. Vehicle identification
 3. Onpremise parking

J. Theft and fraud prevention: 8 hours
 1. Internal theft—Theft by employees
 2. External theft
 3. Alternative prevention programs

K. Information security and computer security: 4 hours
 1. What is information security?
 2. Principles of computer security
 3. Information and computer security methods

L. Disaster control: 4 hours
1. The need for emergency planning
2. How to develop an emergency disaster plan
3. Organization liaisons and mutual aid planning
4. Management responsibilities
   a. Operation shutdown and restoration
   b. Emergency evacuations
   c. Public relations
   d. Emergency and interim headquarters
   e. Management succession
5. Emergency warning systems
6. Testing and updating the plan

M. Strikes and labor disputes: 4 hours
1. Prestrike planning
2. Policy decisions by management
3. Protection of employees and property
4. Security's role during strikes and labor disputes

N. Special problems: 4 hours
1. Kidnapping, extortion, and terrorism
   a. Preventive measures
   b. Security's responsibilities
2. Security's role in management
   a. Security planning
   b. The security budget
   c. Security as a management function
3. Relations with public agencies
   a. Cooperation with police departments
   b. Cooperation with fire departments
   c. Hospitals-ambulances

One final detail that must be considered when a training curriculum for security officers is being developed is that not all of the officers attending will have the same type of job or assignment to go back to. This is especially true if the training is developed for contractual guards or officers employed by organizations large enough to have various assignments, locations, and/or facilities. With this thought in mind, the Private Security Task Force proposed the following as a standard: "To evaluate the effectiveness of training activities, tests as related to job descriptions should be developed."

The Task Force adds another element to the problem of specific training by saying that training classes are also not usually composed of a homogeneous group. To counter this complex problem, the Task Force mentions that efforts should be made by organizations to develop job descriptions from which they can easily, accurately, and effectively evaluate training needs. Through the use of well-defined job descriptions, training can become specifically job related and, thereby, help the organization give the proper training to the right officers.

CHAPTER 26

Operations

To guarantee the peak effectiveness of the security function within an organization, it is vitally important that all security personnel be informed and updated regularly on the conditions within the facility that directly affect them and their performance. In addition, it is virtually impossible for security personnel to learn the first day at an installation or on a new assignment all the policies and procedures that can come to bear on their jobs. This is even more true if any contractual personnel are used.

To aid management in averting the negative consequences of these situations, the following outline is offered as a general guide to the type of information that should be furnished to security personnel. Again, keep in mind that this is only a guide and individual adaptations will probably be necessary.

If each security officer is supplied with a copy of the completed guide/ outline, many questions can be answered before they arise and many problems eliminated before damage is done. The distribution of the completed document also means that additions and deletions can be made by simply distributing supplemental sheets that refer to the original section(s).

SECURITY OPERATIONS OUTLINE

I. **Emergency telephone numbers:**
    A. Municipal Police Department   _____
    B. County Sheriff's Department   _____
    C. State Police or Highway Patrol   _____
    D. Local Fire Department   _____
    E. Ambulance service (paramedics)   _____
    F. Company physician   _____
    G. Hospital   _____

II. **Management representative to be contacted in the event of:**
    A. Fire   Name   _____
                                Title   _____
                              Phone _____

B. Crime   Name _____
                                   Title _____
                                   Phone _____

C. Major accident—   Name _____
    natural disaster   Title _____
                                   Phone _____

D. Equipment malfunctions—   Name _____
    maintenance problems   Title _____
                                   Phone _____

E. Other emergencies   Name _____
                                   Title _____
                                   Phone _____

III. Security officials:

A. Director of Security   Name _____
                                   Phone _____

B. Assistant Director   Name _____
                                   Phone _____

C. Operations Supervisor   Name _____
                                   Phone _____

D. Shift Supervisor—1   Name _____
                                   Phone _____

            2   Name _____
                                   Phone _____

            3   Name _____
                                   Phone _____

E. Security headquarters   Phone _____

IV. Patrol procedures

A. If watchclock key stations are used as part of your patrol proce-
    dure, it is important that a list be made of the key station num-
    bers and where they are located.

B. Describe in detail patrol activities for each assignment. Example:
    1. Assignment 2—motor patrol—Section 1 and 2
        a. Patrol each section at least once each hour, punching key
           stations 1A, 1B, 1C, 1D, 2A, 2B, 2C, and 2D on each
           round.
        b. Check with Security Posts 2, 3, and 5 in person at least
           once every thirty minutes. You must sign the appropriate
           time log each time.
        c. Check pressure gauges 288, 298, and 308 every 30 min-
           utes and *key* the watchlock at each station.
        d. Check each exterior door and window *on foot,* to see that
           they are locked and secured on each round.
        e. The same patrol route through Sections 1 and 2 *is not* to
           be used on two successive rounds.

2. Assignment 3—foot patrol—bldg. 4
   a. A complete patrol of the building is to be made at least once every hour, punching key stations 4A, 4B, 4C, 4D, and 4E.
   b. Each interior door lock on the main floor is to be checked every 30 minutes and entry into each room is to be made every hour.
   c. All exterior doors and windows are to be checked and secured once every hour.
   d. When you are not on patrol, you shall station yourself in room 102 (guard post 8).

V. General security procedures:

A. Security procedures for employees
   1. Are employees allowed to leave the premises for lunch?
   2. What is the procedure for admitting employees to the facility after regular working hours have begun (tardiness)?
   3. Are there certain restricted areas where only specifically designated employees can go?
      a. Where are these restricted areas? List them along with the appropriate security classification for each.
      b. Supply a list of those employees with security clearances and which restricted areas they have access to.
      c. What special orders or procedures govern restricted areas?
   4. How are security officers notified when employees are terminated or when they resign?
      a. How up-to-date is the list kept?
      b. Where is the list kept?
   5. What do security officers do when they observe employees violating company rules or regulations?
B. Procedures for security buildings, gates, doors, and so forth
   1. List each individual location with the specific instructions that govern each. Example:
      a. Warehouse 1A—All exterior doors must be locked from 5:00 p.m. until 8:00 p.m. Monday through Friday and all day Saturday and Sunday.
      b. Gate 8—This gate is to be opened only on regular working days (Monday—Friday) 10:00 a.m. until 3:00 p.m.
   2. It is also important to specify how each location is to be secured.
C. Fire protection
   1. What precautions are security officers expected to take to guard against fire hazards?
   2. Are security personnel expected to inspect fire-fighting equipment, sprinklers, and so forth?

3. What procedures are security personnel expected to follow in case of fire?

A. Are they expected to assist fire fighters?

B. Are they responsible for evacuating the facility?

C. What is the procedure for notifying the fire department?

D. Anticrime activities

1. Are security officers authorized to make arrests? when? where?

2. Are security officers authorized to make searches of persons, vehicles, and property? when? where?

E. Miscellaneous security procedures:

1. Are security personnel expected to turn lights and/or equipment on or off?

2. Are security personnel expected to operate weight scale at truck loading docks?

3. Are officers responsible for the security of parking areas?

4. Are security personnel expected to wear special clothing in certain areas of the facility, i.e., asbestos vests, safety goggles, or hard hats?

TIME SCHEDULE OF DUTIES

If not each officer, at least each shift, has special duties and responsibilities. Since many of them are critical to the smooth operation of the whole organization, it is imperative that they be properly performed. To insure that they are taken care of efficiently, it is *initially* the responsibility of management to see that security pesonnel are made aware of what is expected of them. To make management's task easier the following outline is offered as one example of how to inform security personnel.

EXAMPLE

A. Shift 1—0800 to 1600

1. Main gate

a. **0800**   Open employee's entrance

b. **0830**   Open delivery gate 1

c. **1045**   Escort mail truck to administration building

d. **1600**   Close and secure delivery gate

2. Post 1: Administration Bldg.

a. **0800**   Open main door

b. **1600**   Lock and secure doors 2, 4, and 5

3. Post 2: Delivery and Dock Area

B. Shift 2—**1600 to 2400**   It is essential that the schedule be as concise and inclusive as possible for each shift and/or assignment (post).

I. **Security assignments**: It is just as important for your security officers to know *where* they are supposed to be as it is for them to know *what* they are supposed to do. The following section of this outline gives an example of how this information can be disseminated.
  A. Shift 1
    1. Main gate—5th and Elm
      a. Number of officers assigned
        1. Armed—unarmed?
        2. Vehicle assigned?
      b. Officer in charge/supervisor
    2. Assignment 1—Motor Patrol—Sections 1–2
      a. _____
        1) _____
        2) _____
      b. _____
      c. Section 1 is the N.E. quadrant of the main plant area including:
        1) Administration Bldg.
        2) Warehouses A1 and A2
        3) Loading Docks A, B and D
  B. The same procedure should be followed for each assignment or post of each shift.

II. **Security instructions by post or assignment**:
  A. Main gate
    1. ID badges are used.
      a. All badges must have red or blue color codes.
      b. All badges must have an identification code beginning with M1, M2, or M3.
        1) M1 = Main gate, shift 1
        2) M2 = Main gate, shift 2
        3) M3 = Main gate, shift 3
      c. All ID badges must be worn externally.
    2. All employees and visitors must sign the appropriate log with name, date, and time in and out.
    3. All vehicles entering the plant through the main gate must have a company decal displayed in the upper left corner of the windshield.
      a. All individuals in the vehicle must be company employees with proper credentials.
      b. All vehicles are subject to search before permission can be given to enter.
      c. All individuals must sign the appropriate log/register.

      d. All vehicles must be logged in on the vehicle register with the appropriate information.

    4. All logs and registers must be approved and signed by the supervisor at the end of each shift.

III. **Shift schedules for Security personnel and special employees:**
    A. Shift 1
        1. Start   _____
        2. Lunch break   _____
        3. Coffee break   _____
        4. End   _____
    B. Shift 2
        1. Start   _____
        2. Lunch break   _____
        3. Coffee break   _____
        4. End   _____
    C. Shift 3
        1. Start   _____
        2. Lunch break   _____
        3. Coffee break   _____
        4. End   _____
    D. Maintenance and repair personnel are in the facility from _____ to _____
        1. Which areas are they in and at what time are they there?
            a. Administration building   From _____
               (Circle) M T W Th F Sa Su   To _____
            b. Plant A   From _____
               (Circle) M T W Th F Sa Su   To _____
        2. How many individuals are assigned to maintenance and repair in each area?
        3. Are all of these individuals company employees? If not, who do they work for?
    E. Cleaning crews are in the facility from _____ to _____
        1. ⎫
        2. ⎬ Same as for D above.
        3. ⎭

SCHEDULING SECURITY PERSONNEL

A. To determine the time assignment of security personnel (applicable to both loss investigation and specialized enforcement) the following steps should be followed:
    1. Obtain *loss totals* for the period under study.
        a. You need enough quantity to be significant; *one full year* is recommended rather than the most recent week, month, or

quarter. If more than a year is needed in order to obtain significant totals, then selective assignment of specialized units may not be warranted. In such cases it is better to obtain the desired selectivity through training and adequate instruction to the security personnel normally assigned.

    b.   Where there is extreme *seasonal variation* such as in some locations or where extreme climatic changes are a controlling factor, then special seasonal studies may be warranted. Ordinarily, however, the year's experience is the best basis.

2.   *In smaller facilities,* where specialized security personnel frequently do other work, such as general patrolling, safety, or individual investigating, you cannot plan time assignments on the basis of loss statistics alone but must include in your considerations the amount of nonsecurity work that they may be expected to perform.

3.   Tabulate the *hours of occurrence* of known losses.

    a.   Distribution can be shown by hour of day—24 hours. In this case, the five weekdays, Monday through Friday, can frequently be averaged as being approximately equal, but Saturdays and Sundays should be tabulated separately because the time pattern will not conform to the weekday average.

    b.   In larger organizations distribution may be more effectively and accurately shown by considering distribution by hour of the week—168 hours. Where this is done, assignment of personnel must be based on the weekly cycle rather than on a daily cycle. (Illustrations that follow will use the *average weekday* cycle.)

4.   *Determine the percent of total known losses,* by category, that occur in each hour. Smaller facilities may find that the percent that occurs in each two-hour (sometimes each four-hour) period is adequate for their purpose because (1) the total is small, and (2) they cannot assign personnel at closer intervals than that.

5.   Identify the *periods of maximum occurrences of known losses.*

6.   Determine the *number of personnel available* for specialized assignment throughout the day and/or the week. For example:

Security Officer		S	M	Tu	W	Th	F	S
A.	Johnson	X	O	O	X	X	X	X
B.	Roberts	X	X	O	O	X	X	X
C.	Cline	X	X	X	O	O	X	X
D.	Hogan	X	X	X	X	O	O	X
E.	McDonald	X	O	O	X	X	X	X
F.	White	X	X	X	O	O	X	X
G.	Green	O	O	X	X	X	X	X
Available Daily		6	4	4	4	4	6	7

Note: To make this effective, it is important to assign days off proportionally to the expected load. For seasonal variations, vacations should not be permitted during the season of highest experience.

7. *Personnel available should then be assigned* to work at times that will keep the number on duty approximately proportionate to the loss distribution curve. For example:
   a. If only *one officer* is available, the most effective time for such unit work would be approximately 2:00 pm to 10:00 pm.
   b. If *two officers* are available, one could work from 11:00 am to 7:00 pm, and the other from 3:00 pm to 11:00 pm, thus bracketing the 3:00 pm to 7:00 pm peak.
   c. With *three officers* available, one unit from 7:00 am to 3:00 pm, another from 3:00 pm to 11:00 pm, and the third from 2:00 pm to 10:00 pm, would effectively cover the heaviest portion of the day.
   d. With *four officers* available, the fourth unit could complete the round-the-clock coverage or be assigned thus:
      1) One officer, 6:00 am to 2:00 pm
      2) One officer, 2:00 pm to 10:00 pm
      3) One officer, 10:00 am to 6:00 pm
      4) One officer, 4:00 pm to 12:00 am
   e. The procedures can be used for the assignment of five (or more) officers.

8. In all cases, there should be *experimentation and flexibility* until the *best time-assignment* pattern is found. This is particularly true where a large number of officers are available and in cases where other public policing units can be depended on to provide a basic level of enforcement or loss investigative work.

9. Certain *guiding rules* should be kept in mind. Important among these are:
   a. Avoid having shift changes occur at peak periods. The time lost in making the change may be small, but it can disrupt the planned pattern. If possible, have shift changes occur ahead of the peak periods rather than just after.
   b. Consider the shift changes of other company employees when you are establishing basic shift periods.
   c. Avoid using split shifts. A man should not be required to work his eight hours in two chunks—four and four or two and six—with a break in between. This is a morale breaker and is normally more costly. If an officer is needed only for a four-hour peak, then he should be utilized in other work for the time before or after this peak to make an eight-hour tour of duty.
   d. Do not rotate principal shifts more often than once per month. An officer who has to change his or her habits of eating, sleeping, and recreation oftener than once per month will be wasting his or her strength making the adjustment and will not be a wholly effective worker. Minor shifting of time (up to four hours) can

be made as frequently as desirable as this will not disrupt an officer's living habits seriously.

e. Do not expect to obtain a *perfect matching* of the number of officers on duty with the frequency of incidents. The actual load will vary from day to day, and you cannot predict these changes precisely. The fewer the number of officers available, the less precisely can you match a loss curve. An approximate matching is enough.

f. Since officers often need vehicles, the number of different shifts and special peak-coverage assignments must be geared to the availability of vehicles.

10. In making the assignment of officers to various shifts, it is important that they be *instructed as to the essential points of the assignment.* For example, investigators will need to know in advance when they may expect their heaviest load; patrol officers must be instructed as to when to place their heaviest emphasis on taking specific enforcement action; and must know the specific demands of their posts. This information is necessary so that these officers can plan their own activities within their eight-hour assignments, and not be doing followup or work of lesser priority when the demands of their shift are at or near their *peak.*

11. Once having been established, the *time assignments* of officers should be checked against actual distribution of *losses* from time to time. However, only if a strong continuing trend shows up in the time pattern of losses should any major revision of time assignment of officers be made. The reason for this time change should be studied, and it will probably be found to go hand-in-hand with a change in place, which we shall discuss next.

B. To determine *place assignment* of specialized personnel:
1. The basic need is accurate information and *description of location* on the Security Incident Report, plus a system for recording and indexing the location in a manner to facilitate reference and study.
2. Find out *where various types of losses are occurring.* You will need enough total experience to give a reliable picture of the distribution; 12 months is considered a good period of time.
3. The *most practical device* to show location visually, as well as to facilitate comparative studies of geographic distribution, is the *spot map* or pin map.
   a. For small and medium facilities, one large-scale site plan is usually enough.
   b. For very large facilities, facilities with special or unusual localized problems, or those with security areas with large areas, two or more separate maps or building floor plans may be needed. Some Security Departments have found it desirable to show

distribution within the various floors or areas by means of separate maps.

    c.   In using maps for the study of special problems, the spot map should supplement rather than replace the basic map or floor plan of the facility.

    d.   The simpler the code of pins (or spots) used, the easier (and often the more reliable) the map is to use. It complicates the map unnecessarily to show *all* classifications of loss (e.g.: type, time, amount involved, and so forth) by means of variously colored or differently shaped pins. These classifications can better be studied from data in tabular form, leaving the map to show only *where* accidents are occurring.

4.   Identify the *locations of high loss experience* as revealed by the concentration of pins. These may be areas such as a finished goods area; they may be principal offices or locker rooms; or they may show up at parking lots or near gates. The analyst should supplement this with explanations as to principal circumstances of these, as it is likely they will vary considerably as to type, time, and officers involved.

5.   Experiment with dividing the map into areas that would make up *suitable assignments for individual officers,* keeping in mind facility, patrol, or building or fixed post assignments. Keep in mind the purpose of any special assignments to be made:

    a.   For loss investigation officers, you need to plan the parcelling out of the entire area under study, unless specialized loss units will handle investigations only in the most concentrated places, leaving the sparser areas to be covered by the regular patrol officers.

    b.   For enforcement assignment, especially when the specialized officers are expected to focus only on enforcement programs and regular patrol officers are required to provide basic enforcement and service throughout the facility and around the clock, the areas that are selected for assignment may include only those locations of highest loss experience and constitute only a relatively small portion of the total facility area.

6.   *Practical limitations in dividing the map* must be adhered to and these techniques should be considered:

    a.   Set up the proposed assignments on the basis of the maximum number of officers available at any one time and so that a lesser number may be adapted to cover these assignments with reasonable flexibility.

    b.   Recognize the kind of problem, as to whether it is mainly one of area coverage, or spot coverage and consider establishing some special assignments to handle them. For example, a main gate exit from a facility, because it has heavy employee traffic, may need specialized constant support for spot inspections and vehicle searching.

    c.   Overlapping of adjoining patrol assignments, in three or four locations where there are sufficient patrol areas that adjoin at a particular point, may effectively cover for high-incidence locations.

    d.   The worst problem location may be quite different at one time from where it is at another time of the day or week. For example, during business hours, highest experience may be in the locker room and parking lots; at quitting time it may be at main exits or shipping dock areas and concentrated near production areas; at Saturday midnight it will most likely be in warehouse or yard areas. These will not be revealed on the general spot map, and may be lost in the averages of density of pins.

7.   After deciding on the best plan for dividing the facility into areas or clock routes, or grouping the problem locations into suitable officer assignments, *a simple system of identification* of such areas or assignments must be provided. These need to be described in an appropriate general order, defining the boundaries or limits thereof, and clearly shown on a large map.

8.   Plan for the *coverage of these areas* by available specialized officers. When fewer than the desirable minimum number of officers are available, it is better to abandon some of the lesser problem locations in favor of concentrating on places of the most serious immediate need than to try to spread such units so thinly they become ineffective.

    a.   Such temporarily abandoned special assignments will then need to be covered by the regular patrol until enough specialized officers are again available.

    b.   The thin spreading of loss investigation personnel, however, is not necessarily poor practice unless (1) they become overloaded and cannot handle all calls, or (2) the distances they have to travel in responding to incidents reduces their ability to respond or to provide service as it is needed.

9.   *Make area assignments.* In instructions to the officers assigned, *you cannot separate the problems of time from those of place.* In other words, officers assigned to areas or patrols must know not only when and what areas they are assigned to, but must also know *where within that area* and at *what specific times* their attention will need to be concentrated. This usually requires detailed instruction coupled with close supervision until the officer becomes acquainted with the peculiar conditions and needs of the assignment.

10.   Revision of area or beat boundaries may need to be done from time to time. This will rarely be needed, however, although evaluation and comparison should be made quarterly in order to become aware

of changes as they occur. Major changes will usually parallel shifts in employee population, opening of new facilities or production centers, changes in facility use, or the addition of new product lines. In any case, careful analysis of the reason for the change must be made before relocation of area or patrol boundaries is done.

C. To determine the type of loss activities or conditions that should be given priority attention by officers:

1. There is a *direct relationship between regulation or policy violations and losses*. The more violations can be cut down, the more losses can be prevented. It follows that since *you cannot enforce for all violations* with equal force, wherever and whenever they may occur throughout the facility simply because you will never have enough officers available to do this, then your enforcement effort must be *concentrated primarily against* those *violations that appear most frequently* with significant losses.

2. From *Security Incident Reports* of the year just concluded *tabulate all policy or regulation violations* that are entered. These should include not only violations for which an employee (or nonemployee) is prosecuted or violations that are provable in a legal sense, but all those that, *in the opinion of the investigator,* were believed to have been factors in known losses that occurred.

3. Of the violations listed, which may be anywhere between a dozen and a hundred types, *select some 8 or 10 that occur most frequently,* and list them in the order of their frequency. For example:

Violation	Number of Violations	Percent of Total
Exterior doors left open or unlocked	452	15.1
Fire doors blocked open	375	12.5
Exterior lights burned out	321	10.7
Tools found in lunch boxes	287	9.6
Cars parked in unauthorized locations	96	3.2
Finished products found in trash container	82	2.7
Unauthorized persons in office areas	74	2.5
Improper stacking of materials	74	2.5
Improper shipping documents	56	1.9
Employee horseplay	27	.9
Misc.		
TOTAL	3,002	100.0

4. Often a noticeable break will occur after the third to the sixth violation from the top of the list. In the example above, there is a break between the fourth and fifth violations listed ("tools found," 9.6 percent and "cars parked," 3.2 percent). We can call these top

four, then, *high risk violations,* since they make up some 47 percent of all violations noted in accidents. If no sharp break occurs, then draw a line at the point where approximately 50 percent of the violations would be included, and consider those above the line as the high risk violations.

5. These high risk violations will be the *principal enforcement targets.* In order to direct officers' efforts against them, prepare training materials that will identify what these violations are and instruct the officer what to do about them.

   a. Such bulletins or instructions should indicate the period for which the particular order is to be effective.

   b. It must not direct or imply that officers will give their attention exclusively to these violations; it must indicate the need to maintain reasonable enforcement pressure against the "all other" or nonpriority classes of violations.

   c. If it is nowhere else defined, the company's policy on arrests, reporting, and so forth should be indicated as well as policy and/ or specific rules involved. The need to maintain quality must also be conveyed to the officer. The bulletin or instruction should avoid giving the appearance that this is a drive, a campaign, or enforcement quotas being established, but that this enforcement is part of a long-range, continuing program of reducing loss through specific attention to high risk activities.

6. Checking and followup will be needed to maintain pressure against these *target violations* to the desired degree. To do this *keep records on enforcement* and tabulate the data in the same ways in which loss data is tabulated, by time, place, and type of violation.

   a. To show time distribution of enforcement effort, draw a graph showing the amount of enforcement distributed around the clock (or over the 168-hour week, whichever you use). Compare this with the graph that shows the distribution of accidents by time. For direct comparison draw both graphs on the same sheet, in which case expressing the distribution in percent will eliminate the need for using separate scales for enforcement and for losses.

   b. For evaluating place (area distribution) of enforcement, the most practical device again is the spot map or pin map. A direct comparison of the enforcement map with the accident map will show how closely you are applying enforcement pressure at the places where it is needed. For example, if the loss map shows a concentration of pins in a given area, and the enforcement map shows only a light scattering of pins in that location, then you know that enforcement needs to be increased there. If enforcement pins show heavy concentrations at places where few, if any, losses are reported, then it is likely that this enforcement effort should be applied at other places with better results.

Enforcement maps should show significant distribution within two or three months, thus enabling the administrator to evaluate and control the work of the men in the facility.

Spotting of enforcement on a continual basis may be costly in larger facilities because of the very high volumes involved. In such cases it is enough to make occasional spot checks to see whether enforcement is being applied where it is needed.

c. For determining whether enforcement effort is adequately distributed by type of violation, make up a table showing enforcement in the same way that violations in accidents are shown in the example in C–3, above. Compare the percentages, rather than the raw numbers, since the figures for enforcement actions taken should normally be several times as large as the figures for violations occurring in losses.

7. *Summary. Reasonable matching* by time, place, and enforcement action *is all that is warranted.* To require exact or unreasonably close matching is not realistic (1) because it is all but impossible to obtain and (2) because to seek it would impose artificial and unreasonable controls over actions of the officers. This would make it a mechanical and mathematical function rather than one requiring the utmost in initiative, interest, and good judgment by security officers.

CONTRACTUAL V. PROPRIETARY PERSONNEL: OPERATIONAL CONSIDERATIONS

Like so many other options that can become a part of an integrated security program, the type of security personnel to employ also requires decision making. The two primary alternatives from which to choose are:

1. Proprietary (inhouse) security personnel, or
2. Contractual (for hire) security personnel.

Both types come with their own advantages and disadvantages. The final decision is actually determined by what the organization is really looking for in its security force.

Some of the advantages and disadvantages applicable to each follow.

A. *Proprietary personnel*
   1. Advantages:
      a. Typically more loyal to the company they protect—their employer
      b. Quality of personnel can be determined easily through
         1) Effective hiring practices
         2) High standards for personnel hiring or retention

3) Effective, ongoing training
c. Control of their performance is easier
d. Proprietary personnel are usually more reliable—more trustworthy
e. There is a certain prestige associated with having an inhouse security force
2. Disadvantages:
a. Costlier than contractual personnel
b. Less scheduling flexibility
B. *Contractual personnel*
1. Advantages:
a. Fewer direct and ancillary costs for the client company
b. Client company does not have to be concerned about the administration of a contractual security staff
c. Unlimited manpower to meet a client's changing needs
d. More impartial than their proprietary counterparts
e. Subject the client company to less liability, both criminal and civil
2. Disadvantages:
a. Typically a high rate of attrition—always new people on the job
b. Invariably they come to the job with less training
c. Their performance evaluations are usually minimal, not promoting quality

Most recently, a growing number of organizations are attempting to get the best of both worlds. They are utilizing contractual security personnel for actual protection duties but hiring their own proprietary managers to run the program and supervise the contract staff. To date, this type of *shared* security operation appears to be working effectively.

USE OF FIREARMS BY SECURITY PERSONNEL

Many companies arm their security officers. Yet, the decision to have security officers carry firearms must be based on the protective needs of the company and the degree of risk assumed by the officers in carrying out their responsibilities.

If they are to be armed and all applicable legal requirements for carrying a weapon are met, a comprehensive policy statement should then be prepared. This statement should set forth, in detail, the circumstances under which officers may use their weapons in carrying out their protective responsibilities. This, in turn, protects the company from unnecessary legal risk as a result of officer actions while specifying to the officers what they may and may not do while carrying a firearm.

Firearms

I. *Scope*
   A. Effective immediately *all* security personnel shall strictly adhere to this order. Violations of policies and procedures set forth herein will result in disciplinary action.
   B. This policy shall be effective at all times, regardless of location.

II. *Policies*
   A. Sidearms *will not be removed from the holster* or otherwise drawn unless there is an immediate threat of death to the officer or other persons present. The sidearm or any other such weapon *will not be fired* except to protect the officer's life or the lives of other persons.
   B. *Warning shots will not be fired* under any circumstances.
   C. Officers may draw their sidearms when they reasonably feel that there is danger of being killed or that someone else might be killed.
   D. If any shots are fired under situations as indicated above, a full report shall be initiated by the officer(s) involved specifically documenting the circumstances under which the shots were fired.

III. *Sidearm specifications*
   A. The duty sidearm for uniformed officers shall be a revolver capable of firing .38 caliber special ammunition. The barrel length shall be not less than three and one-half inches nor more than six inches.

IV. *Safety requirements*
   A. Safety should be the primary concern when using firearms. Officers shall at all times handle firearms in a safe manner and as specified in weapons training. There will be no careless or reckless handling of, or horse play with, firearms.
   B. Firearms will not be taken from the holsters or from carrying cases while in the security office. Exceptions would be for the protection of life, if the situation warrants it, or for cleaning purposes. Cleaning will be done in the squad room only.
   C. Weapons shall be cleaned and in good working order at all times.

V. *Exceptions*
   A. The policies set forth above do not apply to approved, company-authorized training situations.

CHAPTER 27

Performance Evaluations

The security officer evaluation forms that follow provide a format for the evaluation of an officer's performance. The first treats the following areas:

1. Appearance
2. Communication skills
3. Public relations
4. Judgment
5. Ethics
6. Self-perception
7. Service-orientation
8. Stability and flexibility
9. Practical knowledge
10. Work analysis

A rating scale is provided for each factor with a built-in requirement that the evaluation be reviewed with the officer. This insures that it is used not only for evaluation but also as a worker improvement device.

The second and third evaluation forms are more concise in design, but, like the first, use both the checklist and narrative formats.

FORM 1: CHECKLIST FOR SECURITY OFFICERS

1 = Superior
2 = Above Average
3 = Average
4 = Poor

Appearance

Is the manner of this officer's dress appropriate for the requirements of the present assignment?

Does this individual's appearance give an immediate impression of a professional security officer?

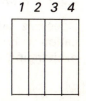

1 2 3 4

Does this officer's bearing elicit a positive response from the public?

Does this officer's appearance reflect a positive self-image and pride?

Is this officer properly uniformed? (see Department Manual Procedure _____ through _____)

Are this individual's uniforms and equipment clean and serviceable?

Measure this officer's personal appearance, personal hygiene, weight, hair style. (see Personal Appearance Guide Chart)

Is this individual physically fit?

Comments

Communication skills

1 2 3 4

Does this individual express ideas with clarity, poise, and relevance?

Is this individual empathetic when speaking to people on a person-to-person basis?

Is this officer tactful in dealing with others?

Does this individual have the verbal ability to reduce tension through persuasion?

Does this officer have the verbal ability to express authority and allay fears?

Does this individual effectively express himself/herself in group interactions?

Is this individual able to communicate his/her point of view to others?

Does this individual maintain open lines of communication with other security and police personnel by exchanging information with them whenever possible?

1 2 3 4

Does this individual listen to what others say and
extract relevant information?

Are this officer's written reports complete, concise,
accurate, and qualitative?

In preparing reports, does this individual comply with
department procedure?

Comments

Public Relations

1 2 3 4

Is this officer aware of, and sensitive to, the various
social and ethnic groups?

Does this officer have an insight into the incipient
problems that may affect the organization?

Does this officer's performance and interaction with
the public reflect favorably on the image of the
organization and its security department?

In interacting with employees and the public does this
officer empathize with their plight by being friendly,
tactful, and understanding?

Does this officer try to look at things from the other
party's point of view?

Does this officer give people adequate time to explain
their problems?

Are employees and the public generally satisfied with
the way this officer handles situations?

Is this officer able to give consolation and emotional
support to people in times of crisis?

When possible, does this officer try to explain or give
a rationale to people before taking action?

Does this officer use persuasion rather than his
authority whenever possible?

1 2 3 4

Does this officer recognize impartiality as part of being a professional?

Does this officer offer equal service to *all* people without regard to their ethnic or racial background, economic class, sex, or position?

Is this officer sensitive to the human rights of individuals?

Does this individual recognize stereotyping as a shortcoming?

Does this officer avoid a condescending or contemptuous attitude?

Does this officer maintain a favorable relationship with other security personnel by being cooperative whenever possible?

Comments:

Judgment

1 2 3 4

Does this officer avail himself/herself of all possible relevant information before making a decision?

Are decisions and actions in accord with command policies and concerned with community response?

Does this officer consider alternative and implications of actions?

Is this individual able to establish correct priorities?

Are this officer's decisions logically sound as opposed to emotional or impulsive?

Is this officer able to integrate his/her decisions with those of peers and supervisors in order to coordinate his/her functions with command goals?

Can this individual make decisions under stress?

Does this officer assimilate information readily permitting him/her to get to the crux of matters quickly?

1 2 3 4

Does this individual make decisions within a reasonable time?

Is this officer's judgment exercised with the welfare of the people involved as the primary concern?

Is this officer able to exercise restraint?

Does this individual use discretion in making arrests?

Is this officer able to make firm decisions despite past errors?

Comments

Ethics

1 2 3 4

Does this officer actively support the police?

Does this officer view ethics as an essential ingredient of professionalism?

Does this individual's deportment and performance reflect a high level of integrity?

Is this individual willing to be unpopular among peers in order to adhere to positive principles?

Is this individual aware that cynicism has a negative effect on ethical standards and work performance?

Is this individual loyal?

Can this individual be relied upon to fill sensitive positions?

Comments

Self-Perception

1 2 3 4

Does this officer value and take pride in his/her work as a police officer?

Does this individual's deportment suggest an officer who possesses self-assurance and who is not easily threatened or antagonized?

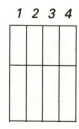

1 2 3 4

Is this individual's self-assurance clearly demonstrated by performance?

Is this officer a willing worker?

Does this individual display proper attitudes in all work contracts?

Is this officer a self-motivator requiring a minimum of supervision?

Does this individual have confidence in his/her own ability?

Is this officer willing to take reasonable risks?

Is this officer's self-image in line with reality?

Comments

Service-Orientation

1 2 3 4

Is this individual's general outlook geared to providing service to the public?

Does this individual go out of his/her way to give assistance to the public?

Does this officer place a high priority on public satisfaction?

Is this individual aware of the needs and feelings of the people he/she services?

Is this officer effective in attempting to address these needs once they are recognized?

Is this officer aware of various service agencies available to help people in need?

Does this individual answer service calls and complaints with dispatch?

Does this officer give respect to get respect?

Does this individual place a positive emphasis on the personal treatment of citizens?

Comments

Stability and Flexibility

	1	2	3	4

Is this officer a stable individual?

Is this officer able to maintain control in incidences of stress?

Is this individual able to control his/her emotions?

Is this officer mature enough to withstand verbal abuse?

Does this officer employ necessary force when appropriate but only as a last resort?

Does this officer engage in enforcement activity (arrest and summonses) in accordance with departmental and local command policies rather than as a personal action?

How does this officer react to unforeseen events?

Can this individual adapt to changing circumstances?

Is this individual able to adapt his/her approach to attain objectives?

Comments

Practical Knowledge

	1	2	3	4

Is this individual aware of the criminal hazards and other conditions that exist in his/her assigned area?

Does this individual direct service efforts toward these hazards and conditions?

Is this officer able to perceive potential security hazards and act against them before they become actual hazards?

Is this individual able to separate the usual from the unusual in recognizing hazards in his/her assigned area?

Does this officer have an immediate and instinctive perception of security conditions?

Does this officer have a grasp of patrol techniques, and is this individual innovative in their application?

Is this officer versatile in his/her patrol function effectively handling a variety of situations (crime, traffic conditions, vice, lost children, and so forth?)

Does this officer patrol in an intelligent manner directing his/her efforts toward command priorities and utilizing slow service periods for secondary functions?

Does this officer respond intelligently to scenes of crime and emergency situations (e.g., respond without siren in burglary cases and respond with caution in emergency situations?)

Is this individual able to defuse potentially bad situations?

Does this officer, by taking effective action, eliminate the need to take stronger enforcement action?

Does this officer have a grasp for investigative techniques, and is the individual innovative in their application?

Is this officer versatile in the investigative function, effectively handling a variety of investigations?

Is this officer adept at recognizing evidence, and is this individual able to assure its validity through a proper chain of control?

Is this individual able to develop sources of information?

Comments

Work Analysis

	1	2	3	4

Does this individual consider service as a most important part of the job?

Does this officer respond as quickly as possible to service calls?

Is this officer knowledgeable of the _____ where he/she can refer people for assistance?

Are this officer's interactions and interventions with _____ on service calls received favorably?

Is this individual aware of all the sources of information available (e.g., internal and external indices—preliminary investigation?)

Does this individual analyze data and assemble facts and information with accuracy and attention to detail (preliminary investigation?)

Is this individual persistent in pursuing his/her investigations and ensuring justice to the best of his/her ability?

Is this officer aware of department policies and procedures?

Does this individual handle investigations promptly and thoroughly?

On investigative calls with _____, does this individual make a serious effort to ameliorate the situation by making appropriate referrals?

Are this individual's interactions and interventions while he or she is on service calls favorably received?

Does this individual work well?

Does this individual tie fragmented information together and assimilate pertinent data developed internally and externally (outside agencies?)

Does the individual analyze data and assemble facts and information with accuracy and an attention to detail?

Is this individual persistent in pursuing his/her investigations and ensuring justice to the best of his/her ability (e.g., alert to the possibility of false identification of perpetrator?)

Does this individual elicit and develop pertinent information from witnesses, complainants and suspects through his/her skill as an interviewer?

Is this individual able to seek out and develop sources of information?

Is this officer aware of court decisions affecting his/her functions as an investigator and does this individual maintain the standards set by the court? (e.g., Miranda and Wade cases)

Does this individual have a knowledge of the law and does this officer apply the spirit of the law?

Comments

Recommendations

Signature of inspecting officer
Date

Officer's Comments

Signature of officer
Date

FORM 2: SECURITY OFFICER EVALUATION

NAME:

DEPT:

TITLE:

REVIEW DATE:

1 = Provisional

2 = Adequate

3 = Competent

4 = Commendable

5 = Distinguished

+ = Strong

− = Weak

√ = Average/Acceptable

N = Not observed

Performance Factors	Ratings		Comments
	Weight	Score	
Quantity			Examples of work well done; superior or above average performance
____ Amount of work done	25	*	
____ Work completed on time			
Quality			
____ Accuracy	25	*	
____ Neatness			
____ Thoroughness			
____ Oral communication			
____ Written communication			

Performance Factors	Ratings		Comments
	Weight	*Score*	
Work habits	*		Performance deficiencies; suggestions for improvement
___ Punctuality			
___ Attendance			
___ Adherence to policy			
___ Follows instructions			
___ Takes direction	15		
___ Interest/willingness			
___ Initiative			
___ Resourcefulness			
___ Attentiveness			
Personal traits	*		General comments
___ Emotional stability			
___ Maturity			
___ Attitude			
___ Tact/diplomacy	15		
___ Compatibility			
___ Personal appearance			
___ Professional demeanor			
___ Loyalty			
Adaptability	*		
___ To new situations			
___ To stressful situations	10		
___ To freedom			
___ To learning			
___ To authority			

Job-related knowledge
_____ Techniques
_____ Procedures
_____ Skills

* 10

* Weight & Score GENERAL categories
* Rate INDIVIDUAL items (+, −, √)

100%

Supervisor/Director

_____ Date

Charge person/Sergeant

_____ Date

Security officer

_____ Date

FORM 3: EMPLOYEE EVALUATION FORM

Name _____ Date Due _____ 90 Day

Department _____ Job Title _____ Annual

_____ (OTHER)

Check the appropriate square which most nearly describes this employee's performance:

Quality of work—Consider neatness, accuracy, and degree of excellence.

☐ Unsatisfactory, careless   ☐ Borderline   ☐ Satisfactory   ☐ Above average   ☐ Outstanding

Quantity of work—Consider the amount of work produced.

☐ Unsatisfactory   ☐ Below average just enough to get by   ☐ Average   ☐ Above average   ☐ Outstanding, eager to do more than assigned

Attendance—Consider absenteeism and tardiness.

☐ Frequently absent   ☐ Frequently late   ☐ Satisfactory   ☐ Above average   ☐ Never absent or late

Attitude—Consider ability to get along with others and willingness to cooperate with supervisors and to conform to rules of work.

☐ Unwilling to cooperate, troublesome or indifferent
☐ Sometimes difficult to work with, occasionally indifferent
☐ Normal, usually tactful, works well with others
☐ Congenial and cooperative
☐ Always willing, highly cooperative

Knowledge of work—Consider how well the employee is equipped with the knowledge essential to the performance of his or her work.

☐ Insufficient for job
☐ Lacks knowledge of some phases of work
☐ Adequate for position
☐ Understands all phases of position
☐ Comprehensive knowledge of all phases of job

Dependability—Consider the extent to which the employee can be counted on to do assigned tasks and degree of supervision required.

☐ Unreliable, needs constant supervision
☐ Sometimes requires prompting
☐ Usually completes tasks with reasonable promptness
☐ Very dependable, needs little supervision
☐ Thoroughly dependable and trustworthy

Initiative—Consider willingness to assume responsibility.

☐ Puts forth no effort, always waits to be told
☐ Puts forth little effort, needs prodding
☐ Average, does assigned work well
☐ Hard worker, willing to do more than assigned
☐ Exceptionally diligent, never waits to be told

Personal appearance—Consider cleanliness, neatness, general grooming, and appropriateness of attire.

☐ Always untidy, improper dress
☐ Sometimes untidy and careless
☐ Generally neat and clean
☐ Well groomed
☐ Very neat, extremely well groomed

Adaptability—Consider ability to adjust to changing situations and work assignments and ease with which he or she learns new duties.

- [ ] Cannot adjust to changing conditions
- [ ] Has difficulty, requires detailed and repeated instructions
- [ ] Satisfactory, minimum instruction on most new duties
- [ ] Very adaptable, quick to learn and understand
- [ ] Exceptionally keen in adapting to new jobs and changing situations

Rate only persons with supervisory responsibility:

Leadership—Consider effectiveness in getting people to accomplish objectives, follow methods, and accept direction.

- [ ] Sometimes fails to exercise effective direction and guidance
- [ ] Generally wins confidence and loyal support
- [ ] Often fails to motivate people
- [ ] Leads people well, wins and holds enthusiasm
- [ ] Provides leadership, motivation, and direction under most conditions

Overall rating:

At his/her level this employee is rated:

- [ ] Outstanding
- [ ] Above average
- [ ] Average
- [ ] Marginal
- [ ] Unsatisfactory

If salary is being considered complete the following—recommended for:

- [ ] Salary increase
- [ ] No increase
- [ ] Reevaluation

If placed on probation or recommended for reevaluation—Date to be reviewed again.

Additional remarks by evaluator:

Date: _____

Signature: _____

Employee remarks

☐ Concur with rating ☐ Do not concur

Date: _____

Signature: _____

Reviewed by personnel office—Remarks

QUALITY AND QUANTITY OF SECURITY
ENFORCEMENT ACTIVITIES

Enforcement activities have long been an important responsibility given to security personnel. How well those responsibilities are performed directly impacts on the overall effectiveness of a security program. Consequently, individual security personnel must be regularly evaluated on both the *quality* and *quantity* of their enforcement activities.

In addition, it should also be remembered that enforcement activities must serve a well-defined purpose. As a result, the *selective* nature of a security officer's enforcement efforts must be evaluated as well.

To aid in this undertaking, the following outlined material on security enforcement activities is offered.

I. Possible purposes of security enforcement (the molding or modifying of behavior)
   A. To punish the violator
      1. To identify those persons who have violated policy or the law
      2. To gather sufficient evidence to support successful administrative handling or prosecution
      3. To present objectively such evidence in such a way that the violator will be found guilty
   B. To create a deterrent effect upon those who might consider violating policy or law at a later date
      1. By seeing officers engaged in businesslike contacts with employees, visitors, or others
      2. By gaining and deserving the reputation of firm, fair, impartial, consistent enforcers of organizational policy or the law
      3. By appropriate use of oral and written warnings
   C. Briefly, the purpose of enforcement is to cause those people who use the protected facilities to realize that: (1) there are rules of approved safe conduct that are reasonable and in the organizational and/or public interest and that must be complied with, (2) deviations from designated patterns of behavior that are dangerous, and (3) getting caught in such misbehavior will bring about consistent enforcement action
      1. Security enforcement strives for compliance rather than obedience.
      2. It endeavors to get people to do the right thing because it is the right thing to do rather than from fear.
II. What is meant by *quality* security enforcement activity
   A. That which accomplishes the desired results most effectively with the least effort and for the longest period of time

B. Selectivity of enforcement (putting the water at the base of the fire)
    1. Definition of selective enforcement—enforcement proportional
        to loss conditions or locations with respect to place, time, and
        type of violation.
    2. Must be based upon knowledge derived from loss records of the
        facility
        a. Best information regarding loss experience comes from the
            work of the investigators
        b. Volume reports, submitted by officers, point up elements of
            time and place fairly well
        c. Information regarding causes and violations can best come
            from objective investigation.
    3. Manpower limitations make it impossible to give full attention
        to all violations at all locations at all times of the day, every day
        of the year
        a. Patrol strength is drained away by
            (1) Access control activities
            (2) Investigations
            (3) Parking control activities
            (4) Special assignments and details, and so forth
        b. Managerial pressure and/or employee demands do not al-
            ways permit the greatest efficiency of the department
        c. Not all administrators base enforcement programs on loss
            experience. Some base programs on whims, past experiences
            or prejudices
        d. Some tend to emphasize those violations that they personally
            feel more important than others
    4. Trends and patterns of loss experience tend to be quite similar
        in many organizations from the standpoint of time. Certain types
        of behavior occur almost universally, such as horseplay, drinking
        on the job, and theft. These factors, while important, are of
        small value in planning selective enforcement since the local
        experience must be pinpointed
C. About the degree to which the enforcement is to be proportional to
    the loss experience.
    1. Manpower can be spread out to parallel losses in reference to
        time—hours of day and days of week.
        a. Sometimes requires splitting up of activities—doing one
            activity until a certain time, stopping that activity long enough
            to give attention to specific types of loss behavior in a certain
            location for a certain length of time, and then returning to
            the first activity or taking up another
        b. Sometimes requires irregular work periods
        c. Sometimes requires unpopular and expensive split shifts

2. Manpower can be assigned to parallel loss experience in reference to locality—by specific assignment
3. It is more difficult to direct enforcement attention at those violations that have been associated with the loss experience of the particular locality at the time under consideration.
   a. Presence of security officers in area at time reduces violations
   b. Loss producing violations should not exclude other violations. For example, trash accumulation has been associated with losses in a given location. Officers should not limit their attention to only trash violations
   c. Contacts with any type of violator provide opportunity to
      (1) Influence that person to correct his or her behavior with respect to other loss producing violations as well as the violation for which he or she was contacted.
      (2) Suggest to other persons that the one contacted has committed the loss producing violation, that the security force are working on this type of violation, and that compliance is expected
4. It is virtually impossible to predict in advance the occurrence of a specific loss with pinpoint accuracy
5. Summary—the important factors in selective enforcement are, (1) the times and (2) places of the greatest number of losses and (3) the violations causing them. The objective is to be at these places at the times of occurrence and giving particular attention to those violations that are most prominent in causing the losses

D. Quality of security services
   1. Policy of enforceable and inspectional procedure must be reasonable, based upon factual foundation, consistent, impartial, and objective
   2. Employee contacts must be carried out so as to obtain desired effect
   3. Deviation from established policy regarding enforcement action must be well justified in policy itself
   4. Other factors influencing efficiency of security officers
      a. Management indifference in its many forms
      b. Supervisors neglecting to follow up on violators
      c. Lack of support and understanding by supervisory personnel or by management.
      d. Lack of support and understanding by managerial personnel
      e. Poor or ineffective policy or work rules
   5. Officer error, by reason of
      a. Lack of knowledge
      b. Lack of interest

      c. Poor supervision

      d. Improper presentation of findings

III. Quantity of enforcement

    A. Concept of an enforcement performance standard

        1. Enforcement performance standard—the number of violations discovered for hazardous violations per loss incident

           a. Violations discovered means personnel actions or prosecution action resulting in disciplinary action, a court finding of guilty and defendant being fined (adequately) or jailed, and/or restitution required

           b. Hazardous violations excludes those relating to theft, misappropriation, vandalism, and trespass as well as those actions that set up conditions that could cause major losses such as personal injury accidents, fires, or thefts by outside parties.

        2. Impact of security officers on loss experience may be determined by their proportional contribution to the established enforcement performance standard

    B. Concept of carryover effect of enforcement

        1. Strict attention to the enforcement of *all* security policy and procedures has a beneficial effect in preventing those violations that contribute to losses

        2. All security policy and procedures are important.

           a. To employees, supervisors, and management, lack of attention to the enforcement of certain policies they know and understand is an indication that the security department is not concerned about *all* traffic laws

           b. It is impossible to notify employer that less attention is to be given to certain offenses than to others since they can justifiably ask: "Who are the security officers to say which policies and procedures are important?"

           c. The level of understanding of the purposes of specific security policies (other than the fundamentals) is generally low.

    C. Kinds of enforcement action by the security officers

        1. Merely being seen has a strong deterrent effect

        2. Visiting and talking, not necessarily to violators, has the effect of impressing on potential violators the need for compliance with policy

        3. Oral warnings have some value, depending upon the nature of the offense, the locality, the person involved, the way in which the warning is issued, and any record kept of the warning.

        4. Written warnings have much greater value than oral, because (a) they can be forwarded to the violator's supervisor, (b) passing

employees know that the violator is getting a violation, (c) they indicate the kinds of violations that are noted in the area and time under consideration, and (d) they tend to have a more powerful and longer-lasting effect upon the violator.

   5. Taking into custody—used infrequently and pretty much reserved for serious offenses.
D. About quotas or productivity—
   1. In police or security parlance, the term "quota" refers to:
      a. A demand or instruction by the supervisor that the officer produce a certain volume of activity, warnings, or other units of enforcement, or
      b. A standard of volume of production set by the individual officer that he decides to meet each day or each month.
   2. *Quotas* in either of the above definitions are not good for the individual, organization, officer, supervisor, department, or security operation. It is virtually impossible to predict what violations will be on any given shift of any given day or of any particular month or year. It is likewise equally impossible to compute in advance the amount of enforcement activity that will be required to accomplish the desired goal.
   3. It is, however, possible to gather general ideas about the volume of certain violations in certain areas of the facility and to evaluate the work of the individual security officers concerned to determine if they are doing as much as can be done. It is thus possible, in general terms, to measure the effectiveness of a given quantity of enforcement action in correcting the conditions that have contributed to the loss picture.
E. About uniformity of enforcement action
   1. It is desirable that similar violations receive similar treatment regardless of the officer who sees them
   2. Such uniformity should exist within the department and among all facilities in all cities.

IN BRIEF:
EXAMPLE OF SPECIAL ADMINISTRATIVE
ORDER ON SELECTIVE ENFORCEMENT

TO: SUPERVISORY OFFICERS
FROM: DIRECTOR OF SECURITY
SUBJECT: *Improvement of Quality of Enforcement*

The Security Department has a primary objective to improve the quality of enforcement with respect to high risk conditions that promote losses.

To accomplish this end, immediate attention must be given to assure a continuing current evaluation by effective supervision of answers to the following questions:

1. Is a complete and continuing accurate analysis of known loss experiences being maintained?
2. Is this analysis being properly used to determine the high-risk violations involved in losses and the times and locations of these losses and to provide a sound basis for deployment of security personnel by time and location?
3. Are deployed personnel properly provided with complete written assignment instructions that contain information about:
    a. Predominant loss-involved violations being committed in the assigned area?
    b. High frequency loss locations in the assigned areas?
    c. The times when loss frequency is the highest on this assignment and day to day change, if any?
    d. Problems peculiar to the assignment such as heavy activity days, hours and places, Saturday and Sunday problems, seasonal or climatic hazards or problems, and so forth?
4. Are these written assignment or post instructions continually evaluated and the information contained therein maintained on a current basis?
5. Is the officer's activity properly evaluated as to:
    a. Quantity and quality in relation to the loss in the assigned area?
    b. Distribution of enforcement action throughout the tour of duty?
    c. Location with relation to the high loss-frequency locations of the area?

SECTION VII

Security Technology

With budgetary restrictions having an ever-increasing impact on both the quality and quantity of security equipment that can be purchased, systematic approaches to purchases can make major cost savings possible. Although there is no easy way to offer definitive information on specifically what types or brands of hardware are best suited for an individual situation, guidelines for decision making do exist, and they are presented in this section.

Advances and improvements in the high technology industry have brought improved equipment to security managers. However, far greater skill is also required in order to select that which is *best* to meet specific protection needs. This section, therefore, also provides basic technical information on alarm systems, electronic access control devices, and closed circuit television (CCTV).

Additionally, checklists to aid in selecting security hardware for individual environments and circumstances are also provided. These checklists include important questions that should be asked, and answered, prior to making final decisions on hardware that is routinely considered essential to security programs.

CHAPTER 28

Intrusion Alarm Systems

Not long ago, electronic security systems were of primary concern only to larger organizations or corporations. They were used almost exclusively to protect money, sensitive items, or highly confidential information, or, in special circumstances, to protect irreplaceable art objects, antiquities, or personal valuables. Yet, the use of electronic security systems has now become a realistic preoccupation for every business, large and small.

The commission of every crime depends on one factor—timing. Simply stated, the property to be taken must be readily accessible to the thief at the precise moment that the crime is to be committed. What happens during these very few seconds or minutes determines the success or failure of a criminal act. Also, psychiatrists who study the habits of prison populations are impressed by the amount of time spent learning the operational details of safes, locks, and burglary alarm systems. Regardless of the years a criminal spends behind bars, he or she dreams of becoming so skillful he or she will escape apprehension in the future. But just below the mask of bravado, there is a deep fear of being caught. Basically, the criminal fears surprise. Therefore, remember that no alarm system will prevent an actual intrusion, *but* the fear of its presence can psychologically discourage all but the most skilled criminals.

Alarm systems are intended only to signal the condition that their sensors were designed to detect, such as opened doors or windows, movement, or environmental changes. These conditions, then, cause the sensor to activate a circuit that, in turn, annunciates the system. However remember that alarm systems do *not* create their own remedial action; they require response from humans' hopefully sound judgment. These systems, being mechanical, are *not* infallible—none have yet been designed.

The selection of a proper alarm system is not a simple matter because the needs vary. Some factors that determine the requirements of an individual alarm system and the questions that must be answered when selecting a system include:

- The threat or risk—what is the system to protect against?
- The type of sensors needed—what will be protected?
- What methods are available to provide the level of protection needed?
- The method of alarm signal transmission—how is the signal to be sent and who will respond to it?

Most of the confusion regarding intrusion detection systems is a result of the variety of methods available to accomplish the proper protection needed. The combination of detection devices ranges into the thousands. An intrusion detection system may serve to deter a would-be intruder. However, the primary function of the alarm system is to signal the presence of an intruder. An intrusion detection system can be just a portion of the overall protection needed. Many large businesses supplement them with security guards and other security personnel. The successful operation of any type of an alarm system depends upon its proper installation and maintenance by the alarm installing company and the proper use of the system by the customer.

COMPONENTS OF ALARM SYSTEMS

Sensing devices are used in the actual detection of an intruder (see Figures 28–1 and 28–2). They each have a specific purpose and can be divided into three categories: perimeter protection, area/space protection, and object/spot protection.

Perimeter Protection*

Perimeter protection is the first line of defense in detecting an intruder. The most common points equipped with sensing devices for perimeter protection are doors, windows, vents, skylights, or any openings to a business or home. Since over 80 percent of all break-ins occur through these openings, most alarm systems provide this type of protection. The major advantage of perimeter protection is its simple design. The major disadvantage is that it protects only the openings. If the burglar bursts through a wall, comes through the ventilation system, or stays behind after closing, perimeter protection is useless.

The types of perimeter protection are:

1. *Door switches (contacts)*. These devices are usually magnet-operated switches. They are installed on a door or window in such a way that opening the door or window causes the magnet to move away from the contact switch that activates the alarm. They can be surface-mounted or recessed into the door and frame. A variety of types of switches are manufactured for all types of doors or windows.
2. *Metallic foil (window tape)*. This method is widely used to detect glass breakage in show windows, doors, and transoms. When the glass cracks and breaks the foil, it interrupts the low voltage electrical circuit and activates the alarm.

---

*From Lawrence J. Fennelly, *Handbook of Loss Prevention and Crime Prevention*, Stoneham, Mass.: Butterworth Publishers, 1982.

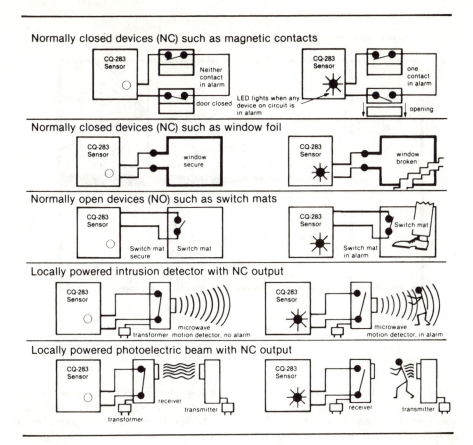

Figure 28–1 Typical application of the use of magnetic contacts, window foil, switch mats, motion detection, and photoelectric beam. (Courtesy of Aritech Corporation.)

3. *Glass break detectors (window bugs).* These detectors are shock-sensing devices that are attached to the glass and sense the breakage of the glass by shock or sound.

4. *Wooden screens.* These devices are made of wooden dowel sticks assembled in a cage-like fashion no more than four inches from each other. A very fine, brittle wire runs in the wooden dowels and frame. The burglar must break the doweling to gain entry and thus break the low voltage electrical circuit, causing the alarm. These devices are used primarily in commercial applications.

5. *Window screens.* These devices are similar to regular wire window screens in a home, except that a fine coated wire is a part of the screen and, when the burglar cuts the screen to gain entry, the flow of low voltage electricity

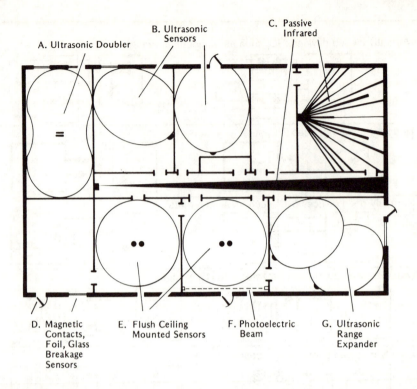

Figure 28–2   Sensors. A. *Ultrasonic doubler*. Back-to-back ultrasonic transceivers provide virtually double the coverage of single detectors at almost the same wiring and equipment cost. With more than 50 by 25 feet of coverage, the doubler is your best value in space protection. B. *Ultrasonic sensors*. Easy to install, no brackets needed. Mount it horizontally or vertically or in a corner, surface or flush, or with mounting feet on a shelf. Each UL listed sensor protects a three-dimensional volume up to 30 feet wide and high. C. *Passive infrared*. For those zones where the lower cost ultrasonic sensor is inappropriate, there is no need to buy a complete passive infrared system. Both ultrasonic and passive infrared can be used in the same system. D. *Magnetic contacts, foil, glass breakage sensors*. The building's perimeter protection detectors can be wired into the system via universal interface sensor. There is no need for running a separate perimeter loop. E. *Flush ceiling mounted sensors*. Only the two small two-inch diameter transducer caps are visible below the ceiling tiles. Designed for where minimum visibility is needed for aesthetic or security purposes. F. *Photoelectric beam*. The universal interface sensor allows the connection of any NO or NC alarm device into the system for zoned annunciation. It can be used with photoelectric beams, switch matting, microwave motion detectors, and many other intrusion detectors. G. *Ultrasonic range expander*. Adding an ultrasonic range expander can increase the coverage of an ultrasonic sensor by 50 to 90 percent, depending on where it is positioned and the surrounding environment. (Courtesy of Aritech Corporation.)

is interrupted and causes the alarm to sound. These devices are used primarily in residential applications.

6. *Lace and paneling.* The surfaces of door panels and safes are protected against entry by installing a close lace-like pattern of metallic foil or a fine brittle wire on the surface. Entry cannot be made without first breaking the foil or wire, thus activating the alarm. A panel of wood is placed over the lacing to protect it.

Area/Space Protection

These devices protect interior spaces in a business or home. They protect against intrusion whether or not the perimeter protection was violated. It is particularly effective for the stay-behind intruder or the burglar who cuts through the roof or bursts a block wall. Space protection devices are only a part of the complete alarm system, not the whole thing. Space protection should always be supplemented with perimeter protection. The major advantage of space protection devices is that they provide a highly sensitive, invisible means of detection. The major disadvantage is that improper application and installation by the alarm company can result in frequent false alarms (see Figure 28–3).

The types of area/space protection are:

1. *Photoelectric eyes (beams).* These devices transmit a beam across a protected area. When an intruder interrupts the beam, the beam circuit is disrupted and the alarm is initiated. Photoelectric devices use a pulsed infrared beam that is invisible to the naked eye. Some units have a range over 1,000 feet and can be used outdoors.

2. *Ultrasonic detectors.* Movement of an intruder in a protected area disrupts a high-pitched sound (ultrasonic) wave pattern that, in turn, activates the alarm signal. Ultrasonic motion sensors generate signals in the range between 19 and 40 kilohertz, which is above the frequencies that the average human can hear. Ultrasonic energy is contained completely in the area in which it is operating. It will not penetrate walls or windows but is absorbed by carpet, draperies, and acoustical tile. Obstructions within a room will reflect the ultrasonic energy and distort its shape pattern. Typical detection range of ultrasonic units is 20 feet wide by 30 feet long in a room with a ceiling up to 12 feet high. More complex ultrasonic systems can detect movement anywhere within the protected area. Ultrasonic devices can be mounted either on the ceiling or on the wall. Ultrasonic detectors can be prone to false alarms due to excessive air currents and other extraneous ultrasonic noises. Proper application and installation of this equipment is very important.

3. *Microwave detectors.* These detectors use high frequency radio waves (microwaves) to detect movement. The most commonly used frequencies are

Environmental and other Factors Affecting Sensor Usage	(Encircle one)	Effect on Sensor Ultrasonics	Microwave	Passive I/R	Recommendations and Notes
1. If the area to be protected is enclosed by thin walls, or contains windows, will there be movement close by the outside of this area?	Yes No	None	Major	None	Avoid using a microwave sensor unless it can be aimed way from thin walls, glass, etc., which can pass an amount of microwave energy.
2. Will protection pattern see sun, moving headlamps, or other sources of infrared energy passing through windows?	Yes No	None	None	Major	Avoid using a passive I/R sensor unless pattern can be positioned to avoid rapidly changing levels of infrared energy.
3. Does area to be protected contain HVAC ducts?	Yes No	None	Moderate	None	Ducts can channel microwave energy to other areas. If using a microwave sensor, aim it away from duct openings.
4. Will two or more sensors of the same type be used to protect a common area?	Yes No	None	None, (See Note)	None	Note: Adjacent units must operate on different frequencies.
5. Does area to be protected contain fluorescent or neon lights that will be on during Protection-On period?	Yes No	None	Major	None	Microwave sensor, if used, must be aimed away from any fluorescent or neon light within 20'.
6. Are incandescent lamps, that are cycled on-and-off during protection-on period, included in the protection pattern?	Yes No	None	None	Major	If considering use of passive I/R sensor, make a trial installation and, if necessary, redirect protection pattern away from incandescent lamps.

Environmental and other Factors Affecting Sensor Usage	(Encircle one)	Effect on Sensor Ultrasonics	Microwave	Passive I/R	Recommendations and Notes
7. Must protection pattern be projected from a ceiling?	Yes No	None, but only for ceiling heights up to 15'	Major	Major	Only ultrasonic sensors can be used on a ceiling, but height is limited to 15'. At greater ceiling heights, either (1) use rigid ceiling brackets to suspend sensor so as to maintain 15' limitation, or (2) in large open areas try using a microwave sensor mounted high on a wall and aimed downward.
8. Is the overall structure of flimsy construction (corrugated metal, thin plywood, etc.)?	Yes No	Minor	Major	Minor	Do not use a microwave sensor! Where considerable structural movement can be expected, use a rigid mounting surface for ultrasonic or passive infrared sensor.
9. Will protection pattern include large metal objects or wall surfaces?	Yes No	Minor	Major	Minor (major if metal is highly polished).	1. Use ultrasonic sensor. 2. Use passive I/R sensor.
10. Are there any nearby radar installations?	Yes No	Minor	Major when radar is close & sensor is aimed at it.	Minor	Avoid using a microwave sensor.

Figure 28–3 Motion sensor survey checklist

Environmental and other Factors Affecting Sensor Usage	(Encircle one)	Effect on Sensor			Recommendations and Notes
		Ultrasonics	Microwave	Passive I/R	
11. Will protection pattern include heaters, radiators, air conditioners, etc.?	Yes No	Moderate	None	Major, when rapid changes in air temperature are involved.	1. Use ultrasonic sensor, but aim it away from sources of air turbulence. (Desirable to have heaters, etc., turned off during Protection-On period). 2. Use microwave sensor.
12. Will area to be protected be subjected to ultrasonic noise (bells, hissing sounds, etc.)?	Yes No	Moderate, can cause problems in severe cases	None	None	1. Try muffling noise source and use an ultrasonic sensor. 2. Use a microwave sensor 3. Use passive infrared sensor.
13. Will protection pattern include drapes, carpets, racks of clothing, etc.?	Yes No	Moderate, reduction in range.	None	Minor	1. Use ultrasonic sensor if some reduction in range can be tolerated. 2. Use a microwave sensor.
14. Is the area to be protected subject to changes in temperature and humidity?	Yes No	Moderate	None	Major	1. Use an ultrasonic sensor unless changes in temperature and humidity are severe. 2. Use a microwave sensor.
15. Is there water noise from faulty valves in the area to be protected?	Yes No	Moderate, can be a problem.	None	None	1. If noise is substantial, try correcting faulty valves and use an ultrasonic sensor. 2. Use a microwave sensor. 3. Use a passive I/R sensor.
16. Will protection pattern see moving machinery, fan blades, etc.?	Yes No	Major	Major	Minor	1. Have machinery, fans, etc. turned off during Protection-On period. 2. Use careful placement of ultrasonic sensor. 3. Use passive infrared sensor.

Environmental and other Factors Affecting Sensor Usage	(Encircle one)	Effect on Sensor			Recommendations and Notes
		Ultrasonics	Microwave	Passive I/R	
17. Will drafts or other types of air movement pass through protection pattern?	Yes No	Major	None	None, unless rapid temperature changes are involved.	1. If protection pattern can be aimed away from air movement, or if air movement can be stopped during Protection-On period, use an ultrasonic sensor. 2. Use a microwave sensor. 3. Use a passive I/R sensor.
18. Will protection pattern see overhead doors that can be rattled by wind?	Yes No	Major	Major	Minor	1. If protection pattern can be aimed away from such doors, use an ultrasonic sensor. 2. Use a passive I/R sensor.
19. Are there hanging signs, calendar pages, etc. which can be moved by air currents during Protection-On period?	Yes No	Major	Major	Moderate, can be a problem.	1. Use ultrasonic sensor, but aim pattern away from objects that can move or remove such objects. 2. Use passive infrared sensor.
20. Are there adjacent railroad tracks that will be used during Protection-On period?	Yes No	Major	Minor	Minor	A trial installation is required if using an ultrasonic sensor.
21. Can small animals (or birds) enter protection pattern?	Yes No	Major	Major	Major (particularly rodents)	Install a physical barrier to prevent intrusion by animals or birds.
22. Does area to be protected contain a corrosive atmosphere?	Yes No	Major	Major	Major	None of these sensors can be used.
Approximate ADT cost per square foot of coverage:	—	(3¢)	(4¢)	(6¢)	—

Figure 28–3 (continued)

between 915 and 10.525 megahertz. The microwave energy will penetrate and pass through all building construction material (wood, sheet rock, cinder block, plastic, glass, and brick) and is reflected by metal. Because microwave energy will penetrate, application and installation is very critical. Microwave has a much greater range than ultrasonic and can be used outdoors.

4. *Infrared detectors.* These detectors are passive sensors because they do not transmit a signal for an intruder to disturb. Rather, a source of moving infrared radiation (the intruder) is detected against the normal radiation/temperature environment of the room. They sense the radiation from a human body moving through the optical field of view of the detector.

5. *Pressure mats.* These mats are basically mechanical switches. Pressure mats are most frequently used as a backup system to perimeter protection. When used as *traps,* they can be hidden under the carpet in front of a likely target or in hallways where an intruder would travel.

6. *Sound sensors.* Sound sensors detect intrusion by picking up on the noise created by the burglar during an attempt to break into a protected area. These sensors consist of a microphone and an electronic amplifier/processor. When the sound level increases beyond the limit normally encountered, the unit signals an alarm. Some units have a pulse-counting and time-interval feature. Other types have the capacity for actually listening to the protected premises from a central monitoring station.

Object/Spot Detection

Object/spot detection is used to detect the action or presence of an intruder at a single location. It provides direct security for *things.* Such a detection method is the final stage of an indepth system for protection. The objects that are most frequently protected include: safes, filing cabinets, desks, art objects, models, statues, and expensive equipment.

1. *Capacitance/proximity detectors.* The object being protected becomes an antenna, electronically linked to the alarm control. When an intruder approaches or touches the object-antenna, an electrostatic field is unbalanced and the alarm is initiated. Only metal objects can be protected in this manner.

2. *Vibration detectors.* These devices utilize a highly sensitive and specialized microphone called an electronic vibration detector (EVD). The EVD is attached directly to the object to be protected. It can be adjusted to detect a sledge hammer attack on a concrete wall or a delicate penetration of a glass surface. It will sound the alarm only when the object is moved, whereas a capacitance device will detect when the intruder is close to the protected object. Other types of vibration detectors are similar to tilt switches used in pinball machines.

ALARM CONTROLS

All sensing devices are wired into the alarm control panel that receives their signals and processes them. Some of the most severe burglary losses are caused, not by a failure in equipment, but simply by someone turning off the alarm system. The type of control panel needed is dependent upon the sophistication of the overall intrusion alarm system. Some control panels provide zoning capabilities for separate annunciation of the sensing devices. They may also provide the low voltage electrical power for the sensing devices.

Included in the control panel is backup or standby power in the event of an electrical power failure. Batteries are used for standby power. Some equipment uses rechargeable batteries, whereby the control has a low-power charging unit—a trickle charger—and maintains the batteries in a fully-charged condition.

The alarm control unit will normally incorporate a key-operated switch to turn the system on or off. Some control panels will accept a remote on-off switch so that the system can be turned on and off at more than one location.

If the alarm control panel is connected to a central monitor station, the times that the system is turned on and off are recorded and logged. When the owner enters the building in the morning, the alarm is activated. If this happens at a time that has been prearranged with the central station, it is considered a normal opening. If it happens at any other time, the police are dispatched.

It is possible for the owner or other authorized persons to enter the building during the closed times. The person entering must first call the central station and identify himself or herself by a special coding procedure. Records are kept at the central station company for these irregular openings and closings.

Tamper protection is a feature that can be incorporated into alarm systems that provides an alarm signal to be generated when there is an attempt to compromise the system in any way. Tamper protection can be designed into any or all portions of the alarm system (control panel, sensing devices, loop wiring, or alarm transmission facilities.)

ALARM TRANSMISSION/SIGNALLING

The type of alarm transmission/signalling system used in a particular application depends upon the location of the business or residence, the frequency of police patrols, and the ability of the customer to afford the cost. Remember that, after deterrence, the purpose of an alarm is to summon the proper authorities to stop a crime during the act of commission or to lead to the apprehension of the intruder. It is very important that the response by proper authorities to the alarm comes in the shortest possible time. There are four types of alarm signalling systems in general use:

1. *Local alarm* is one where a bell or light indicates that an attempted or successful intrusion has taken place. The success of the system relies on

someone hearing or seeing the signal and calling the responsible authorities. The local alarm also serves to notify the burglar that he has been detected. This may be advantageous in frightening off the less-experienced intruder.

2. With a *central station system* the alarm signal is transmitted over telephone lines to a specially-constructed building, called the *central station*. Here, trained operators are on duty 24 hours a day to supervise, record, and maintain alarms. Upon receipt of an alarm, the police are dispatched, and, in some cases, the alarm company guard or runner. This recordkeeping function and guard-response assure thorough documentation of any alarm signal. Alarm transmissions to the central station are of six types. Each type of transmission has certain advantages and disadvantages which must be considered in determining the risk. The transmission of an alarm signal to the UL-listed central station is generally regarded as the most reliable method for reducing burglary losses.

    a. *Direct wire systems.* High-risk locations (banks, jewelers, furriers) are generally protected with a direct wire system. A single dedicated telephone line is run from the protected premises to the central station or police station where a separate receiver supervises only that alarm. A fixed DC current is sent from the central station to the protected premises and is read on a meter at the central station. The advantage of a direct wire system is that problems can be very quickly traced to a specific alarm system. This makes compromising the alarm signal by a professional burglar more difficult.

        The disadvantage of such a system is the high cost of leased telephone lines. This becomes a more serious economic factor as the distance from the central station to the protected premises increases. Proper transmission of the alarm signal to the central station is essential. Problems can result on these telephone lines from shorts and broken wires. Most central stations expect these problems and are well equipped to rapidly make repairs. However, some of today's burglars are more sophisticated. They know they can prevent the transmission of the alarm signal to the central station by shunting or jumpering out the leased telephone line. Special methods are used by the alarm company to protect against jumpering of the alarm signal. Alarm systems having this special *line security* are classified as "AA Grade Central Station" alarms by Underwriters Laboratories.

    b. *Circuit (party line) systems.* Alarm signals transmitted over circuit transmission systems can be compared to a party line where several alarm customers defray the cost of the telephone line by sharing it. With a circuit transmission system, as many as 15 alarm transmitters may send alarm signals to a single receiving panel at the central station over the same line or *loop*. The alarm signals at the central station are received on strips of paper. Each alarm has a distinct code to identify it from the others. The advantage of a circuit-loop alarm transmission system is the lower telephone line cost. Thus, a central station can make its services available to more customers by subdividing the cost of the telephone line among different users. The disadvantage of circuit-loop alarm transmission systems is that problems on a leased telephone line are more difficult to locate than with a direct wire system.

c. *Multiplex systems*. This system is the newest method used by central station companies to receive alarm signals. The multiplex system is designed to reduce leased telephone line charges while at the same time providing a higher degree of line security than circuit-loop alarms. Multiplex systems have introduced data processing—computer based techniques—to the alarm industry.

d. *Digital communicators*. This type of alarm transmission equipment is a computer-based type that sends its signal through the regular switch line telephone network. The alarm signal transmitted is a series of coded electronic pulses that can only be received on a computer-type terminal at the central station.

The signals are then displayed visually and also provide a hard copy printout of the activity received. The receiving terminal can also provide additional data for the alarm operator.

e. *Telephone dialer*. The dialer delivers a prerecorded, verbal message to a central station, answering service, or police department when an alarm is activated. Many of the earlier tape dialers were a source of constant problems to police departments, because of their lack of sophistication. Basically, they were relabeled tape recorders. It was not uncommon for the tape dialer to play most of the message before the police could answer the phone. The police knew that an alarm signal had been sent, but did not know its location. The newer, modern tape dialers have solved these problems and are reasonably reliable.

f. *Radio signal transmission*. This method takes the alarm signal from the protected premises and sends it via radio signals to either a central station or police dispatch center. Additionally, the alarm signal can be received in a police patrol car.

APPLICATION GUIDELINES FOR EXTERIOR INTRUSION DETECTORS*

Many false alarms can be prevented by selecting the proper sensor for the application and by using good installation practices. Guides listed below should be considered in the intrusion detection system design along with the guides recommended in the manufacturer's installation manual for the specific equipment being installed.

---

*From Robert Barnard, *Intrusion Detection Systems*, Stoneham, Mass.: Butterworth Publishers, 1981.

Before listing guides for specific exterior detectors, some generation guidelines are listed that are applicable for all detectors. The guides are not listed in any order of priority.

---

1. *General*
   a. Check all equipment for shipping damage prior to installation.
   b. Check the equipment after installation for damage.
   c. Check that all electrical connections are secure.
   d. Mount detector transducers, especially active motion detector transducers, rigidly on vibration-free surfaces.
   e. Adjust detector sensitivity level for adequate detection in the worst case operating environment.
   f. Areas containing sources of electromagnetic energy (radio transmitters, radar, electrical switches, large motors, generators, and so forth) could cause severe operational problems.
   g. Avoid adjusting any detector sensitivity so high that it will be susceptible to false alarms.
   h. Detector enclosures should be tamper-protected and the tamper alarms monitored continuously.
   i. Detector processor units installed out of doors should be in weatherproof enclosures and the circuit boards should be conformal coated.
   j. All interconnecting cables should be installed in sealed conduit and, where applicable, buried in the ground.
   k. Exterior detection zone lengths should be limited to about 300 linear feet.
2. *Fence disturbance sensors*
   a. The fence fabric should be reasonably tight and the fence posts well anchored.
   b. All fence signs should be removed or secured so they will not rattle.
   c. Gates should be well secured so that they will not rattle.
   d. Bottom of fence fabric should be in close proximity to the ground or, better yet, anchored down.
   e. All brush and tree branches should be cut or removed so they will not rub against the fence.
3. *Microwave detectors*
   a. Ground should be level with no dips or obstructions between the transmitter and receiver.
   b. Zones of detection should be overlapped (approximately twice the distance from the transmitter to where the beam touches the ground.)
   c. Grass should be removed or maintained at a length of no greater than 4 inches between the transmitter and receiver.

    d. Snow should not accumulate more than about 4 inches.

    e. Detectors should be located far enough from the fence that the fence will not interfere with the microwave beam.

4. *Infrared detectors*

    a. Ground should be level with no dips or obstructions between the detector columns.

    b. Bottom beam should be no greater than 6 inches above the ground.

    c. Top infrared beam should be at least 4 feet above the ground.

    d. Zones of detection should be overlapped or top of detector columns protected with pressure switch.

5. *Electric-field detectors*

    a. When detector is installed on chain-link fences, the fence fabric should be reasonably tight.

    b. All vegetation must be removed from under the electric-field fence.

6. *Geophone sensors*

    a. Locate sensor to avoid objects anchored in ground that could move in the wind.

    b. Backfill dirt for geophone trench should be well tamped.

7. *Strain/magnetic line sensors*

    a. Locate sensor cable to avoid objects anchored in the ground.

    b. When crossing over or under power lines with the sensor line cannot be avoided, cross perpendicular to them.

    c. Avoid routing signal and power cables in the same trench with the transducer cable.

    d. Backfill dirt should be well compacted.

APPLICATION GUIDELINES FOR INTERIOR INTRUSION DETECTORS*

The intent of this summary is to present a list of basic guidelines that should be considered in the selection, design, installation, and operation of interior intrusion detectors.

---

1. *Ultrasonic motion detectors*

    a. Avoid using ultrasonic detectors in areas with large volumes of moving air caused by open windows, doors, vents, and so forth.

    b. Avoid directing the transceivers at large glass windows, nonrigid partitions, warehouse doors, and so forth that might vibrate and cause false alarms.

---

*From Robert Barnard, *Intrusion Detection Systems*, Stoneham, Mass.: Butterworth Publishers, 1981.

    c. Avoid directing transceivers directly at each other unless they are separated by an adequate distance to prevent interference (usually about 60 feet).

    d. Avoid locating individual receivers or transceivers close to air conditioning and heating registers.

    e. Position the transceivers and separate receivers at least 10 feet from telephone bells or any type of bell (unless otherwise indicated by the manufacturer.)

2. *Microwave motion detectors*

    a. Avoid locating detectors closer than 10 feet to bare fluorescent lamps, especially if the detector will be pointed toward the lamp, without first determining that the fluorescent lamps will not affect the detectors.

    b. Avoid directing the transmitted energy toward nonrigid metal partitions, thin metal walls, or large metal doors that might be vibrated by wind, passing trucks, airplanes, and so forth.

    c. Avoid directing the transmitted energy toward windows, wooden walls, or any wall that the energy can penetrate and perhaps detect outside movement.

    d. Avoid directing the transceivers toward rotating or moving machinery.

    e. After an installation is complete, check movement outside the protected area that might cause alarms. (Remember, cars and trucks are larger targets and can cause alarms at greater distances than can human movement.)

3. *Sonic motion detectors*

    a. Consider the fact that sonic detectors generate an audible high frequency tone that might be heard several hundred feet from the area being protected, depending on the building construction.

4. *Infrared motion detectors*

    a. Avoid directing the detectors toward heat sources that cycle on and off.

    b. Avoid directing the detectors toward burning incandescent lamps.

    c. Avoid mounting the detectors over heat sources such as radiators or hot pipe lines.

    d. Avoid directing the detectors toward windows where sunlight enters.

5. *Audible detectors*

    a. Avoid locating the receivers close to inside noise sources or near outside walls or doors where exterior noises could be a problem.

6. *Vibration detectors*

    a. Both structural and glass breakage detectors should be well secured to the surface where they are detecting penetrations.

    b. Structural vibration detectors should be connected to a pulse-accumulating supervisory circuit that can be adjusted for the specific application and not alarm on a single impact.

7. *Operable opening switches*
   a. Doors and windows should be well secured to prevent excessive motion that might cause false alarms.
8. *Photoelectric detectors*
   a. Mount transmitters and receivers along with any mirrors securely on vibration-free surfaces.
   b. Avoid using mirrors with detectors covering long ranges or ranges over 100 feet.
   c. Conceal transmitters and receivers to reduce compromise.
9. *Capacitance/proximity detectors*
   a. Avoid using wooden blocks to isolate the protected metal object from the ground plane.
   b. Reference ground plane should be well grounded to provide adequate electrical potential differential between the metal object and ground.
10. *Pressure mats*
    a. Conceal pressure mats to reduce compromise.

INTRUSION ALARM SYSTEM

The following checklist is used to assist in determining the type of intrusion detection equipment required in a facility. It is most often used in conjunction with the Alarm System Procurement Outline to insure that all protective requirements are detailed before they are summarized. This checklist further insures that all desired or necessary specifications for the alarm system are detailed and documented.

FACILITY SURVEY CHECKLIST FOR INTRUSION DETECTION ALARM SYSTEMS*

1. Facility
2. Location
3. Unit conducting survey
4. Individual's name (person preparing inquiry)
   a. Title
   b. Address
   c. Phone

---

*General Services Administration, Federal Protection Services, Washington, D.C., 1972.

5. Date of survey conducted
6. Purpose (State what you want to protect, classification of data, weapons, storage, and monetary or other intrinsic value.)
7. Name and general description of outdoor areas, buildings, indoor areas, and objects to be protected:
   a. Size of outdoor area
      1) Fencing type and height
      2) Patrol roads or footpaths (type)
      3) Security lighting (type and intensity)
      4) Describe terrain
      5) Environmental extremes (temperatures and climate and adjacent activities)
   b. Types of buildings
      1) Number of doors (List each type and its use, i.e., personnel, vehicle, overhead, emergency exit, and so forth; also list any special construction such as Dutch, glass, vault, roll-up, and so forth.)
      2) Number, type, and size of windows (List quantities of each size and type separately; also structural barriers over windows.)
      3) Number, type, and size of accessible openings other than windows and doors (List all openings greater than 96 square inches in areas that have a minimum dimension in excess of six inches, include all ducts, grills, panels, vents, and so forth that do not provide physical barriers equivalent to the walls, floors, and ceilings in which they are located.)
   c. Indoor areas: Dimensions, shapes and utilization of indoor areas to be provided with space or motion detection (Explain type of furnishings, height, and configuration of shelving or other storage.)
      1) Type of construction (wood, metal, or masonry)
      2) Temperature extremes and extreme air velocities
   d. Objects: Furnish size, shape, location, and composition of objects to be protected
8. Total number of areas or zones to be protected (number of separate circuits to be individually annunciated):
9. Type of system preferred:
   a. Local alarms
   b. Central station alarms
   c. Remote annunciator
10. Type of guard system to be supported:
   a. Fixed post sentries
   b. Foot sentry-roving
   c. Foot sentry-fixed patrol
   d. Sentry-dog team

    e. Motorized patrol
    f. One man patrols
    g. Buddy system
    h. Size of sabotage alert team
    i. Size of backup alert force

11. Surveillance interval (in minutes):
    a. One man surveillance interval
    b. Duress response interval (response time of second guard)
    c. Sabotage alert team response
    d. Backup alert team response

12. Travel distance (miles):
    a. Perimeter of patrolled area
    b. Motorized patrol tour
    c. Maximum foot tour
    d. Distance from sabotage alert station to furthest protected item (travel route)
    e. Distance from backup alert force station to the furthest protected item
    f. Distance between communication points (phones, radios or fixed sentry stations)

13. Communications available for guard use:
    a. Vehicle radio
    b. Personnel radio
    c. Guard telephone or net telephones
    d. Phone jacks
    e. Automatic ringdown
    f. Dial station
    g. Watchman call stations
    h. Tour clock stations
    i. Telephone circuits, aerial
    j. Telephone circuits, underground

14. Electrical power:
    a. Commercial
    b. Standby generator
    c. Emergency generator
    d. Emergency battery power
       1) Security lighting
          a) Perimeter
          b) Area
          c) Building
       2) Electrical service to buildings (list all areas, buildings, and objects to be protected where normal electrical service is *not* available)

15. Access controls: Will alarm system be required to provide:

a. Intrusion detection only?
b. Positive authorized ingress control?
c. Positive authorized egress control?
d. Protection against system compromise by personnel authorized access to area?

16. Protection reliability: Will alarm system be required to provide automatic alarm signals for the following conditions:
    a. Forced entry only?
    b. Unintentional improper operation or accidental damage?
    c. Disablement by operations personnel during authorized access?
    d. Complete fail-safe reliability against any/all above exposures?
    e. Other (explain)?

17. Performance tests: Will system performance be subject to tests and verification by:
    a. The system's internal fail-safe features only?
    b. Guard personnel on sentry duty?
    c. Guard supervisory personnel monitoring the alarm system annunciation?
    d. Operational personnel authorized access to protected items?
    e. Maintenance personnel responsible for the alarm system?

18. Alarm annunciation and supplementary signaling desired:
    a. Local audible (distance in feet)
    b. Local visual (visual distance)
    c. Central station audible and visual alarms (alarm signal only)
    d. Secure condition indicators
       1) Local
       2) Central station
       3) Remote station
    e. Authorized access (open) signals
       1) Local
       2) Central station
       3) Remote station
    f. Deactivated (unmanned) condition signals (not available for local alarm systems)
       1) Central station panel
       2) Remote station panel
    g. Hold-up signals
       1) Manual from protected areas to central station
       2) Manual from central station to response forces

19. Remote annunciation requirements: Will alarm system require one or more of the following:
    a. Local alarms automatically transmitted to guard office?
    b. Central station alarms automatically transmitted to remote annunciator for other alert force?
    c. Will remote alarm signals be:

        1)   Common alarm (single annunciator for all alarm systems of the protected area?)

        2)   Area alarm (one annunciator for each group of buildings or several circuits in one building?)

        3)   Zone alarm (individual remote annunciators for each zone or circuit at each protected premises?)

20.   Furnish any special considerations not covered by the foregoing questions:

ALARM SYSTEM PROCUREMENT OUTLINE

This outline provides the guidelines for determining the type of intrusion equipment desired for a facility, a format for determining the locations for each type of device, and an inventory sheet for preparing either bid specifications or placing equipment orders.

Figure 28–4 provides a summary sheet for listing all equipment to be used in the facility. The information required to complete this sheet is obtained from both this outline and the Facility Survey for Intrusion Detection Alarm System Outline.

Initially, it may well be useful to develop a graphic representation of where an alarm system is to be placed to insure that all portions of the facility are adequately protected. Therefore, Figure 28–5 is offered as an example of a typical floor plan of a location equipped with various alarm components and the zones each protects.

ALARM SYSTEM PROCUREMENT OUTLINE*

1.   Functional description of Intrusion Detection System requirements: (Explain general requirements of the system desired to include preparing a zone chart, establishing the precise number of zones required with types of equipment desired per zone, and diagraming actual location of each zone (see Figures 28–4 & 28–5.)

2.   Requirements of monitoring facilities:

    a.   Type of monitor panels

        1)   Class A (qty)

        2)   Class B (qty)

        3)   Class C (qty)

        4)   Emergency power indicator (qty)

---

*General Services Administration, Federal Protective Services, Washington, D.C., 1972

Zone Number	Location of Zone		Electro-Mechanical Systems												
	Building	Room	Foil			Protective Wiring					Magnetic Switch		Heat Detector	Hold Up Device	
			Window	Door	Wall	Window	Door	Wall	Vent	Other (Explain)	Simple	Balanced		Button	Foot Rail
1	214	Front doors										X			
2	214	Back doors										X			
3	214	Wading Dock										X			
4	214	109										X			
5	214	109													
6	214	112										X	X		
7	214	112													
8	214	111										X			

Zoning Chart For BUILDING 214, 1st Floor

Figure 28–4   Alarm system outline

Access/Secure Control	Photo Electric	Audio Detector	Vibration Detector	Door Grid	Window Grid	Duct Grid	Other (Explain)	Sonic/Ultrasonic	Micro-wave	Emergency Power Indicator	Class "A" Supervision	Class "B" Supervision	Class "C" Supervision	Remote Test	Security Telephone	Remarks
							Capacitance System		Motion Detection System			Monitor Cabinet				
X												X				
X												X				
X												X				Roll-up door
			X	X	X						X					Metal Clad door
									X	X	X					
			X			X					X					Vault door
								X		X	X					
X												X				Steel door

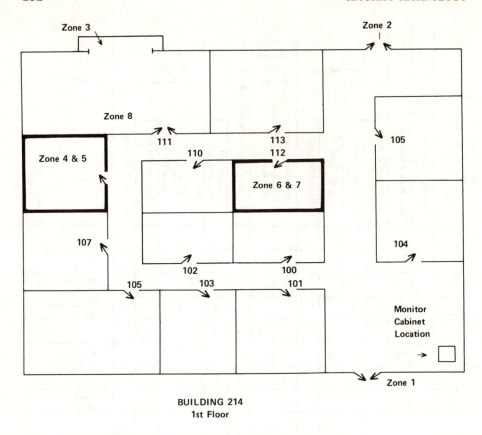

Zone 3

Zone 2

Zone 8

Zone 4 & 5

111

113   105

110

112

Zone 6 & 7

107

104

102

100

105   103   101

Monitor
Cabinet
Location

Zone 1

BUILDING 214
1st Floor

Figure 28–5   Typical drawing and zone chart

    b. Security telephone system
        Required (qty of instruments)
        Not required
    c. Event recorder
        1. Standard
        2. With Options
    d. Monitor cabinet (Combination of active and spare zones should
        be an even multiple of 10)
        1. Number of active zones
        2. Number of spare zones
    e. Description of any special requirements such as: remote panels,
        status maps, and so forth
3. Standby power requirements (check one)
    a. 12 hours (Standard)
    b. 24 hours

    c. 36 hours
    d. 48 hours
4. Remote test
    a. Required
    b. Not required
5. Conduit requirements (check appropriate items)
    a. None
    b. E.M.T.
    c. Rigid
    d. Location of Conduit (check one)
        1) Entire system
        2) Between control unit and monitor cabinet
6. Description of existing intrusion detection systems (if new system is to tie in with existing system):
7. Description of government furnished items:
    a. AC power: Furnished or not furnished?
        1) To nearest disconnect switch
        2) To locations as specified by contractor
    b. Signal lines: Furnished or not furnished
        1) Leased telephone lines
        2) Proprietary telephone lines
        3) Direct wire runs
    c. Government furnished equipment (describe).
8. Types of detectors required (check applicable items)
    a. Electro-mechanical devices
        1) Access/secure control unit
        2) Magnetic switch
            a) Simple
            b) Balanced
        3) Foil
        4) Protective Wiring
        5) Hold-Up Devices
            a) Push button
            b) Foot rail
        6) Heat detector
    b. Photo-electric system
    c. Vibration detection system
    d. Audio detection system
    e. Capacitance detection system
    f. Motion detection system
        1) Ultrasonic
        2) Microwave
        3) Other

CHAPTER 29

Automated/Electronic Access Control Systems

Automated access or electronic access control systems have been developed to enhance identification and control of movement in conforming with company policies. Access control must be tied to an adequate identification system to: (1) permit or deny entrance to a location, (2) protect the company from unauthorized observation or entry, (3) prevent injury or damage to persons or property, and (4) control rate of access to a location.

Automated systems can provide access control more cost effectively. Yet electronic control system must also be: (1) reliable, (2) easy to use, (3) resistant to counterfeiting, and (4) physically adequate.

Automated electronic access control systems include the following types of systems: (1) standard comparison devices, (2) magnetic readers, (3) dielectric readers, (4) embossing readers, (5) optical character readers, (6) Hollerith readers, (7) palm recognition, (8) fingerprint matching, and (9) *smart* cards. Fingerprint and palm recognition devices are biometric devices being perfected and used for high security access control applications.

In their simplest forms automated access control systems replace the personal identification of the guard with an electronic system for allowing access on a preprogrammed basis if a certain set of identifiers are presented to the system. Identifiers include identification cards, badges, and entering coded series of numbers through an electronic keyboard or some biometric characteristic of the individual. If the electronic system recognizes the characteristic being presented to it, it will allow the person to activate the locking mechanism and enter the protected area. Most electronic systems provide for the recording of each transaction that the system accomplishes. Many systems allow for access and egress activities to be controlled by time, location, and type of person. The recording of transaction information is done through microcomputers, minicomputers, mainframe computers, or by a simple numeric time sequence logging of this data.

It is essential that, whatever type of security application is required, the cost for providing it be considered in the development of the system. Each type of technology has specific costs associated with it and specific performance characteristics that can be expected.

294

ACQUISITION AND INSTALLATION OF
ELECTRONIC ACCESS CONTROL SYSTEMS

Properly developed, installed, and maintained electronic access control systems can measurably enhance the overall quality of virtually any security program. Not only can they contribute significantly toward a more secure and risk-free environment, but a good system can also appreciably reduce costs associated with general access control responsibilities otherwise taken on by security personnel.

However, such benefits will only be realized if the access control system utilized is, indeed, both (1) appropriate to the environment it is to protect and (2) implemented in a manner that facilitates and promotes maximum efficiency. In other words, if the system is too cumbersome, difficult, or inconvenient to use; too prone to mechanical problems; or too easy to compromise its effectiveness will diminish accordingly.

To minimize the likelihood of any of these problems occurring, a simple, straightforward approach to the purchase and installation of an electronic access control system should be followed.

1. Determine initially *why* there is reason to have an electronic access control system on the premises.
2. Through an appropriate audit, identify *what* specific security-related problems will be reduced or eliminated as a result of the installation of an electronic access control system.
3. Define, specifically, *how* you want the system to work. What do you want it to do for you?
4. Determine *how much* deterrent effect you want the system to have. Is it to be a high visibility system or simply incidental to other components of your security program?
5. Determine what *backup systems* are going to support the system. Locking devices? CCTV? Security personnel? Computer?
6. Determine how you want the system to actually control *traffic flow*.
7. Determine what *type(s) of accountability or documentation subsystem(s)* are needed to supplement the access control system.
8. Evaluate the access control system requirements that have been generated thus far and from them develop (or have developed) system specifications.
9. Submit those specifications for cost estimates.
10. Review cost estimates with *cost-benefit* in mind.
11. Select *reputable* equipment manufacturers, distributors, and installers with proven track records.

CHAPTER 30

Fire Suppression Systems

A **system**, by definition, is intended to be a *group of devices or several individual items joined together as an organized whole in order to serve a common purpose or to perform a common function*. Consequently, a single bucket filled with water and labeled "in case of fire" is *not* a system. However, a series of sprinkler heads linked together by water-filled, pressurized pipes would be one. Fire suppression systems, whether manual or automatic must, by design, be integrated, interrelated, and coordinated.

The National Fire Protection Association (NFPA) is the primary source for standards for fire suppression systems. Even though NFPA standards are advisory, they are, nonetheless, widely accepted by both government and insurance agencies alike. Yet, whether they have been fully adopted by those in your area or not, NFPA standards still provide a good yardstick by which to measure your systems.

The following commonly-used types of fire suppression systems are discussed in NFPA standards.

1. *Sprinkler systems*. These systems continue to have a commendable reputation for effectiveness. The simplest type of sprinkler system is a *wet-pipe*. These systems activate when the fusible link melts, allowing water to flow freely through the sprinkler head. These fusible links are rated by temperature—usually in increments from 150° to about 200°—and will melt at the rated temperature. When water begins flowing, a *clapper valve* in the water pipe actually activates the fire alarm. Thus, when a fire produces sufficient heat to melt the fusible link, the system activates, *then* the alarm will annunciate.

A *dry-pipe* sprinkler system does not have water in the system all of the time. Instead water is held back from the sprinkler piping by an air pressure valve. When the sprinkler fuses, air (rather than water) escapes and trips the valve, allowing water into the pipes and through the open sprinkler head(s). Since no water actually sits in dry-pipe sprinkler systems they are frequently utilized in areas where temperatures below freezing are common.

Deluge sprinkler systems have sprinkler head orifices open all of the time. These systems use a supplementary automatic detection system to actually initiate the flow of water. Most frequently, heat or smoke detectors are used to activate the deluge system's control valve.

Obviously, sprinkler systems can only be used to extinguish Class A fires.

2. *Foam suppression systems.* Foam systems have been in extensive use for many years, most notably in the petroleum industry for the suppression of flammable liquid fires. The two basic types of foam suppression systems employed most often are chemical and mechanical systems.

Chemical systems involve the mixing of powders—either aluminum sulphate or bicarbonate of soda—with liquid foaming agents. The catalyst reaction then produces bubbles containing carbon dioxide gas that separates combustible vapors from the oxygen needed for combustion.

Mechanical or air foam systems, on the other hand, mix a liquid foam concentrate with water and *mechanically expand* it with air bubbles.

Both types of foam systems work effectively on Class A and B fires.

3. *Dry chemical systems.* Most dry chemical systems are designed to handle flammable liquid and electrical fires. Since dry chemicals are nonconductive this type of system is often used for protecting oil-cooled electric transformers, electric motor equipment, and kitchen grease fires. However, such systems should *not* be used on any delicate or sensitive electronic equipment that could be affected by the corrosive residue left behind by dry chemicals. Dry chemical systems can be activated either manually or automatically by heat or smoke sensors. Once activated the dry chemical typically travels through either hoses or pipes, from storage tanks, to discharge over the fire.

4. *Carbon dioxide* (CO_2) *systems.* CO_2 is an odorless, inert, nontoxic, noncorrosive, and electrically nonconductive gas that suppresses fire by reducing the level of oxygen in the environment to the point where it will not support combustion. Consequently, CO_2 systems have been used quite effectively for over six decades for all kinds of commercial applications.

Carbon dioxide was used initially for extinguishing flammable liquid fires in confined areas where the CO_2 could effectively displace air. More recently its use has been expanded to include protection for special situations such as computer facilities, paint spray booths, or restaurant range/grill hoods. NFPA recognizes four types of CO_2 systems:

- Total flooding systems
- Local application systems
- Hand hose-line systems
- Standpipe systems with a remote storage supply

CO_2 systems work effectively on both Class B and C fires.

The only problem with CO_2 systems is that their discharge is extremely cold and very noisy.

5. *Halon 1301 systems.* Halon is a colorless, odorless, electrically nonconductive vapor that puts out fires differently than any other extinguishing

agent. Halon works chemically rather than physically to suppress fires. It is low in toxicity and, as a result, will not damage delicate electronic or computer hardware. Halon also leaves no corrosive residue to clean up. Additionally, Halon is effective on all three primary classes of fire.

Halon 1301 is actually a liquid when stored in tanks and only discharges as a vaporous gas. In this way it functions much like CO_2. However, Halon has been found to be two to three times as effective as CO_2. It is also widely accepted to be as effective as sodium-based dry chemical systems. Unfortunately, Halon is a good deal more expensive than any of the other fire suppression agents.

CLASS OF FIRE

Classes of fire are based on the types of extinguishers necessary to combat a specific fire (see also Figure 30–1). The three classes you are likely to encounter include:

A. Class A are fires in ordinary combustible materials such as wood, cloth, paper, rubber, and many plastics. Extinguishers suitable for this class of fire are identified by a triangle containing the letter "A". If they are colored, the triangle will be green.

B. Class B are fires in flammable liquids, gases, and greases. Extinguishers suitable for this class of fire are identified by a square containing the letter "B". If they are colored, the square will be red. *Do not use water to extinguish this class of fire.*

C. Class C are fires that involve energized electrical equipment. Extinguishers suitable for this class of fire are identified by a circle containing the letter "C". If they are colored, the circle will be blue. *Do not use water to extinguish this class of fire.*

KIND OF FIRE	APPROVED TYPE OF EXTINGUISHER							HOW TO OPERATE
DECIDE THE CLASS OF FIRE YOU ARE FIGHTING.... THEN CHECK THE COLUMNS TO THE RIGHT OF THAT CLASS	MATCH UP PROPER EXTINGUISHER WITH CLASS OF FIRE SHOWN AT LEFT							
	FOAM Solution of Aluminum Sulphate and Bicarbonate of Soda	CARBON DIOXIDE Carbon Dioxide Gas Under Pressure	SODA ACID Bicarbonate of Soda Solution and Sulphuric Acid	PUMP TANK Plain Water	GAS CARTRIDGE Water Expelled by Carbon Dioxide Gas	MULTI-PURPOSE DRY CHEMICAL	ORDINARY DRY CHEMICAL	
CLASS A FIRES USE THESE EXTINGUISHERS ORDINARY COMBUSTIBLES • WOOD • PAPER • CLOTH ETC.	B	✗	(yes)	(yes)	(yes)	B C	✗	FOAM Don't Play Stream into the Burning Liquid. Allow Foam to Fall Lightly on Fire
CLASS B FIRES USE THESE EXTINGUISHERS FLAMMABLE LIQUIDS, GREASE • GASOLINE • PAINTS • OILS, ETC.	B	B C	✗	✗	✗	B C	B C	CARBON DIOXIDE Direct Discharge as Close to Fire as Possible. First at Edge of Flames, and Gradually Forward and Upward
CLASS C FIRES USE THESE EXTINGUISHERS ELECTRICAL EQUIPMENT • MOTORS • SWITCHES ETC.	✗	B C	✗	✗	✗	B C	B C	SODA ACID Direct Stream at Base of Flame. PUMP TANK Place Foot on Footrest and Direct Stream at Base of Flames. DRY CHEMICAL Direct at the Base of the Flames. In the Case of Class A Fires, Follow Up by Directing the Dry Chemicals at Remaining Material That is Burning.

Figure 30–1 Types of fire and approved fire extinguisher

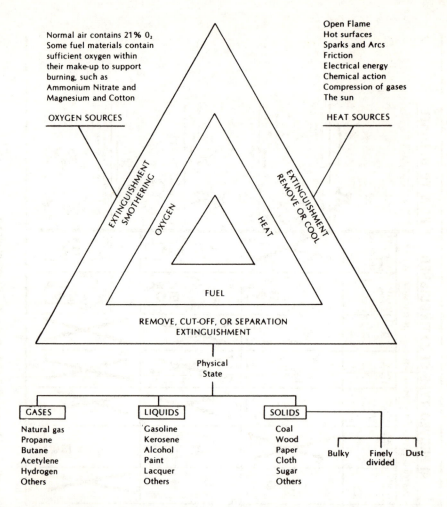

Figure 30–2 **Fire triangle. Most fires occur as the result of a chain of events. Recognizing this potential chain and breaking it is the key fire prevention concept.**

Pressurized Water Extinguisher — Class A
Discharge time: 60 seconds
Range: 30-40 feet
Size: 2 1/2 gal. water

Special features: Intermittent use. Pressure gauge will show the pressure remaining in the unit. It will be usable as long as pressure and water remain.

Dry Chemical Extinguisher — Class A, B & C or B & C
Discharge time: 10-25 seconds
Range: 5-20 feet
Size: 10-20 lbs.

Special features: Intermittent use. A pressure gauge will show how much pressure is left. Discharge is a fine powder which spreads immediately. Clean up with a dry vacuum and when only a light film remains, flush with water.

Carbon Dioxide (cO²) Extinguisher — Class B & C
Discharge time: 8-30 seconds
Range: 3-10 feet
Size: 5-100 lbs.

Special features: Intermittent use. Discharge is extremely cold and noisy. Do not touch metal portions of the discharge horn because of the extremely low temperature.

Halon 1211 Extinguisher — Class A, B & C
Discharge time:
Range:
Size: 2 1/2-20 lbs.

Special features: Intermittent use. Very good for computer rooms because it leaves no residue, is clean and non-conductive. As safe as CO_2 and 2-3 times as effective.

Figure 30–3   Hand-held fire extinguishers

CHAPTER 31

Closed Circuit Television (CCTV) Systems

Closed circuit television is utilized to monitor controlled areas, provide surveillance to large areas cost effectively, reduce the number of officers required for patrol, and provide a permanent record of access events or other security matters. Closed circuit television systems can vary in size from one that utilizes a single camera and a monitor to systems with hundreds of cameras that operate in low light, record transactions on video tape, and are activated by motion detection alarms built into the systems. Closed circuit television cameras are most often used for area surveillance in access/egress control points to provide positive identification of individuals.

The decision to utilize closed circuit television should be based on need, suitability of this type of technology, and cost and value to the security program. The closed circuit television system cannot be used as a total security system. It is merely one aspect of a program to enhance the use of guards, increase surveillance, or cost-effectively increase security coverage.

Current technology allows the television picture to be transmitted from remote locations across voice-grade telephone lines, normal coaxial cable, microwave and laser transmissions, or multiplexed applications.

System cost can vary dramatically with small single camera/single monitor systems costing less than $1,000. Low light cameras can range upwards of $5,000 for the camera alone, plus the environmental housing required to heat/cool cameras, provide protection against inclement weather, and provide protection against vandalism and theft. These cameras are being used with increasing frequency on an integrated basis with access control/intrusion detection and related facility control technology.

The planning for the use of closed circuit television should be in line with development of operating systems that mutually support effectiveness and can be effectively coordinated by security personnel.

Miniaturization and transistors have resulted in cameras that are small enough to conceal with lenses no larger than a pinhole, utilizing fiber-optic technology. They are used for specialized surveillance applications in elevators, in reception areas, or wherever it is undesirable to have a visible camera.

AREAS OF COVERAGE*

In planning a CCTV installation it is important to select the proper locations for camera placement in order to provide maximum coverage of the most sensitive areas. The areas to be covered are (1) those requiring continuous surveillance, (2) those multiple areas requiring close inspection but requiring too heavy a burden in terms of patrol activity and man-hours expended by employees or security officers, and (3) those requiring additional coverage, expanding the total protection of the premises both through the observation and deterrence value of CCTV.

Those areas most frequently selected for CCTV coverage include:

1. Interiors of highly sensitive areas such as file rooms or rooms containing vaults with classified materials
2. Loading docks (interior)
3. Shipping rooms
4. Stock and storage areas
5. Interior hallways terminating at doors leading to the outside
6. Cashier booths or rooms containing large amounts of cash or other valuables
7. Exterior perimeters and parking areas
8. Exterior views of loading areas, showing trucks and loading activity
9. Any other area considered sensitive enough for constant surveillance

HORIZONTAL RESOLUTION

After determining the location of the camera, the second most important factor to be considered is the degree of clarity or detail necessary for the camera to project. This factor is known as *resolution,* and in television cameras it is measured by the number of lines of *horizontal resolution.* The image on a television monitor is actually composed of hundreds of horizontal lines. The average home television receiver has a minimum of 380 horizontal resolution lines. Closed circuit television receivers also begin at that point, and increase from there: the more horizontal lines, the more detailed the picture. The better cameras will transmit more horizontal lines, and the better receivers are sensitive enough to receive those additional lines in order to preserve the clarity of the image. It should be emphasized that the more horizontal lines of resolution, the more expensive the television camera.

---

*From David Berger, *Security for Small Businesses,* Stoneham, Mass.: Butterworth Publishers, 1981.

LENSES

All cameras require a lens to focus the light from the scene being monitored. The camera transforms this light into an image and then converts it into an electrical signal. This signal is then transmitted to the picture tube of the monitor and reconverted to an image on the monitor's screen.

There are two features that should be considered when selecting a lens. The first is the speed of the lens. A very fast lens allows more light to enter the camera, thus allowing the camera to operate at lower light levels. The lens speed is indicated by the f-number. The smaller the f-number, the faster the lens.

The second important feature of the lens is the focal length. This is a measure of the viewing angle of the lens. Table 31–1 lists some of the standard focal lengths available and the corresponding field of view. The lower the focal length, the wider the field of view. A wide-angle lens provides excellent coverage for larger spaces such as storage areas and parking lots. When a small area is being monitored from a distance and a great deal of detail in the image is required, a narrow-angled telephoto lens would be most effective.

MOTION FEATURES

Other features available on CCTV cameras are those that effect the movement of the camera in order to select the direction, height, and specific area to be viewed.

Pan: The pan feature, by operation of a switch at the control monitor, will rotate the camera from right to left.

Tilt: The tilt feature, operated at the same control, raises or lowers the lens of the camera.

Table 31–1   How to choose the right lens: Relate focal length to field of view

Lens Focal Length, mm	*Subject Width When Subject Distance Is:*							
	5 ft.	*10 ft.*	*15 ft.*	*20 ft.*	*30 ft.*	*50 ft.*	*80 ft.*	*100 ft.*
12.5	5	10	15	20	30	50	80	100
25	2.5	5	7.5	10	15	25	40	50
50	1.25	2.5	3.75	5	7.5	12.5	20	25
75	0.83	1.67	2.5	3.33	5	8.33	13.33	16.7
100	0.62	1.25	1.87	2.5	3.75	6.25	10	12.5
150	0.42	0.83	1.25	1.67	2.5	4.17	6.67	8.3
300	0.21	0.42	0.62	0.83	1.25	2.08	3.33	4.2

Source: Cosmicar Lens Div., Pentax Corp.

Zoom: The zoom feature selectively brings distant images close, like a tele-photo lens, or reverses the operation for more distant wide angle image—maintaining a constant focus at all times.

All three features, used in conjunction with each other, can enable the camera to effectively scan a large area such as a parking lot.

TAMPER-PROOF HOUSING

Cameras, particularly those installed outdoors, should be fitted in tamper-proof housings, eliminating the possibility of the units' being intentionally put out of commission. The housings will also act as weatherproofing, providing additional protection for the camera against natural elements.

It is also recommended that the cameras be placed high—as additional protection against tampering, and, more importantly, because the added height provides a better visual angle for viewing a large area.

MONITORS

The appropriate size of the monitor actually depends upon how many monitors are planned for the console. There are two basic approaches to monitoring. The first is to use a single monitor (or possibly two) that automatically switches from one camera location to another. Such a system normally allows the officer to hold any one view if unusual activity has been detected during the sweep and to switch to and hold any camera location if an additional alarm indicates trouble in that particular area. When such a system is utilized, a larger screen, such as 19-inch or 24-inch, should be considered.

The second monitoring approach is to use one monitor for each camera. This system is generally preferable. When an individual monitor is used for each camera location, it is possible for the employee viewing the monitors to scan and study each individual image at his own choosing, based on the activity being projected. He can still be aware, through peripheral vision, of any movement on other screens or check other screens with a quick glance. The use of a single monitor on a rotating sequence could allow sufficient time between successive views from one camera for some important activity to be missed.

The use of one monitor for each camera does have its limitations. Tests have provided convincing evidence that no more than ten monitors can be scanned effectively by a single individual assigned to monitoring duty. When the one-camera, one-monitor system is used, it is probably better to use smaller screens, such as 9-inch ones, in order to avoid spreading the viewer's scanning range too far.

ONE CAMERA WITH MANY MONITORS

Video Monitors

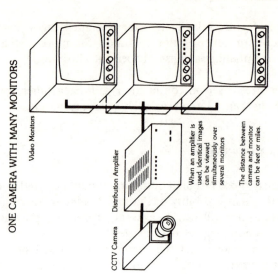

Distribution Amplifier

When an amplifier is used, identical images can be viewed simultaneously over several monitors

The distance between camera and monitor can be feet or miles.

CCTV Camera

ONE CAMERA WITH ONE MONITOR

Video Monitor

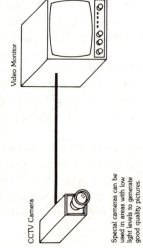

CCTV Camera

Special cameras can be used in areas with low light levels to generate good quality pictures.

MANY CAMERAS WITH ONE MONITOR

Video Monitor

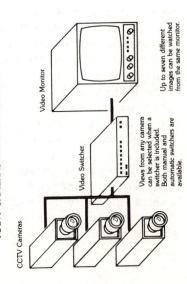

Video Switcher

CCTV Cameras

Views from any camera can be selected when a switcher is included. Both manual and automatic switchers are available.

Up to seven different images can be watched from the same monitor.

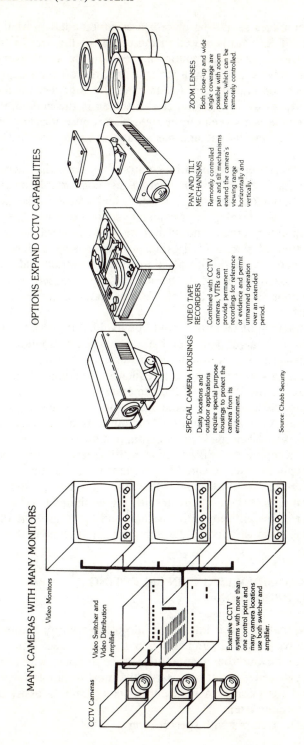

OPTIONS EXPAND CCTV CAPABILITIES

ZOOM LENSES
Both close-up and wide angle coverage are possible with zoom lenses, which can be remotely controlled.

PAN AND TILT MECHANISMS
Remotely controlled pan and tilt mechanisms extend the camera's viewing range horizontally and vertically.

VIDEO TAPE RECORDERS
Combined with CCTV cameras, VTRs can provide permanent recordings for reference or evidence and permit unmanned operation over an extended period.

SPECIAL CAMERA HOUSINGS
Dusty locations and outdoor applications require special purpose housings to protect the camera from its environment.

Source: Chubb Security

MANY CAMERAS WITH MANY MONITORS

Video Monitors

Video Switcher and Video Distribution Amplifier

Extensive CCTV systems with more than one control point and many camera locations use both switcher and amplifier.

CCTV Cameras

Figure 31-1 CCTV systems ranging from the simple to the complex. Systems can be expanded as needed for specific surveillance applications. (Courtesy of Chubb Security.)

1. The monitors should be placed in a curved configuration directly in front of an officer who is seated in the center of the arc. In this arrangement, the officer's eyes are continually equidistant from every screen. If the monitors were placed in a straight line, the officer would have to refocus his eyes continually from (as an example) four feet for the first screen on the left, to two feet for the closest screen in the middle, then back to four feet for the last screen on the right. Constant refocusing of the eyes causes headaches and fatigue and has an almost hypnotic effect after a period of time.
2. The officer's chair should be comfortable—one that swivels from right to left, rolls freely, allows his feet to rest comfortably on the ground, leans back on a moderate spring tension, and adjusts in height so that he can select an eye level of approximately six inches above the monitors.
3. The monitor screens should not be tilted upward, as this will catch the reflection of overhead lighting, superimposing a lighted image on the projected picture. Such reflections cause eyestrain and are disorienting.
4. A polarized filter should be placed over the screen to further reduce reflections of light. Most of the new monitors come equipped with this feature.
5. The stacking of monitors should be avoided if possible. Rather than stack monitors, it might be preferable to use a single monitor that switches from one camera location to another as discussed earlier.
6. Screens should be placed in a sequence providing a logical continuity with relation to the location of the cameras.
7. Officers assigned to console duty should be given additional tasks to perform, such as log entries, communications, emergency phone-call response for the purpose of calling municipal services, or dispatching patrol units. Keeping the officer active will increase his efficiency and eliminate the hypnotic effect created by constant staring at the screens.
8. Officers at this post should be rotated for two reasons: (1) to allow all personnel to become familiar with the equipment, which forms the nerve center of the entire security system, and (2) to give the officers a break in routine from what could develop into a monotonous task.

MAJOR CONSIDERATIONS IN SELECTING CCTV COMPONENTS

1. Insure that CCTV is integrated into other security features in the facility.
2. Is the system being purchased expandable to meet future needs?
3. Are you buying from a large, full-service company with service guarantees?
4. The low bidder is not necessarily the most desirable for your needs.
5. Consider retaining an independent consultant to assist in developing an appropriate system.
6. Get a written bid with specifications.

7. Insure that service agreements are available from the supplier or manufacturer.
8. Insure that you develop appropriate specifications that will support your efforts and are manageable by your security personnel.

SECTION VIII

Security Situations and Procedures

Even though every security program must be designed, implemented, and maintained to confront those unique and ever-changing problems that adversely affect individual organizations, there are also those that are likely to, in some manner, affect almost all. For example, such problems as employee theft, burglary and robbery prevention, disaster planning, and access control are generic in nature. Consequently, Section VIII presents these and other issues of importance in practical terms, offering, in addition, examples of procedures that can be adapted to fit specific business settings.

CHAPTER 32

Internal Theft

The complacency of management toward employee theft has been a long-standing problem in both business and industry. For whatever the reasons managers have largely ignored the dishonest habits of their employees. Yet now, as economic conditions in the business community worsen, programs to curtail this profit-reducing problem are surfacing with ever-increasing frequency. Unfortunately, however, many of these programs are haphazardly organized, ill-planned combinations of mismatched loss-reduction efforts and activities that may or may not produce the successful results sought.

Nonetheless, employee theft, even though it is a serious problem, is something that management can and should be able to counteract effectively. What is needed, first and foremost, in such a counter-offensive is a well-thought out plan of action designed specifically to deal with the employee theft problems that either currently affect or have a potential for affecting your organization in the future. Ideally, the logical place to begin organizing for such a theft-reduction program is with a security audit.

Yet, before beginning an audit effort, it is also important initially to obtain management's input regarding their perceptions on:

1. *Where* employees are stealing,
2. *What* is being stolen,
3. *Who* is doing the stealing,
4. *When* such thefts are occurring,
5. *Why* such thefts are occurring, and
6. *How* employees are committing the thefts.

A lack of management perception, in a good many cases, contributes significantly to both the number and extent of thefts committed by employees. Also, a lack of genuine interest in theft control and prevention on the part of management can impact on the volume and intensity of thefts by employees.

Therefore, a genuine interest in loss prevention must be considered of paramount importance in any loss-reduction program. Very simply, the attitudes and levels of honesty among employees are influenced, in good part, by the example set by management. Consequently, if management's support of security and its loss prevention efforts is perceived by employees as weak and superficial, its efforts to assist in these efforts are very likely to be similar. Therefore, management participation and support must be not only genuine but also visible and ongoing.

Also, it is important to evaluate just where the security function fits into the organization's system of priority programs and activities. Often management is reluctant to participate wholeheartedly in loss-reduction efforts because, traditionally, losses were merely treated as a cost of doing business. Historically, to recover the costs associated with such losses, many businesses would simply pass them on to the client or consumer in the form of higher prices. Unfortunately, this type of activity cannot continue.

The quickly escalating costs of doing business can no longer be recovered by regularly increasing costs. Such higher costs will only serve to affect already depressed profits, further reducing profit margins. Consequently, management has no option other than to develop programs that operate cost effectively to curtail theft levels.

The immediate question, therefore, is how to deter individuals from committing thefts—in this case, thefts committed by employees. The first step in this arduous task is to determine exactly why employees steal. Even though the reasons for employee theft are numerous and complex, nonetheless an understanding of employee behavior is essential when the company is attempting to develop a program to reduce employee thefts.

It is generally agreed that people's actions are often influenced by their situations and their dispositions. Here, "situation" means the environment in which employees find themselves. For example, working conditions may be inadequate, thus causing morale problems to surface among employees. Once morale begins to deteriorate, then increases in employee theft typically result.

"Disposition" includes those personality traits that act independently from situational circumstances. To compile a list of these traits that is exhaustive would require significant time and effort. However, personality traits that typically cause employees to resort to dishonesty and theft include:

- Fear
- Anger
- Dissatisfaction
- Hostility
- Greed
- Revenge
- Disillusionment
- Uncertainty

The cases of employee theft can also be attributed to external circumstances, such as inflation and the resulting decrease in an employee's purchasing power. Others steal to gain status among peers, and still others, simply on impulse because the opportunity presents itself. Yet, whatever the reason for the theft might be, what must be remembered is that employees will only steal when:

1. They have the opportunity to do so, and
2. They feel that they are able to steal without fear of detection or punishment.

The audit checklist presented later will identify a variety of locations and procedures that, when properly controlled, can have a very definite positive impact on the incidence of employee theft, by restricting *opportunity*.

For now, concentrate on the notion that the way in which employees perceive management sanctions against employees caught stealing will also appreciably affect the incidence of these thefts. If sanctions are not present, appear not to be present, or are imposed in a lax manner, thefts are most certainly going to mean a profit-reducing problem for management. In contrast, if sanctions imposed by management are both swift and fair, the number of thefts can be expected to decline. However, it should also be noted here that research indicates that employees who are young and not married are likely to be less susceptible to these management sanctions—including dismissal. Consequently, management cannot afford to depend too heavily on their enforcement program alone to appreciably curtail employee theft.

The ways in which employees rationalize their stealing are also important to consider when formulating a program to prevent losses attributable to the dishonest employee. Unfortunately, these rationalizations can often indicate to management that the problem is much larger than originally perceived. If, for example, employees are rationalizing thefts by saying:

- "They'll never miss it"
- "They owe it to me"
- "Everyone else is doing it"
- "I need it more than they do"
- "They have it coming to them"

they may well indicate that they do not fully understand management intentions or the organization's objectives. They may also indicate that employees feel that their wages and benefits are something less than what they consider adequate and, therefore, they feel justified in stealing in order to help them make up for what they are not getting legitimately from their employers.

The latter rationalization may well signal that employees feel that they are being treated unfairly, for example, in disciplinary actions or in compensation for overtime work. If this is occurring, personnel policies should be carefully evaluated to see if grievance procedures are (1) available to employees and (2) invoked fairly and appropriately. More importantly, it must be determined if employees look upon these procedures as a charade or facade or as fully supported and adhered to by management.

Still, the most important concern must be for control of theft by dishonest employees. Therefore, the following Employee Theft Checklists are offered in order to provide materials useful in preventing the theft of cash and merchandise. They can also assist in the development of internal control procedures, and the identification of preventive actions for reducing the risk of employee theft.

THE THEFT OF CASH AND MERCHANDISE

Cash is typically handled by sales personnel, cashiers, bookkeepers, and credit department personnel. Employee theft by these people can be discouraged by a management that is both alert and able to enforce a good system of rules.

Methods of Theft

The following is a listing of some of the principal methods of employee cash theft:

1. *Underring* the cash register. The clerk does not give the customer a sales receipt and pockets the money later.
2. Failing to ring up sales. The clerk leaves the register drawer open, puts money directly into the register without ringing up certain sales, and takes out the stolen money later.
3. Ringing up *no sale* on the register, voiding the sales check after the customer has left, and pocketing the money.
4. Overcharging customers so that cash overages can be stolen.
5. Taking cash from a *common drawer* register.
6. Cashing bad checks for accomplices.
7. Making false entries in the store's records and books to conceal theft.
8. Giving fraudulent refunds to accomplices or putting through fictitious refunds.
9. Stealing checks made payable to cash.
10. Pocketing unclaimed wages.
11. Paying a creditor's invoice twice and appropriating the second check.
12. Failing to record returned purchases and stealing an equal amount of cash.
13. Padding payrolls as to rates, time worked, or number of employees.
14. Forging checks and destroying them when they are returned by the bank.
15. Pocketing collections made on presumably uncollectible accounts.
16. Issuing checks on *returned* purchases not actually returned.

17. Raising the amount on checks, invoices, or vouchers after they have been officially approved.
18. Invoicing goods above the established prices and getting a kickback from the supplier.

Thefts of merchandise by employees may range from the simple pocketing of an item to larger-scale stealing concealed by intricate accounting manipulations. The problem becomes more difficult when there are weaknesses in stock control sytems.

Methods of Theft

The more frequent methods of merchandise theft are included in the following list:

1. Passing out merchandise over the counter to friends or accomplices.
2. Trading stolen merchandise with friends or accomplices employed in other departments.
3. Hiding merchandise on one's person, in a handbag, or in a parcel and taking it out of store at lunchtime, on relief breaks, or at the end of the day.
4. Hiding goods in stairways, public lockers, and corridors for later theft.
5. Taking unlisted packages from delivery trucks.
6. Stealing from warehouses with the cooperation of warehouse employees.
7. Stealing from stockrooms by putting goods on one's person or in packages.
8. Stealing from returned-goods rooms, layaway rooms, and similar places where goods are kept.
9. Making false entries to pad inventories so shortages will not be noticed.
10. Giving employee discounts to friends or accomplices.
11. Putting on jewelry, scarves, or jackets to model; then wearing them home and keeping them.
12. Shoplifting during lunch hour or relief periods.
13. Stealing special *property passes* to get stolen articles out of store.
14. Taking sales slips from training rooms or supply areas to put on stolen goods.
15. Stealing trading stamps.
16. Getting stolen goods through the mailroom by slapping on *customer's own* label normally used to ship out altered goods.
17. Putting *return to manufacturer* labels on goods and sending them instead to the employee's own address.
18. Picking up by a sales clerk of a receipt discarded by a customer and

putting it on stolen goods that the clerk then keeps or turns in for refund.
19. Intentionally soiling garments or damaging merchandise so the employee can buy them at reduced prices.
20. Printing one's own tickets for stolen goods by marking-room employees.
21. Clerks spurring sales with unauthorized markdowns, in order to get kickbacks from manufacturers.
22. Employees stamping their own mail with the store postage meter.
23. Shipping clerks sending out stolen goods to their own disguised post office boxes.
24. Smuggling out stolen goods in trash and refuse containers.

INTERNAL THEFT PREVENTION

In many businesses, one person or department is frequently given the combined responsibility for both collection and disbursement of funds. Moreover, in such businesses, management's time is so often taken up with nonsupervisory activities that they are unaware of the extent to which theft is taking place. Consequently, a plan that concentrates on reducing the incidence of such stealing must be implemented.

Preventive Actions to Take

Good internal control requires that work be divided so that there is little opportunity for inside theft without collusion. The following are suggestions specifically for such businesses.

1. All cash receipts should be deposited intact daily.
2. All disbursements should be by checks that are countersigned by the manager.
3. Each month the manager should personally reconcile the bank accounts.
4. During the first few days of each month, the manager should receive and open all incoming mail.
5. The manager should compare all cash receipts with the deposits shown on the bank statement.
6. Someone other than the bookkeeper should do all of the receiving and shipping of merchandise.
7. The mail should be opened by someone other than the cashier or cash receivable bookkeeper.

8. Cash registers should be locked so that employees cannot read the totals.
9. All refunds and sales checks should be numbered.
10. A control should be kept of all salesbooks and refund books.
11. Rigid control should be maintained on petty cash disbursements.

Honest employees will not be outraged by efforts to prevent thievery. Meanwhile, the small group of potentially dishonest employees will find it more difficult to steal if they are confronted with an effective system of control and detection.

Preventive Actions to Take

The following is a list of actions and policies suggested for curbing employee thefts:

1. Screen new employees carefully, insisting on references that can be checked.
2. See that supervisors set a good leadership example; alert them to the employee theft possibility.
3. Give special attention to employees who appear to have financial or other personal problems that might increase the temptation to be dishonest.
4. Set up retraining classes for employees who make numerous sales-check errors.
5. Check employees who arrive early or stay late when there is no need to do so. (When losses by theft appear very high, consider setting up after-hour plants. Use honest shopping, for example, *Wilmark*—for testing salespeople.)
6. Permit no employee to make sales to himself.
7. Require that all employee purchases be checked in the package room.
8. Restrict all employees to a single exit if possible.
9. Give each salesperson his or her own cash drawer, but permit no one to do final tally on his or her own cash register.
10. Use care in allowing employees free access to storerooms or other sensitive areas.
11. If confronted with a theft problem, do not completely eliminate the possibility that friends or relatives of management are involved. They, too, may have personal problems and resentments that will provoke them to dishonesty.
12. Beware of *theft contamination*. Dishonesty, once it gains a foothold in a business, can spread.

13. Have fixed policies about discipline for dishonesty. Failure to take decisive action or failure to be consistent can have an adverse effect on other employees.

14. Have a good system of controls, including an effective internal audit system.

15. Have a tight control of employee packages. Also check packages found on delivery platforms, loading docks, and similar locations to see if they have correct shipping labels.

16. Use tamper-proof packaging with all price tags inside the wrapping.

17. Have a sound refund system, and be sure it is being followed.

18. Keep valuable items locked up with the appropriate manager in possession of the keys. Also, keep all storerooms locked.

IN BRIEF

Employees typically steal from their employers using one of six different methods. In order to prevent losses from each of these six methods, the following preventive measures are suggested:

I. Employees will carry stolen items off company property.
   A. Personal items, including attaché cases, purses, boxes, and packages, should be inspected before employees are allowed to enter or leave company property.
   B. Employees should be required to enter and exit through specific *employee doors*.
   C. Employees typically should not be allowed to take personal items, such as coats, lunch boxes, or purses to the work area with them.
   D. Employees should not be allowed access to work areas before or after their scheduled work times.
   E. Only authorized employees should be permitted to remove trash from the premises.
   F. All vehicles entering or leaving company property should be subject to inspection.

II. Employees will engage in collusion with others and have them assist in pilfering company property.
   A. Separate sensitive functions and responsibilities.
   B. Require accountability of every employee.
   C. Restrict accessibility to valuable assets.
   D. Control interaction between employees and nonemployees such as vendors, service representatives, or delivery personnel.
   E. Inventory control is vital.

III. Employees will wear company property that they want to steal. For example, nurses will wear hospital-owned scrub suits, or retail clerks will wear clothing stolen from the store's sales racks.

    A. Do not allow employees to wear company-owned clothing off the premises.

    B. Retail employees should not be allowed to try on merchandise during their work hours.

    C. Company-owned clothing worn by employees on the job should be prominently stenciled, monogrammed, or in some other manner identified as such.

IV. Employees will mail or ship stolen items off the property to either themselves or confederates.

    A. Restrict the number of employees who are authorized to mail or ship merchandise.

    B. The shipping function should be part of an integrated system based on accountability and documentation.

    C. Two or more employees—or independent functions—should be involved in every *ship* order.

    D. UPS, parcel post, or U.S. mail personnel should be required to pick up all packages to be sent. Employees should *not* be allowed to carry merchandise to the shipper.

V. Employees will steal cash.

    A. Require that all employees who handle money be properly investigated to better ensure their level of honesty.

    B. Limit the number of employees who do handle money.

    C. Implement and enforce procedures based upon both accountability and proper documentation.

    D. Employees who request or receive company funds should not be the same as the ones who authorize or distribute those funds.

    E. Bank deposits should be made *at least* daily.

VI. Employees will write fraudulent documents.

    A. No single employee should be able to authorize and issue documents that can assist in the commission of theft.

    B. Regularly audit the company's entire paperwork process.

CHAPTER 33

External Theft

Companies can experience the consequences of external theft in a variety of different ways. However, three seem to be the most prevalent—causing the greatest losses.

1. Robbery
2. Burglary
3. Retail theft

For this reason, the material that follows discusses, in detail, these specific problem areas that continue to create significant concerns for today's security managers. In order to give added benefit, the majority of this material also concentrates on preventive strategies.

ROBBERY PREVENTION

Robberies often occur because management has made it easy and convenient for the robber by poor housekeeping, poor cash-handling methods, and/or a general lack of planning toward the possibility of robbery. While it is impossible to eliminate robberies completely, it is management's responsibility nonetheless, to deter the would-be robber as much as possible through good operational practices.

Preventive Actions

1. Keep the interior and front and rear entrances well lighted.
2. Keep advertising and merchandise out of the windows as much as possible. This will permit a clear view into the building.
3. Keep the rear and/or side doors locked at all times.
4. Maintain a record of decoy currency (bait money), by serial number and series, in the cash register.
5. Be sure alarms are working at all times.

6. As far as possible, do not open the place of business *before* or *after* regular business hours.
7. Call the police if a request is received to open the place of business after regular hours.
8. Keep cash exposure and cash on the premises at the lowest possible level.
9. Keep checks separate from cash when you are making a bank deposit.
10. When making bank deposits:
    a. Go directly to the bank;
    b. Conceal the money, if possible;
    c. Do not leave the deposits or withdrawals unattended in an automobile;
    d. Do not go to the bank alone;
    e. Vary time and routine of bank trips; and
    f. If possible, make deposits in daylight hours.
11. Do not keep large sums of money on the premises—bank all receipts as often as possible.
12. Do not keep large sums in the cash register or where it may be exposed to the view of others.
13. Beware of bell tapping—the procedure whereby one person distracts the attention of the cashier while an accomplice steals from the cash register.

The speed with which a robbery normally takes place makes it difficult for the businessman or his employees to give helpful information to the police. Consequently, be prepared for the possibility of a robbery by deciding in advance what is to be done and who is to do it.

Preventive Actions

1. Be alert for persons attempting to hide on the premises at closing time.
2. Instruct all employees in the use of the alarm system.
3. Call the police if a suspicious person is observed on or near the premises. If he or she is driving a car, get the license number.
4. Make plans in advance about who will take certain actions if a robbery occurs:
    a. Who calls the police;
    b. Who makes observations;
    c. Who protects the evidence at the scene;
    d. Who detains witnesses.
5. Some employees are gifted in the art of observation. These persons should be alerted to make observations during a holdup.
6. Practice identification with coworkers.
7. If possible, install height markers, e.g. black plastic tape, at varying heights on door frame to identify approximate height.
8. Discuss with employees what they might do if a robbery occurs.

The chance of apprehending a robber is considerably enhanced if victims are able to give accurate descriptions of the person or persons. Consequently, victims must be prepared to observe the robber, usually within a time period spanning a minute or less. By remaining calm during a robbery, the victim's power of observation will increase while the danger of injury will be minimized.

Preventive Actions

1. Observe the physical characteristics of the robber.
   a. Race, age, height;
   b. Facial characteristics, complexion, and hair;
   c. Clothing worn, head to foot;
   d. Physical carriage;
   e. Speech;
   f. Marks, scars, deformities;
   g. Robber's method of operation.
2. Look for accomplices.
3. Note method of escape.
4. Describe escape car, model, make, year, and license number.
5. Ascertain direction of travel.
6. Describe type of weapon used.
7. If more than one robber is involved, study the nearest one. Do not try to observe all in detail.
8. Comparison of the robber with someone the victim knows aids in recalling details.

Most robberies take place in approximately one minute. During that time, victims must do the robber's bidding and be observant enough to give the police useful information. To the average person, however, a robbery is a frightening experience. The robber is generally armed and should be considered capable of committing bodily harm.

Preventive Action

1. Take no action that would jeopardize personal safety.
2. If the robber displays a firearm, consider it to be loaded.
3. If possible, activate the silent alarm.
4. Attempt to alert other employees by use of prearranged signals.
5. Attempt to delay the robber if at all possible, but without sacrificing personal safety.
6. Try to maintain possession of the hold-up note if one is used.

AFTER-ROBBERY INSTRUCTIONS

These instructions provide guidelines for proper employee conduct after a holdup (robbery) to assist the police in making an arrest as well as protecting their own personal safety and that of customers.

General Instructions

1. Call local:
   a. Sheriff's office: Phone Number _____
   b. police: Phone Number _____
   Be prepared to give a brief but complete description of robbers and getaway car.
2. Close the facility.
3. Protect the area of the holdup, marking off exact spots where the bandits may have left prints. Do not touch any objects bandits may have left.
4. Call facility owner, _____, (or at home).
5. Obtain names and addresses of all witnesses in the area, or outside and ask them to fill out a description card.
6. Ask each employee to fill out a description card.
7. Make cash count to determine the amount of loss. This cash count must be made by two employees, one of which must be the manager.
8. The facility should not be kept closed any longer than necessary. Generally, a cash count should be completed and the permission of the law authorities obtained before reopening.
9. Public relations:
   a. All contacts should be routed through facility management.
   b. Do not make statements to the press or curious public.
   c. Do not allow press or public in work areas.
   d. Pictures of the quarters are permissible; however, pictures of employees should be discouraged.
   e. Do not give out estimates of the amount taken or information about how much was overlooked.

Proper Employee Conduct

With respect to proper employee conduct during and after a robbery, employees should be instructed:

1. To avoid actions that might increase danger to themselves or others;
2. To activate the robbery alarm system or the surveillance system during the robbery if it appears that such activation can be accomplished safely;

3. To observe the robber's physical features, voice, accent, mannerisms, dress, the kind of weapon he or she has, and any other characteristics that would be useful for identification purposes;

4. That if the robber leaves evidence (such as a note), to try to put it aside and out of sight, if it appears that this can be done safely; retain the evidence, do not handle it unnecessarily, and give it to the police when they arrive and refrain from touching, and assist in preventing others from touching articles or places the robber may have touched or evidence he may have left, in order that fingerprints of the robber may be obtained;

5. To give the robber no more money than the amount he demands and include *bait money* in the amount given.

6. That if it can be done safely, to observe the direction of the robber's escape and the description and license plate number of the vehicle used, if any;

7. To telephone the local police, if they have not arrived, or inform a manager or other employee who has this responsibility that a robbery has been committed.

8. That if the robber leaves before the police arrive, to assure that the manager or other employee waits outside the facility, if it is safe to do so, to inform the police when they arrive that the robber has left;

9. To attempt to determine the names and addresses of other persons who witnessed the robbery or the escape and request them to record their observations or to assist a designated officer or other employee in recording their observations; and

10. To refrain from discussing the details of the robbery with others before recording the observations respecting the robber's physical features and other characteristics as above described and the direction of escape and description of vehicle used, if any.

BURGLARY PREVENTION

Those concerned about security for their organization should know as much as possible about the alternatives available to them in burglary protection. Basically, they need to be prepared to make decisions relating to the following:

1. The kind of alarm system that is best suited for their kind of business. The cost of maintaining an alarm system must also be measured against the expected savings in insurance or the average loss from a typical burglary in his kind of business.

2. The adequacy of locks on entrances to the building is important also. This includes locks on windows, sidewalk entrances, roof openings, and doors. Too often, locks are not changed for long periods of time and the businessman may not actually know all who have keys to the building. It should also be a practice to change locks or tumblers on locks as often as it

becomes necessary to give adequate protection. Further, the types of locks should be such as to give maximum protection. Window locks should be given the same thorough inspection as door locks. Counseling with a competent locksmith often will eliminate many unforeseen problems.

3. The establishment of a routine for total protection, with assigned responsibility to others in the absence of management is also essential. There is no substitute for good housekeeping in burglary protection. Management should establish a fixed daily routine to assure that every precaution is being taken. This includes such measures as:
   a. Leaving the cash register or safe open at night;
   b. Turning on lights inside and outside the building before leaving;
   c. Checking to see that no one is hiding in the building at closing time;
   d. Doublechecking all doors and windows; and
   e. Checking to see that the alarm is turned on and is operating properly.

Essentially, management's function in burglary prevention is to increase the time needed to gain entry. What must be remembered is that the individual manager's effort is the most important part of prevention. By installing adequate lights, locks, alarms, and other devices, the physical security of any business will deter, at best, or delay, at least, the efforts of even the most determined burglar.

But no business is secure unless it is totally protected. The most intricate alarm system is of no use if it fails to cover even the smallest roof opening. The strongest door will do little good if the burglar can quickly enter an unlocked window. Anything short of total protection means inadequate protection.

Poor general housekeeping or lack of controls are invitations to burglary. Therefore, management should establish basic policies and operational routines to reduce the risk of burglary. They should also be simple enough that responsible, dependable employees should be able to carry out the functions in management's absence.

Preventive Actions

1. Keep a record of serial numbers of all merchandise and equipment.
2. Policy numbers and serial numbers of large denominations of bills should be recorded.
3. Before locking up each night, check to see that no one is hiding in the building.
4. Leave the cash register or safe open at night to prevent unnecessary damage.
5. All checks should be logged and marked "For Deposit in Account of ——" as soon as they are received.

The following Burglary Prevention Checklist provides information on all major aspects of burglary prevention including:

1. Lighting
2. Locks
3. Doors
4. Windows
5. Safes
6. Building exteriors
7. Alarm systems
8. What to do if a burglary occurs

The majority of burglaries occur at night, and, naturally, the criminal welcomes darkness to conceal his presence and his actions. Three out of four commercial burglaries are committed in buildings that have either no lights or inadequate lights. The would-be burglar can be discouraged and perhaps thwarted by adequate lighting inside and outside a building.

Preventive Actions

1. Place a night light over the safe or vault.
2. Alleys and the rear of the facility should be well lighted.
3. Illuminate all entry points well.
4. Keep night lights on inside the building.
5. Night lights should be wired so that the alarm is set to go if they go out.
6. Install inside lights in such a way that an intruder's silhouette can be seen from the street.

The easier the method of entry, the greater the chance of burglary. Locks that can be forced, duplicated, or easily opened increase the likelihood of burglary. Experienced would-be burglars can quickly size up the ease of entry by casual observation of locks on doors, storage, windows, and so forth. The burglar-proof lock has not yet been invented, but adequate locks are available and will deter even the most determined.

Preventive Actions

1. Modern, cylinder-type locks are preferable.
2. Proper installation should prevent prying, cutting, and twisting.
3. Lock bolts should be protected against being pushed back with a thin instrument.
4. Control of keys is important.

5. Hinge pins and hasps should be installed to prevent removal of pins and screws.
6. High-grade steel hasps will prevent prying, twisting, and cutting.
7. Padlocks should be locked in place at all times to prevent key duplication.
8. Lock bolts should be flush and point inward.

Most burglaries occur by forcing a natural opening in the building, such as a door or a window. Inadequate doors offer the burglar easy access to the premises. Doors too fragile for adequate protection, improper fit of doors into jambs, antiquated locking mechanisms—all these add to the problem. Strength and security can be had without sacrificing looks. Protection, however, should overweigh appearance.

Preventive Actions

1. Panels and glass should be protected against being kicked or knocked out.
2. Put bars on the inside of doors to prevent breaking the entire door.
3. Double doors should be flush-locked with a long bolt.
4. If the door has glass that can be broken, install a double-cylinder lock requiring key both inside and out.
5. Install sheet metal on the inside and outside of basement doors.
6. Install door frames that cannot be pried off hinges or removed.
7. The cylinder ring of lock should be recessed to discourage use of a lock puller.

Windows offer easy access to the building unless they are adequately protected. Display windows or large plate-glass windows are susceptible to hit-and-run tactics. Other windows, poorly protected, permit the burglar to enter the building, often undetected, particularly when the windows are poorly lighted. Windows should offer light, ventilation, and visibility, but *not* easy access.

Preventive Actions

1. Properly installed grates give maximum security.
2. Glass bricks are highly effective on windows not needed for ventilation.
3. Locks must be designed and located so they cannot be reached and opened by breaking the glass.
4. Heavy merchandise and equipment piled in front of unused windows will give some protection.
5. Cleaning windowsills periodically will help assure that fingerprints are left by a burglar.

6. Avoid, wherever possible, window displays or stored material that obstruct the view into the building.
7. Expensive or small items left visible overnight invite burglaries.

Given the alternative, the burglar prefers cash to other property. Yet, far too many businesses have safes that are inadequate for company needs, have not had combinations changed for years, or are easily opened or removed by a skilled burglar. Hiding the safe will serve only to give the burglar better working conditions. Money needs more protection than records.

Preventive Actions

1. The safe should be easily visible from the outside of the building.
2. Lightweight safes should be secured to the structure to prevent being carried away.
3. Cash should be kept at a minimum by frequent banking.
4. Never leave the written combination where it can be found.
5. When employees with the combination leave the firm, change the combination.
6. Keep a light burning over the safe at night.
7. Lock safe securely when leaving the premises by turning the dial several times in the same direction.

The enterprising burglar will take every advantage to gain entry into the building, especially if entry points are poorly protected. The alert manager needs to ask himself, "If I were determined to gain entry to this building, what are all the possible ways I could do it?" The outward appearance and security of the building will often determine whether or not it will be attacked. Every opening represents a hazard—inspect and correct wherever possible.

Preventive Actions

1. Fences should be strong, in good repair, and kept free of debris and boxes.
2. Weeds around the outside of the building or fence provide a good hiding place.
3. Ladders should be kept locked up.
4. Blind alleys afford protection for the burglar.
5. Sidewalk openings and their frames should be securely and properly locked.
6. Skylights and ventilators on the roof are easy access points unless they are protected.
7. Fire escapes and exits should be designed for quick exit but difficult entry.
8. Utility poles offer easy access to roofs.

Obviously, 24-hour vigilance by management is not practicable; consequently, they must rely on other means of detecting any real or attempted burglary. An adequate alarm system may give constant protection whether the management is on or off the premises.

Preventive Actions

1. All openings should be covered by alarms.
2. Periodic tests will insure that the alarm is in proper working order at all times.
3. Power sources should be hidden, protected, checked, and tested regularly.
4. Designate an employee who is to notify authorities if the alarm goes off.
5. Properly installed alarms can result in lower insurance premiums.
6. The type of alarms should be adequate to the needs of the facility.

Finally, in the event of an actual burglary, adhere to the following basic rules:

1. Do not disturb anything at the scene. The chances of apprehension are greatly increased if the scene is left completely intact.
2. Preserve all clues.
3. Call the police immediately.
4. Be prepared to assist the police in every way.
5. Be prepared to provide information about items missing.

BURGLARY PREVENTION CHECKLIST FOR BUSINESS PLACES*

Exterior

1. Are all of the points where a break-in might occur lighted by street lights, signs, or your own *burglar* lights?
2. Have you protected blind alleys where a burglar might work unobserved?
3. Are piles of stock, crates, or merchandise placed so as not to give burglars hiding places?
4. Are windows protected under loading docks or similar structures?
5. Have the weeds or trash adjoining your building been cleared away?
6. If a fence would help your protection, do you have one?

*From "Crimes Against Small Businesses," Small Business Administration.

7.   Is your fence high enough or protected with barbed wire?
8.   Is your fence in good repair?
9.   Is your fence fixed so that an intruder cannot crawl under it?
10. Are boxes, materials, and so forth, that might help a burglar over the fence placed a safe distance from the fence?
11. Are the gates solid and in good repair?
12. Are gates properly locked?
13. Are the gate hinges secure?
14. Have you eliminated unused gates?
15. Have you eliminated danger from poles or similar points *outside* the fence that would help a burglar over?
16. Have you protected solid brick or wood fences that a burglar could climb and then be shielded from view?
17. Do you check regularly to see that your gates are locked?
18. Do you regularly clean out trash or weeds on the outside of your fence where a burglar might be concealed?

Doors

19. Have you secured all unused doors?
20. Are door panels strong enough and securely fastened in place?
21. Is the glass in back doors and similar locations protected by wire or bars?
22. Are all of your doors designed so that the lock cannot be reached by breaking out glass or a lightweight panel?
23. Are the hinges so designed or located that the pins cannot be pulled?
24. Is the lock bolt so designed or protected that it cannot be pushed back with a thin instrument?
25. Is the lock so designed or the door frame built so that the door cannot be forced by spreading the frame?
26. Is the bolt protected or constructed so that it cannot be cut?
27. Is the lock firmly mounted so that it cannot be pried off?
28. Is the lock a cylinder type?
29. Do you remove valuable merchandise from unprotected display windows at night?
30. Have you considered the use of glass brick in place of some windows?

Other Openings

31. Do you have a lock on manholes that gives direct access to your building or to a door that a burglar could open easily?
32. Have you permanently closed manholes or similar openings that are no longer used?

33. Are your sidewalk doors or grates locked securely?
34. Are your sidewalk doors or grates securely in place so that the entire frame cannot be pried up?

Walls

35. Are your walls actually as solid as they look? Have you eliminated insecure openings in otherwise solid walls?
36. In checking walls, have you paid particular attention to points where a burglar can work unobserved?
37. Is your roof either secure or protected by an alarm system?
38. Have you eliminated weak points in your walls where entrance could be gained from an adjoining building?

Safes

39. Is your safe designed for burglary protection as well as fire protection?
40. Is your safe approved by the Underwriters Laboratories?
41. If your safe weighs less than 750 pounds, is it fastened securely to the floor, the wall, or set in concrete?
42. Is your safe located so the police can see it from outside?
43. Is your safe lighted at night?
44. If you have a vault, are the walls as well as the door, secure?

Alarms

45. Have you investigated the use of a burglar alarm system?
46. If you have a system, is it fully proved by the Underwriters Laboratories?
47. Was it properly installed by competent workmen?
48. Is your burglar alarm system tested regularly?
49. Does the system cover your hazardous points fully?
50. When your building was remodeled, was the burglar alarm system remodeled, too?

Security Officer

51. Did you investigate your security officer when you hired him/her?

RETAIL THEFT

The Shoplifting Problem

1. How big is the shoplifting problem and who does it?
   a. One out of 20 shoppers is probably a shoplifter (from nationwide surveys).
   b. The novice is the most frequent offender and takes items for personal use.
   c. The professional shoplifter is the most costly offender and takes high-value items for resale. Drug addicts very often fall into this category.
   d. The kleptomaniac has a psychological compulsion to steal and is very rare.
2. What items do shoplifters go for most?
   a. Cigarettes are taken more than anything else.
   b. Meat, health and beauty aids, and candy follow in that order.
3. When do shoplifters operate?
   a. During busy times when employees are occupied up front.
   b. When employee or management apathy to the problem is apparent.
   c. The days and times to be most watchful are Fridays between 3 PM and 6 PM, and Saturdays around noon. Sundays are also frequent since store personnel is at a minimum.
4. How do shoplifters operate?
   a. Concealment of items in clothing and purses.
   b. Changing containers, lids, or labels with lower priced merchandise.
   c. Transferring merchandise to bags carried in from other stores.
   d. False bottomed boxes (booster box), hooks inside coats, and so forth, are used by professionals.
5. How can a shoplifter be recognized?
   a. A shoplifter will usually pay more attention to the people in the store than the merchandise. (people shoppers)
   b. Bulky or unseasonal clothing to conceal items is a clue.
   c. Women shoplifters often carry their billfolds separately from the purse to avoid opening the purse at the checkstand.
   d. Loitering around high-value merchandise is an indicator.
   e. Open packages or large purses in the top of the shopping cart are used to conceal merchandise.
6. Wears a long outercoat and conceals articles between legs.
7. Walks to an unattended section, or one near a convenient exit, grabs merchandise and hastily departs from the store.
8. Two or more shoplifters may work together as a team. One or more occupy the attention of the clerks; the others, who appear to be just waiting, are actually shoplifting.

Combating the Shoplifter

The Problem

Even with the best policies and practices, some shoplifting is bound to occur in any store. However, there should be an effort to hold it to the minimum. The businessman must depend on his employees and on himself to detect shoplifting. All should be trained in alertness and effective detection.

Preventive Actions to Take

The following is a checklist of policies and practices to curb shoplifting:
1. Serve all customers as promptly as possible. Customers approached immediately will appreciate the service. Shoplifters will be served notice that this is not the time or place to attempt theft.
2. When a salesperson is busy with a customer and another customer enters the store or department, the salesperson should acknowledge his or her presence by saying something like, "I'll be with you in a moment."
3. The salesperson should never turn his or her back on the customer. This is an open invitation to shoplifting, if the customer is so inclined.
4. Keep an eye on people loitering or wandering in the store.
5. Never leave the store or department unattended. This offers a golden opportunity for theft.
6. If possible, give each customer a receipt for every purchase. This will help prevent shoplifters from obtaining cash refunds for stolen merchandise.
7. Develop a warning system so that all employees can be alerted when presence of shoplifters is suspected. In a small store, this might be a code word.
8. Also develop a procedure for employees to notify the office or some clerical location when they suspect thieves are present.
9. Lock up expensive merchandise that is attractive to shoplifters in a showcase displayed in a position where it can be viewed by more than one salesperson.
10. Do not stack merchandise so high on counters or in aisles that it blocks the view of salespeople.
11. Arrange merchandise so customers must pick it up. If it is not so arranged, a thief can push it off the counter into some type of container.
12. When merchandise is made up of pairs, display only one of the pair.
13. Whenever possible, attach merchandise in some way to make its removal difficult.
14. Keep counters and tables neat and orderly.
15. Place the telephone so that salespeople can view their sales area while using the telephone.

16. Return to stock any merchandise that was taken out for customer's inspection and not sold.
17. As a deterrent to shoplifting, keep service fast and efficient, especially when you are waiting on juveniles.
18. Keep each area clear of discarded saleschecks. Shoplifters may use them as apparent evidence of purchase.
19. To deter till tappers, establish definite cash register procedures: (a) Keep register open while it is actually being used to ring up a sale; (b) close the drawer before wrapping the merchandise; (c) do not allow any customer to distract the cashier.

Apprehension and Prosecution of Shoplifters

1. What should be done if a shoplifter is observed?
    a. First, notify the management. (A prearranged signal is helpful.)
    b. Keep him in sight at all times and know *what* has been taken and *where* it is concealed.
    c. Stop the shoplifter after he or she has passed the last place to pay and still has the goods in his or her possession. (at the *out* door is best)
    d. When you approach the suspect, say (for example) "There is a private matter we would like to discuss. Please come to the office with me."
    e. Question the suspect in private *with a witness present.* (A woman witness, if the suspect is female.)
    f. *Do not* say "steal," "shoplift," or similar words.
    g. *Do not* attempt to physically hold the subject and *do not* search. The police will do that.
    h. Get a written confession if you can, on the official form.
    i. Write down exactly what happened and attach it to the report.
    j. Call the police and make a complaint on all cases where the merchandise is valued at over $1.00, the suspect is uncooperative, does not sign the confession, or you expect trouble.
    k. Forward a report to Regional Security on all shoplift apprehensions.

IN BRIEF:

Prevention of Shoplifting

1. Shoplifting can be prevented through the vigilance, interest, and involvement of all store personnel.
2. What can a checker do to prevent shoplifting?
    a. Check the bottom of shopping cart.

    b. Handle magazines by the binding edge. This will cause concealed items to fall out.

    c. Beware of the customer who insists on holding packages in his or her arms. Be firm but gentle in asking that these packages be put with other purchases.

    d. Know what items are most often pilfered in your store and their prices.

    e. Ask price checks on items that you suspect of label switching.

    f. Be alert for customers that request a refund without a register tape.

    g. Notify the manager of all cases of *suspected* or known shoplifting.

3. How do department heads, stock clerks, and baggers aid in shoplifting prevention?

    a. Scan aisles as you work. Be alert for the customer that is observing people instead of merchandise.

    b. Offer assistance to the "people shoppers." It is extremely difficult to steal when an employee is attentive to shoppers' needs.

    c. Be alert for:

        (1) loiterers,

        (2) customers carrying open packages or large purses open or in the top of the shopping cart;

        (3) customers with heavy or bulky clothing during warm weather;

        (4) customers who keep returning to a particular aisle and apparently are not selecting items on each visit to that aisle;

        (5) notify the manager in all cases of *suspected* or known shoplifting.

FRAUDULENT CHECKS

It has often been said that fraudulent checkwriting is the safest crime the individual can engage in—all he or she has to carry is a loaded pen. It is also one of the most difficult to control.

Check cashing is a service provided by a wide range of businesses, but not necessarily associated with the purchase of merchandise. Checks are cashed as a convenience to customers, whether or not the person has made a purchase and whether or not he or she even intends to make a purchase. It is this service that has made fraudulent checks the widespread problem they are today. Laxity on the part of the businessman, combined with the desire to increase sales volume has been a principal cause of the problem.

As a matter of management, the businessman must make some very basic decisions about permitting the cashing of checks at his or her place of business:

1. *Whether checks will be cashed for more than the amount of purchase.* In certain kinds of stores, especially food stores, there is a tendency to permit

checks to be cashed for more than the amount of purchase. Knowing this, checkpassers make small purchases as a ruse to cash a check. There is no assurance, however, that exact payment will guarantee the check's genuineness. This is particularly true for items that can be easily disposed of at a price satisfactory to the *purchaser*. It must be remembered that several days may elapse before discovery that a bad check has been accepted. In the meantime, the person passing the check may have departed the area.

2. *The extent to which checks will be cashed as a service to the store's customers*. It is not uncommon for certain types of stores to cash checks for amounts totaling considerably more than the gross sales of the business. These will include payroll, pension, social security, welfare, and allotment checks. It is uncertain whether the increase in sales resulting from the check cashing service is sufficient to offset the losses experienced by accepting uncollectable checks.

3. *The kind of a procedure the business institutes to insure that the check is genuine and collectable*. Insistence on certain kinds of identification, care in examining the check for accuracy in all detail, and other pertinent factors are suggested to exercise all due caution in cases where the clerk is not personally acquainted with the person desiring to cash a check. If the clerk is not totally satisfied that the check is authentic, he or she should refuse to cash it. There is a common fear among many businesses that a stringent check cashing policy will serve to alienate the store's customers, causing a greater loss of business than that experienced through bad checks. No substantive data has as yet been advanced to prove this claim, however.

4. *Whether or not to use protective devices in cashing checks*. There are numerous devices available to the firm cashing checks, based on the principle of photographing the check and the person simultaneously. Firms that produce this equipment assert that the device has a strong deterrent effect on professional checkpassers. Thus, the cost of the equipment is more than offset by the reduction in number of fraudulent checks presented for payment. It is this deterrent quality, more than the possibility of apprehension, that gives the device its sales appeal.

5. *A decision on the action to take when an uncollectable check has been accepted*. Technically, uncollectable checks can be classified as due to (a) insufficient funds or (b) intent to defraud. The former category suggests a significantly different treatment than the latter. Yet, from the businessman's point of view, both represent a loss of revenue.

In the case of fraudulent checks, the businessman must decide the course of action to take and the extent to pursue it. This includes notifying the proper law enforcement agency, signing a complaint, and prosecuting the check passer if and when he or she is caught.

One of the common complaints among merchants is on the complications arising from bringing a check passer to trial: Testifying in court only to have the person acquitted, the case set aside or postponed, and causing undue delay and expense on the part of the merchant. In those areas, however, where a firm stand has been taken by the merchants and the courts, reduction in fraudulent check passing has been noticeable. Laws governing fraudulent checks and strict prosecution of offenders, however, will not arbitrarily reduce bad check losses unless the business that accepts checks establishes a firm policy and adheres to it.

For every careful merchant who refuses to accept a check because it is improperly written, contains abbreviated information, or lacks sufficient identification, many other merchants will cash the same check without hesitation.

Principal Causes of Losses

1. The lack of a check-cashing procedure
2. Failure to examine every check
3. Failure to record certain information on the check
4. Indiscriminate cashing of checks
5. Fear that a sale would be lost unless checks are cashed without undue complication.

Establishing a Check Cashing Procedure

The Problem

Most small businesses have no set policy for doing business by check. It is essential that the businessman establish a procedure that will give the greatest possible protection against bad checks and then hold to that policy without deviation.

Preventive Actions

1. Establish a firm policy regarding the cashing of checks for amounts over the cost of the merchandise (or service).
2. Assign the responsibility of cashing checks for amounts higher than the purchase only to certain employees.
3. Examine *every* check carefully.
4. *Require* a suitable amount of identification.
5. *Require* an address and telephone number of the *maker* and *endorser* of every check.
6. Record identification numbers on the check.
7. Assign the cashing of checks to new or young employees only when under the supervision of experienced employees.

Identification

The Problem

Most checks are cashed in situations where the passer is not personally known to the businessmen, who must rely on some form of proof presented that the passer is the legitimate owner of the check. Usually this decision must be reached quickly under hurried conditions and often by someone not skilled in detecting fraudulent checks. It is doubtful if foolproof identification exists anywhere in the world since all types now in use can be counterfeited.

Preventive Actions

1. Be sure to ask for identification.
2. Identification should be requested if the passer is not *personally* known.
3. The best types of identification now being used include:
   (a) Driver's license,
   (b) Military or government identification, or
   (c) Some airline and national credit cards.
4. Always require *at least one* type of physical description identification such as a driver's license.
5. Never accept social security cards, lodge cards, hunting and fishing licenses, employment records, or birth certificates alone.
6. Compare the physical description on the identification to the person presenting the check.
7. Compare the signature on the identification to that on the check.
8. Record the identification number somewhere on the check.
9. Require just as much identification with certified checks, cashier's checks, money orders, government checks, and state warrants as on personal checks.
10. Try not to give the impression of suspicion when asking for identification.
11. A good customer will not object to the need to ask for identification.
12. Be sure all identification used is current.
13. In the absence of a sufficient amount of good identification or none at all, do not cash the check.
14. Be cautious if the person presenting the check becomes angry when asked for identification.
15. If an out-of-state driver's license is used as identification, be sure to record the name of the state issuing the license.
16. Never cash a check for a stranger until positive identification is established. Insist on local references, then check them carefully.
17. Do not accept a combination of identification that is too readily offered.
18. Ask for identification that is not ordinarily carried, such as paid utility bills, a tax statement, or a statement from a retail store.

Examining the Check

The Problem

Most fraudulent checks are passed because the businessman does not take the time to examine the check thoroughly. Establishment of identification is not enough. Care must be taken to be sure the check is correct in *all* respects. Examine every check before it is cashed.

Preventive Actions

1. Examine the dateline.
   (a) The check must be dated.
   (b) The check must not be postdated.
   (c) Establish a policy regarding the cashing of checks over thirty days old.
2. Examine the payee line.
   (a) Be sure name of the payee and the endorsement can be read and that the endorsement is written exactly as appears on the front and includes address and telephone number.
   (b) Be sure payee/endorser identification establishes identity.
   (c) Do not accept checks with second endorsements from strangers (two-party checks).
3. Examine the digit and written amounts.
   (a) These amounts should correspond exactly.
   (b) Do not accept the check if either shows signs of alteration.
   (c) Do not accept the check if *any* part has been altered.
4. Examine the maker.
   (a) The maker's name should be legible and should include address and telephone number.
   (b) Beware of checks if any part of the maker's name extends past the space allotted.
   (c) If the maker's name cannot be read, ask that the check be written again.
   (d) Beware of titles preceding the maker's name. These are often meant to distract attention from the check, the passer, or the identification.
5. Examine the name of the bank section.
   (a) It should be imprinted on the check. If not, be sure the name of the bank and city of location are written out completely—not abbreviated.
   (b) Be sure the check is a bank check and not from a savings and loan association or some other kind of business.
6. Examine the endorsement.
   (a) The endorsement should be written exactly as it appears on the payee line on the front of the check.
   (b) The endorsement should be legible and include an address and telephone number.
   (c) If already endorsed, ask that the check be endorsed again in the receiver's presence.

Additional Precautionary Measures

The Problem

Losses in merchandising to bad check artists are a serious and costly problem. Carelessness causes most of them. The best way to keep bad check losses to a minimum is to follow sound and sensible practices and to always use caution and common sense whenever a check is accepted. The cashing of a check for a stranger should be treated in the same way an unsecured loan would be made. Take nothing for granted.

Preventive Actions

1. Beware of checks that have a company name stamped with a rubber stamp or typewritten.
2. Refuse to cash a check that has the word "hold" written anywhere on it.
3. Watch out for the "I'm an old customer" routine.
4. Do not be misled if the passer waves to someone, particularly if it is another employee.
5. Beware of the big name dropper.
6. It is not good business to cash a check for an intoxicated person.
7. If a check is cashed for a juvenile, be sure he or she, or the parents, are well known to the person cashing the check.
8. Never assume a check is good because it *looks* good.
9. Beware of personal checks bearing unusually low or high sequence numbers.
10. Beware of checks far in excess of the amount of purchase.
11. The person cashing the check should initial it so that it can later be identified in court if necessary.
12. Report all check law violators to the proper local law enforcement agency.
13. Follow through with prosecution on all check cases after a complaint has been signed.
14. The businessman should protect his or her own blank checks, cancelled checks, bank statements, and check protector from theft.
15. Review own canceled checks for unauthorized signatures or altered amounts.
16. Every businessman who cashes checks should be familiar with the state laws governing fraudulent checks.

CHAPTER 34

Computer Security

The computer has rapidly become one of the key elements in the management of a company. The computer and the entire data processing effort in an organization often represent its single largest expenditures in money, time, and effort. The systems and the information contained in them are often considered critical to the successful operations and profitability of the company.

For this reason the protection of a computer and its programs should be thought of as essential to insuring the company's investment. This investment is not only limited to the hardware of the system, the computer itself, and the peripheral equipment such as printers and data terminals, but also extends to the software developed for use with it and the actual information contained in the system. It is, therefore, essential that a security effort for data processing include methods for protection of the hardware and of all other facets of the system including the software, data files, database management systems documentation, and the personnel working with the information in the data center.

Threats to data are not only from fire, theft, earthquakes, weather, water leaks, bombings, riots, and so forth, but also include such things as electrical failures, hardware or software problems, operator error, and misuses of the system. They also include the compromising of data in the system, embezzlement, forgery, burglary, sabotage, extortion, and kidnapping. Unfortunately, any or all of these events can occur in any corporation at any time. Unfortunate, too, is the fact that sometimes more than one of these problems occur simultaneously.

Like any other aspect of a company's activities, the *criticality* of a system to company operations and its *vulnerability* to loss, damage or compromise are key factors in determining the extent and sophistication of the protection required.

With the growing complexity and diversity of data processing, greater attention to security planning, enforcement, and awareness is essential. Further, with lower costs for hardware, software, and communications networks, terminals and/or computer equipment are being located in all areas of a company. This computer equipment located in plants, warehouses, service centers, stores, and even in noncompany facilities affords many direct access to programs and databases, making good security even more necessary.

The previously identified systems for vulnerability assessment can, however, be easily applied to the computer data processing function. Controls required for protection of this particular company asset include:

1. Physical access control
2. Physical security
3. Environmental controls
4. Communications security
5. Operating controls over software
6. File access controls
7. File backup and recovery procedures
8. Off-site storage of data
9. Surveillance systems
10. Audit trails and record keeping
11. Disaster control

There are several methods for conducting a vulnerability assessment for data processing systems. They include the same elements as for any other aspect of the business but focused on the data processing problem. The identification of threats, an assessment of the impact of those threats, and an environmental assessment to determine what is the possibility of an incident actually occurring should be done initially. The effect and the severity of the effect of an incident upon operations should also be assessed. A vulnerability assessment of the impact on the business that is caused by an interruption of production or nonprovision of services, if any adverse events take place, likewise needs to be done.

Many of the firms that sell computer hardware and software systems provide no-cost or low-cost consulting services for the development of security systems and data recovery. When available, these should be reviewed for applicability to a company's needs, and even if an independent review is to be done by the computer firm, it should be utilized as a *second opinion* provided at minimum cost to the company. Likewise, many of these firms will provide samples of data processing programs or policies that might be tailored to meet a company's specific needs at no cost. These should also be explored and reviewed for appropriateness to your company's situation.

NEED FOR A POLICY

It is essential that a company develop effective policy for the development of Electronic Data Processing (EDP) or Automated Information Systems (AIS) security controls and procedures. Such policy must take into account the impact of data processing on the entire organization and of the loss of these services within the organization should an adverse event take place. Then a strategy must be developed and set forth for minimizing the exposure and effects of an incident should it occur.

The existing and growing complexity of the EDP and AIS communications/database environment commands increasing attention to its management in general. Included in this need for increased management attention is the addressing of security planning and controls. All activities must be pursued in such a manner that they are compatible with security objectives.

As developing technology is integrated into the computer environment, careful evaluation and planning is essential to insure maintenance of achieved levels of security.

Recent and future system development efforts involve the provision of direct access to data processing equipment, programs, and data files to a large population of noncomputer-involved employees. Therefore, an EDP or AIS security program must interface with the management and operation of *all* company functions that are users of computer services. Thus, the requirement exists for a broad-based exposure of security activities throughout a company and for a coordinated, flexible approach to computer security activities.

STATEMENT OF POLICY

It should be the policy of any EDP or AIS operation to address its security responsibilities through a structured, unified, integrated computer security program. The program should be structured through definition of tangible elements for which responsibility can be clearly established; it should be unified by common philosophy, objectives, and policies, and integrated with other activities of the computer operation and with activities making use of computer services.

The security program should be objective driven. All activities of the program should be evaluated on the basis of their ability to contribute to the achievement of its objectives. The objectives of the program should be to:

1. Minimize the probability of security incidents.
2. Limit the loss, damage, and/or injury if a security incident does occur.
3. Provide the capability to recover rapidly from any loss or damage resulting from a security incident.
4. Verify and improve the organization's ability to achieve the above objectives.

Having to meet the needs for greater audibility and control, as well as government regulations such as the Foreign Corrupt Practices Act, also serves to increase the need for effective policy on computer security. Such policy should set forth a control mechanism for the review, updating, and enforcement of security practices relative to EDP and AIS. It should establish a realistic, applicable, and consistent commitment to computer security. By doing so, the responsibility for ensuring that EDP and AIS security is effectively and efficiently accomplished will be more clearly defined.

EDP AND AIS SITE CLASSIFICATION POLICY

Given the wide variety and complexity of computer sites within the EDP and AIS community, it is imperative that a successful security program for each be classified. This will assist in proper planning, control, and resource allocation by exposure level.

The following classifications are recommended:

A. Major data center
B. Local data center
C. Remote job entry (RJE) facility
D. Application processor facility
E. Online terminal or time sharing terminal
F. Process control installations

Responsibility for compliance with this policy should rest jointly with the director of EDP or AIS and the manager responsible for security operations.

EDP AND AIS APPLICATIONS CLASSIFICATIONS

Currently one of the major problems is identifying the exposure level in the area of backup processing. This policy should require that all systems be classified at the development stage as to their criticality to the company. This will then support proper contingency planning, resource allocation, and backup processing considerations.

These classifications are recommended:

Classification	Definition
Vital:	Company existence depends on data or process.
Critical:	Loss of major revenue producing capability or cash flow mechanism (i.e., order processing, invoicing, collection.)
Essential:	Loss of functional capability not directly related to cash flow. Research and development, accounts payable, purchasing.
Deferrable:	Must be run eventually for record keeping.
Interruptible:	(for duration of outage)

Responsibility for ensuring compliance with this policy should be in the hands of the Director of EDP or AIS.

EDP AND AIS CONTINGENCY PLANS

It is essential that each data processing facility develop a contingency plan that revolves around its respective site classification and application classification policies. These policies should ensure that each facility has considered potential risks and developed and tested viable data processing alternatives. Specifically, these recommendations should be included in these policies:

A. Each site will have a documented contingency plan that is consistent with the need defined in the site and applications classification policies.
B. That the contingency plan will be reviewed and tested annually to ensure viability.
C. Copies will be maintained onsite and submitted for initial approval to the director of EDP or AIS and the manager responsible for security operations.
D. Reviewed and approved by top management.

APPLICATION OF POLICY

A computer security program should recognize that security is essentially a line management responsibility. While acknowledging the EDP or AIS obligation to provide support and coordination, the computer operation should not fully assume responsibility for noncomputer functional continuity, for protection of noncomputer functional information resources that may be in its guardianship, or for protection of data processing resources not under its direct control.

A computer security program must seek to maximize the use of line resources in addressing security and to minimize the involvement of security staff personnel while, at the same time, supporting line management through centralization of objective definition, policy setting, and development of standards.

Finally, a computer security program has to provide flexibility in the implementation of security activities in order to recognize differences in the value and scope of resources to be protected. It must develop an awareness of, and a sensitivity to, security issues through the provision of appropriate training programs. And, it should include the development and continued assessment of security plans and systems in order to ensure that data processing capabilities and information resources are protected to the extent that is commensurate with their value to the company.

AIS AND EDP SECURITY PROGRAM ELEMENTS

Philosophy: A definition of the environment in which the program exists, that is, the structural, responsibility, and operational aspects of the program. The philosophy of the program is embodied in the *Application of Policy* and the *Responsibility of Authority* sections of this policy.

Objectives: Criteria by which other elements and activities of
                               the program are evaluated for effectiveness.

Policies: Security-related policies should be published as part
                               of the company's *AIS and EDP Services Policy
                               Manual.*

Standards: Security standards are issued to document standard
                               practices and minimum acceptable levels of protec-
                               tion to be afforded by security activities. Therefore,
                               security standards should be published as part of
                               the company's policy manual.

Security Support System: A combination of controls and procedures designed
                               to achieve one or more of the objectives of the AIS
                               and EDP security program. The controls and pro-
                               cedures incorporated in a security support system
                               may be automated or manual and may be active or
                               passive in nature. Each security support system is
                               designed to address one specific area of security at
                               a given site.

Security Support Plans: Security-related plans that are necessary for the
                               effective management of the security program. In-
                               cluded are contingency plans, security project plans
                               and security capital expenditure plans.

The following material is offered as a sample version of appropriate policy and
procedures applicable to a computer security program. Although every computer operation should be considered unique unto itself, this material should,
nonetheless, provide ample food for thought.

I.   *Physical protection*
     A.   *Responsibilities.* The manager of the facility in which a computer
          data center will be installed should be responsible for advising on
          construction of the computer data center including environmental
          security support systems. The manager of the computer data center
          should also be responsible for proper maintenance of all security
          support systems.
     B.   *Standard practices*
          1.   *Location.* A computer data center should be located away from
               outside walls, clear of any piping and in areas of the building
               not subject to rising or falling water. If it is not possible to avoid
               locations containing such hazards, special precautions must be
               taken to protect the equipment.
          2.   *Construction.* A computer data center should be constructed in
               accordance with applicable building codes. Partition walls and
               ceilings should be constructed of fire retardant material. The

primary access to the machine room should be from an anteroom under environmental control rather than from a public corridor.

If the machine room floor is constructed of raised metal panels, the panels should form a NEMA-rated enclosure for electrical power cables and interconnection cables between computer system components.

Machine rooms containing raised floors should also include a ramp to provide a means of installing and removing equipment.

3. *Air Conditioning.* Air temperature, humidity, and flow for the enclosed area should be designed to conform with local codes for office environments for the basic room. To this load will be added the manufacturer's cooling/heat dissipation requirements for major components. In the event that a vendor's requirements for temperature, humidity or air flow are more stringent than the local codes, the vendor specifications should apply.

4. *Electrical service.* Electrical service should be provided from a central distribution panel dedicated to the computer room area. This panel should be located within the controlled access area. The incoming service, panel, and breakers should be sized and located to conform with national and local electrical codes and the hardware vendor's specifications.

5. *Telecommunications.* Telecommunications service should be provided by a dedicated cable direct from the building distribution frame. No service for any telephones or equipment, other than those in the machine room, should be connected to this cable.

In complex teleprocessing installations, a NEMA-rated metal enclosure should be provided to house the modems, interconnecting, and access equipment.

6. *Fire suppression.* The manager of a computer data center should be responsible for evaluating the need for permanent fire suppression equipment over and above local code requirements. However, acquisition of such equipment should be approved by the Director of Security.

In addition to any permanent suppression equipment, a data center should also have portable extinguishers of the proper size and type according to National Fire Protection Association (NFPA) guidelines.

7. *Fire and smoke detection.* Computer data centers should also be equipped with UL approved smoke detectors installed in sufficient numbers to provide proper coverage based on local codes or manufacturers' recommendation, or one for each room smaller than the minimum protection area.

If a system alarm system exists in the facility, the detection system must be connected to it. Fire detection and automatic suppression equipment must be interconnected as well.

8. *Water detection.* Any raised floor areas and any machine room areas at or below grade level must be equipped with UL approved water detectors.

9. *Housekeeping.* The equipment rooms should be cleaned on a regular basis in order to prevent the accumulation of dust and debris that could harm the equipment.

Further, any and all filters should be cleaned in accordance with the manufacturer's instructions. Waste materials must be discarded into fire safe containers that should be emptied daily. No more than a two-day supply of paper should be stored within the equipment room. Any paper that must be stored within the equipment room should be in metal cabinets.

II. *Access control*

A. *Responsibilities.* The manager responsible for the operation of a computer data center should also implement a security support system designed to control access to the computer room, data entry areas, offsite storage areas and supporting equipment areas. The security support system should include the necessary controls and procedures to achieve required minimum levels of protection and to implement the required standard practices described in this chapter.

B. *Standard practices*

1. *Required minimum levels of protection*

   a. A computer data center should be located and equipped so that entry of unauthorized persons can be detected during both operating and nonoperating hours.

   b. Access to a computer data center should be restricted to the following authorized personnel:

      1) Employees having job assignments within the computer data center.

      2) Employees having job assignments that require regular access to the computer data center.

      3) Nonemployees, such as vendor maintenance personnel and couriers, who require entry to the computer data center on a regular basis.

   c. Authorization for access should be effective only during those periods when a person legitimately requires access to the computer data center.

   d. Access to the computer data center by unauthorized persons should be approved on a visit-by-visit basis. Such access should be recorded on a visitor register and visitors should be escorted by an authorized person at all times while in the data center.

2. *Restricted area.* The computer data center (including computer room, data entry areas, offsite storage areas, and supporting equipment areas) should be designated as a *restricted area.*

3. *Access authorization procedure.* A formal procedure should be established for authorizing individuals to have access to the computer data center.
4. *Access authorization identification.* A method should also be devised that allows persons controlling access to know who has been authorized access and to positively identify individuals having such authorization.

C. *Guidelines*

1. *Construction.* The location and construction of a computer data center should be such that some degree of destructive force is necessary for unauthorized, undetected entry. Consequently, avoid locating the data center adjacent to building windows, and also avoid the use of glass in data center walls. Care should also be taken to ensure that the data center walls extend from the structural floor to the structural ceiling.

2. *Detection measures.* Measures that can be taken to detect intrusion into the data center *restricted areas* should typically include use of closed circuit television cameras, sonic devices, and/or scheduled checks by security officers.

3. *Restriction methods.* Access to the computer data center has to be restricted to authorized persons. Choice of a method should be based on cost and appropriateness to the local situation. Some possibilities are:
   a. Visual recognition of authorized persons by an employee controlling computer data center entrances.
   b. Assignment of special ID badges to authorized persons.
   c. Installation of door locks opened only by keys, cards, or combinations that are issued under control to authorized personnel.

III. *Program control*

A. *Responsibilities.* The manager responsible for the operation of a computer data center must implement a security support system designed to protect computer programs from destruction, unauthorized use, and unauthorized revision. All programs (purchased, leased, or developed) that are used or controlled by the computer data center must be protected.

B. *Standard practices*

1. *Required minimum levels of protection*
   a. A current executable copy of all production programs, including systems software, must be maintained at a location remote from the computer data center.
   b. Source programs in machine-readable form or current copies of program documentation must also be maintained at a location remote from the computer data center.
   c. Use (execution) of programs must be restricted to authorized

purposes (i.e., for company business, for production processing according to documentation, or for testing during
maintenance or modification).

2. *Documentation.* Program revisions must be documented according to predetermined and standard practices.

3. *Computer usage.* A record of all computer usage must be maintained for verification of authorized execution.

IV. *Information protection*

A. *Responsibilities.* The manager responsible for the operation of a
computer data center must develop and implement an information
security support system designed to protect all computer-readable
information processed in the center.

B. *Standard practices*

1. *Information to be protected*

a. *Computer input/output.* Computer-generated information that
resides on paper, carbon paper, microfilm, or other permanent visual media should be subject to special security
standards. This includes all system documentation, procedures, and forms used for the application.

b. *Systems operations.* Information regarding the operation of
systems in a computer data center *must* be restricted on a
need-to-know basis.

2. *Information classification.* All information processed or to be
processed in a computer data center must be reviewed to determine the applicability of information classifications defined by
security standards. This review will be performed in concert with
EDP or AIS support groups and the organizations owning the
information.

3. *Stored computer information.* All removable computer storage
media containing restricted information must be externally labeled with the appropriate classification. Therefore, physical
access controls must also be established to prevent removal of
the storage medium.

4. *Restricted information*

a. *Processing.* Restricted information must be processed on
employee-controlled computers unless a contractor providing the service signs a legal proprietary agreement.

b. *Transmission.* Transmission of restricted information must
be controlled to limit access only to authorized individuals.

c. *Destruction.* Controls must be implemented for monitoring
the destruction of restricted information to ensure compliance with predetermined policy.

d. *Access approval.* Nonemployees must be denied access to
all restricted information unless prior approval is obtained
from the owner of the information.

e. *Access records.* A record of accesses to restricted information must be maintained so that an audit trail can be reconstructed for the purpose of verifying authorized access.

6. *Strictly private information.* Information of this classification must be controlled according to requirements determined by the originator.

7. *Information sharing.* Sharing of information between systems controlled by different organizational units must be approved by the owner of the data.

8. *Access control.* Access codes used to restrict access to protected information must not be printed or displayed on a terminal. If appropriate access controls are not available in operating software, they must be incorporated into appropriate, written application programs.

9. *Security systems.* Obviously, computer data centers that have equipment or operating systems with security capabilities must utilize those features in their security support systems.

V. *Contingency planning*

A. *General information.* Interruption of computer processing operations can be caused by a variety of conditions that result in outages from a few hours to an extremely long period of time. Efficient recovery of the computer processing facility can only be accomplished by having established contingency plans. The degree of advanced preparedness has a significant impact on the efforts expended and on the cost, length of disruption, and security exposure incurred recovering from service disruptions. Consequently, standard operating procedures must be designed to respond to day-to-day minor operating problems as well as major disruptions and disasters.

B. *Standard practices*

1. *Responsibilities.* The manager responsible for the computer data center should be responsible for developing a contingency plan that details emergency measures in the event of a major disruption or disaster.

2. *Contingency plan contents.* The contingency plan should include:

a. *Emergency response plan.* This details steps to be taken to protect life and property and to minimize the impact of any emergency such as bomb threats, tornados, flooding, fire or explosion, civil disturbances, and/or strikes.
1) Emergency procedures
2) Emergency equipment
3) Facility layout
4) Responsibility and authority

b. *Administrative action plan.* This details steps to be taken in the event of a disaster. These plans should cover damage assessment, activation of disaster contingency plans (items c and d below), disaster organization structure, and a notification system.

1) Emergency notification procedure
   a) Notification contact list
   b) Order of contact regarding decisions
2) Damage assessment procedures
   a) Notify assessment team members from a predetermined contact list
   b) Specify place of assembly
   c) Assess site damage
3) Backups and recovery implementation decision criteria
   a) Discuss decision-making process
   b) Criteria to attempt normal recovery
   c) Criteria to implement backup/recovery plan
4) Responsibility and authority
   a) Decision-making authority
   b) Approval requirements
   c) Proposed action documentation

c. *Backup processing plan.* In the event of a disaster, this plan should provide for alternate processing capabilities for all affected EDP and AIS applications at service levels commensurate with their predesignated criticality classification.
   1) Application criticality—processing priorities
   2) Configuration requirements
   3) Relocation procedures and schedule
   4) Starting procedures and schedule
   5) Organizational responsibility and authority
   6) Manning requirements/assignments
   7) Application recovery instructions
   8) Backup data file inventory

d. *Recovery plan.* This provides for smooth and rapid restoration of an Automated Information System (AIS) database or EDP site following a disaster.
   1) Situation assessment
   2) Immediate protective/security measures
   3) Vendor contact list
   4) Recovery team members
   5) Organizational responsibility and authority
   6) Planning and implementation

e. Copies of routine preemergency procedures that are implemented in support of, and are necessary for the initiation of, the contingency plan.
   1) Offsite file backup protection
   2) Operating and program documentation

       f.   Information required to execute the contingency plan, such as contact names and phone numbers, location and inventory of backup supplies, and so forth.

C. *Classification of service disruptions*

    1. *Major disruption.* The disruption is classified as a major disruption when conditions exist that disrupt or disable critical demand processing but do not require physical recovery of equipment, media, and facilities.

    2. *Disaster.* The disruption is classified as a disaster when conditions exist that totally disable computer processing services and require physical recovery of equipment, media, and facilities. Conditions constituting a disaster include but are not limited to fire, bombing, civil disturbances, and natural disasters.

D. *Preparing a contingency plan*

    1. *General.* A plan should be of a general enough nature to allow the interface of detail plans during and after the occurrence of a disruption/disaster. It should specify actions to be taken, individuals or organizational functions responsible for those actions, and respective time relationships of the actions. Of major importance is the preidentification of the recovery teams that will relocate application production and of who will recover the data center facility. Remember that this contingency plan must also satisfy the current requirements of both the user and computer operations department.

    2. *Elements of the contingency plan for major disruptions.* The following documentation in the contingency plan is provided, primarily to ensure continued processing or resumption of processing in the event of a major disruption:

        a. *Operational procedures.* Establish written procedures to be followed when responding to major disruptions. Specify actions to be taken by operations management, vendors, and supporting functions such as power and air conditioning. Provide contact phone numbers (both office and home) and equipment lists that identify vendors and vendor maintenance personnel.

        b. *Backup processing procedures.* Under certain circumstances, the need for service level continuation in support of critical and semicritical systems will require initiating backup processing procedures during a major disruption. A procedure for backup processing must be established.

    3. *Elements of the contingency plan for disasters.* The following documentation in the contingency plan is provided, primarily to ensure personnel safety, continued processing capability, and physical recovery in the event of a disaster:

a. *Emergency procedures.* The safety of EDP and AIS personnel is foremost during the initial phase of a disaster. Formal emergency procedures are required to ensure a safe and proper evacuation of personnel.

b. *Interim production planning procedures.* An interim production plan must be implemented immediately after the occurrence of a disaster to resolve disposition of processing load and minimize the impact on critical applications. The procedures for production demand planning and must be predeveloped as an element of contingency planning.

c. *Data center recovery planning procedure.* Recovery of the data center must address equipment, software, and physical facilities. Since the initial concern will be continuity of computer processing, this plan will normally be implemented after the initiation of the processing demand plan. The procedure for data center recovery planning must be predeveloped as an element of the contingency plan.

4. *Storage and distribution.* Once developed, the plan should be maintained in a contingency plan manual divided into two major sections: "Major Disruption" and "Disaster." Further division of each section should be made as required to address the subelements defined in this chapter. Copies of the manual should be distributed to members of the recovery team as well as maintained in offsite storage.

E. *Data center recovery team.* The data center recovery team should be comprised of personnel from functional areas both within and outside of the company that can assist in the efficient and timely recovery of the facility. Team members should be selected jointly by the Director of Security, the manager of the computer data center, and appropriate top management administrators.

COMPUTER SECURITY CHECKLIST

The following checklist provides a format for determining the vulnerabilities of a data processing operation. It is often used as a supplementary checklist when a full-scale audit of a facility is being conducted. However, it can also be used separately for a computer center only when the balance of the facility is properly protected while the special protective needs of this high-risk activity indicate additional security. It is offered here to provide you additional help in determining exactly what security needs are appropriate for your computer operation.

COMPUTER SECURITY CHECKLIST

1. Is the enforcement of security procedure within the data processing department a specific function of the security department?
   YES _____ NO _____
2. Are there internal security procedures enforced by supervisory personnel within the data processing department?
   YES _____ NO _____
3. Are all employees working in, or having access to, the data processing department given security clearances commensurate with the work that they perform?
   YES _____ NO _____
   If yes, explain the security clearance system.
4. Are security investigations used to determine the security clearances to be assigned to data processing employees?
   YES _____ NO _____
   If yes, explain the investigative process.
5. Are these investigations conducted by security department personnel?
   YES _____ NO _____
   If no, by whom?
6. Once security clearances have been given are they regularly reviewed and updated?
   YES _____ NO _____
   How often?
7. Are specific employees given the responsibility for the control and maintenance of data processing disks, tapes, programs and manuals?
   YES _____ NO _____
   If yes, who has the responsibility?
8. Is access to tape and disk storage facilities restricted?
   YES _____ NO _____
   If yes, explain in detail the procedure governing access.
9. Is a log kept showing identification, time issued and returned, and the person receiving the property for all computer data files, programs, tapes, disks, and manuals?
   YES _____ NO _____
   If yes, explain procedure and include location of log(s).
10. Are computer operators/programmers given access to programs, data files, disks, tapes, and manuals not required for their current operation?
    YES _____ NO _____

11. Are operational computer programs kept in secured restricted storage areas?

    YES _____ NO _____

    If yes, explain.

12. Who has authorized access to storage areas for the operational computer programs?

13. Are duplicate copies of operational computer programs made?

    YES _____ NO _____

    If yes, when are they duplicated?

    Where are the duplicate programs kept? (They should be kept in an off-premises location.)

14. Are safes or vaults used to store computer programs, tapes, disks, and manuals?

    YES _____ NO _____

    If yes, explain conditions.

15. Are storage areas for computer programs, tapes, disks, and manuals rated for fire resistance of at least two hours?

    YES _____ NO _____

    Are they kept in fire retardant filing cabinets having at least a "C" or "D" rating from UL?

16. Are regular inventories made of stored programs, tapes, disks, and manuals?

    YES _____ NO _____

    If yes, how often and by whom are inventories made?

17. Is there a specific route used to transport duplicate computer programs to offsite storage?

    YES _____ NO _____

    If yes, who transports the data and how are they transported?

    How often is the route changed?

18. Are security measures taken to safeguard data placed in the offsite storage facility?

    YES _____ NO _____

    If yes, explain measures in detail.

19. Are confidential or sensitive computer programs, tapes, disks, and manuals disposed of by burning or shredding?

    YES _____ NO _____

20. Is the process conducted under the supervision of security personnel?

    YES _____ NO _____

21. Are all carbon paper copies and other duplicate copies of sensitive or confidential data disposed of in a similar fashion?

    YES _____ NO _____

    If yes, explain the procedure in detail.

22. Are all outside doors and windows to the data processing center locked and secured after normal working hours?
    YES _____ NO _____
23. Are all data processing or computer programs, tapes, disks, and manuals logged in and out of the data processing center?
    YES _____ NO _____
    If yes, explain the procedure including all the information that is required to properly fill out the log.
24. Is there a daily review of computer console printouts made by supervisory personnel to check for:
    a. Improper operating procedures?
    b. Suspicious or unauthorized runs?
    c. Suspicious or unapproved reruns?
    YES _____ NO _____
25. Are all console typewriters controlled by a central operating system that requires a specific time and program code to activate and log on the system?
    YES _____ NO _____
26. Do all data processing consoles have time meters that accurately record the time logged on the computer system?
    YES _____ NO _____
    Are the meters safeguarded against tampering?
    YES _____ NO _____
    If yes, how often and by whom?
27. Is a register of program operating times maintained and then examined regularly for accuracy?
    YES _____ NO _____
28. Are written procedures provided to instruct console operators about which activities are authorized and/or approved and which are not?
    YES _____ NO _____
29. Are computer operators prohibited from making any program modifications without a supervisor's authorization?
    YES _____ NO _____
30. Are there audit trail procedures for handling error rejects, accounting errors, and entering corrections and adjustments?
    YES _____ NO _____
    If yes, explain the procedures.
31. Are there procedures for posting credits or adjustments in customer accounts?
    YES _____ NO _____
    If yes, explain the procedure.
32. Are there classification procedures for handling uncollectable accounts?
    YES _____ NO _____
    If yes, explain the procedures.

33. Are there formalized systems of security measures in effect to see that data processing processes are properly adhered to?

    YES _____   NO _____

    If yes, explain.

34. Are credit authorizations checked regularly by an internal audit section to see that the authorizations are legitimate?

    YES _____   NO _____

    If yes, who conducts the audits, and when are they done?

35. Are balances and transactions monitored by an internal audit section before they are sent to data processing and again after they have been programmed?

    YES _____   NO _____

    If yes, who conducts the audits, and when are they done?

36. If a data processing/computer system is used on a time-share basis, are there any security safeguards in force to insure the integrity of your system element?

    YES _____   NO _____

    If yes, explain the security safeguards.

37. Are mailing lists and customer names and addresses kept in a secure location to prevent unauthorized access or use?

    YES _____   NO _____

    If yes, explain where they are kept and who has access to them.

38. Are formal steps taken to educate data processing and computer personnel on the security regulations and procedures that govern their work in the data processing/computer center?

    YES _____   NO _____

    If yes, explain the type and duration of training.

CHAPTER 35

Executive Protection

Hostage taking for political or criminal purposes is a major weapon of terrorists throughout the world. The use of this tactic has been on the increase for several years, primarily because it serves several purposes for the terrorist:

1. Obtaining the release of fellow terrorists in jail or prison.
2. Increasing visibility and recognition through worldwide publicity.
3. Having psychological impact by showing capability to *strike*.
4. Highlighting the corporation's or government's inability to provide protection.

This hostage-extortion-kidnap tactic is also fundamental to the raising of money for terrorist purposes. Although there are a relatively small number of these incidents, they have cost hundreds of millions of dollars in ransom in recent history.

Consequently, it is essential that many companies, while providing an overall protection program for their facilities and personnel, also provide comprehensive programs of executive protection and crisis management. These programs should include not only political risk assessments, sound physical security programs, and development of crisis management plans for the organization, but also training in hostage survival and a course of bargaining for its key personnel.

A comprehensive program should also insure that employees are provided with the best available risk information about various overseas environments in which they might operate. It further needs to provide advisory information to assist the employee to better protect himself or herself through advanced planning and preparation. By doing so, it puts a company in a much better position to respond effectively to a crisis situation should it develop, deal effectively with the situation if it does develop, and then, if necessary, do everything possible to safely recover a kidnapped employee. Lastly, it insures that those who might be kidnapped are provided with enough information to survive a kidnapping situation by insuring physical and mental conditioning, an understanding of terrorist goals/objectives, and a sensitivity to the company's role and posture in dealing with ransom kidnapping situations.

The key elements of an executive protection—crisis management program should include:

1. Proactive planning and activities
2. Procedures for dealing with a threat situation
3. Training of employees
4. Ongoing risk assessment

A political risk assessment program should include the maintenance of up-to-date political risk, crime, and terrorism information on each of the countries in which a company does business and sends travelers or technical and sales personnel. This material should be provided to company employees on a regular basis prior to travel to these locations. This will insure that anyone traveling to these locations is aware of the risks associated with that trip, making them better prepared to deal with such risks. Along with this activity, maintenance of appropriate liaison, where possible, with host government police, security, or military contacts should be developed or maintained.

Travelers and executives should also be briefed on what to do in the event of a crisis situation, trained in countersurveillance, what to do in the event of a hijacking, or, more generally, how to stay out of trouble while they are traveling overseas.

These two activities should, for the most part, provide employees with the tools necessary to be cautious and maintain a low profile while they are traveling. This also goes a long way toward discharging a company's responsibility to warn employees of dangers that they know might be present in an employee's work environment.

If, despite the best efforts of the company to provide good advisory information, an incident occurs, a crisis management plan should exist. It should be noted that even when the best protection methods are employed, a determined terrorist group can and will be effective in committing a kidnapping, extortion, or terrorist act for financial gain. Consequently, there can be no guarantees given that an employee will be safe even if he or she follows all the company's advice. The world is not a safe place. There is no such thing as 100 percent security. The best an executive protection program can do is provide good information, minimize exposure to risk, and provide the best possible advice on self-protection.

A PROGRAM FOR EXECUTIVE PROTECTION

Since all countries are different and since a company's operations and resources are different in each country, a program of executive protection must reflect these basic differences. It is, therefore, essential that each country in which company employees live as expatriates or travel have a country-specific executive protection plan developed and ready for use. In addition to these plans, a program for the company, as a whole, for dealing with a threat situation should be developed, distributed, and reviewed regularly through careful audit programs to insure its readiness and timeliness. This plan should include:

1. The organization of a crisis management team
2. How the team will be administered, equipped, and supported by the organization
3. Who will participate in negotiations
4. Who will control the overall crisis management effort
5. Where and under what conditions ransom will be paid
6. Determination of whether kidnap and ransom insurance should be purchased and put into effect
7. Who should handle press relations
8. Decisions regarding family or friends of the victim
9. Government relations in the country of occurrence and U.S. State Department liaison
10. Negotiation process and ransom payment
11. Victim recovery
12. Victim postevent handling

All of these activities are equally important parts of the overall effectiveness of an executive protection program. The following sections provide examples of how each one of these areas can be effectively handled and, taken as a whole, could constitute a framework for the development of an effective executive protection program in a company.

The Terrorists' Target

In selecting a target, whether for the purpose of extortion or kidnapping, terrorists have been known to evaluate their chances of success using the following criteria:

1. *Accessibility.* Obviously a *hard* target executive will stand a greater chance of being left off a hit list than an *easy* or *soft* target executive.
2. *Prestige.* The relationship and respect an executive enjoys with his peer group and subordinates influences his desirability as a target.
3. *Visibility.* An executive with wide media exposure, through newspapers, television, and so forth is a highly desirable target because of the publicity value.
4. *Financial.* The ability of the executive or his or her company to pay a ransom or extortion demand may be an important consideration of the terrorists.
5. *Family.* The mutual closeness and strength of family bonds serves as an added attraction to such groups.

6. *Health.* The ideal target executive will be in good health, not require any special medication, and be able to stand the rigors of prolonged imprisonment.

Therefore, it is vitally important that a company also consider these same criteria when developing an executive protection plan.

Developing A Plan

One must remember that no executive protection plan can be expected to be totally effective if it is not first and foremost comprehensive in nature. Your plan literally will be no stronger than its weakest link. Therefore, when developing an executive protection plan to protect company employees and executives from hostage-extortion-kidnap tactics, certain key elements must be considered for inclusion in the plan:

1. Office Security

The tenor of public opinion can turn both the executive and his or her offices into prime targets for terrorist groups. Virtually any executive can be a target of such terrorist tactics as forced entry, building occupation, kidnapping, sabotage, and even assassination. However, executive office space can present effective barriers, both psychological and physical, against terrorist activities. Acceptability of routines, sufficient security funds, space isolation and access control, and established security policies can give the modern executive the psychological advantage and make executive office space a hard target.

The executive office should provide some type of barrier between the executive and visitors. This barrier can be a secretary or receptionist or some type of physical barrier such as electromagnetically operated doors. In addition, use of a silent *trouble alarm* button, with a signal terminating in your security department or at the secretary's desk should be considered.

One of the most effective means to be employed in connection with executive protection in the office is the close screening of visitors, both at the reception desk in the main lobby and, again, at the executive's office itself. The secretary should not admit visitors unless they have been positively screened in advance or they are known to the secretary from previous visits. If the visitor is not known and not expected, he or she should not be admitted until satisfactory identification is established. In such instances, your security department should be called and an officer asked to come to the scene until the visitor establishes a legitimate reason for being in your office. If the visitor cannot do so, the officer should be asked to escort the visitor out of the building.

Unusual telephone calls, particularly those in which the caller does not identify himself or herself or those in which it appears that the caller may be misrepresenting himself or herself, should not be put through to the executive.

Note should be made of the circumstances involved, (i.e., incoming line number, date and time, nature of call, name of caller and so forth.) This information should then be turned in to the security department for followup investigation.

Under no circumstances should an executive's secretary reveal to otherwise unknown callers the whereabouts of the executive, or his or her home address or telephone number.

When you are working alone in the evening, on weekends, or on holidays, it is suggested that this fact be made known to the security department by advising the desk officer of how long you will be in your office. Checking out with the security department when you leave is also a good idea.

2. Home Security

Protection of the family and the home presents unique problems that makes security difficult to maintain. Social and business activities tend to change the family security profile. Teenagers are an excellent example as they tend to resist strict routines and close supervision. Not only must personal problems be solved, but the home security plan must also answer questions of fire, medical emergency, and natural disaster. The primary purpose of the home security program, including plans, safety equipment, and alarm systems, is the personal safety of the executive and the family. A sound home security program must concentrate on making the home target *high risk,* thus directing the terrorist elsewhere.

One of the primary tactics of extortion and terrorism is the adverse psychological pressure of telephone harassment. This psychological pressure is designed to upset, infuriate, and break the overall stability of the family. Telephone harassment should be discussed openly between the executive and the family, and family members must be convinced that such verbal abuse is not directed toward themselves as individuals but at the family unit, which represents some social, economic, or political target. It is the family's inner strength and self-discipline that must be used to combat this form of terrorism. Report all instances of repeated telephone harassment to the security department so that appropriate action may be taken to correct this problem.

Kidnapping and terrorism are painful battles of nerves and stress, and most terrorists are psychologically better prepared than are the executive's family. The solution to this form of crisis is basically twofold: (1) training the family to be a stronger psychological unit, especially under stress, and (2) establishing a home security program that is based on proven security principles and hardware and reinforced with dedicated family participation. Not only must the entire family voluntarily be motivated to accept security restrictions, but they must also closely adhere to the routine and details of these restrictions. The preliminary step in developing a home security program is an indepth security survey with both husband and wife present. Your security department should be able to arrange for such surveys of your executives' residences upon request.

Individual family members must understand and feel that they are part of, and contribute to, the home security program. Security awareness is one area that is normally very weak; yet, every family member can develop a special sense for observing their surroundings and spotting potential security problems. All members of the executive's family should become inherently aware of the following everyday situations and recognize their potential danger. For example:

A. When a child is to be picked up at school, the school should have an established procedure with which to verify this action with the home or office.

B. When you are calling the school about an emergency situation, always give your name and then your location. Next, proceed with an explanation of the problem.

C. Terrorist victims are normally under surveillance for a number of days before any action takes place so be aware of possible surveillance activities.

D. Do not establish routine patterns of social activity involving such areas as club meetings, sports, and restaurants.

E. Consider telephones as possibly being *bugged* and limit the amount of important security information given out. Always answer the telephone with "hello" and establish the identity of the caller before giving such information as your name, address, and who is at home. Unrecognizable callers identifying themselves as *old friends* and *business associates* should be referred to an office telephone number.

F. Family members should never unlock doors or permit the entry of strangers. Service personnel should be verified by telephone with their respective companies before they are allowed to enter the residence. If forced entry is attempted, the family should retreat to a home *safe-room* equipped for such emergency use.

The special problems of home security are many, and the need of a good security program with contingencies to meet specific terrorist threats cannot be overemphasized. The above concepts can help build the psychological framework for stronger family security involvement, and the following specific *Security Checklists* and information will help make the home a high-risk target the terrorist will avoid.

HOME SECURITY CHECKLIST

As a self-test have your executives review these safeguards as they relate to their individual situations. Then evaluate your company's needs for remedial action or improved response capabilities.

1. The executive should consider having a well-equipped home *safe-room,* preferably a second floor interior room with deadbolt locks,

telephone, and duress signal. In some instances, a second hiding place somewhere outside of the residence should be considered.

2. The executive should maintain emergency contingency plans containing important information on the family, health, neighbors, and social activities and current personal photographs. This material should be locked in a storage cabinet located in the home safe-room, and be duplicated in the security department files.

3. Residence doors, including garage doors, should be kept locked at all times. Before allowing entry of strangers, utility and service people, and salespeople, their identities should be verified by telephone with their respective companies.

4. Before leaving the residence for extended periods of time, the following precautions should be observed:

   a. Leave the residence with a *lived in* appearance. Leave a few inexpensive items such as toys in the front yard.

   b. Have the mail, packages, and trash picked up daily. Have neighbors set out some garbage to indicate occupancy in your residence.

   c. Discontinue services, such as newspapers and telephone.

   d. Arrange for lawn care services to continue on a regular basis.

   e. Leave a set of keys to the residence, storage buildings, and alarm system with a neighbor (never under flower pots, mats, or other obvious places) and inform the police of their name and address and your plans.

   f. Utilizing either manual or electronic timers, have different lights, and a radio or TV, turned on every evening.

   g. Upon returning, if you find evidence of a break-in, do not enter the residence. Instead call the police.

5. Fire and safety equipment such as ABC fire extinguishers, first aid kits, blankets, flashlights with spare batteries, and water hoses should be stored for emergency use and inspected on a regular basis.

6. Water and gas utility shutoff valves and electrical distribution boxes should be located inside the residence. Fuse and circuit breaker boxes should be kept locked and a flashlight and spare fuses should be readily available.

7. Emergency procedures should be practiced in private and they should involve all members of the family. Security business and emergency family plans should not be discussed outside the home.

8. Emergency telephone numbers of police, fire, medical, and ambulance service should be available at each telephone.

9. Children should be trained in good security procedures such as traveling in groups, refusing rides with strangers, avoiding isolated play areas, keeping parents informed as to time and destination, reporting all strange events and attempted molestation, and how to get help or call the police.

10. When you use one animal inside and one animal outside the house, guard dogs can provide an excellent deterrent to terrorism. However, they should receive routine training and not be treated as pets.
11. The executive should consider very carefully the ramifications of having firearms in the home security program. If it is decided to include a firearm, a shotgun is recommended; and all responsible members of the family must be trained in firearm safety and use.
12. Home telephone numbers should be unlisted whenever it is practicable to do so.
13. Maids, cleaning women, and other domestic workers should, whenever possible, be subject to security checks. They should be instructed not to admit strangers to the house, to refuse information to strangers inquiring about the activities or the whereabouts of family members, and not to accept packages or other items unless they are sure of the source.

---

3. Vehicle and Travel Security

Threats of terrorism and kidnapping are serious problems involving all aspects of security management, and effective management dictates that available resources be used wisely and concentrated on security weak points. Terrorists, such as the late Carlos Marighella, are very quick to point out the security weakness of business, family, and pleasure travel. At their best, protection strategies dealing with vehicles and travel are perhaps the hardest to formulate, and the advantage tends to be with the terrorist. Current statistics indicate that the greatest danger from acts of terrorism occurs while the executive is traveling to or from the office and just before reaching his or her destination.

The inherent security problems of passenger vehicle travel are many. Vehicles are easily recognized by year, make, and model, and the trained terrorist can accurately assess any protection modifications and security devices. Using adequate resources, vehicles can be discreetly followed, therefore making possible repeated dry runs of potential attacks with very low risk of detection. Under these conditions, different methods of attack can be formulated and tested until success is ensured. Vehicles are often left in driveways, on streets, at service centers, and other isolated areas with no form of control or protection, allowing easy access to terrorists. While traveling in a passenger vehicle, the executive has limited protection resources upon which to rely and often is dependent on fixed security manpower. This makes it easier for terrorist groups, which are geared to mobility, to ensure numerical superiority.

The attack potential against the executive in travel rests heavily on psychological instability and human weakness. The shock of surprise attack is greatest at points of changing surroundings, crossroads and when entering or exiting vehicles. These are situations of constant change, and points of activities where the executive has a tendency to be mentally off balance. Through illegal entry to the vehicle, the terrorist can gain a number of attack points: sabotage with the intent to maim or injure, sabotage with the intent to execute, and sabotage to ensure the success of future attacks. These psychological factors make the vehicle the ideal place to apply scare tactics, warnings, and gain initial control of the executive.

Even though travel problems provide the greatest number of security and psychological variables, there are actions and policies that can be developed to minimize the executive's risk and complicate the terrorist's plans. The basic travel policy can be divided into three areas: (1) normal travel procedures, (2) vehicle equipment, and (3) vehicle defense strategy. The following checklists will aid in formulating and evaluating an effective travel security policy.

VEHICLE EQUIPMENT GUIDELINES

1. The executive vehicle designed to meet the terrorists' threat should be a hard top model with the following special equipment:
   a. Inside hood latch,
   b. Locked gas caps,
   c. Inner escape latch on trunk,
   d. Steel-belted radial tires with inner tire devices,
   e. Radiator protection,
   f. Disk brakes, and
   g. An antibomb bolt through the end of the exhaust pipe.
2. Positive communications can be insured with a two-way radio or a car telephone.
3. It is recommended that the executive vehicle designed to meet the terrorists' threat carry the following safety equipment:
   a. Fire extinguisher,
   b. First aid kit,
   c. Flashlight,
   d. Two spare tires,
   e. Bomb blanket,
   f. Armored blanket,
   g. Large outside mirrors, and
   h. A portable high intensity spotlight.
4. For additional protection, the vehicle should have an alarm system protected with a standby battery.

ROUTINE TRAVEL GUIDELINES

1. Executives and their drivers should be trained in antiterrorism strategy and defensive driving. This means established responsibility and contingency plans.

2. There should be a simple duress procedure established between executives and their drivers.
3. Never overload a vehicle. All persons should wear seatbelts.
4. Always avoid routine times and patterns of travel. Avoid driving in remote areas after dark, and keep to established, well-traveled roads.
5. Arrange vehicles in advance so they may be carefully inspected. Always park vehicles in parking areas that are either locked or watched, and never park overnight on the street.
6. Occasionally use public transportation. When using taxi services, the taxi company should be varied. Never take the first vehicle in line. Insure that the driver follows direct routes, yet varies the route according to the executive's directions.
7. Always restrict travel plans to a need-to-know basis, minimize newspaper coverage, and travel in groups when you are attending social functions.
8. Avoid driving closely behind other vehicles, especially service trucks, and be aware of activities and road conditions two or three blocks ahead.
9. Keep the ignition key separate from other keys, and never leave the trunk key with parking or service attendants.
10. Before each trip, the vehicle should be inspected to see that:
    a. The hood latch is secure,
    b. The fender wells are empty,
    c. The exhaust pipe is not blocked,
    d. No one is in the back seat, and
    e. The gas tank is at least three-quarters full.
11. Establish a firm policy regarding carrying and using firearms.

In parts of Europe and Latin America the increasing incidence of violent crimes against persons, particularly kidnapping, robbery, and personal assaults, has been widely reported in the press and by other news services. Therefore, you need to alert your company's overseas travellers and prospective expatriate employees about these trends and to suggest some precautions that can be taken when in these areas.

Many of these crimes are the work of political terrorists whose objectives are to disrupt the local civil government, to gain publicity for their causes, and to obtain the cash to pay for their political activities. However, similar crimes are committed by nonpolitical, or so-called "common," criminals who are interested merely in money. To the unfortunate victims, of course, the motive of the criminal makes little difference.

A profitable kidnapping or robbery, whether by terrorists or by common criminals, ordinarily requires careful planning and coordination. Consequently, the casual overseas traveller, tourist, or new resident is not especially vulnerable to these crimes. However, he or she is now becoming much more vulnerable to street crime such as assault, robbery and theft—about to the same extent he or she would be likely to encounter these in most of the big cities in the United States.

We believe that the risk of becoming the victim of a crime in an overseas location can be minimized by practising the following precautions:

1. Try to remain as inconspicuous as possible, in dress, social activities, and choice of cars. Try to blend into the local crowd and avoid attracting attention or publicity whenever possible. In chauffeur-driven cars, riding in the front seat is preferable to riding alone in the back seat. Avoid bars, restaurants, or other public places of the type where provocative incidents might occur that could identify you as a visiting *rich* American.
2. Walk, whenever possible, with one or more companions and on well-lighted main streets where other people are present. Limit sightseeing and shopping to the popular local tourist attractions and the main market areas.
3. Limit the number of persons who know of your meeting schedules and further travel plans to those who need to know. Avoid unnecessarily identifying yourself with a company by not using luggage stickers, not wearing jackets with company emblems, and so forth. Always speak of your activities, business affairs, and travel plans in the vaguest terms possible, or say nothing when you can, particularly to suspiciously friendly hotel maids, bartenders, bellboys, cab drivers, and chauffeurs.
4. Keep important documents and money, except what is needed for that day, in a hotel safety deposit box.
5. Pay attention to the advice of the local management regarding security matters.

FOREIGN TRAVEL GUIDELINES

1. Maintain a low degree of visibility. Wear clothing that is casual and consistent with the area being visited.
2. Keep two sets of business cards. In areas of concern, use business cards with innocuous titles such as Manager, Engineer, and so forth, rather than Vice President, Director, and so forth.
3. Use business visas for business travel to preclude entry or exit problems from the country.
4. Executives should not meet at the airport in high-risk countries. Rides to the airport should not be accepted from expatriates or business associates. And, wherever possible, travel to and from airports alone.
5. Advance notice of foreign visits should be made on an extremely limited need-to-know basis. Itineraries should be closely controlled. There

should be no press coverage in advance of the visits, and receptions should not be attended if they are publicized in advance.

6. If travel is to high-risk countries, advance security planning must be done, and if countries are particularly sensitive, security department personnel should provide advance trip planning to insure appropriate trip arrangements.

7. Overseas travel should be on commercial airlines rather than on corporate aircraft whenever possible.

8. Arrange precoded messages to check in with your office or home via telex when you are on extended trips. This is to insure that planned itineraries are being followed and deviations, quickly noted.

STATEMENT OF POLICY

Owing to the current threat of terrorism throughout the world, every company should desire to take all reasonable precautions for the protection of their personnel and property most likely to be possible targets for acts or threats of violence by terrorists, or other radical or revolutionary groups. Such acts or threats may include:

1. Kidnapping
2. Assassination
3. Extortion
4. Bombings
5. Ambush
6. Harassment

Consequently, it should be the policy of a company to provide all reasonable protection to its employees against the foregoing acts or threats, but particularly to those executives who are more vulnerable targets of terrorism due to their position with the company, their travel to or residence in a high-risk country, or their high public visibility.

Unfortunately, there is no proven method to predict which executive may become a target for terrorism. However, as a sound business practice, it is prudent to take measures to minimize the risk. For this reason, company executives at both domestic and overseas locations, as well as overseas travelers, should be provided with recommendations for reducing the likelihood that they may become targets for terrorist-directed action.

In furtherance of this policy, an executive protection plan should be established:

I. *Crisis management plan*
   A. *Overview.* If individual protective measures fail and a crisis situation results, the crisis management plan must be activated.

The decision to implement the crisis management plan in any given geographical area will be made by the chairman of the board, or the president, or the chairman of the executive protection committee. In the event that none of the three executives is available, the decision will be made by the president of the affected division, as appropriate, based on the recommendation of the director of security.

Implementation of the crisis management plan should normally be based on verification by a senior executive at the scene of the incident (country, city, or facility) that an act of terrorism, as defined in the statement of policy, has occurred. Verification should also include the threat involved, the person(s) or organization(s) making the threat, the location from which the threat was made, the location of the victim(s), and the existence of any propaganda accompanying the threat,

1. The emergency plan for the country in which the incident has occurred should be implemented.
2. The security department's emergency operations plan should be implemented.
3. The crisis management team should be convened as specified in the executive protection plan.
4. An onsite team consisting of a senior member of management appointed by the chairman of the board or the president in the former's absence, the director of risk management, and the director of security or his or her designee should proceed to the site of the incident. A previously designated negotiator will join them there to begin negotiations for the release of the victim (if a kidnapping is involved).
5. Once the victim has been recovered or the emergency situation otherwise terminated, the postincident portion of the plan should be implemented.

B. *Crisis management team.* It must be assumed that any act of terrorism directed against a company will be well planned, carried out with dedication and zeal, and will result in the targeted executive being caught off guard with little or no opportunity to take evasive action. The result undoubtedly will be an initial time period of confusion and chaos that calls for a planned and efficient response to the disruptive effects of the terrorist act.

The crisis management team should, therefore, be organized to provide the means for quick response capability to any terrorist act that is intended to cripple or otherwise significantly disrupt the normal operations of the company. This capability must be such as to facilitate a coordinated and effective response to acts of terrorism that can normally be expected to be directed against executives.

Members of the crisis management team are expected to function in a decision-making capacity on behalf of the company insofar as an act of terrorism may be directed against the company. The team is charged with the responsibility of effecting the implementation and carrying out of the policies and procedures contained in the overall executive protection plan.

In order to reduce the likelihood of confusion under the stressful conditions accompanying a crisis situation, the make-up of the crisis management team must be restricted to a relatively small number of individuals who represent the varied and oftentimes highly specialized skills required to counteract the effects of a crisis situation.

1. *Threat analysis.* The primary focus of the threat analysis function is to determine the validity of the threat and its seriousness. In addition, threat analysis should attempt to determine whether the threat originated with a terrorist, a criminal, or someone who is mentally deranged. Answers to these questions will determine the intensity of the response called for to alleviate the problem. Much of the analytical effort will be directed from onsite evaluations and intelligence gathering techniques employed.

    Once the threat has been determined to be a valid one and the level of the threat established together with the identity of the threateners, it becomes necessary to ascertain the extent to which company personnel and assets are in danger.

    Once these questions are answered, attention must be given to establishing the origin of the threat, the location of company personnel mentioned in the threat and others who might also be threatened, the goal of the threatener (the real goal as differentiated from the stated goal, if this is the case), and the validity of our negotiations (do they appear to be realistic in terms of the stated demands of the terrorists?)

    After arriving at answers to the above, the crisis management team must then turn to considering the steps necessary to neutralize, or at least reduce, the threat and guarantee the safety of company personnel and assets. Again, these decisions will be affected, to a great extent, by information and action originating with the negotiating team.

2. *Negotiating team support.* Depending on the location of the incident, the crisis management team will be required to provide varying degrees of support to the negotiating team. It may be necessary, for example, to provide a medical analysis of the health status of the victim of a kidnapping or details of personnel records to be used in establishing a means of verifying that the victim is still alive and is, in fact, the actual person being held by the kidnappers. Other staff support functions, such as communications, photographic, and so forth, may be required

to provide specialized support and the crisis management team will be responsible for making such support available as needed.

C. *Executive protection committee.* There should be an executive protection committee established that will:

1. Insure that adequate security procedures for the protection of company executives (domestic and foreign) are in effect throughout the company.

2. Provide for training, formal instructions, and controls.
   a. All members of the executive protection committee, and their alternates, will receive familiarization training in matters of executive protection.
   b. The members and alternates of the crisis management team, in addition to the above, will receive specialized training in crisis management and participate in a mock negotiation session under professional direction.

3. Provide the means for maintaining a level of operations necessary for implementing and carrying out management policy in the event of a major incident.

4. Be normally comprised of any or all of the following (each person to designate an alternate:)
   a. Chairman (primary contact with the negotiator),
   b. General counsel, or company legal advisor,
   c. Treasurer,
   d. Vice president for employee relations,
   e. Vice president for operations,
   f. President of the company,
   g. Vice president of administration,
   h. Director of security,
   i. Medical director,
   j. Vice president for corporate communications,
   k. Director of risk management.

The chairman of the executive protection committee will be appointed by the chairman of the board. The person selected as chairman should be a member of the management committee.

D. *Negotiating team.* As a general rule, no two negotiating situations with terrorists will be alike. The terrorists' demands may differ, their threats may differ, and their strategies and objectives will vary from one situation to another. However, the one consistent factor in all negotiating situations is that negotiating involves the possibility of at least partial defeat on the part of the negotiating team (payment of ransom) and, hopefully, at least some compromise on the part of the terrorists (release of the victim). In a negotiating situation involving terrorism, the willingness to negotiate implies a willingness to compromise and carries with it an indication that the other side can expect to receive something in return.

It is imperative that the negotiating team be permitted to engage in their negotiations with a clear understanding of the limits to which they can commit company resources. They must be free from hindering influences and must have total control over the negotiating process. Consequently, the person designated to be the negotiator must be in a position to speak with authority and not be subject to the influence of local management. His one communication channel, other than to the terrorists, will be to the chairman of the crisis management team (or direct to the chairman of the board or the president, as the case may be). No other management personnel will be permitted to influence or otherwise interfere with the negotiator's role. The onsite security department and risk management department representatives will provide up-to-date intelligence and other types of guidance to the negotiator and, for all practical purposes, will be the only company representatives providing input to him or her except as the negotiator may request such input from others. Realistically, the negotiator must be free to operate without restraint as the official representative of the chairman of the board.

E. *Onsite command post team*
    1. *Negotiator.* The position will be filled by a third party selected by the director of security and the director of risk management and will handle all negotiations and direct contacts with the terrorists. The incumbent must be proficient in the local language and have an intimate knowledge of the local political situation and legal processes. Whenever possible, this position will be filled by a local attorney or other negotiator experienced in matters of this sort.
    2. *Security.* The director of security (or his or her designee) will fill this position and be responsible for maintaining security channels/means of communications, liaison with U.S. embassy officials, and other intelligence and law enforcement agencies and officials.
    3. *Risk management.* The director of risk management or his or her designated representative will provide necessary assistance in those matters of risk analysis peculiar to the given situation. The incumbent will also be responsible for certain activities jointly designated by the director of security and the director of risk management.
    4. *Management.* This position normally will be filled by a senior management official designated by the chairman of the board or the president. He may be a senior management official from the country of occurrence or from the U.S. as is deemed appropriate.

F. *U.S. command post team*
    1. *Chairman.* This position is responsible for insuring complete coordination of the actions called for in the executive protection

plan. The chairman will serve as the primary point of contact with the onsite command post. He or she will also be responsible for interpreting the risk/liability aspects of the problem. The chairman will be appointed by the chairman of the board from among the members of the management committee.

2. *Legal.* This position will be filled by an attorney designated by the general counsel. He will advise the chairman in the matters of employee relations and the legality of the measures employed in meeting the demands of the terrorists.

3. *Security.* A representative of the director of security will provide assistance in implementing the executive protection plan and provide liaison with U.S. State Department, FBI, or other intelligence, counterintelligence, and law enforcement agencies as required. He will also coordinate actions called for by the director of security operating from the onsite command post.

4. *Financial.* This position will provide guidance and assistance in obtaining whatever financial support may be required as a result of the onsite negotiations.

5. *Public relations.* This position will be responsible for all contacts with the news media and will be subject to direction of the chairman.

6. *Others.* As called for, from time to time, support will be provided to the U.S. command post by the following:

   a. *Medical.* Medical records will be reviewed by the medical department and, where required, medical advice and/or instructions to protect the victim will be passed on to the negotiating team.

   b. *Personnel.* Necessary personnel records will be provided to the appropriate command post for use by the negotiating team.

   c. *Communications.* Incoming lines, recording devices, and other communications equipment and services will be made available by the director of telecommunications.

   The crisis management team (U.S.) will have two basic functions: Analyze the threat; and Support the on-site negotiating team.

II. *Overseas locations.* All foreign locations must have a specific emergency operating program for their operations. As a minimum, this emergency operating plan should provide for the following:

A. Family emergency readiness plan that includes:

   1. The persons to be contacted in an emergency;

   2. Location of wills, securities, insurance policies, and other assets; or the name, address, and telephone number of authorized persons having access to these items;

   3. Special instructions in event of emergency;

   4. A list of personal and household effects in the country;

     5.   Sufficient traveler's checks on hand to finance emergency travel out of the country and related expenses.

B. *Official responsibilities*

    1.   All expatriate personnel must:

       a.   Register at the U.S. Embassy (or other embassies in case of third country nationals).

       b.   Maintain contact with embassy personnel for current information, recommendations, and suggestions concerning safety precautions, evacuation procedures, and so forth.

       c.   Verify that personnel files, and other necessary information, are kept current.

       d.   Maintain current travel itineraries for themselves and family members. Information should include exact mode of travel (flight number, and so forth), dates of departure and location arrival, contact points, and so forth.

       e.   Maintain valid air travel cards or open airline tickets for themselves and each dependent.

    2.   All exit formalities should be prearranged to the greatest extent possible and each employee should be periodically briefed on these requirements and procedures.

    3.   A member of the local manager's staff should be designated to maintain a list of all passports, visas, and vaccination certificates to insure that these are maintained in valid condition. In some countries visas for bordering countries should be obtained and kept current. Each child should have his or her own passport in case of separation.

C. *Evacuation plan* (Developed by local management and approved by the security department.)

    1.   Specific assignments will be made for alternate modes of communication of emergency evacuation action plans for employees.

    2.   Modes of evacuation travel and alternates will be selected and specific instructions for their use made. Commitments from carriers should be obtained, if possible, and kept current.

    3.   An alternate location for housing employees and their families will be selected in the most accessible safe country or region, preferably one in which a company operation can assist in obtaining temporary housing, communication facilities, and so forth.

    4.   An assembly point for groups of employees to travel to the embarkation point will be designated with alternate locations in the event the designated point becomes insecure.

    5.   An embarkation point and alternate points will be selected and arrangements made, if possible, to protect the site and verify the presence of all employees and their families.

6. Emergency first aid survival kits will be prepared for each family member. These kits should include any special medication needed and materials that the specific country may require and as suggested by the local U.S. embassy. Such a list might include: medicines, compass, water purification tablets, blankets, freeze-dried meal pouches, signalling devices, and flashlights. These kits must be light enough to carry, and family members should be instructed in their use.

7. Instructions for essential personal belongings with priorities established to insure that only minimum requirements are taken. These instructions will provide for an alert to families for packing these essentials for standby purposes.

8. ID bracelets should be available and worn during any alert.

D. *Emergency awareness and communications*

1. The local manager will regularly report to the U.S. embassy any factors uniquely affecting the position of the company in the event of, or in the midst of, a crisis.

2. A mutual aid association with other multinational companies that have similar situations should be contemplated and, if arranged, will be tested periodically.

3. Rumors of other companies preparing to leave or leaving an area will be verified and reported.

A terrorist incident can occur in spite of the best efforts of both the company and its employees to protect themselves properly. Should such an incident occur, the crisis management plan must be immediately activated. This plan represents the coordinated response to a crisis situation. Specific instructions for action to be taken by management personnel should be provided by the security department.

III. *Executive protection program*

A. *Executive protection plan.* To protect those company executives who are likely to become targets for terrorist groups or other similar groups or individuals, the following protective measures will be available at all company overseas locations as well as in the United States.

1. Security surveys of executive residences must be provided by the security department.

2. Executive travel patterns must be analyzed to identify critical areas that can be exploited by terrorists.

3. Security briefings and training must be provided as it becomes appropriate.

4. Appropriate security measures must be instituted in all company facilities.

5. Reference material concerning terrorism and crime prevention for residents and travelers should be available to all managers.

6. The negotiating/security team and the victim (when applicable) will be evacuated from the country of occurrence.

7. The emergency plan will be concluded.

B. *Kidnapping response plan—domestic*

1. The person first receiving word that a kidnapping has occurred will immediately notify the security department who will immediately notify the director of security.

2. One member of the security department will be designated as the "duty officer" for the crisis management team each calendar month. Security will initially report a kidnapping occurrence to the duty officer or an alternate designate duty officer.

3. Upon receipt of notice of a kidnapping, the duty officer will convene the crisis management team and notify the chairman of the board and the president of the incident.

4. The security department representative will establish immediate contact with the nearest FBI office and the local police department involved.

5. Negotiations for the release of the victim will be initiated based on the principles outlined for release negotiations for overseas victims.

C. *Kidnapping response plan—overseas.* In the event of a kidnapping overseas, the following action will be taken:

1. Immediately upon receiving word of the incident, the facility's manager, or his designee, should implement the local emergency plan and notify appropriate top management.

2. The person in (1) above will also notify the director of security (or his or her designee) after obtaining all available information.

3. The director of security will specifically inform the chairman of the board and the president.

4. Members of the crisis management team will be contacted by the director of security and will report to a predetermined command post location, depending on where the victim is from and where the incident has occurred.

5. After review of the known details with the chairman of the board and the president, a senior member of management, the director of risk management, and the director of security should consider the advisability of travel to the country of occurrence.

   a. All communications, including travel arrangements, should be handled by the use of *safe* phones, in accordance with specific instructions contained in the emergency plan for the location involved. Preselected code words should be used when necessary.

   b. The chairman of the crisis management team will be designated as contact representative for receiving all messages from the negotiator at the scene.

6. Upon arrival, the security department representative will evaluate the situation and assume responsibility for efforts directed toward securing the early release of the victim. He or she must also:
    a. Insure that safety and precautionary measures have been taken on behalf of the family of the victim and other executives and their families as outlined in the local emergency plan.
    b. Consult with law enforcement officials of the host country, *if this is deemed prudent.*
    c. Consider consultation with the U.S. embassy and consular officers. (See country plan.)
    d. Endeavor to keep the crisis management team in the United States informed.
7. Any news releases to news media, U.S. and foreign, should also be under the control of the negotiator.
8. Every effort must be made to insure that the methods utilized to secure the release of the victim will not be divulged to the press or made public.
9. At the time that the negotiator believes that the victim will definitely be released, he or she will advise the company so that arrangements can be made for transportation to a neutral location.
10. The emergency plan for each location will embody the names and telephone numbers of the go-between designates, protection and evacuation measures for the remaining family members, and means to protect other key personnel and their families. This plan is to be on file in the company's main office in the U.S., the security department, and the homes of:
    a. The chairman of crisis management team
    b. The director of security

D. *Payment of ransom.* The decision whether or not to pay ransom, if demanded by the terrorists, will be the responsibility of the chairman of the board or the president in the absence of the chairman of the board. This will be based on the onlocation assessment by the negotiator of the situation as it develops. Limitations on the amount of ransom that can be paid should be determined by the chairman of the board, or the president on the chairman of the board's behalf. Once the negotiator has received authorization to negotiate the release of the victim of a kidnapping or pay the amount specified in an extortion attempt, the amount so authorized may not be increased without further authorization of the chairman of the board, or the president on the chairman of the board's behalf.

In an extreme situation, when neither the chairman of the board nor the president is available to decide upon the payment of ransom, the chairman of the executive protection committee shall be authorized to approve ransom payment not to exceed that specified by the board of directors.

The decision to accede to the demands of the terrorists/kidnappers should only be made by one of the executives authorized to do so and, even then, only after several requirements are satisfied. These include:

1. That the company agreed to pay ransom (or extortion) money or other considerations only under duress and
2. That, prior to making such payment, the company made every reasonable effort, under the circumstances, to:
    a. Determine positively that the threat to kill or injure the victim(s) was genuine; and
    b. Notify the FBI or the local law enforcement official (in the case of a domestic incident) of the demand for ransom payment or other considerations and to comply with any recommendations and orders that they may have given, as soon as practicable, keeping in mind the concern for the safety of the victim(s).

When a ransom has been agreed upon, the negotiator must inform the company's executive committee of this fact as well as the stipulations from the terrorist/kidnappers as to the type of currency, size of bills, method of delivery, and so forth. Depending upon the requirements for U.S. or foreign currency, arrangements will be made for a transfer of necessary funds to a company representative specified by the executive committee chairman in the country agreed to as the exchange point. Because of the likelihood that laws in the country of occurrence will prohibit the exchange of ransom money there, it may be necessary for the exchange to take place in a third country. Arrangements for the transfer of funds or the obtaining of necessary cash, if U.S. currency is specified, will be under the direction of the treasurer.

In the event that it is necessary to transport the ransom money in cash from one country to another, privately-chartered aircraft, rather than commercial aircraft, should be utilized and arrangements made to deliver the ransom in accordance with instructions issued by the security department.

If the ransom payment is to be made in the United States, the money must be photographed, serial numbers recorded, and packaged according to specific instructions from the FBI. Unless otherwise specified by the security department, similar arrangements are not required for ransom payments made outside the United States. Similarly, if U.S. funds are specified to be turned into an exchange bank in another country for exchange into foreign currency, the requirements for photographing, recording serial numbers, and packaging the money, need not be followed.

Care must be taken to insure that all money removed from the United States is handled in accordance with U.S. Customs regulations that require registration of the removal of more than $5,000 in U.S. currency.

CHAPTER 36

Bomb Threats

Experts and publications in law enforcement and security alike, indicate that incidents involving explosive or incendiary devices are likely to increase. Consequently, organizations must prepare themselves as best they can for the possibility that they might become targets selected by a bomber.

Yet, how do you know where a bomber will strike or why? How can you determine who he or she is or what organization he or she might belong to? These are questions that need to be answered. However, it would be most unwise to spend a great deal of time in this research while forgetting to prepare for the possible results of an actual bombing incident. Still, by keeping these questions in mind, a better plan for the security of a facility against a bomb situation can be developed. One is likely never to know precisely where a bomber will strike. Attacks, threats, and hoaxes are received by airports, libraries, hospitals, schools, and entertainment centers almost every day. Unfortunately, there seems to be no hard and fast rule governing the type of institution or organization that may be the next target of a bomb threat. Sometimes, however, the target selected by the bomber will indicate the particular motive or the kind of dissident or terrorist group. Any organization may receive a bomb threat but because of location, ownership, size, or product, some businesses *may be* more likely to be bombed than others. For example, certain government or political centers, fuel or chemical installations, power stations and certain public places may be considered higher risk targets for both bomb threats and actual bombings.

As was mentioned before, a bomber's target may give a clue to the motive of the bomber. If a political headquarters is bombed, it would be fairly safe to assume that there may be political reasons for the attack. However, some terrorists or terrorist groups will attack unlikely targets. Their motive appears to be purely psychological. These attacks have a disruptive effect upon society and are even enough to cause panic in extreme cases. The aim of terrorists is typically to make a government and its officials appear helpless in the face of such attacks. If these officials appear discredited, the terrorists then feel that their organization becomes more appealing to the average citizen.

A bomber may be a terrorist or nothing more than a disgruntled employee, a member of the lower class or a member of the upper class, or well-educated and employ technical wiring and detonating devices or be poorly educated and use a crude but effective pipe bomb. As this basic information illustrates, there is indeed a great deal to plan and prepare for if an organization is to effectively curtail the efforts of a bomber.

Initially, very simple things can be done to make a building safer and more resistant to bomb attacks. Basically, the best defense that any security director has is common sense. Many measures that can be taken to improve security can be done for very little money or no money at all. For example, do not allow workers to stockpile any parts or products near a fence. This creates an easy stair-step method of entry for a possible bomber or burglar. Also, try to keep the same sort of materials away from the walls of the building as this would furnish a ready-made stepladder to windows or the roof of a structure. There should be as few trash receptacles as possible situated on the outside of the building. They should be emptied and inspected regularly as well.

Another thing to be very concerned about is the quantity, quality, and placement of security lighting. These very basic, straight-forward items are the types of things that can make a real difference between an organization being the unfortunate target of bombing and being safe. If an organization can make it just a little difficult for a bomber, that bomber may very well decide that it is not worth the risk and give up the notion of planting a device in a company building. Still, it is important that every security director realize that no building is perfectly secure. This is especially true when a building must remain open, providing access to perhaps hundreds of employees every day, very possibly at every hour of the day.

Regrettably, if a bomber is intent upon placing an armed device within the perimeter of a building, he or she can undoubtedly get the job done. However, there are things that can be done to make it a great deal more difficult. Also, preparations *can* be made for the day when such a thing might happen.

Therefore, security directors must look at the buildings that they are responsible for and ensure that they are secure.

Employees must also be ready to take action the minute a bomb threat is received. Operators, specifically, should know how to handle such calls and obtain all of the information possible about the bomb from the caller. They should also be instructed to contact the police and/or fire departments promptly. Police, in turn, should determine whether the assistance of a bomb disposal unit will be necessary. Consequently, organizations should contact local police departments to ensure that, in the event of a bomb situation, they will be able to assist in searches and subsequent investigations. Probably, though, your own people can search as well as, if not better than, the police because they are more familiar with the area that is going to be searched. However, police should always be asked to help in the evacuation if a bomb has been located in building. It is also essential that strict procedures be enforced if genuine security is ever to become a reality. This is best demonstrated by the importance of establishing procedures for inspecting incoming packages. Placing explosives inside packages and letters has long been a favorite method of both vengeful bombers and terrorists. Therefore, secretaries to executives and personnel in mail rooms must be instructed about how to identify possible letter bombs. They should be especially watchful for such things as:

1. Mismatching names and titles.
2. Envelopes that are extremely rigid.
3. Envelopes marked "Photographs—do not bend."
4. Envelopes with no return address.
5. Envelopes received with return address unknown by the recipient and from an unfamiliar source.
6. Excessive amounts of postage.
7. Protruding materials.
8. Envelopes marked "Personal—open by addressee only."
9. Envelopes marked "Hand cancel only."
10. Unprofessionally wrapped packages.
11. Stains on the material or envelope.
12. Distinctive odors.
13. Uneven weight or bumpy envelopes.
14. Packages that are too large or too heavy.

Unfortunately, by using letter bombs, a bomber can be miles away at the time of the explosion and never has to see the result. A bomb is also effective in destroying any possible evidence of the crime. When it explodes, almost every shred of evidence is destroyed in the blast. This all makes subsequent investigations very difficult.

Letter and package bombs are especially hard to detect and can cause a great deal of damage. As a result, packages must be controlled and screened if they are going to be moved into critical areas. Personnel must also be controlled *prior to* entering critical areas by making them wear identification badges that are color coded to tell which departments they are allowed in.

Additionally, representatives from both police and fire departments should be asked to go through your facility with appropriate people who will be responsible for conducting any searches should the need arise. Areas where explosives are likely to be concealed should be prime areas of concentration during such visits. Particular attention should be given to elevator shafts, rest rooms, closets, storage areas, furnace rooms, or hose rooms where fire fighting supplies are stored. Basically, areas should be kept in mind where it would be possible for a bomber to enter and work on the device undetected for a period of time. Keep in mind that not all devices are armed before entering the target. Some devices must be armed after they are in place.

Security and maintenance personnel must also be properly instructed to inspect such likely places to check for unfamiliar objects or persons. They must also be instructed to watch for persons who appear to be checking out the area. If such a person is seen, security personnel *must* check the person for a company ID card or some other form of positive identification.

Further, it is the duty of a director of security to see that adequate protection is specifically given to classified documents or other information that is vital to the company. A company should never rely solely on computers for the storage of information. Recently computers have been singled out as primary targets for bombers.

If a bomb threat is actually received, there should be thorough searches of all suspected areas of the facility. Personnel, typically, should be responsible for searching the area immediately around their desks or work areas. If any strange or out-of-place objects are found, they should immediately point this out to their supervisor. Under no circumstances are they to touch or handle the object. The supervisor will make the decision whether or not to continue the search or whether to evacuate. This is also a good time to point out that personnel should never assume that only one device has been planted. If a suspicious object has been located, under general conditions, the search will continue until the entire area has been completely searched.

The logic behind the workers searching their own work areas is that they can often tell at a glance what objects do and do not belong there. However, trained security or police personnel should oversee the entire search operation to ensure that it is done properly and completely.

In conducting a search for a possible explosive device, everyone should remember a few basic safety rules. Even though a search should be conducted expeditiously, there is still no margin for carelessness or stupidity. Specifically, in conducting searches:

1. Never use more searchers than absolutely necessary.
2. Use a maximum of two searchers per room.
3. Use searchers in alternate rooms or areas.
4. Never assume only one device has been planted; continue operations until the entire area has been searched and found to be clear.
5. Clearly mark (using tape or some similar method) areas or rooms that have already been searched.

In order to ensure that the search being conducted is both safe and effective, certain search techniques should be employed. Again, it would be well to point out that certain techniques are more likely than others to ensure both safety and effectiveness. For example:

1. Never touch a strange or out-of-place object. A note should be made denoting its location and description, and this information should be turned over to the search coordinator.
2. If a danger zone is located, it will be blocked off or barricaded with a clear zone of three hundred feet in every direction until the object has been removed or disarmed.

3. The use of any electronic equipment will be prohibited. No one will be allowed to have a portable radio or walkie-talkie within the area under threat of a bomb. These devices can cause premature detonation of an electronic initiator (blasting cap).

If a company should receive a bomb threat and it does become necessary to initiate an actual bomb search, a two-person team approach is recommended. In using this system, a team of two persons—one of whom should be either a security or police officer—are assigned to search specific areas.

Should a device or a suspicious object be located, the search teams should be instructed to use the following procedures:

1. They are to report to the director of security with a description of the device and an accurate description of its location. If the police are handling the situation, then this information should be immediately relayed to the officer in charge. If they were not notified earlier, this information will then be relayed to the police and fire departments.
2. Once the device is located, sandbags or mattresses will be placed carefully around the object so as not to disturb it. *A danger area of 300 feet around the object will be established.* This includes any area *above* or *below* the device.
3. Once the device has been cushioned in this manner, the searchers must be instructed to make sure all doors and windows have been opened to minimize damage from either a primary blast or secondary fragmentation. This should be done by the searchers as they are evacuating the building.
4. Once outside, no one should be allowed to enter or reenter the building. This will permit the bomb squad to remove or to disarm the device without the added worry of unauthorized people being in the blast area.

Finally, remember that there are events that may occur that would change how a security director would respond in a given situation. However, if this general information is available and known by all personnel, then a company would certainly be a safer, more secure place in which to work.

PROCEDURES FOR BOMB THREATS

Proper actions are essential if a bomb threat is made against a facility. The person receiving the threat must be prepared to deal with the caller, get accurate information about the alleged bomb, and assist the authorities in identifying the caller. The use of the Bomb Threat Report Form in Figure 36–1 will better

INSTRUCTIONS: BE CALM. BE COURTEOUS. LISTEN, DO NOT INTERRUPT THE CALLER.
NOTIFY SUPERVISOR/SECURITY OFFICER BY PREARRANGED SIGNAL WHILE CALLER
IS ON LINE.

Date _____ Time _____

Exact words of person placing call: _____

_____

_____

QUESTIONS TO ASK:

1. When is the bomb going to explode? _____

2. Where is the bomb right now? _____

3. What kind of a bomb is it? _____

4. What does it look like? _____

5. Why did you place the bomb? _____

_____

TRY TO DETERMINE THE FOLLOWING (CIRCLE AS APPROPRIATE)

Caller's identity: Male   Female   Adult   Juvenile   Age _____ years

Voice: Loud   Soft   High pitch   Deep   Raspy   Pleasant   Intoxicated   Other _____

Accent: Local   Not local   Foreign   Region

Speech: Fast   Slow   Distinct   Distorted   Stutter   Nasal   Slurred   Lisp

Language: Excellent   Good   Fair   Poor   Foul   Other _____

Manner: Calm   Angry   Rational   Irrational   Coherent   Incoherent   Deliberate   Emotional
          Righteous   Laughing   Intoxicated

Background Noises: Office machines   Factory machines   Bedlam   Trains   Animals   Music   Quiet
                     Voices   Mixed   Airplanes   Street traffic   Party atmosphere

ADDITIONAL INFORMATION: _____

_____

ACTION TO TAKE IMMEDIATELY AFTER CALL: Notify your supervisor/security officer as instructed. Talk to
no one other than instructed by your supervisor/security officer.

_____   _____
RECEIVING TELEPHONE NUMBER   PERSON RECEIVING CALL

Figure 36–1 Sample bomb threat report form.

insure that all relevant information is collected from the caller. These forms
should be distributed to all telephone users and used *while* the caller is talking
(if possible).

Evacuation and search procedures as well as the policy for contacting the
authorities should also be prepared.

IN BRIEF

These specific procedures may help to evaluate the legitimacy of a bomb threat and, when necessary, to respond to it appropriately:

A. *Receiving a bomb threat*
    1. Keep the caller on the line as long as possible. Ask the caller to repeat the message and try to record the words spoken by the person making the call. (The local telephone company should also be contacted to ascertain the availability and legal usage of equipment for recording bomb threat calls when calls become repetitive in nature.)
    2. If the caller does not indicate the location of the bomb or the time of possible detonation, the person receiving the call should *ask* the caller to provide this information.
    3. It is advisable to inform the caller that the building is occupied and that the detonation of a bomb could result in death or serious injury to many innocent people.
    4. Pay particular attention for any strange or peculiar background noises such as motors running, background music, and any other noises that might give even a remote clue as to the place from which the call is being made.
    5. Listen closely to the voice (male—female), voice quality, accents, and speech impediments, drunkenness, and so forth.
    6. Immediately after the caller hangs up, report the information to the security director (or his or her designee).
    7. The person receiving the call must document the time, date, and so forth of the call and make a verbatim record of the conversation immediately after notification to the emergency coordinator.
    8. The security director must seek police and/or fire department assistance as determined appropriate under the exigencies of the circumstances. However, the nearest law enforcement agency *must* always be alerted immediately to any threat and advised of the details and circumstances surrounding the threat.
    9. All such incidents must be promptly reported to the security department.
B. *Initial action after receipt of the threat.* An emergency must be dealt with by persons present or immediately available. The best approach is to establish a list of persons authorized to deal with the problem in the order of preference for notification. Ideally, the emergency coordinator and his or her alternates should be given first consideration.

C. *Evaluate the threat.* In planning a sound bomb defense, *available data* cites a compelling reason to concentrate upon *prevention* rather than threat response. It is 5 times more likely that a real bomb will not be preceded by a threat than that it will. It is 100 times more likely that when a threat is received, it will not involve a real bomb than that one is present.

This is the single most important step in the bomb procedure. The key to whether we deal rationally with a threat or rush into overreaction depends upon the skill with which the threat is analyzed. Although the decisions will always depend upon the facts in the particular case, there are some general assumptions that will be helpful.

1. Actual explosive devices are more likely to be found in buildings that are completely or partly accessible to the public than in those that are not.

2. The more effective the controls on admittance of persons and materials, the less likely it is that an actual explosive device will be found in a given facility.

3. The favored places in which explosives will be placed are those in which a member of the public might expect to find privacy or shelter while placing the device. Lavatories, utility closets, electrical and mechanical lockers, stairwells and elevator shafts, pulley houses, entrance doors, reception areas, and exterior perimeters of the building should be considered as prime areas.

4. If a device is planted and does explode, damage is more likely to be confined to a specific area than it is to involve the entire facility. This is especially true in very large facilities and in those with good, firm dividers or strong bearing walls.

5. Remember that a dramatic response to a warning or threat, such as evacuating all or a part of a building, is often likely to be followed by additional threats.

6. The more detailed and credible the warning, the greater the likelihood that an actual explosive device is involved. If a warning is given in connection with a genuine bomb, it is because the bomber is intent on avoiding or reducing injuries to persons. One intending death or injury will *not* warn.

7. A nonspecific or inherently incredible warning (for example, from a child, a drunk, a giggler, or an incoherent person) is not likely to involve an actual explosive.

8. In all cases the police and fire organizations must be notified. However, they should not be expected to provide any significant help between the time a warning is received and the time an actual device is found. Most facilities will be dependent on their

own resources, both as to decisions to be made and postwarning precautions to be taken.

9. Because of the possibilities for diguise and concealment, the only persons likely to locate an actual device through a search are those who are intimately familiar with the area being searched. Prior to evacuation all personnel should make a cursory search of their own work areas. The only reliable criterion in conducting a search is that any object capable of being or concealing an explosive device (generally anything the size of a typical lunch box thermos bottle) is suspect until identified by a person who recognizes it.

D. *Search procedures.* Once the bomb threat has been received and evaluated as being real, the main objective would be to locate the device if it does in fact exist and to prevent or minimize any damage from it, all without injury to or death of personnel. To accomplish these objectives, the following procedures are suggested:

1. The suspected area should be evacuated to the extent feasible, and persons should be stationed to prevent unauthorized personnel from entering.

2. Personnel assigned to the exterior search should be divided into one team or unit for each building or, where insufficient personnel are available, a single exterior search unit should process each building in sequence. A thorough search of exterior areas is extremely important because they are the most accessible areas to the bomber, especially at night when the building is closed.

3. Search personnel should make an immediate check of those interior areas most likely to attract a bomber. This includes areas open to the public and areas containing cleaning equipment. Reception rooms, lobbies, elevators, stairs, and rest rooms are frequent bomb targets and must be closely screened. The searchers should move systematically from floor to floor up through the building. Areas searched should be marked to eliminate duplication or omission or search by others.

4. Those engaged in search activities should systematically search each room or area of the building, beginning with public and utility areas. These searches should be augmented by members of the janitorial or maintenance force who will be familiar with their initial areas of search. When all the areas on one level have been searched, the detailed room search teams should move up to the next level and conduct a search of that area. This system of search should continue until the entire structure has been searched.

5. Utility and service areas are generally located in the basement or subbasement and may be prime target areas for the bomber.

Destroying a building's utility area puts the building out of operation with small risk of killing or injuring the occupants. Whenever possible, search of utility areas should be at least guided by maintenance personnel familiar with the facility. Furnace rooms, electrical control centers, telephone switching rooms, auxiliary power plants, central air conditioning units, and elevator shafts and wells should all be searched as well as any storage or maintenance areas.

E. *Evacuation.* In handling bomb threat situations, the evacuation of facilities may become necessary. When such situations occur, compliance with the following procedures is vitally important.

1. As time and circumstances permit, the emergency coordinator must report the known facts to the manager (or his or her designee) responsible for the operation of the facility.

2. Depending upon the time and circumstances, the manager, or other executive management indicated in 1. above, *will* make the decision to evacuate employees from a building or facility. Such decisions must weigh the danger and risk involved where there is nonevacuation against the lost man hours when such threats are a hoax.

3. The evacuation signal may be the same as that used for a fire. However, there is one consideration in this regard that must be evaluated. The normal procedure in the case of fire is to close all doors and windows. In the case of a bomb explosion, closing doors and windows could increase damage. Where the capability exists, it is preferable to use voice communication for evacuation purposes. Such announcements must be made calmly and personnel should be instructed to leave all windows and doors open.

4. Routes of evacuation will be based on the type of building and the location of personnel within building.

5. Priority consideration must be given to identifying safe routes of evacuation in the event a bomb is located. In addition to the immediate danger area, in multistoried buildings, personnel on floors above the danger area should be evacuated first. This can be simultaneous with the evacuation of lower levels provided it can be done in an orderly manner.

6. If an evacuation is made and personnel held on standby pending completion of the search, an evacuation or holding area must be established and controlled. This area should be at a distance far enough away from the building to protect personnel against debris and so forth, in the event of an explosion.

7. The member of top management, after consultation with the security director, and police or fire personnel, will make the decision when to have employees return to their work stations. A suitable means of communication must be established to notify

employees when it is safe to return to work. In connection with bomb threat evacuations, additional procedural aspects regarding shutdown measures must be considered.

8. If the building is to be evacuated, a decision must be rendered as to whether all electricity, gas, and fuel lines should be shut off at main switches or valves. Such emergency shutdown and restart procedures must be accomplished by personnel who are entirely competent to shut down or restart such processes.

CHAPTER 37

Terrorism and Civil Disturbances

A major problem that confronts the private security community in dealing with terrorist groups is that these groups do not generally resemble the *typical* criminal or criminal group. In many instances the only thing these groups have in common with the groups with which security and law enforcement agencies generally deal is the criminal aspect of their activities. However, in a great many cases the education, dedication, and sophistication of the majority of the members of these groups present a problem quite new to law enforcement agencies. The constant changing of targets by these groups is an added problem. Even those security departments that have faced this problem for the past few years are still developing techniques for dealing with the problem. While there has been effort on the part of both security and the police to better understand the problems associated with the phenomenon of urban terrorism and to develop effective countermeasures, there is a need, in the face of the rapid growth of the activity, for additional focus and attention in the form of concentrated training to deal more effectively with the problem.

Unfortunately, terrorism as a means of achieving an end or as an activity in itself is not limited to either an individual or an organization as a target. Both are likely targets. Likewise, terrorist activity is not limited to *leftist* or revolutionary individuals or organizations. Terrorism is also an activity of *rightist* or reactionary individuals or organizations. As unpalatable as it may be to our thinking, terrorism *is not* the *sole province* of the *out groups*. Terrorism is sometimes the mode of operation of the regime—regime used here in the generic sense, i.e., government at any and all levels.

TERRORISM AND THE PRIVATE SECTOR

Revolution as a concept, of course, is not new to the world and certainly not to the United States nor is the association of terrorist activity as a part of revolutionary tactics. However, what is relatively new to the business community is the concept of using guerrilla warfare tactics as an approach by the urban terrorists operating in the private sector. Certainly terrorism is not new to the public law enforcement community. However, the terrorist's activities that they have traditionally had to deal with have generally been associated with the activities of organized groups of criminals for whom terrorism was merely another business tactic, e.g., protection or muscle to take over business. There has also been the occasional individual or group involved in some form of terrorism either as a manifestation of some mental disorder or even for kicks. The law enforcement community has had some success in the development of both countermeasures and investigative techniques to either prevent or apprehend those involved in such acts of terrorism.

A major problem for private security in dealing with terrorist activities is to be able to establish the balance between strategic and tactical analyses in order to be able to be effectively proactive as well as reactive to such activities and, at the same time, not violate the accepted principles of privacy and security.

Quite obviously, if security departments operate only in a reactive mode, they will not fulfill their assigned mission nor will they be effective in dealing with criminal terrorism as an activity. At the same time, if there are not adequate guidelines about the point(s) at which the agencies can institute active intelligence gathering so that they can be effective in proactive mode, they may violate the accepted principles of privacy and security.

The law enforcement community is confined to dealing with criminal acts and violations of criminal law. Terrorism as an activity has many facets that are difficult to identify within the definition of criminal action or even violation of civil law. However, there may be instances where a violation of civil law is much clearer than a violation of criminal law. In such cases private companies must recognize and be prepared to utilize the appropriate avenues to transfer the matter to civil proceedings. For example, terror itself is a state of mind. This state of mind can be brought about by actions that may be very difficult to define as criminal acts. Implied threats, for example, are most difficult to first define and then prove. However, there may be elements of civil law violation involved that could be exploited.

CITIZEN SUPPORT

Additionally, some forms of terrorism and some targets of terrorism may receive implicit sanction from given segments of the otherwise law abiding segments of the community. Many individuals, while not moved to such acts themselves, may not be too perturbed about acts of terrorism carried out against organizations (businesses or people), especially those that they feel do not function in the best interests of the public as they define it. This means that while the terrorist group may not get direct support from such individuals neither will the law enforcement community. This amounts, in effect, to support of the terrorist group by apathy.

Still another dilemma which faces the business community is the fact that terrorism as a tactic is not confined to the *leftist* side of the picture. Terrorism is all too frequently also the tactic of the reactionary groups. Frequently, this terrorism is a form of *revolutionary tactics* with individual companies caught in the middle. This situation is one in which the citizen support problem can be very real and create an extremely sensitive, volatile, and potentially explosive atmosphere for the security department involved. There may be strong sentiment among a reasonably large segment of the population that such action is the only way to deal with revolutionaries. The law enforcement agency must protect the target group from such terrorist actions or investigate and seek prosecution for such actions if they occur. Public sentiment may directly oppose these efforts.

TODAY'S PROBLEMS

It is also recognized that the problems being faced today are different from those surrounding the civil disruptions and riots of the late 1960s. While some of the same social and economic conditions are being identified as the basis for the current terrorist activities, the resultant action is quite different. True, there were bombings, i.e., molotov cocktails in stores and automobiles, in the 1960s. However, they were more targets of opportunity than planned targets for the purpose of creating terror. Likewise, looting as a part of the total riot scene had a different purpose from burglary of an arsenal or bank robbery for the securing of arms and money on a planned basis. This means that even those law enforcement and security agencies that experienced such disorder in the late 1960s cannot assume that they are totally prepared to meet the challenge of current terrorist activities.

We see, then, that the problems related to criminal acts of urban terrorism are very complex and have a different character than the criminal activities that have traditionally been faced by law enforcement agencies even when these activities include traditional criminal activities—kidnapping, robbery, extortion, burglary, and narcotics trafficking. The elements of education, commitment, and sophistication add very difficult dimensions to the problem. They also make it a *very different* problem from that of the riots and civil disturbances of the late 1960s.

New technology, changing social conditions, and the demands for new services create ever-increasing pressures on both law enforcement and private security for better programs. The problem of providing such programs is multifaceted and complex. A major portion of the solutions to these problems rests in the training and education of both law enforcement and security personnel.

Urban terrorism as an activity of organized groups, who may or may not in their other activities be considered under the normal classification of *organized criminal gang,* certainly cannot be considered a simple problem facing both police and private security. When it is a tactic of groups whose activities are generally classified as organized crime, the problem is more recognizable. However, this does not make dealing with these groups any simpler. In both instances, there are frequent overtones of political, and even religious, activities that create very real problems. These problems evolve from the need to recognize and respect legitimate political and religious activities of groups that may, in fact, be being used as a cover by certain segments of not-so-legitimate groups for their criminal activities. In other cases the political or religious element may be introduced by the terrorist groups to deliberately create a facade of legitimacy.

In any case it is becoming increasingly evident that terrorism as a tactic of certain groups is a reality that the law enforcement community must face. Likewise, it is equally evident that terrorism as an organized group activity is on the increase. Protective services, in general, must satisfy a varied and subtle set of objectives. Dealing with the problem of urban terrorism has the appearance of an activity with less subtle objectives. Still it involves a varied set of objectives and to some extent some very real and difficult subtleties. Unfortunately, guidelines for action and methods for dealing with such activity cannot be derived in any straightforward fashion, either from the criminal/legal codes or from the public sentiment about law, order, and justice. On the other hand, programs for dealing with this problem, even more than many other security programs, cannot be a matter of pragmatic decision making with guidelines or goals stated explicitly. Rather, every program must be designed to meet the specific terrorist problems that it is most likely to encounter.

CIVIL DISTURBANCES

Unlike terrorist attacks, civil disturbances can, in most instances, be prepared for with a generic plan. An example of such a plan follows.

EMERGENCY PLAN OUTLINE AGAINST CIVIL DISTURBANCES*

I. *Purpose.* The following items should be included in the purpose of the plan:
    A. Orderly and efficient transition from normal to emergency operations.
    B. Delegation of emergency authority.
    C. Assignment of emergency responsibilities.
    D. Assurance of continuity of operations.
    E. Indication of authority by company executives for actions contained in the plan.

---

*From the National Association of Manufacturers.

II. *Execution instructions.* This should include the elements of who, what, when, where, and how for executing the plan:
   A. Individual(s) having authority to execute the plan.
   B. Conditions under which the plan may be partially executed.
   C. Conditions under which the plan may be fully executed.
   D. Coordination between all responsible individuals to assure an efficient sequence of execution.

III. *Command control center.* The command control center is the plan command post—the focal point for directing all emergency actions. If more than one control center is established, for decentralized operations, all emergency actions should be coordinated through the central control center.
   A. *Location.* The primary location should be in a well-protected area of the facility where access can be controlled with a minimum of manpower. An alternate location, also well protected, should be selected in the event of damage or inaccessibility to the primary location.
      1. Primary.
      2. Alternate.
   B. *Chain of command.* Assure the legal continuity of leadership and direction. Prepare a management succession list to assure leadership and supervision in the event executive and administrative personnel and key employees are incapacitated or unable to report to work. Assure that management continuity and other emergency modifications of the organization are in accord with state corporate laws and the charter or bylaws of the company.
      1. Emergency organization.
      2. Continuity of management and key employees.
      3. Designation of successors.
      4. Prepublished company orders constituting emergency authority.
      5. Establishment of orders in accordance with state corporate laws and charter or bylaws of the company.
   C. *Planning coordination and liaison.* This element of the plan is designed to assure mutual planning approaches and objectives. It also provides a means of keeping you abreast of the social climate and receiving advance warning of the imminence and possible magnitude of a disturbance. Coordination and liaison should be maintained with:
      1. Local and state officials.
      2. Fire departments.
      3. Adjacent plants and business firms.
      4. Local utilities.

          5. Employee union officials.

          6. Local news media for news release policy.

    D. *Communications.* Internal and external for command control units.

          1. Internal.

             a. Adequate coverage of plant area.

             b. Complement primary system with two-way radios, walkie-talkies, field telephones, or megaphones (bull-horns).

             c. Controlled usage.

          2. *External.* Local and state law enforcement agencies (consider police radio monitor).

             a. Fire departments.

             b. Hospitals.

             c. Adjacent plants and business firms.

             d. Management and key employees.

             e. Switchboard operators trained in emergency procedures.

    E. Maintain a log of all emergency actions taken.

IV. *Personnel*

    A. An inventory should be made of employee secondary skills.

          1. Apply secondary skills to possible emergency requirements based on emergency organization.

          2. Determine degree of competence.

          3. Develop accelerated training where necessary.

    B. *Availability.* Keep switchboards open and operators available. Designate male operators as alternates for female operators who may not report. The cascade system of notification is very effective. This is accomplished by having the switchboard operator, or whatever means are available, notify two or more key persons. They in turn will notify a designated number of employees, who in turn will notify others until all employees have been notified.

          1. System of notification (cascade system).

             a. Recall to work.

             b. Reporting instructions.

          2. Rendezvous or reporting points. Central assembly points for employees should be preselected, if possible, in areas of relative safety. Employees should be informed of the location of these areas and instructed to report to them if routes to the plan are inaccessible. Transportation, i.e., busses or trucks, should be provided from assembly points to the plant.

             a. Primary—out of emergency area.

             b. Secondary—alternate for primary.

      c. Inform employees of location(s).
3. Transportation.
    a. Company-owned.
    b. Contract needs.
    c. Mutual needs with other facilities.
    d. Escort by law enforcement agencies.
    e. Preselected routes from reporting points to and from the facilities. (Plan for escort of female personnel—car pools should be considered.)
4. Training.
    a. Emergency functions.
        1) Primary and/or secondary skills (related to inventory of secondary skills).
        2) Immediate emergency repairs.
            a) Internal.
            b) External.
    b. Situation briefings. Employees should be briefed daily as to the impact of the riot on the facilities and the overall status of the community. These briefings must be factual in order to dispel rumors and speculation.
        1) Preemergency.
        2) During the emergency.
            a) Reacting to crowd pressure. Employees should be prepared psychologically to remain on the job. They should be advised that management needs their loyalty. Self-restraint must be emphasized: don't irritate the mob; don't associate with rioters; in essence, ignore the overtures of the mob. Act only upon, and as directed by, management or local law enforcement officials. The pressures of the mob may be overwhelming; thus this type of training is essential.
                1) Psychological preparation.
                2) Self-restraint.
                3) Act only upon direction of management or law enforcement officials.
                4) Report all rumors to supervisor
                5) Loyalty to the organization.
            b) Postemergency.
                1) Recognition of exemplary performance.
                2) Impact of emergency on plant.
                3) Employment continuity.

V. *Evacuation routes.* Predesignated routes to evacuate buildings and/or the plant should be included. All employees should be informed of these routes and of procedures for evacuation.

A. *Buildings.*
    1. Evacuate by departments if practicable.
    2. Exits.
        a. Primaries.
        b. Alternates.
B. *Location.*
    1. Primary—away from emergency area.
    2. Alternates—away from emergency areas.

VI. *Electric power.* Coordinate this portion of the plan with local electric power companies.
A. *Transmission lines.*
    1. Location of transformer banks.
    2. Alternates—away from emergency area.
B. *Emergency power.* An auxiliary source for providing sufficient emergency power for lighting and other essentials. This should not be construed to mean a standby capability to continue full production operations. The following items are suggested:
    1. Generators.
        a. Show size and location.
        b. Fuel supply.
        c. Operators.
    2. Battery-powered.
        a. Flashlights.
        b. Lanterns.
        c. Other battery-powered sources of illumination.

VII. *Security.* The essential elements of this portion of the plan are:
A. *Organizational plans.*
    1. Develop plant security organization.
    2. Put security plans and procedures in writing.
    3. Provide for reporting promptly to the FBI any actual or suspected acts of espionage or sabotage.
    4. Liaison with the local and state law enforcement agencies.
    5. Have supervisory personnel attend plant protection training courses.
B. *Guard force.*
    1. Organize the guard force.
    2. Prescribe qualification standards.
    3. Insure that guards are:
        a. Trained.
        b. Uniformed.
        c. Armed. (Examine the authority and legal liability during civil disturbances. Check with local officials.)
        d. Deputized (if necessary).
    4. Assure that the guard force is on duty at all times.
    5. Issue written orders to the guard force.

6. Have an internal communication system for the exclusive use of the guard force.
7. Plan for an auxiliary guard force for use in an emergency. (This may be accomplished by designating and training company employees. If contract guards are to be used, advance arrangement should be made.)

C. *Perimeter barriers.*
   1. Check the facility security fences (or other perimeter barriers) to insure that they are:
      a. Properly maintained.
      b. Inspected regularly.
   2. Vehicle parking should be located outside of the security fence or wall. (This reduces the fire potential from gasoline in vehicle tanks and minimizes the hazard of explosives and incendiary devices that are easily concealed in a vehicle.)
   3. There should be adequate protective lighting to illuminate critical areas.
   4. Intrusion detection devices may also be used.

D. *Control of entry.*
   1. Develop procedures for positive identification and control of employees. (Samples of identification media should be given to local law enforcement officials. This is essential for getting through police lines and during times of curfew.)
      a. Identification cards (sample to police).
      b. Badges (sample to police).
      c. Personal recognition (may be used for routine admission of employees to plants with less than thirty employees per shift).
   2. Develop procedures for control of visitors.
   3. Admittance to the facility should be controlled by the guard force.
   4. Exercise control over movement and parking of vehicles.

E. *Protection of critical areas.* Identify and list critical areas within the plant.
   1. Enclose critical areas with physical barriers.
   2. Designate specific personnel who are to have access to critical areas.
   3. Admittance to critical areas should be controlled by:
      a. The guard force or
      b. Supervisory personnel.
   4. Protect unattended critical areas by:
      a. Locks. (Locks should be rotated upon notification of impending civil disorder or other emergency.)
      b. Intrusion detection devices.
   5. Develop a key control system.

      6.   Develop package and material control procedures.

      7.   Institute procedures to protect gasoline pumps and other dispensers of flammable material. (Disconnect power source to electrically operated pumps.)

  F.   *Personnel security.*

      1.   Conduct preemployment investigations of applicants.

      2.   Make personnel checks of persons who are authorized access to critical areas.

      3.   Brief employees regarding the importance of plant security and the need for exercising vigilance.

VIII. *Fire prevention.* These measures are of utmost importance in preventing or minimizing fire damage resulting from civil disorders.

  A.   Post and enforce fire prevention regulations.

  B.   Extend fire alarm system to all areas of the facility.

  C.   Determine whether the municipal fire department can arrive at the facility within:

      1.   Five minutes after the report of an alarm.

      2.   Ten minutes after the report of an alarm.

  D.   Have a secondary water supply system for fire protection.

  E.   Have facility fire protection equipment onsite and insure that it is properly maintained.

  F.   Determine from local fire department the feasibility of using mesh wire or other screening material to protect roofs from fire bombs, Molotov cocktails, or other incendiary devices.

  G.   Organize employees into fire fighting brigades and rescue squads.

  H.   Store combustible material in a well-protected area.

  I.   Instruct employees in the use of fire extinguishers.

  J.   Conduct fire drills periodically.

  K.   Maintain good housekeeping standards.

  L.   Implement recommendations in the latest fire insurance inspection report.

IX. *Vital records protection.* Develop procedures for classification and protection of vital corporate records and protection of cash and other valuable items.

X. *Property and liability insurance.* Review property and liability insurance against potential loss or obligation resulting from riots and other destructive acts.

XI. *Emergency requirements.* These requirements should be based on estimated needs for the duration of the emergency. These items should be prestocked because conditions may preclude their procurement during the emergency. Unused portions can be carried over for postemergency use.

  A.   Food.

  B.   Water.

    C. Medical supplies.
    D. Quarters.
        1. Sleeping.
        2. Separate male and female employees.
    E. Sanitation.
    F. Administrative supplies (office equipment).
    G. Emergency repair tools and equipment.
    H. Procedures for employees to purchase gasoline from plant supply in case local stations are closed.

XII. *Testing the plan.* Frequent testing and correcting the plan will improve its effectiveness upon implementation under actual conditions. An emergency plan, like a chain, is no stronger than its weakest link.
    A. Types of tests:
        1. Partial—testing individual segments of the plan.
        2. Complete—testing entire plan.
    B. Tests should be unannounced.
    C. Weaknesses should be noted and the plan revised to include corrective actions.

CHAPTER 38

Emergency and Disaster Planning

This material outlines the emergency planning for the protection of company assets and those that are on the company's property during or after a disaster.

EMERGENCY PLANNING PROGRAM

Initially, it is imperative that *all* operating entities within your organization maintain up-to-date emergency programs. Also, keep in mind that the widespread dispersal of facilities and personnel often increases the potential exposure to which an organization can fall victim.

However, experience has proven that casualties and damage can be minimized through careful advance planning. Effective planning and implementation of an emergency program begin with an evaluation and utilization of existing resources. The major areas requiring consideration and written plans are:

1. Administration
2. Personnel
3. Emergency services
4. Vital records
5. Continuity of operations
6. Restoration of facilities
7. Reporting

   I. *Administration.* Emergency plans should provide for:
      A. The appointment of coordinators who have responsibility for the overall program on a divisional/subsidiary, as well as location, level.
      B. The appointment of an advisory staff (where appropriate) to represent various departments of the plant, laboratory, office, or other locations involved.
      C. The designation of management succession to provide for continuity of management.
      D. The training of personnel in fire, first aid, rescue, damage control, and evacuation.

    E.   The designation of both onsite and offsite emergency control head-
quarters.

    F.   The procedures for emergency shutdown of the facility.

II.   *Personnel.* Plans should provide for locating, accounting for, communi-
cating with, and rendering appropriate assistance to employees both at
home and at work. The following should be considered:

    A.   Personnel reporting centers or procedures as required by local
conditions.

    B.   Assignment of personnel to operate such centers.

    C.   Advice to employees concerning the plan as it affects their welfare.
Employee-manager meetings, individual letters to employees, location and divisional newspapers, bulletin boards, and so forth
may be used.

    D.   Evacuation procedures and the designation of available shelter
areas.

    E.   Provision for emergency funds to meet payroll and operating ex-
penses.

    F.   Immediate availability of current personnel listings. Listings should
include home addresses, position classification, and other personnel
data that would be helpful in an emergency.

    G.   Ability of a manager to reach employees at home during nonwork-
ing hours.

III.   *Emergency services.* It is necessary to provide adequate personnel and
proper equipment to respond immediately to an emergency condition.
This is the first line of defense in limiting the extent and seriousness of
injuries and damage. Therefore, advance training, specific assignments,
and planning are necessary for:

    A.   Facility protection,

    B.   Fire protection,

    C.   Vital services and supplies,

    D.   Emergency alert system,

    E.   Rescue teams,

    F.   Damage control units,

    G.   First aid teams,

    H.   Emergency equipment,

    I.   Emergency transportation,

    J.   Communications facilities,

    K.   Medical personnel and supplies, and

    L.   Emergency numbers for police, fire, hospital, ambulance, utility
companies, and military or police explosive unit.

IV.   *Vital records.* To ensure continued operations, each location should
provide a program for the protection of vital records based on requirements to reconstruct and resume activities after a disaster.

V.   *Continuity of operations.* Planning should include the resumption of
operations (production, development, marketing, and so forth) at an

alternate site. While immediate standby facilities cannot be provided, contingency plans should be maintained in respect to leased space or other company facilities. This, together with a planned course of action and offsite vital records, will assist in the prompt resumption of operations.

Particular attention should be given to backup facilities for data processing, reproduction, and microfilming operations as well as supporting parts procurement, manufacturing processes, and engineering records that support manufacturing. Current documentation to support vital data processing operations is critical to disaster recovery.

VI. *Restoration of facilities.* Necessary plans or blueprints for each facility should be protected as part of the vital records program. Provision should be made locally for restoring a damaged facility as quickly as possible with consideration given to availability of extra contractors and materials. Personnel should be assigned responsibility for liaison with supply and service organizations, e.g., power, light, water, telephone.

VII. *Reporting.* In addition to offering every reasonable assistance to company employees, one also must consider clients, customers, and the general population in the event of an emergency. When a disaster occurs, it should be promptly reported up the line organization. When appropriate, it will be the line organization's responsibility to advise the corporate office. Preliminary reports must be made at the earliest possible time and should be followed by detailed information as soon as it becomes available. Reports should include the nature and extent of the emergency, injuries to employees, damage to employees' property, damage to company property, damage to customers' offices and installed equipment, and action taken or recommended.

Consequently, conditions affecting the welfare and/or safety of employees should be promptly reported to top management by the director of personnel or the director of security.

Other company locations in the immediate area and those that normally have day to day business with the affected location should be advised any time a location closes due to an emergency or experiences a serious situation that could cause injuries or otherwise affect nearby company locations. (Examples: fire, explosion, threat, inclement weather, power failure.)

A. *Testing.* Periodic tests of the vital records program should be conducted at locations by the company's records management division. These tests necessarily include those parts of emergency planning that bear on resumption/continuity of operations. Operating units should encourage locations to test their own vital records/emergency planning programs. These tests are especially effective for emergency services, continuity of operations, facility restoration, and so forth.

B. *Review of Planning.* The company's lawyers should be responsible for reviewing division and subsidiary planning to ensure that it is not only complete but also adequate enough to avoid the potential for liability. Additionally, records management should be responsible for reviewing and testing the vital records program. Divisions and subsidiaries should also be responsible for reviewing plans of their locations.

C. *Emergency work rotation plan.* The purpose of this plan is to permit the dispersal of employees during any grave emergency or disaster, either internal or external. The emergency plans at every location must contain procedures that give assurance that their plan can be activated within 24 hours.

Upon receipt of instructions from top management to activate the plan, locations will assign employees to one of five teams on either a departmental or functional basis. Each team, representing 20 percent of the normal work force, will work its customary hours two days a week, so that 40 percent of the work force will be at work and 60 percent will be dispersed. During the period that the plan is in operation, no employee is to receive less than regular salary.

This will be maintained as an *on the shelf* plan with no ongoing implementation.

D. *Disaster support.* Financial or other assistance to company employees affected by a disaster should be based on individual consideration. Immediate action should be taken if the situation is urgent. If time permits, recommendations should be made by the location manager and approved by the division.

In cases of disaster, organizations such as the American Red Cross and the Salvation Army usually mobilize their forces in the area to alleviate hardships to the best of their ability. The company should cooperate with such organizations, and contribute to relief funds occasioned by the disaster. (Follow corporate guidelines on making contributions.)

E. *Emergencies affecting the community.* Areas containing a number of company facilities require additional planning for emergencies (e.g., civil disorders) affecting part or all of the community.

An area coordinator should be appointed to act as a central dissemination point for communications and to serve in an advisory capacity to the other locations.

Liaison with police and other authorities should also be centralized to avoid unnecessary inquiries from other company managers. On an individual location basis:

1. Designate those individuals authorized to declare an emergency closing.

2. Assure that employees understand they are not required to enter a troubled area and may leave such an area if a disturbance develops.

3. Make sure that employees are not placed in a position of violating curfews imposed by the authorities.

In order to further explain the specifics associated with effective emergency and disaster planning, the following questionnaire is offered. It identifies a variety of important considerations that need to be taken into account when designing or implementing such a plan.

EMERGENCY PREPAREDNESS QUESTIONNAIRE

A. Emergency plan organization and communications
   1. Who is delegated decision making authority?
      a. Name
      b. Title
      c. Home address
      d. Home telephone number
   2. List order of delegation as indicated in plan.
      a. Name
      b. Title
      c. Home address
      d. Home telephone number
         1) Who is delegated authority after normal working hours and how is this person contacted?
         2) Is one organization functional for decision making with regard to all emergencies?
   3. What are criteria for determining at the time of the emergency whether the location will be:
      a. Operated on a normal basis (possibly with some modification to guard and protection tours)?
      b. Operated on a limited basis (designate functions that will operate)?
      c. Closed down and manned solely by supervisory and plant protection personnel?
      d. Closed down and unmanned for the duration of the emergency?
   4. Is there a procedure for advising employees of the decision to activate the plan?
      a. What method is used?
      b. Describe.

5. What is the possibility of a disaster or emergency affecting your company?
   a. What is the geographic proximity to troubled, sensitive, or potentially hazardous areas that might cause emergencies or disasters?
   b. Is the company located in a geographic area that is particularly susceptible to weather-related emergencies or disasters?
   c. What is the probability of an internal emergency or disaster?
   d. Can plant be reached by public transportation?
6. Have all sources of advance civil disturbance information been explored?
   a. Local Government agencies.
      1) Name
      2) Title
      3) Agency
      4) Telephone number
   b. Civil Defense
      1) Name
      2) Title
      3) Agency
      4) Telephone number
   c. Local law enforcement and state police
      1) Name
      2) Title
      3) Agency
      4) Telephone number
   d. Local fire department
      1) Name
      2) Title
      3) Agency
      4) Telephone number
   e. National Guard
      1) Name
      2) Title
      3) Agency
      4) Telephone number
7. Is location working with neighboring industry in the formation of a united front?
   a. List neighboring industry involved.
   b. Who is the company's representative?
   c. What significant items have developed from these discussions?

B. Security personnel
   1. Are all security personnel fully instructed on their responsibilities

prior to, during, and after an emergency, whether it is external or internal?

    a. Verbally?

    b. Written instructions?

2. Are training sessions scheduled so that personnel will be thoroughly familiar with all safeguards and protective devices provided in the plant?

3. Are security personnel sufficiently equipped for self protection?

    a. Emergency lights?

    b. Battery operated megaphones? Public address system?

    c. Transceivers (walkie-talkies)?

    d. First-aid kits?

    e. Battery powered AM/FM receiver tunable to police band?

    f. Metal helmets?

    g. Bulletproof vests?

    h. Other?

4. Have emergency procedures been established for both operating and nonoperating hours? Do security personnel fully understand these procedures?

5. Can guard force be supplemented rapidly?

    a. Guard contractors?

    b. Other company locations?

    c. Company management employees?

6. Are living arrangements and supplies available on the premises should circumstances dictate?

C. Interior protection

1. Are all areas protected by automatic sprinkler systems, including outside receiving and shipping platforms?

    a. What protection is afforded flammables?

    b. Are flammables inaccessible from outside the building?

    c. Are extra sprinkler heads on hand to meet any foreseeable replacement requirement?

2. Are control valves equipped with central station or proprietary supervision? Are these checked daily?

3. Is there adequate distribution of fire extinguishers and hand hoses? Are locations accessible and distinctly marked?

4. How are important services secured? *(normal/emergency)*

    a. Electricity

    b. Gas

    c. Water

    d. Steam

    e. Chilled water

    f. Oil

    g. Boiler equipment

    h. Air conditioning equipment

       i. Switchgear and transformers
       j. Telephone equipment
      k. Vital business records
      l. Data processing and tape storage
     m. Internal communications
      n. Fire protection devices
      o. Fire pumps

5. Has an emergency generator been provided? Does the generator have capacity to handle essential services?
   a. Elevators?
   b. Lighting (emergency)?
   c. Security systems? CCTV? Intrusion alarms?
   d. Fallout shelter area?
   e. Public address systems?
   f. Fire alarms?
6. Are supplies of materials maintained on hand—plywood, lumber, and so forth—sufficient to repair broken doors, windows, roofs, and so forth?
7. Does location have sensitive manufacturing operations?
   a. How would these be protected during a disorder?
   b. Can areas be isolated?
   c. Have plans been made to close off any area where an internal disaster has occurred?

D. Emergency operations
   1. Has an alternate operating location been established away from the disaster area for use by key management personnel? Where?
   2. Has the emergency plan included diversion of incoming shipments to locations outside the disaster areas?
   3. Has an alternate means of carrying on critical functions been established?
   4. Has a means been established for emergency evacuations?
      a. Have emergency routes been established for personnel access and egress?
      b. Have designated employee entrances been established?

CHAPTER 39

Security Incident Reporting

Today, more than ever before, it is essential that security departments properly document the activities of their personnel *and* the security-related incidents that they investigate. Unfortunately, litigation associated with claims of inadequate security has been growing rapidly during the 1980s. As a result, security departments must be constantly prepared to defend those allegations. One of the very best ways of doing so is through carefully-prepared quality reports.

Therefore, the following policy and procedures and security incident report forms are offered to aid in this very important endeavor. Although the policies and procedures are fairly generic, having value to virtually all, the report forms run from the rather simple and straightforward to the more complex (see Figures 39–1 through 39–5.)

SECURITY REPORTS

Every security officer is required to complete an incident report for every event he encounters as specified in the security department's *Policy and Procedure Manual*. Items 1 through 8 should be completed on every report before the officer goes off-duty. All reports are to be printed or typed.

A. The following are explanations of what is *required* in each item:
   1. Specify the subject of the report being filed:
      a. Vehicle accident
      b. Personnel security violation
      c. Personal injury
      d. Missing or stolen property
      e. Unauthorized entry
      f. Criminal activity
   2. Specify both the complete date (month, day, year) of the incident's occurrence and its report.
   3. Specify time using 24-hour military time.
   4. When giving the location of the incident be as specific as possible. Give specific addresses, building numbers or exact distances from

1. Subject of the Report: _____

2. Date of the Incident: _____

3. Time of the Incident: _____

4. Location of the Incident: _____

_____

5. Names and Addresses of <u>all</u> Parties Involved: _____

_____

_____

6. Explain Details of the Incident: _____

_____

_____

_____

_____

_____

7. Explain Corrective Action Taken: _____

_____

_____

_____

_____

Figure 39–1   Security department incident report.

designated locations. (Example: 123 N.W. 45th Street, Warehouse 14-A, 125 yards south of Gate 4)

5. Give the full names and complete addresses of all persons involved in the incident. Also, specify what part each person played in the incident. Examples:
   a.   Robert E. Brown—Driver, Vehicle 1, 678 North 9th, Newtown
   b.   William Green—Victim (Acme Employee), Department 42—Shift 2

6. Details of the incident should be brief but answer the who, what, when, where, why, and how of the event. (Examples: Who was involved; who filed the report; who discovered the violation; what took place; when did the incident take place; when was the situation

OFFENSE CATEGORY		DATE-TIME RECEIVED	DAY OF WK.	DATE MO. DAY YR.	TIME AM. PM.	INVESTIGATION NO.

FORCED ENTRY	COMPLAINANTS NAME	HOME PHONE

THEFT:
- PERS. PROP.
- COMPANY PROP.
- COIN MACHINE
- AUTO

ADDRESS   BUSINESS PHONE

ROBBERY

STATUS   ☐ VISITOR   ☐ EMPLOYEE   ☐ OTHER (SPECIFY)

ASSAULT

RAPE | DATE-TIME OF OFFENSE | DAY OF WK. | DATE MO. DAY YR. | TIME AM. PM. |

MANSLAUGHTER   PLACE   WEAPON USED

DISTURBANCE

VANDALISM

TRAFFIC   TRADEMARK

OTHER (SPECIFY)

VICTIMS NAME   ADDRESS

SEX AGE RACE	STATUS
☐ M ☐ F	☐ VISITOR ☐ EMPLOYEE ☐ OTHER (SPECIFY)

MEDICAL TREATMENT
☐ YES (EXPLAIN)
☐ NO

DESCRIPTION OF LOST PROPERTY   VALUE

DESCRIPTION OF OFFENDER(S)

NO. 1	SEX ☐ M ☐ F	RACE	HEIGHT	BUILD	EYES	HAIR	GLASSES ☐ YES ☐ NO	COMPLEXION
	MARKS				AGE	HAT	COAT	SHIRT

NO. 2	SEX ☐ M ☐ F	RACE	HEIGHT	BUILD	EYES	HAIR	GLASSES ☐ YES ☐ NO	COMPLEXION
	MARKS				AGE	HAT	COAT	SHIRT

WITNESS NAME 1.	ADDRESS	TELEPHONE
WITNESS NAME 2.	ADDRESS	TELEPHONE

LAW ENFORCEMENT AGENCY NOTIFIED	TIME	PERSON
1.	A.M. P.M.	
2.	A.M. P.M.	

NAME OF PERSON ARRESTED 1.	ADDRESS
NAME OF PERSON ARRESTED 2.	ADDRESS

CHARGES

1.   2.

WAS PHYSICAL FORCE USED   ☐YES   ☐NO

SIGNATURE OF REPORTING OFFICER   DATE | FOR SECURITY OFFICE USE ONLY
APPROVED _____
DATE NAME CARD COMPLETED _____

Figure 39–2   Security department incident report.

NARRATIVE - BE SPECIFIC IN WRITING OF THIS REPORT. BE SURE TO USE THE GUIDELINES: "WHO", "WHAT", "WHEN", "WHY", "WHERE", "HOW". DESCRIBE OFFENSE IN DETAIL. INCLUDE INITIAL STATEMENTS UTTERED BY VICTIM, WITNESSES AND SUS-PECTS. EXAMPLE: IN CAR THEFT, WHAT WAS VICTIM'S RESPONSE TO DIRECT QUESTION, "WAS CAR LOCKED?"? DESCRIBE SCENE OF OFFENSE AND CONTRIBUTORY CONDITIONS SUCH AS POOR LIGHTING, EXTREME ISOLATION, ETC. LIST EVIDENCE FOUND AT SCENE AND ALL OTHER RELEVANT INFORMATION SUCH AS SOBRIETY OF VICTIM, WITNESSES AND SUSPECTS. SAFE-GUARD REPORT FOR REFERENCE.

FOR SECURITY DEPARTMENT USE ONLY

THIS OFFENSE IS DECLARED:

UNFOUNDED ☐

CLEARED BY ARREST ☐   SIGNED_____ DATE_____

EXCEPTIONALLY CLEARED ☐   SECURITY DIRECTOR

INACTIVE (NOT CLEARED) ☐

Case # _____

SECURITY DEPARTMENT

INCIDENT REPORT

Type of Incident: _____   Location of Incident: _____

Name, Address, and Telephone Number of Complaintant/Victim(s): _____

_____

Time and Date of Incident: _____   Officers or Unit Responding, and Police
                                         Report Number: _____

Name and Address of Suspect(s) or Arrestee(s):

_____

_____

_____

Name and Addresses of Witness(es):

_____

_____

_____

Details of Incident:

_____

_____

_____

_____

_____

_____

_____

Officer(s) Responding: _____

Signature of Officer Filing Report: _____   Date: _____

Director of Security: _____   Date: _____

Division Administrator: _____   Date: _____

Figure 39–3   Unusual incident report.

CASE NUMBER:
CASE CODE:

SECURITY INCIDENT REPORT
SECURITY DEPARTMENT

TIME OF OCCURRENCE:	DATE OF OCCURRENCE:	DOW:	TIME REPORTED:	DATE REPORTED:	DOW:

LOCATION OF INCIDENT:		LOCATION CODE:	AREA CODE:

CODES FOR PERSONS: 1 C = Complainant S = Subject V = Victim W = Witness 2 E = Employee V = Visitor P = Patient O = Other

NO.	CODE 1	2	NAME LAST	FIRST	M.I.	RACE	AGE	SEX	ADDRESS OR DEPARTMENT	TELEPHONE NO. OR EXTENSION

SUBJECT (s)

NO.	WEIGHT	HAIR COLOR	EYES	DISTINGUISHING FEATURES
	HEIGHT	HAIR STYLE	SKIN TONE	CLOTHING
NO.	WEIGHT	HAIR COLOR	EYES	DISTINGUISHING FEATURES
	HEIGHT	HAIR STYLE	SKIN TONE	CLOTHING
NO.	WEIGHT	HAIR COLOR	EYES	DISTINGUISHING FEATURES
	HEIGHT	HAIR STYLE	SKIN TONE	CLOTHING
NO.	WEIGHT	HAIR COLOR	EYES	DISTINGUISHING FEATURES
	HEIGHT	HAIR STYLE	SKIN TONE	CLOTHING

PROPERTY

QTY.	TYPE OF PROPERTY	CODE 1	2	MANUFACTURER	MODEL NUMBER	SERIAL NUMBER	COLOR	VALUE

CODES FOR PROPERTY: 1 S = Stolen M = Missing 2 O = Unaccounted for R = Recovered

(Continued on reverse side)

Figure 39–4 Security incident report.

NARRATIVE

(blank ruled lines)

NOTIFICATIONS

SECURITY MANAGER:		POLICE AGENCY:	
TIME:	DATE:	TIME:	DATE:
DEPARTMENT MANAGER:		ADMINISTRATOR ON CALL:	
TIME:	DATE:	TIME:	DATE:
REPORTING OFFICER:		SECURITY MANAGER:	
TIME PREPARED:	DATE PREPARED:	TIME APPROVED:	DATE APPROVED:
CHARGE OFFICER:		TYPED:	
TIME APPROVED:	DATE APPROVED:	TIME:	DATE:

Figure 39–4   (continued)

OFFENSE CATEGORY _____ INVESTIGATION NO. _____

COMPLAINANT   (LAST NAME)   (MIDDLE NAME)   (FIRST NAME)

ADDRESS

ADDITIONAL DETAILS OF OFFENSE, PROGRESS OR INVESTIGATION, ETC.

_____

_____

_____

_____

_____

_____

_____

_____

_____

_____

_____

_____

_____

_____

_____

_____

_____

_____

THIS OFFENSE IS DECLARED:

   UNFOUNDED   ☐   SIGNED _____ DATE_____

   CLEARED BY ARREST   ☐   INVESTIGATING OFFICER

   EXCEPTIONALLY CLEARED ☐   SIGNED _____ DATE_____

   INACTIVE (NOT CLEARED)   ☐   SECURITY DIRECTOR

THIS FORM IS USED BY OFFICER ASSIGNED TO A CASE TO REPORT PROGRESS AFTER THREE AND SEVEN DAYS AND WEEKLY
THEREAFTER ALSO TO REPORT SIGNIFICANT DEVELOPMENTS.

Figure 39–5　Supplementary offense report.

     discovered; where was the property taken from; why did the incident
occur; how did the incident occur; how was the situation discovered?)
7. Describe corrective action taken (if any) following the same criteria
    as outlined in Item 6.
8. Officer must sign each report and include his identification or badge

number. The officer's signature indicates that the report is complete and the information is accurate.

B. A Security Supervisor is to complete information covered in items 9 through 12.

9. Details of any followup action is to be explained using the same criteria as in Item 6.

The supervisor is to review the officer's report for completeness and accuracy of information and add any facts about action in addition to that done by the officer.

10. Any information not factual or relating directly to the incident or the report should be placed here.

11. The supervisor's signature indicates that the report is complete and that he is satisfied with both the report and the corrective action taken (if any).

12. Supervisor should indicate what departments and/or individuals receive copies of the report.

IN BRIEF

What should be included in an Incident Report?
1. Subject
2. Victim
3. Date and time of occurrence
4. Date and time reported
5. Location
6. Motive
7. Method of operation
8. Articles taken
9. Accused—suspect
10. Complaintant—victim
11. Vehicle used
12. Property recovered and disposition
13. Action taken
14. Witnesses
15. Additional leads to be investigated
16. Summary of case
17. Pictures, charts, diagrams
18. Status of the case
19. Officer writing report
20. Authorizations and approvals

CHAPTER 40

Access Control and Identification

An effective access control procedure is the cornerstone to building and maintaining an effective security program. It is, therefore, necessary to establish a standard for access control that will be applied at all of a company's locations, assuring admittance only to persons on legitimate business while precluding or detecting persons who should not be admitted.

POLICY AND PROCEDURES

A. *Employee access*
1. *Official company ID cards.* Employees are isssued standardized official photo identification cards for the following purposes:
   a. Identification at all company facilities.
   b. Card reader access admittance at controlled doors, gates, and so forth, where they are in use.
   c. Proper identification in the event of onsite disasters or emergencies.
2. *Use of ID cards for access.* In order to insure that tight access controls are in effect at all company facilities, employees are required to show their identification cards to a security officer when they enter those company facilities where there are perimeter and/ or building access control programs. That is, each facility utilizing a guard, receptionist, and so forth, to screen persons entering a facility or building will institute procedures to have the guard or receptionist check employee ID cards for access.
3. *Forgotten or lost ID cards*
   a. *Forgotten ID cards.*
      1) Procedures will be established at each location for the issuance of temporary ID cards when an employee has forgotten his/hers.
      2) Those locations or facilities that do not use encoded ID cards in conjunction with card readers will use one-day (nonencoded) cards as a temporary ID card. At locations

or facilities using encoded photo ID cards with card readers, temporary nonphoto plastic cards will be used.

3) Tight security accountability and issuance controls must be established for all one-day, temporary ID cards whether they are encoded or nonencoded.

4) Issuance procedures for one-day temporary ID cards will be consistent with the following minimum standards:

    a) The employee will be required to give the guard or receptionist his/her name, department, and payroll number.

    b) Where the employee is not known to the security officer some other form of positive identification must be produced such as a driver's license with a photograph.

    c) The security officer will verify the employee's employment status to insure that he/she is a current employee of the company.

    d) A temporary ID card will be issued to the employee who will be advised that he/she must return it to the issuing access control point before the close of business that day.

b. *Lost ID cards.* When an employee has lost his/her ID card (rather than having forgotten it), the following procedures will apply:

1) A lost identification card report must be completed by the employee.

2) The employee will be issued one-day, temporary cards for a period not to exceed two weeks from the date of issuance.

3) The temporary ID card must have the dates for which it is valid clearly indicated on the face of the card.

4) If during the valid time period, the employee's ID card is not found or returned to the personnel department, a permanent replacement card will be made and the employee notified as to where and when to pick up his/her new card.

4. *Terminations, transfers, and leaves of absence*

a. An employee who *terminates* his/her employment with the company must surrender his/her photo ID card at the exit interview.

b. An employee who *transfers* to another company facility or location should retain his/her photo ID card. The new location will issue a new photo ID card for that location, retrieve the former photo ID card and return it to the personnel department.

      c. An employee who *transfers* from one group or division to another within the company should retain his/her photo ID card.

      d. An employee on a *leave of absence* must surrender his/her photo ID card prior to the commencement of such leave. The card may be reissued to him/her when he/she returns to work.

  5. *After-hours access*

      a. *Logging.* Other than during regular shift change times, after-hours or off-shift access will require in and out logging. Times when such logging is required are as follows:

        1) 5:30 P.M. to 6:00 A.M. Monday through Saturday.

        2) All day Sundays and holidays.

        3) At all times for visitors.

      b. *Controlled access (24-hour access authorization).* Other than for assigned shift personnel, after-hours admittance (as indicated in (a) above) will be on an *official business* and controlled basis.

  6. *Employee visits to other facilities, locations, or departments.* Company employee photo identification cards will be used as a standardized means of identification at all company locations and may be used in lieu of a visitor's badge. Restricted access areas may require that employees also adhere to certain additional procedures.

B. *Visitor access.*

  1. *Normal Visiting Hours* (May vary at different facilities or locations).

      a. Normal visitor access hours are as follows:

        1) 8:00 A.M. to 4:30 P.M.—Monday through Friday

        2) 8:00 A.M. to 2:00 P.M.—Saturdays

      b. Visitor admittance during other hours *must* have the approval of the manager for the facility being visited or comply with other established local procedures.

      c. *Visitor's badges*

        1) Visitors must be identified through the use of a visitor's badge.

        2) Nonemployee visitors will be issued a one-day visitor's badge.

        3) It is intended that visitor's badges be conspicuously displayed by visitors while on company property. A one-day visitor's badge is a card pocket insert. It may be placed in a plastic holder with clip and attached to the visitor's outer garment in the event that the visitor's clothing has no suitable pocket in which to display the visitor's badge.

        4) Unless personally known to the person *registering* the visitor, each visitor will be required to show identification

such as his/her own company identification or a driver's license *prior* to the issuance of the visitor's badge and visitor registration.

5) Provisions *must be made* to permit the visitor upon completion of the visit to surrender his/her visitor's badge at the visitor control point of entry where it was issued.

d. *Escorting.* Nonemployee visitors should be escorted at all times by an employee while on company property. First consideration must be given to having nonemployee visitors met by the host or his/her designee at or near the visit control point.

e. *Visitor removal of property.* Visitors who are issued a one-day visitor's badge can have noncompany property carried into the premises cited on the lower portion of their visitor's badge at the time of admittance. However, should they be given company property during their visit, a property/package pass must be completed by the issuing department.

2. *After-hours access.* The procedures for nonemployee visitors (either one-day, short-term, long-term, servicer, or contractor) who will require admittance into the facility after normal daytime business hours are:

a. *Logging.* After-hours or off-shift nonemployee access will require in and out logging at all times.

b. *One-day visitors.* When the initial admittance of a one-day visitor will be after normal business hours, the visit must be arranged beforehand, as follows:

1) A memo from the department head concerning authorizing the visit must be sent to the security department. The memo must list the following:
   a) Times and dates of visit
   b) Building and area to be visited
   c) Names of visitors
   d) Employee host
   e) Location where entry will occur

2) The Security Representative will arrange to have the appropriate visitor's badge prepared after verifying the legitimacy of the visit.

3) The one-day visitor's badge will be annotated with the notation "after hours" on the face of the card.

4) Visitors will pick up their badges at the access control point and log in at the time of ingress.

5) One-day visitor's badges will be surrendered at the access control point when leaving.

c. *Short-term visitors*

1) The written request to the issuing office must include the

        additional information regarding the requirement for after-hours admittance as previously described.

    2) The short-term visitor's badge should have the notation "after hours" on the face of the card.

  d. *Long-term visitors.* Long-term visitors with photo ID cards who require after-hour access will have a "24" designation on their ID cards, where this form of authorization is used, or be authorized such access in accordance with local access control procedures.

  e. *Servicers and contractors.* Servicers and contractors who will require after-hour access must have such access requirements determined by the purchasing department at the time of the procurement.

  f. *Personal visits and group tours*

    1) The initial approval request for after-hours access in connection with personal visits and group tours must indicate in the request that the access will be after hours.

    2) When they are prepared, the visitor's badges should be annotated with "after hours" on the face of the cards.

C. *Personal visits*

  1. *Approvals.* At those facilities where personal visits by employee friends, relatives, former employees, and so forth are permitted, there must be a formalized procedure for obtaining management approval prior to admittance being granted. As a minimum, the sponsoring employee's department head should be designated as the approving authority for such visits.

  2. *Hours of admittance.* Unless otherwise authorized by the facility's manager, personal visits will be limited to normal daytime business hours.

  3. *Limited access.* Because of OSHA and company requirements, personal visits within company facilities must be limited to nonrestricted and nondangerous areas.

  4. *Escorts.* Once authorization for the visit is obtained, the host employee must meet the visitors at the access control point and escort such guests at all times. The host is responsible to insure for the safety and proper conduct of the visitors while they are on company property.

D. *Group tours or visits*

  1. *Approvals*

    a. The company's top management must authorize group tours into their facilities. All group tours must have a designated member of management who will be responsible for security and safety measures attendant to such visits. All visiting groups must have a company escort throughout the duration of the tour.

b. It is important to remember that the safeguarding of proprietary and company intellectual information must be given primary consideration when admitting nonemployees to tour a company facility.

c. In addition to the protection of company secrets, safety requirements and the company's liability toward such invitees in case of injury or accident must also be considered.

2. *Badging.* Visitors on group tours should be provided with visitor's badges at the point of entry into the facility and a record should be made of the admittance.

E. *Servicers and contractors*

1. *Servicers (general)*

a. *Definition.* Servicers are outside personnel who require intermittent and continuing access into a company facility to perform work under a purchase order. Such service will generally consist of installation, repairs, or maintenance to machinery or equipment.

b. *Coordination.* The purchasing department personnel involved in arranging such service contracts will provide the security department with an up-to-date list of those servicing concerns with whom there are service contracts in effect. The information to be provided is as follows:

1) Name of the firm

2) Business address and telephone number

3) Servicer contact for access coordination matters

4) Nature and duration of the services

5) Company location (Bldg./Dept.) where services are to be performed

c. *Access control measures*

1) In order to facilitate ease of access into company facilities, servicers will be encouraged to furnish a list of personnel who can be anticipated to perform services under such procurement. This listing will include the names of personnel requiring access.

2) At the time of procurement, the procuring office should ascertain whether the servicer's organization issues company identification cards. Where such cards are used, a copy and/or complete description should be obtained for access identification purposes.

3) Either one-day visitor's badges or nonemployee ID cards (with or without photos) can be issued. These badges will be worn by servicers while on company property.

d. *Servicer access to restricted and other secured areas.* Servicers must be escorted by the using department while in restricted areas.

2. *Contractors (general).* Facilities using outside contractors for in-plant construction, nonservicer maintenance, remodeling, and so forth, should establish procedures that include:

a. *Coordination.* Information regarding the contractor's name, address, the type of contract work, and areas where the work can be expected to be performed will be furnished to the security department by the using department head and/or procuring office concerned.

b. *Access control measures*

1) In order to facilitate ease of access into company facilities, contractors will be encouraged to furnish the using facility with a list of their personnel who can be anticipated to perform the work under the procurement. This listing should include the names of contractor personnel. Contractor employees should have acceptable identification on their persons when they are gaining access to the facility.

2) Wherever possible, a specified contractors' gate should be used for entering and leaving the facility.

3) A contractor's in and out personnel registration log should be utilized for contractor employees entering and leaving the plant.

4) Contractor buttons or other suitable identification should be used for identification purposes and worn at all times while within the facility.

5) Contractors' private vehicles should be parked outside of the plant's perimeter, or in a fenced or otherwise limited-access area within the plant, as applicable.

6) Contractor vehicles used inplant should be issued vehicle passes and have periodic vehicle checks by guard personnel when the vehicles exit the premises.

7) Contractor vehicles used or parked inside the plant's perimeter must comply with established vehicle safety and parking regulations.

8) Under no circumstances should the company accept responsibility for the safeguarding of contractor tools or equipment that the contractor leaves inplant overnight.

9) Contractor access into the company's restricted areas will follow the procedures outlined in Section 1, of the *restricted area access* procedure that follows.

F. *Restricted area access*

1. *Access control.*

a. At certain company locations there are specified areas that

require supplemental access control procedures and where access is highly restricted. These areas are identified as *restricted* areas and should be posted accordingly.
b.   This designation is not used in the classified, defense department sense, but is to denote specific areas where admittance is to be tightly controlled and on a company *need-to-know* basis. An example of such an area would be a computer or data processing center at a company facility.

2.   *Limited Access*
a.   Access to all restricted areas are normally limited to those company personnel and specifically identified noncompany personnel, (such as customer service engineers in computer areas) who require such access as part of their regularly assigned duties.
b.   Where employee photo ID cards are in use, a special color-coded restricted area designator should be incorporated into the ID card. Such badges should be used specifically for gaining access to computer facilities.

3.   *Entrance Controls.* All company restricted areas must have a means of controlled entry during working hours and be capable of being locked during nonworking hours. The method of securing and controlling access doors can be any one of the following means:
a.   *Key lock.* Where a pedestrian access door is to be key-operated from the outside, careful consideration must be given to the type of lock to be utilized. It is preferable not to have the lock and key system for restricted areas as part of the facility's overall lock system unless it is a masterkeyed system with interchangeable cores on its own submastered system. Special locks should be considered whenever possible in order to insure for maximum security protection. Regardless of the key lock system, stringent key control and accountability measures must be instituted to include action to be taken when persons who possess keys are transferred or terminated.
b.   *Card readers.* Encoded identification cards/badges with card readers also may be utilized. However, when such a system is to be employed, the capability for voiding or locking out cards when a card is lost or an employee is transferred should be part of the card reader system's capability. The security department should be involved in the selection of card reader systems in order to insure compatability with existing systems companywide.
c.   *CCTV monitored access.* Depending upon the location, remote control access systems can be used utilizing CCTV monitored surveillance from within in conjunction with two-way voice intercom and a remote controlled electromagnetic door lock.

4. *Visitor controls.* Regardless of the facility's perimeter visitor control measures, all noncompany visitors to a restricted area will be identified and escorted at all times while within the area.

5. *Servicer and vendor access.* The procedures for servicers and vendors who require continuing, long-term (semiresident) access to a restricted area are provided in Section E, "Servicers and contractors."

6. *Minimum physical protection standards.*
   a. Each company manager must insure that there is at least a minimum level of physical protective safeguards for all restricted areas. In evaluating such protection, the location of the area is of primary concern. If the area is located on the ground level with one or more of the area's perimeter walls part of the external building wall and readily accessible by unauthorized personnel, greater physical protection measures must be considered to prevent or deter intrusion.
   b. At company locations without tight access control procedures in effect for the entire location, more stringent physical safeguards must be provided for the restricted area location itself.
   c. All restricted areas must be enclosed on all sides, i.e., walls, ceiling, and floor. Construction should be such that entry without use of force is not possible. When outside perimeter walls utilize regular glass, smash-resistant security glass, grills, or security blinds should be considered.
   d. In determining the level of physical protective measures needed, the ease of access through ceilings, walls, roofs and ducts, as well as through the floor beneath, must be evaluated.
   e. Where it is determined that the overall physical protective safeguards are not in and of themselves adequate, consideration should be given to the utilization of an intrusion alarm system. Such an alarm system can be incorporated into the facility's overall alarm system or can be just for the restricted area itself with a local building alarm bell. The security department will assist in determining minimum physical security protective measures and alarm utilization.

G. *Vehicle access*
   1. *Safety.* All vehicles entering company property will be required to adhere to posted speeds, safety regulations, and no-parking signs.
   2. *Commercial vehicles*
      a. Commercial vehicles, such as carriers picking up or delivering materials, contractors, and servicers, will be subject to spot load and/or cab security checks as established by the facility. This may include carrier off-loading to verify shipment documentation.
      b. All vehicles leaving the premises with company property must

have required shipment or removal documentation that will be subject to inspection by guard personnel at exit control points.

c.   A record of all incoming vehicles including the company name, registration number, driver's name, and time in and out will be maintained at the access control point. Vehicle passes will be issued to the driver for conspicuous display behind the windshield while on the premises and will be returned to the guard upon leaving.

d.   Insurance liability requirements for servicers and contractors should be reviewed with risk management.

3.   *Employee inplant parking.* Where permission has been given to an employee to park on company-owned property, the following rules will apply:

a.   All speed, stopping, parking, and issued or posted safety rules will be followed.

b.   Parking will be in designated areas.

c.   Vehicles will be kept locked when unattended.

d.   Vehicle decals will be conspicuously displayed on vehicles at facilities where they are issued.

e.   Liquor, drugs (unless prescribed by a doctor), firearms, weapons, or other dangerous instruments will not be brought in vehicles into company parking lots.

f.   Personal vehicles must meet minimum safety inspection standards in those states having such a requirement.

h.   All personal vehicles leaving the premises with company property must have required shipment or removal documentation that will be subject to inspection by guard personnel at exit control points.

i.   Improper driving or failure to adhere to the above requirements or to those additional requirements established by facility management may constitute grounds for revocation of the employee's privilege to park on company property.

CHAPTER 41

Key Management and Control

The reason for having a standard for key management and control is sound. Keying systems must be well organized and thoroughly controlled in order to achieve maximum security, efficiency, and economy. It is of vital importance to know, at any given moment, who possesses keys and what doors or areas those keys will operate. If this procedure is not followed, the effectiveness of the overall security of the affected company location will be seriously lessened.

To accomplish this objective, standardization becomes necessary. These benefits of standardization are well recognized in terms of security. Standardization also brings about a *substantial reduction in lock expenditures* that is, of course, a very important aspect in any asset protection program.

It is necessary to consider certain factors involved in any masterkeyed lock and key system.

1. In a standardized security keying system the ease of changing locks and combinations, the different types of locks in which the system can be integrated, and the ability to extend or change the system must be considered.
2. Key-operated locks have many advantages over other types of locks, but they must be manufactured so as to be extremely difficult to pick or violate in any way. The keys must be of such construction that it is difficult for any unauthorized person to have them duplicated.
3. In standardization it is important to consider the service and delivery the supplying company can offer, not only on original delivery but also on replacement parts continuous service.
4. The overall quality and dependability of the keying system must be equal, if not superior, to others. This is especially important in connection with the master keying desired for a location.
5. Cost of installing a security keying system can be completely repaid in a few years through maintenance and replacement cost saving, and through far greater protection of all company property.

Standardization of a company's locking systems can be realized very satisfactorily by use of locks containing the interchangeable core, removable by a special master key, such as is manufactured by the Best Lock Corporation.

Other manufacturers, such as Corbin, Sargent, Yale, and Russwin, also provide removable core locks but the cores are not interchangeable among different types of locks.

1. A key-operated, interchangeable core can be completely replaced in approximately ten seconds by another core containing a new combination. Authorized personnel can remove the cores, change combinations, and cut new keys that are ready to be installed at the location of any given lock.
2. The interchangeable core allows the keying system to be incorporated into nearly every type of lock including mortise locks, rim locks, tubular locks, cylindrical or key-in-the-knob locks, padlocks, cabinet locks, panic exit units, and other special locks such as cylinders already equipped with the interchangeable core. Through this key-operated, interchangeable core the system can be expanded almost indefinitely or restricted to fit any specific need, and all within the masterkeyed system proposed. Personnel can be restricted from specific areas and can enter authorized areas through the master keying tailored to fit a location's needs, thus providing excellent key control.
3. In connection with new construction, to be assured of complete key control, the supplier should be required to ship all permanent cores to the company with the keys. These should be withheld from the contractor and not installed until the company takes possession of the building. Meanwhile, the contractor can be provided with his own master key system through the use of construction cores furnished by the supplier. Normally, there is no charge to the company for the construction cores since the contractor will return them for credit.

ESTABLISHMENT OF A SYSTEM

When any company plans to initially lock or relock its premises, a lock company representative will normally be available at no charge to the facility to make a lock survey. A detailed cost proposal will be furnished and if the system is to be acquired, it will be obtained through normal purchasing channels.

Masterkeying systems will be set up on an organizational and *need-to-know* basis. This means that operating managers will have the responsibility of determining which employees will have access to areas under their direct control. Departmental managers and above may authorize interdepartmental key access in the masterkeying system.

Grand master keys for any master locking system can only be issued on the written approval of the manager in charge of that facility. Grand master keys will not be carried by an employee for personal convenience but will be assigned to a responsible person and retained in a secured container for emergency access purposes. Guard tour, maintenance, and custodial access keys will be provided for in the initial master keying survey to be conducted.

SYSTEM OPERATION

To maintain the integrity of the master locking system, a designated person must be assigned the responsibility for establishing and maintaining account-ability control records. This function normally is called the *key control office*. Security department key record cards should be utilized for this purpose. These cards permit easy recording of the keys issued to employees, and can be cross indexed by employee, naming key number, or location.

In addition to maintaining lock and key records, the key control office is responsible for obtaining required approvals for key issuance. Depending on the size of the facility, key request forms will be utilized.

The key control office will also establish a key retrieval system to insure that terminating or transferring key custodians surrender their keys when the keys are no longer needed. In addition, a lost key report form will be utilized when a key is no longer in the control of its custodian. Each employee will be advised when he/she is issued a key that he/she must immediately complete a lost key report form whenever his/her key is lost.

All key duplication and new key cutting will be under the control of the security department and coordinated with the lock supplier, when this is applicable.

System Audit

A key system audit will be made at least once annually at all company locations. Depending on the facility's size and number of employees, security personnel will cite each key charged to an employee verifying key numbers with central accountability key records.

When a key is reported lost prior to, or in connection with, a key audit, the department head responsible for the area concerned will ascertain the extent of the compromise involved and determine whether cores are to be changed and new keys issued to those personnel requiring access into the area.

Access control and loss prevention also depend on a master key system and effective key control (see Figure 41–1.) In most facilities, without regard to size, a changeable core master key system is the most economical and effective component in a security program.

However, the development of effective policy to maintain the integrity of the system is often overlooked. Keys are given out almost without regard to the need of the company, but instead for employees' convenience.

Therefore, the policy statement offered here is specifically written for the purpose of outlining the responsibility of security personnel and the use of master keys. Additional policy should also be developed and put into effect for other employees in the organization. While the specifics might vary it should contain statements concerning:

DATE	TIME OUT	NAME	DEPARTMENT	KEY SET NO.	SIGNATURE	RELEASING OFFICER	TIME IN	DATE	ACCEPTING OFFICER

Figure 41–1   Security department key log.

1. Who is issued keys.
2. What level master key is issued.
3. Development of adequate records for issuance.
4. Establishment of a rekeying schedule.
5. Actions for dealing with lost, stolen, or missing master keys.
6. Procedures for return of keys by terminated employees.
7. Actions to prevent duplication of keys.

KEY CONTROL

I. Scope
 A. Effective immediately all security personnel shall strictly adhere to the provisions of this order. Violations of the policy set forth herein will result in disciplinary action.
II. Purpose
 A. The purpose of this order is to insure the integrity and safe handling of master keys.

B. Master keys permit access to nearly every work space, office, and other area in the facility. Should they fall into the hands of unauthorized personnel, serious damage or loss of property could result.

C. The following policy is not intended to question the integrity of security officers, but rather to protect the officers against possible repercussions resulting from loss or misuse of property.

III. Policy

A. Master keys will remain in the security office keybox at all times except when the officer is on duty.

1. Each officer will take his or her assigned keys from the keybox immediately prior to beginning his or her tour of duty.

2. Officers will take great care to guard their keys against loss and will use them only as is necessary to the performance of their assigned duties.

3. Any loss or damage of master keys will be reported to the supervisor immediately.

4. Each officer will place his or her assigned keys in the keybox upon ending his or her tour of duty and prior to leaving the security office.

B. Any violation of this policy will result in disciplinary action being taken.

CHAPTER 42

Fire Safety and Prevention

Fire prevention inspections are undoubtedly one of the most important non-security activities performed by security personnel. A well-planned and implemented fire safety program, which includes regular inspections conducted by trained security personnel, can indeed prevent many fires. These fire prevention inspections, while less exciting than many other security functions, can nonetheless do a great deal toward achieving the ultimate goal of every security program—effective assets protection and loss reduction.

For all too many years, the amount of cooperation and assistance given to security personnel, concerned about the very real problem of fire, was minimal. Failures far outdistanced successes. People too frequently ignored the fact that fires do not just happen, they are caused by unsafe acts or conditions.

Therefore, the real value of a quality fire prevention program may well have to be proven. Fire safety/security officers can often prove the value of their efforts by carefully recording *and* reporting all fire hazards identified *and* corrected. This lets management know just how vulnerable the organization is to actual fires and to the losses that invariably result.

However, reports that only include the number, location, and extent of fires that have occurred are negative—producing evidence of failures—and do very little to support fire safety efforts. The real goal of fire safety/prevention efforts should be to improve their standing from one of secondary, *incidental* function to one of primary security service deserving of appropriate attention and support.

More specifically, fire prevention activities can be categorized as the interrelated functions: planning, education, and enforcement. Actually, however, these should be viewed not only as functions, but also as goals of fire safety/prevention programs.

PLANNING

By reviewing proposed project plans for new construction or modifications to existing facilities, fire safety/security staff can better ensure that adequate protec-

438

tion measures are properly planned for during preliminary design stages. The cost savings and efficiency that can result from such efforts can be significant.

In addition to assisting in planning for the installation of needed fire suppression systems and fire extinguishers, fire safety/security staff should also plan for:

- The maintenance of fire prevention and suppression hardware
- The inspection and testing of fire prevention and suppression hardware (see Figure 42–1)
- The implementation of an ongoing education (awareness) program that concentrates on quality fire safety
- The maintenance of adequate records and reports in order to provide proper documentation to regulatory or enforcement agencies

EDUCATION

Fire safety and prevention efforts, in cooperation with other security and loss-reduction programs, should develop and present a continuing education program that should be aimed at maintaining a high level of fire safety consciousness. These programs should generally include, but not necessarily be limited to:

A. The active promotion of quality fire safety and prevention through personal appearances of fire safety/security personnel at inservice training sessions
B. The use of all available inhouse media services to promote effective fire safety and prevention
C. The development of special fire prevention programs that center around specific holidays or periods of the year. For example:
1. Fire safety and seasonal decorations at Christmas time
2. Special programs during Fire Prevention Week in October

ENFORCEMENT

Competent, concerned fire safety/security officers can, through their recommendations, effect a great many corrections of fire hazards. Yet, this aspect of enforcement should not be relied upon totally as the only criteria for eliminating fire hazards. If fire safety/security personnel put forth *genuine* effort, they can generally win support for their recommendations *without* resorting to actual or threatened enforcement tactics. However, there are, nonetheless, going to be those cases where one may have to resort to appropriate enforcement actions. For example:

Code: ✓ - item meets standards
     X - deficiencies - see reverse side for comment   Date: _____

Building:

Fire Protection Equipment		Elevators	
Fire Extinguishers		Emergency Signals	
Charged		Door Controls	
Sealed		Penthouses	
Pressure Reading		Motor Rooms	
Hose		Pits	
Tip		C-O-2 Fire Ext.	
C-O-2 Weight			
Hangers		Electrical	
Obstructed		Approved	
		Clearance	
Sprinkler Systems		Covers	
Wet		Operable	
Dry		Appliances	
Anti-Freeze		Pipe Chases	
Heated			
Storage Clearance		Fire Alarm System	
Obstructed		Control Panel	
		Annunciator Panel	
Standpipe Systems		Fire Boxes	
Post Indicator Valve		Gongs	
Open		Obstructed	
Wrench Attached			
Obstructed		Fire Hydrants	
Connections		Capped	
Capped		Obstructed	
Emergency Lighting System		Heat Actuating Devices	
Charge Indicator		Clear of Storage	
Tested		Signs, Decorations	
Operable		Obstructed	
Obstructed			
		Fire Exits	
Building Construction		Fire Doors	
Brick		Closed	
Cinder Block		Panic Bars	
Cement Block		Lights	
Reinforced Concrete		Passage	
Parapet Walls		Stairs	
Wood Frame		Storage Underneath	
		Street Area Clear	
		Ice, Snow	

Figure 42–1 Fire prevention and safety inspection report.

- Dangerous hazards where disastrous consequences could result if they are not remedied immediately
- Situations that have not been properly corrected even after several informal requests for compliance have been offered

Obviously, there will be occasions when a fire hazard cannot be immediately corrected. In those instances, a realistic deadline for compliance should

Building:

Mechanics Locker Room		Shops	
Ventilated		Machinery	
Clothes Hanging		Safety Equipment	
Rolled		Electrical	
Safety Disposal Container		Flammable Liquids	
Rags, Paint, Grease, Chemicals		Safety Cans	
Odors, Fumes		Open Cans	
		Paints	
Storage		Paint Agents	
Aisles		Metal Cabinets Provided	
Floor Space Clear		Oxygen & Acetylene	
Divided Spaces		Burning Equipment	
Fire Walls Clear			
Ceiling Clearance		Dormitories	
Excelsior, Shredded Paper		Drapes, Curtains	
		Fire Resistant	
Kitchens		Tested	
Overhead Vents		Passage	
Ducts		Stairs	
Gas Ovens, Grills		Exits	
Electric Ovens, Grills		Fire Extinguishers	
Grease Disposal System			
Clean		Rubbish	
Insects, Rodents, Vermin		Inside	
C-O-2 Fire Ext.		Outside	
		Containers Empty	
		Approved Containers	
		Covered	
		Grass, Weeds	

FIRE INSPECTOR:

When your observation reveals that those items listed are found in a very satisfactory condition, simply apply a checkmark (√) for that item. Any deficiencies or violations observed, mark that particular item with an (X) and submit a written report to the Director of Security & Safety on this inspection form. **Be complete, precise and clear.**

Department Representative Receiving Copy of Report   Person Making Inspection

Signature: _____   Signature: _____

Title: _____   Title: _____

be provided. Above all, remember that adherence to a company's fire safety standards will come much more quickly when an atmosphere of understanding and cooperation exists. Therefore, it is very important that enforcement activities not be:

- too quick in coming,
- too arbitrary,
- too harsh.

INSPECTION OF FIRE PROTECTION EQUIPMENT*

The following schedule for the inspection of fire protection equipment by inhouse security personnel provides a composite picture of the inspectional and surveillance activities of a security department.

Daily Inspections

A. Trucks:
    1. If engine is started, it is to run until water temperature reaches 180 degrees before being shut off.
    2. Check ammeter operation for generator charging.
    3. Check windshield wipers.
    4. Check vacuum boosters on brakes.
    5. Check engine oil level.
    6. Check water level in radiator.
    7. Check fuel by reading gauge.
    8. Check all lights.
    9. Check horn and siren.
    10. Check foot brake.
    11. Check hand brake.
    12. Check tires (visual).
    13. Check booster tank, water level.
    14. Check radio.
    15. Check pump primer oil.
    16. Report all malfunctions to supervisor.
B. Equipment:
    1. Check equipment on truck against truck checklist to determine that all equipment is on the truck and in its proper place.
    2. Check each piece of equipment to see if it is in proper working condition and check all seals to see that they are not broken.
    3. Check position of valves on mounted equipment.
    4. Check working parts of equipment to see that moving parts are free and easily moved (except cock valves on dry chemical units).
    5. Check equipment for accessibility and removal from truck.
    6. Report all malfunctions and deficiencies to supervisor.
C. Extinguishers:
    1. Check all extinguishers daily to see that they are accessible, noting if any of the extinguishers are damaged.
    2. Check the seals to see if any have been broken. If any seals are broken, weigh the CO_2 extinguisher. If the weight of the extin-

---

*From the National Association of Manufacturers.

guisher shows a decrease of more than 10 percent of the total weight of the extinguisher, the extinguisher must be brought into the station and refilled. If the weight is within the range of full to 10 percent less, it is permissible to reseal the extinguisher and leave it in service. If the extinguisher is a dry chemical type and the seal is broken, the level of the dry chemical must be checked. The cartridge must be removed and inspected to see if it has been punctured. If the cartridge is not punctured and the powder is at the designated level, the extinguisher may be assembled and sealed. If either the powder is low or the cartridge is punctured, the extinguisher must be brought to the fire station and properly recharged.

3. Report all extinguishers in need of service to supervisor.

Weekly Inspections

A. Trucks:
   1. Check tires for proper pressure with tire pressure gauge.
   2. Check batteries using hydrometer. If readings are 1200 or below, connect charger to the batteries.
   3. Flush the booster tanks.
   4. Report all deficiencies to supervisor.
B. Weekend inspection schedule:
   1. Check sprinkler systems using inspector's test valve.
   2. Check fire alarms by operating the alarm, using key to open box.
   3. Check sectional controls valves by actually moving valve to see that valve is in either the open or closed position, whichever it is supposed to be.
   4. Sprinkler control valves to be checked by same procedure as sectional control valves.
   5. Inner control valves to be checked by same procedure as sectional control valves.
   6. Check hydrants by visual inspection. Note if caps are in place, hand tight, if wrench is on hydrant, and that hydrant is not obstructed.
   7. Report all deficiencies to supervisor.

Monthly Inspections

A. Building inspections:
   1. Each building is to be inspected monthly for fire hazards.
   2. Buildings will be inspected with attention given to proper storage pertaining to sprinkler systems, allowing proper clearances for efficient sprinkler operations.

3. Wiring will be checked for temporary hook-ups and dangerous use of extension cords.
4. Poor housekeeping is a contributing factor in causing fires. Check for poor housekeeping practices and ways in which they can be eliminated.
5. When flammable liquids are used or stored in a building, check to see that proper provisions have been made for this type operation.
6. Check storage and operations to see that first equipment is not blocked.
7. Check for violations of smoking rules.
8. Report all deficiencies to supervisor.

B. Operational checks on truck equipment:
1. Dry chemical units will be activated, using as little dry chemical as possible.
2. Foam units will be actuated, condition and quality of foam will be noted. Foam tanks will be cleaned and contaminated foam removed.
3. Report any unusual equipment condition to supervisor.

C. Hose rebedded:
1. Bedded hose will be removed from trucks and rebedded with sections coupled together, hand tight. Fold hose in different places so folds will not be in the hose for a period longer than thirty days.
2. Observe condition of gaskets, butts, and hose at this time.

D. Assigned location extinguishers:
1. Assigned location extinguishers will be inspected monthly.
2. The inspection will consist of general visual condition.
3. Check hose to see if it is defective or obstructed.
4. Check to see that the seals are not broken and for signs of tampering.
5. If the seal is broken, the extinguisher is to be taken apart and checked (except CO_2 extinguishers, which will be weighed.)
6. If all parts are in proper condition, extinguisher may be reassembled and sealed.
7. Report all unserviceable equipment to supervisor.

E. Dry chemical extinguishers
1. Dry chemical extinguishers are to be checked monthly by dumping dry chemical and observing the condition of the powder. If the powder is not lumpy from moisture, its continued use is permissible.
2. The CO_2 cartridge will be removed and checked for proper weight.
3. The hose will be tested for obstructions by blowing air through it.
4. Gaskets will be checked for condition and proper seating.
5. If there are no deficiencies, the extinguisher can be reassembled and marked as shown in the inspection book.

Semiannual Inspections

A. Pumper:
    1. The CO_2 unit on the pumper will be disassembled and cylinders weighed. If the weight is within 10 percent of weight indicated on cylinder heads, they may be marked "OK" and the system reassembled.
B. Fire hose test:
    1. All fire hose will be tested with water pressure every six months.
    2. To test, connect hose to pumper and bleed off the air in the hose. Hose may be tested in any lengths as long as all air is bled from hose.
    3. The 2½ inch double jacket hose will be tested at 200 lbs. pressure for a period of 3 minutes.
    4. The 2½ inch single jacket and the 1½ inch hose will be tested at 150 lbs. pressure for a period of 3 minutes.
    5. During the test, observe the hose for pinhole leaks and for couplings pulled from the hose.
    6. After the test, break *all* hose at couplings, drain, roll into doughnuts and assemble at pumper for bedding. Hose will be coupled hand tight when bedding.
    7. Only dry hose will be reloaded. Wet hose will be hung in tower and replaced with dry hose.
    8. Record test on hose record cards in file.
C. Buildings:
    1. A fire inspection survey has been completed on all buildings. Results of the building surveys are on file in the Fire Protection Office.
    2. Reinspections will be made on these buildings every six months.
    3. The buildings will be checked against the original inspection. Any differences or changes noted in construction or of contents will be noted in a supplemental report and affixed to the original inspection.
    4. Construction changes are to be noted on original drawings.
D. Fire Hydrants: These will be flushed every six months.
E. Control Valves: All sprinkler control valves, sectional control valves, and county connection valves will be closed and opened, once every six months as a preventive maintenance procedure.

Annual Inspections

A. Fixed CO_2 systems:
    1. All fixed CO_2 systems will be dismantled and cylinders weighed.
    2. A check will be made of all moving parts of the system and if they operate satisfactorily, the system will then be reassembled.

    3. If any deficiencies are found, they are to be corrected before the system is reassembled.

    4. Report all unserviceable equipment to supervisor.

B. Extinguisher recharge:

    1. All foam and soda acid extinguishers will be recharged the first month of each year.

    2. Extinguishers will be taken apart and contents dumped, hoses and gaskets will be checked.

    3. The extinguishers will be cleaned and polished.

    4. New charges will be prepared and extinguishers charged.

    5. Extinguishers will then be sealed and condition registered in extinguisher record book.

C. Dry chemical extinguishers:

    1. To check dry chemical extinguishers, disassemble and dump powder, checking for lumps due to moisture.

    2. Check hose for obstruction and weigh the CO_2 cartridge.

    3. If all parts are in good condition, reassemble extinguisher.

    4. If any part is defective, replace it and then reassemble the extinguisher.

    5. Record work in record book.

D. Weigh CO_2 extinguishers:

    1. Weigh all CO_2 extinguishers.

    2. Weight must be within 10 percent of the weight stamped on head of cylinder.

    3. Check hose and horns for breaks and obstructions.

    4. Replace any part that is defective.

    5. Record condition and work done in extinguisher record book.

CHAPTER 43

Safety in the Work Environment

In December of 1970 President Richard Nixon signed into law the Occupational Safety and Health Act (OSHA). The specific purpose of this legislation was to better ensure that American workers were provided with a safe and healthful work environment. As a result, employers not only had to be aware of good safety and health standards, they also had to implement them. OSHA simply mandated such compliance under penalty of law.

Specifically, each regulated employer has the duty and obligation to furnish his or her employees with a workplace that is free from recognized hazards that are known to cause, or are likely to cause, death or serious physical injury. Further, OSHA compliance officers are authorized to inspect and investigate places of business to determine if they are actually in compliance. Consequently, companies are not at liberty to ignore OSHA.

Since its enactment, many companies have chosen to give to their security departments the responsibility for ensuring OSHA compliance internally. The use of this arrangement seems to be growing, with more and more companies following suit. Therefore, it is becoming increasingly important for security managers to have at least a basic working knowledge of OSHA.

The OSHA checklist that follows offers the tool by which one can determine whether or not a particular company generally complies with OSHA standards. However, if additional information is needed, it would be most appropriate to consult the act itself (29 USCA § 651 et seq.) or standards found in the Code of Federal Regulations (start with 29 C.F.R. Part 1910).

OSHA INSPECTION CHECKLIST

	Yes	No
A. *Building exterior*		
1. Are all entrances and dock areas adequately lighted?		
2. Are all outside utility boxes and water valves properly secured?		
3. Are exterior canopies, awnings, and overhangs in good condition and properly secured to the building?		

	Yes	No

B. *Means of entrance/exit*
   1. Are all doors in good condition? Do they not open too hard, swing, or revolve too freely?
   2. Are all *In* and *Out* doors clearly marked as such? Are *Push* and *Pull* signs present on all manually-operated doors?
   3. Are all exits clearly and properly marked as such?
   4. Are doorways and passageways that are *not* exits clearly and properly marked?
   5. Do all fire/emergency doors swing open in the direction of exit travel?
   6. Are all fire emergency doors unlocked from the inside, and each equipped with a panic, or simple type, releasing device? (Exit doors must not be locked or bolted during building occupancy.)
   7. Are vestibule floors clean and free from foreign matter?
   8. Are rubber mats or suitable floor coverings utilized at entrances during inclement weather, and do they create tripping hazards?
   9. Are large floor-to-ceiling windows marked with decals where the possibility exists for a *walk-through* accident?
   10. Are exits clearly visible and the routes to reach them conspicuously marked and unobstructed?
   11. Is there adequate and reliable illumination for all exit facilities?
   12. Do emergency lighting systems work properly?
   13. Are diagrams showing the location of emergency exits and equipment properly posted throughout the facility?
C. *Work area*
   1. Are traffic aisles and hallways unobstructed, with surfaces clean and free from foreign matter or materials?
   2. Is carpeting in good condition, free from tears or holes and with no loose, worn, or missing tiles?
   3. Are floor electrical outlets in good condition, protected and covered to prevent accidents?
   4. Are extension cords, where used, heavy duty type, and do they create a tripping hazard?
   5. Are work counters, glass shelves, and dividers in good condition and free from sharp edges or other defects? Are there protruding extensions that could cause tripping or other injury?
   6. Do metal racks have end caps?
   7. Are pointed objects, particularly pegboard hooks, protruding into aisles at eye level?
   8. Are pallets and platforms situated so that they create tripping hazards. Are safety chains used to adequately secure, where they are needed?

	Yes	No

9. Are boxes and bulk merchandise stacked so goods will not fall when handled?
10. Are *No Smoking* signs posted where necessary? Are the rules appropriately enforced?
11. Are temperatures and air movement within comfort limits?

D. *Stairways*
    1. Are boxes and equipment stored or left on stairs or landings?
    2. Are stairways and landings adequately illuminated with *Use Handrail* signs properly posted?
    3. Are stairs equipped with handrails and treads, and are risers on steps in good repair with no-slip surfaces?

E. *Elevators*
    1. Do all elevators have inspection certificates and capacity plates conspicuously posted (certificates should not be more than one year old)?
       a. Are proper safety devices provided?
       b. Do cars consistently stop at floor level?
    2. Do all elevator cars have adequate lighting and emergency signals?
    3. Do freight elevators, not permitted to carry passengers, have *No Rider* signs posted?
    4. Are elevator penthouses and wells clean and well maintained?
    5. Are elevator *Emergency Stop* controls operative?
    6. Do security and maintenance personnel know the locations of emergency stop buttons?

F. *Stockrooms and warehouses*
    1. Is lighting in passageways and storage areas adequate?
    2. Are trash chute openings protected when they are not in use? Are there gates or bars across the openings?
    3. Are aisles and hallways free of obstructions and debris?
    4. Are areas near switch panels, sprinkler control valves, and fire extinguishers unobstructed?
    5. Are merchandise and boxes so stacked and interlocked as to prevent toppling hazard?
    6. Are storage racks overloaded?
    7. Are clearance signs located where clearance is below 6'8" from floor?
    8. Are portable step ladders maintained, unpainted, and in good condition?
    9. Are metal ladders used where there is a possibility of electrical shock?
    10. Are personnel instructed in the proper use of extensions and step ladders?

G. *Receiving, shipping dock, and maintenance shops*
    1. Are wheel blocks used to prevent the movement of

	Yes	No

trucks and trailers where it is necessary for loading or unloading at locations?
2. Do solid bumpers protect docks from damage?
3. Are dock edges painted yellow (OSHA color code) for contrast?
4. Are dock plates free of defects and used properly?
5. Is lighting adequate in trailers during loading and unloading operations?
6. Is trash removed from buildings immediately, thereby reducing accident and fire hazards?
7. Are conveyors in good working order, *Emergency Stop* controls in operating condition and their locations properly signed, and safety rails installed where they are needed?
8. Are compactors and other automatic mechanical devices properly maintained and *Emergency Stop* controls operative?
9. Are flammable paint and aerosol spray cans stored in metal cabinets? Are those cabinets properly labeled to indicate the storage of flammables?

H. *Special hazards*
1. Are all equipment rooms and mechanical areas equipped with fire doors and labeled as to hazards contained within (*Danger High Voltage,* and so forth), and do they have applicable entrance restriction instructions?
2. Are all electrical outlet boxes provided with covers that effectively protect people from accidental contact?
3. Are extension cords and other temporary wiring breaks fraying, or do they have other defects? (Temporary extension cords should not serve permanently in lieu of an established circuit.)
4. Is there sufficient access and working space provided and maintained around all electrical equipment?
5. Are *critical areas* identified and marked with proper OSHA color code?

ACCIDENT INVESTIGATION*

Supervisors have a responsibility to investigate accidents in an effort to control tomorrow's potential losses as well as to help prevent similar accidents in the future. Proper investigation of an accident can lead to the real or basic cause of the accident so that corrective action can be taken to avoid future mishaps (see Figure 43–1).

From John A. Wanat et al., *Supervisory Techniques for the Security Professional,* Stoneham, Mass.: Butterworth Publishers, 1981.

MORE EFFECTIVE ACCIDENT CONTROL

THROUGH GOOD

INVESTIGATION   AND   REMEDIAL ACTION

BY APPLYING THESE OBJECTIVES

1. To determine all contributing causal factors.
2. To determine the fundamental or basic reason for the existence of each contributing factor.

1. To eliminate or control each contributing cause.
2. To eliminate or control the reason for the existence of each contributing cause.

AND FOLLOWING THESE GUIDEPOSTS

- In case of injury, make sure worker is properly cared for before doing anything else
- When practical, have scene kept as undisturbed as possible
- Investigate as promptly as possible
- Whenever possible, go to scene of accident for initial investigation
- As applicable, have someone else get photographs; make drawings or measurements
- Interview all witnesses, one at a time and separately
- Reassure each witness of investigation's real purpose
- Get witnesses' initial version with minimal interruption; ask for complete version step by step; have them describe and point without doing
- Apply empathy in interviews; make no attempt to fix blame or find fault
- Be objective; don't have fixed opinion in advance
- When witness finishes initial explanation, ask questions to fill in gaps
- Avoid questions that lead witness or imply answers wanted or unwanted
- Summarize your understanding with witness after interview
- Express sincere appreciation to anyone who helped in the investigation
- Record data accurately

(Select appropriate actions)
- Institute formal training program
- Give personal reinstruction
- Institute proper job instruction program
- Institute a safety tipping program
- Temporarily or permanently reassign person/s
- Institute a job analysis program
- Order job analysis on specific job/s
- Revise existing job analysis
- Institute a job observation program
- Order job observation on specific job/s
- Institute new or improve existing inspection program
- Institute pre-use checkout of equipment
- Establish or revise indoctrination for new or transferred employees
- Repair or replace equipment
- Improve biomechanic design of equipment
- Establish biomechanic requirements for new equipment
- Improve basic design or establish design standards
- Improve identification or color code for safety
- Install or improve safeguards
- Eliminate unnecessary material in area
- Institute program of order or improve clean-up
- Institute mandatory protective equipment program or improve existing coverage or design
- Use safer material
- Estabish purchasing standard/s or controls
- Institute incident recall program
- Create safety incentive program
- Improve physical examination program

WILL REDUCE

| INJURIES & DAMAGE | DEFECTS & DELAYS |
| REJECTS & REWORK | MISTAKES & WASTE |

.... Adequate time spent today on proper investigation and effective remedial action is cost reduction effort on tomorrow's losses.

Figure 43–1   More effective accident control. (Insurance Company of North America.)

Not all accidents result in major injuries requiring medical attention. There are those instances commonly known as "near misses" where individuals often escape with minor injuries or no injuries at all. These near misses should also be investigated. Today's near miss may be tomorrow's tragedy. Look on accident investigation as accident prevention.

Every accident should be investigated as soon as possible. The sooner an accident is investigated, the better the opportunity to obtain all of the facts. The greater the time span between the accident and the investigation, the greater the chance for information and evidence to be lost, forgotten, or destroyed.

Make every effort to investigate the accident at the scene. Make clear to everyone involved that the purpose of the investigation is to obtain the facts and not to place blame. The investigation may uncover human error or negligence, or it may uncover an unsafe condition. The investigation itself, however, should be concerned only with the facts.

The investigation, based on accumulated facts, should determine the cause of the accident. Most accidents have multiple causes or contributing factors. The investigator should endeavor to identify all the causes and contributing factors to determine the overriding cause of the accident. Once the major cause of the accident is determined, make a recommendation to correct the cause of the accident. Submit a report to management indicating the cause and recommended corrective action.

A written report of an accident investigation should list the facts uncovered during the investigation. It also should include any action taken or recommendations to management. As with all reports, forms differ with each company or organization. A survey of accident reports lists the following essential questions:

- Who was involved in the accident?
- When did it happen?
- Where did it happen?
- What was the cause of the accident?
- What action was taken?

Reference Bibliography

The importance of doing careful research into a security-related problem, its cause and solutions, cannot be overemphasized. Effective, results-minded managers, prior to deciding on solutions, first take time to review critically what others have learned and what is recommended. These managers do not attempt to reinvent the wheel every time they are confronted by a problem, instead they go to the professional literature.

The following list of reference materials and documents is not all-encompassing or definitive. It is offered as an aid to the manager who wishes to know more in depth about the various protective services subjects. The publications listed are a cross section of what is currently available and in print on security and safety in the private sector.

Since changes in private protective services are happening more rapidly now than ever before in history, this list is limited to those publications that are recent enough to still have worthwhile value and impact for the reader. In addition, there are those seemingly ageless books that appear in every area of literature and they, too, are included.

GENERAL ISSUES

Anderson, Ralph E. *Bank Security*. Stoneham, Mass.: Butterworth, 1981.

Berger, David L. *Industrial Security*. Stoneham, Mass.: Butterworth, 1979.

——— . *Security for Small Businesses*. Stoneham, Mass.: Butterworth, 1981.

Bequai, August. *Organized Crime*. Lexington, Mass.: Lexington Books, 1978.

——— . *Computer Crime*. Stoneham, Mass.: Butterworth, 1978.

——— . *The Cashless Society*. New York: Wiley, 1981.

Bottom, Norman R., and J.I. Rostanoski. *Security and Loss Control*. New York: Macmillan, 1983.

Clinard, M.B. *Corporate Crime*. New York: MacMillan, 1981

Curtis, Bob. *Retail Security*. Stoneham, Mass.: Butterworth, 1982.

Fisher, James A. *Security for Business and Industry*. Englewood Cliffs, N.J.: Prentice-Hall, 1979.

Gigliotti, R.J., and R.C. Jason. *Security Design for Maximum Protection*. Stoneham, Mass.: Butterworth, 1984.

Green, Gion. *Introduction to Security (3rd edition)*. Stoneham, Mass.: Butterworth, 1981.

Hemphill, C.F. *Modern Security Methods*. Englewood Cliffs, N.J.: Prentice-Hall, 1979.

Hemphill, C.F., and R.D. Hemphill. *Security Safeguards for the Computer*. New York: American Management Association, 1979.

Hemphill, C.F. and J.M. Hemphill. *The Secure Company*. Homewood, Ill.: Dow Jones-Irwin, 1975.

Hess, Karen, and H.M. Wroblenski. *Introduction to Private Security*. St. Paul, Minn.: West, 1982.

Hsiao, D.K. et al. *Computer Security*. New York: Academic, 1979.

Keogh, J.E. *Small Business Security Handbook*. Englewood Cliffs, N.J.: Prentice-Hall, 1981.

Kingsbury, Arthur. *Introduction to Security and Crime Prevention Surveys*. Springfield, Ill.: CC Thomas, 1973.

Lipson, Milton. *On Guard*. New York: Quadrangle/New York Times, 1975.

Mason, D.L. *The Fine Art of Art Security*. New York: Van Nostrand-Reinhold, 1979.

Oliver, E., and J. Wilson. *Practical Security for Commerce and Industry*. Brookfield, Vt.: Gower, 1978.

O'Toole, G.O. *Private Sector—Private Spies, Rent-a-Cops and the Police-Industrial Complex*. New York: W.W. Norton, 1978.

Post, Richard, and Arthur Kingsbury. *Security Administration: An Introduction (3rd edition)*. Springfield, Ill.: CC Thomas, 1986.

Ricks, T.A., B.G. Tillett, and C.W. Van Meter. *Principles of Security—An Introduction*. Cincinnati: Anderson, 1981.

Rosberg, Robert R. *Games of Thieves*. Stoneham, Mass.: Butterworth, 1980.

Russell, Lewis A. *Corporate and Industrial Security*. Houston: Gulf, 1980.

Schultz, Donald O. *Principles of Physical Security*. Houston: Gulf, 1978.

Strauss, Sheryl (editor). *Security Problems in a Modern Society*. Stoneham, Mass.: Butterworth, 1980.

Walsh, D.P. *Shoplifting—Controlling a Major Crime*. New York: Holmes and Meier, 1980.

SECURITY MANAGEMENT

Burstein, Harvey. *Hotel Security Management*. New York: Praeger, 1975.

Carroll, John M. *Managing Risk*. Stoneham, Mass.: Butterworth, 1984.

Carson, Charles R. *Managing Employee Honesty*. Stoneham, Mass.: Butterworth, 1977.

Cole, Richard B. *Protection Management and Crime Prevention*. Cincinnati: Anderson, 1974.

Daykin, Len. *Loss Prevention: A Management Guide to Improving Retail Security.* Stoneham, Mass.: Butterworth, 1981.

Finneran, Eugene. *Security Supervision.* Stoneham, Mass.: Butterworth, 1981.

Guy, Edward T., et al. *Supervisory Techniques for Security Professional.* Stoneham, Mass.: Butterworth, 1980.

———. *Forms for Safety and Security Management.* Stoneham, Mass.: Butterworth, 1980.

Healy, Richard J., and Timothy Walsh. *Principles of Security Management.* Long Beach, Cal.: Professional Publications, 1981.

Hopf, Peter S. *Handbook for Security Planning and Design.* New York: McGraw-Hill, 1979.

Mocarski, Donna T. *The Security of Excellence.* Chicago, Ill.: Truhart, 1981.

Morneau, R.J., and G.E. Morneau. *Security Administration: A Quantitative Handbook.* Stoneham, Mass.: Butterworth, 1982.

Neill, W. *Modern Retail Risk Management.* Stoneham, Mass.: Butterworth, 1981.

Rosberg, Robert R. *Security Risk Management.* Stoneham, Mass.: Butterworth, 1980.

Post, Richard, and David Schachtsiek. *Effective Company Security.* Chicago: Dartnell, 1977.

Schweitzer, James A. *Managing Information Security.* Stoneham, Mass.: Butterworth, 1982.

Sennewald, Charles A. *Effective Security Management.* Stoneham, Mass.: Butterworth, 1978.

Ursic, Henry S., and Le Roy Pagano. *Security Management Systems.* Springfield, Ill.: CC Thomas, 1974.

PRINCIPLES AND PRACTICES

Astor, Saul D. *Loss Prevention: Control and Concepts.* Stoneham, Mass.: Butterworth, 1978.

Barefoot, J. Kirk, *Undercover Investigations.* Springfield, Ill.: CC Thomas, 1975.

———. *Employee Theft Investigations.* Stoneham, Mass.: Butterworth, 1979.

Bilek, Arthur, J.C. Klotter, and R.K. Federal. *Legal Aspects of Private Security.* Cincinnati: Anderson, 1981.

Bequai, August. *How to Prevent Computer Crime.* New York: Wiley, 1983.

Broder, James F. *Risk Analysis and the Security Survey.* Stoneham, Mass.: Butterworth, 1984.

Carroll, John M. *Computer Security.* Stoneham, Mass.: Butterworth, 1977.

———. *Confidential Information Sources: Public and Private.* Stoneham, Mass.: Butterworth, 1976.

———. *Controlling White Collar Crime.* Stoneham, Mass.: Butterworth, 1982.

Cole, Richard B. *Principles and Practices of Protection.* Springfield, Ill.: CC Thomas, 1980.

Colling, Russell. *Hospital Security (2nd edition)*. Stoneham, Mass.: Butterworth, 1982.

Curtis, Bob. *How to Keep Your Employees Honest*. Stoneham, Mass.: Butterworth, 1979.

Di Domenico, J.M. *Investigative Techniques for the Retail Security Investigator*. New York: Labhar-Friedman, 1979.

German, Donald R., and Joan W. German. *Bank Employees Security Handbook*. Boston: Warren, Gorham, and Lamont, 1985.

Gorrill, B.E. *Effective Personnel Security Procedures*. Homewood, Ill.: Dow Jones-Irwin, 1975.

Healy, Richard J. *Design for Security (2nd edition)*. New York: Wiley, 1982.

Inbau, Fred, Marvin Aspen, and James Spiotto. *Protective Security Law*. Stoneham, Mass.: Butterworth, 1982.

Knowles, Graham. *Bomb Security Guide*. Stoneham, Mass.: Butterworth, 1976.

Kenda, M. *Crime Prevention Manual for Business Owners and Managers*. New York: American Management Association, 1982.

Monboisse, Raymond. *Industrial Security for Strikes, Riots and Disasters*. Springfield, Ill.: CC Thomas, 1977.

Moore, Kenneth C. *Airport, Aircraft and Airline Security*. Stoneham, Mass.: Butterworth, 1976.

O'Block, R.L. *Security and Crime Prevention*. St. Louis: C.V. Mosby, 1981.

Purpura, Philip P. *Security and Loss Prevention*. Stoneham, Mass.: Butterworth, 1984.

Reid, John E., and Fred E. Inbau. *Truth and Deception: The Polygraph Technique*. Stoneham, Mass.: Butterworth, 1977.

Sapse, Anne-Marie, Peter Shenkin, and Marcel Sapse. *Computer Applications in the Private Security Business*. Stoneham, Mass.: Butterworth, 1980.

Sennewald, Charles A. *The Process of Investigation*. Stoneham, Mass.: Butterworth, 1981.

Skiar, S.L. *Shoplifting—What You Need to Know About the Law*. New York: Fairchild, 1982.

Stoffel, Joseph. *Explosive and Homemade Bombs (2nd edition)*. Springfield, Ill.: CC Thomas, 1977.

Strobl, W.W. *Crime Prevention Through Physical Security*. New York: Marcel Dekker, 1978.

Wanat, John, John Brown, and L.C. Connin. *Hospital Security Guard Training Manual*. Springfield, Ill.: CC Thomas, 1977.

Woodruff, Ronald S. *Industrial Security Techniques*. Columbus, O.: Merrill, 1974.

SECURITY HARDWARE

Bose, Keith W. *Video Security Systems*. Stoneham, Mass.: Butterworth, 1982.

Barnard, Roger L. *Intrusion Detection Systems*. Stoneham, Mass.: Butterworth, 1981.

Hahn, Steven. *Modern Electronic Security Systems*. Rochelle Park, N.J.: Hayden, 1976.

Schnabolk, Charles. *Private Security: The Industry and Technology*. Stoneham, Mass.: Butterworth, 1982.

Sloane, Eugene A. *The Complete Book of Locks, Keys, Burglar and Smoke Alarms, and Other Security Devices*. New York: Morrow, 1977.

Trimmer, William. *Understanding and Servicing Alarm Systems*. Stoneham, Mass.: Butterworth, 1981.

Weber, Thad L. *Alarm Systems and Theft Prevention*. Stoneham, Mass.: Butterworth, 1978.

Walker, Philip. *Electronic Security Systems*. Stoneham, Mass.: Butterworth, 1983.

GOVERNMENT PUBLICATIONS

National Advisory Commission on Criminal Justice Standards and Goals. *Task Force Report on Private Security*. Washington, D.C.: U.S. Department of Justice (LEAA), 1976.

National Institute of Law Enforcement. *Security and the Small Business Retailer*. Washington, D.C.: U.S. Department of Justice (LEAA), 1977.

Private Security Advisory Council. *Model Security Guard Training Curricula*. Washington, D.C.: U.S. Department of Justice (LEAA), 1977.

——— . *Scope of Legal Authority of Private Security Personnel*. Washington, D.C.: U.S. Department of Justice (LEAA), 1976.

——— . *Prevention of Terroristic Crimes*. Washington, D.C.: U.S. Department of Justice (LEAA), 1976.

Index